[91ST CONGRESS, 1ST SESSION . . HOUSE DOCUMENT NO. 91-195]

MEMORIAL SERVICES IN THE

CONGRESS OF THE UNITED STATES

AND TRIBUTES IN EULOGY OF

# Dwight David Eisenhower

LATE A PRESIDENT OF THE

UNITED STATES



*Compiled Under Direction of the*
*Joint Committee on Printing*

UNITED STATES GOVERNMENT PRINTING OFFICE

WASHINGTON : 1970

# Senate Concurrent Resolution No. 16

IN THE SENATE OF THE UNITED STATES,

*April 29, 1969.*

*Resolved by the Senate (the House of Representatives concurring),* That there be printed as a Senate document the eulogies on Dwight David Eisenhower delivered in the Congress; the eulogy delivered by President Nixon and the benediction by the Reverend Doctor Elson in the Rotunda of the Capitol on Sunday, March 30; and the text of the funeral service, including prayers and scriptural selections read by the Reverend Doctor Elson, at Washington Cathedral, on Monday, March 31, 1969.

*Resolved further,* That the copy shall be prepared and bound in such style as the Joint Committee on Printing may direct.

# House Concurrent Resolution No. 368

In the House of Representatives

*September* 25, 1969.

*Resolved by the House of Representatives* (*the Senate concurring*), That there shall be printed with illustrations as a House document a compilation of the eulogies of the late Dwight David Eisenhower delivered in the Congress; the eulogy delivered by President Nixon and the benediction by the Reverend Doctor Elson in the rotunda of the Capitol on Sunday, March 30, 1969; the text of the funeral service at the Washington Cathedral on Monday, March 31, 1969; and the text of appropriate eulogies, messages, prayers, and scriptural selections delivered at the funeral services at Abilene, Kansas April 2, 1969; and that thirty-two thousand two hundred and fifty additional copies shall be printed, of which twenty-one thousand nine hundred and fifty copies shall be for the use of the House of Representatives and ten thousand three hundred copies shall be for the use of the Senate.

Sec. 2. The copy shall be prepared and bound in such style as the Joint Committee on Printing may direct.

Sec. 3. Copies of such document shall be prorated to Members of the House of Representatives and the Senate for a period of sixty days, after which the unused balance shall revert to the respective House and Senate document rooms.

A compilation of addresses and tributes as given in the United States Senate and House of Representatives plus such additional materials, including the texts of eulogies, messages, prayers, and scriptural selections delivered at the funeral services held in Washington, D.C., and in Abilene, Kansas, on the life, character, and public service of the late President Dwight David Eisenhower.

# Dwight David Eisenhower
# (1890–1969)

☆ ☆ ☆ ☆ ☆

Dwight David Eisenhower, Republican, of Gettysburg, Pa., thirty-fourth President of the United States, was born in Denison, Tex., October 14, 1890; son of David J. and Ida Elizabeth (Stover) Eisenhower; attended public schools in Abilene, Kans.; B.S., United States Military Academy, 1915; graduated Infantry Tank School, 1922; honor graduate Command and General Staff School, 1926; Army War College, 1928; Army Industrial College, 1933; married Mamie Geneva Doud, July 1, 1916; children: Dwight Doud (deceased), John Sheldon Doud, United States Ambassador to Belgium.

Commissioned as second lieutenant of Infantry at West Point in 1915 and assigned to 19th Infantry, Fort Sam Houston, Tex.; advanced through the grades to lieutenant colonel, commanding the Tank Corps School at Camp Colt, Gettysburg, Pa., during World War I; assistant executive officer, Office of Assistant Secretary of War, 1929–33; Office of Chief of Staff, 1933–35; Assistant to Gen. Douglas MacArthur in Philippines, 1935–40; Chief of Staff, 3d Division and later IX Corps, 1940–41; Chief of Staff, Third Army, 1941. At the beginning of World War II was named Chief of War Plans Division, War Department General Staff; then Assistant Chief of Staff, in charge of Operations Division; commanded Allied Forces landing in North Africa November 8, 1942, became Commander-in-Chief, all Allied Forces in Northwest Africa the following February; named Supreme Commander, Allied Expeditionary Forces, December 31, 1943; commanded the land, sea, and air invasion of Normandy which began on June 6, 1944; promoted to General of the Army on December 20, 1944; accepted unconditional surrender of Germany on May 8, 1945; commander United States occupation forces in Germany; Chief of Staff, United States Army, November 19, 1945, to February 7, 1948.

President of Columbia University, June 7, 1948, to January 10, 1953; took leave from Columbia December 16, 1950, to become the Supreme Allied Commander, Europe, to forge the integration of the defense forces of the North Atlantic Treaty nations.

Nominated for President of the United States on first ballot of Republican National Convention at Chicago, July 11, 1952; resigned from the Army within the hour of his nomination; elected President on November 4, 1952; reelected President on November 6, 1956; retired to his farm at Gettysburg, Pa., in January 1961.

Author of *Crusade in Europe,* the Supreme Commander's account of World War II; wrote a two-volume memoir, *The White House Years* (Mandate for Change, 1953–56), and *Waging Peace* (1956–61); author of *At Ease,* pre-Presidential reminiscences, and *In Review,* a pictorial autobiography.

As soldier-statesman, was called upon by his successors, Presidents Kennedy, Johnson, and Nixon, as an advisor, especially with respect to international affairs; prominent figure in the active affairs of the Republican Party; supported many charitable and philanthropic activities; member of National Presbyterian Church, Washington, D.C.; died on March 28, 1969, at Walter Reed Army Medical Center, Washington, D.C. Honored by a State Funeral in Washington, D.C., and nationwide observances; laid to rest in The Place of Meditation on the grounds of the Eisenhower Center, Abilene, Kansas.

THE STATE FUNERAL OF

# Dwight David Eisenhower

## 1890–1969

☆ ☆ ☆ ☆ ☆

# *THE STATE FUNERAL OF*
# *GENERAL DWIGHT DAVID EISENHOWER*
## *(1890–1969)*

☆ ☆ ☆ ☆ ☆

General Eisenhower died at Walter Reed Army Hospital during the early afternoon of Friday, March 28, 1969. The Military District of Washington directed the State Funeral in Washington, D.C., and the burial services in Abilene, Kansas, were coordinated by the Fifth Army.

## THE ORDER OF SERVICE

Saturday
March 29, 1969
Washington Cathedral

Prayer
The Very Reverend Francis B. Sayre, Jr.
Dean of Washington Cathedral

Repose
Bethlehem Chapel

Palm Sunday
March 30, 1969

Procession
From Washington Cathedral to United States Capitol, pausing at the South front of the White House, where the casket was transferred from hearse to a horse-drawn caisson

Eulogy
President Richard M. Nixon

Benediction
The Reverend Edward L. R. Elson, D.D.
Minister, National Presbyterian Church and Chaplain, United States Senate

Lying in State
Rotunda of United States Capitol

Monday
March 31, 1969

Procession
From United States Capitol to the Washington Cathedral

Organ Prelude
Chorale-Prelude,
*"Schmucke dich, o liebe Seele"*
JOHANN SEBASTIAN BACH
Chorale-Prelude,
*"O Welt, ich muss dich lassen"*
JOHANNES BRAHMS

The Palms (J. Faure)
The Washington Cathedral Choir
Paul Callaway, Organist

Prayer
The Very Reverend Francis B. Sayre, Jr.
*"A Mighty Fortress Is Our God"*
MARTIN LUTHER, 1529
Congregation Standing and Singing

Psalms 46 and 121
Read responsively and lead by The Reverend Edward L. R. Elson, D.D.

The Apostles' Creed
Congregation Standing and Participating

The Reading of the Scriptures
The Reverend Edward L. R. Elson, D.D.

Psalm 23
Sung by the Washington Cathedral Choir

Memorial and Pastoral Prayers
The Reverend Edward L. R. Elson, D.D.

Benediction
The Right Reverend William F. Creighton
Episcopal Bishop of Washington

"Onward Christian Soldiers"

Congregation Standing and Singing

Honors to the President

Played by the Marine Band

Procession

From Washington Cathedral to Union Railroad Station for journey to Abilene, Kansas

Wednesday
April 2, 1969
Abilene, Kansas
Eisenhower Library

Funeral Service

The Reverend Robert A. MacAskill

Pastor, The Presbyterian Church, Gettysburg, Pennsylvania

Pastoral Prayer

Scripture Reading:
John 14:1–3
II Timothy 4:6–8

Memorial Tribute

Pastoral Prayer

Benediction

Memorial Service

The Reverend Dean W. Miller

Pastor, Palm Desert Community Presbyterian Church, Palm Desert, California

Psalms 121 and 23

Eulogium

Memorial Prayer

The Place of Meditation

Burial Service

Chaplain (Maj. Gen.) Luther D. Miller
Former Chief of Army Chaplains, U.S. Army (Ret.)

Meditation

Pastoral Prayer

21-Gun Salute

Pastoral Prayer

Volley

Taps

Music for the Funeral in Abilene

Repose

Ruffles and Flourishes
Hail to the Chief
God of Our Fathers

Procession

Onward, Christian Soldiers
Stars and Stripes Forever
Lead Kindly Light

Arrival and Funeral Service

Ruffles and Flourishes
Hail to the Chief
National Anthem
A Mighty Fortress is Our God
Army Blue
Lead Kindly Light

Interment

West Point Alma Mater
Carillon:
America The Beautiful
The Old Rugged Cross

## Statement by Former President
# HARRY S. TRUMAN
### upon the death of
# GENERAL DWIGHT D. EISENHOWER

"General Eisenhower and I became political opponents, but before that we were comrades in arms, and I cannot forget his services to his country and to Western civilization. He led the great military crusade that freed Western Europe from Nazi bondage, and then commanded the allied forces that stood guard over liberated lands while they regained their strength and self-reliance.

"For these achievements, which brought him the highest office and the highest honors in the land, he must be long and gratefully remembered."

## Statement by Former President
# LYNDON B. JOHNSON
### upon the death of
# GENERAL DWIGHT D. EISENHOWER

A giant of our age is gone.

Dwight David Eisenhower began his service to his people as a soldier of war. He ended as a crusader for peace.

For both, he will be long remembered by a scarred but hopeful world—a world that loved him well.

The sturdy and enduring virtues—honor, courage, integrity, decency—all found eloquent expression in the life of this good man and noble leader.

I was proud to serve him when he was President. I respected him as a wise and valued counselor during my own days in the White House. I treasured him always as my close and lasting friend. His death leaves an empty place in my heart, as it will in the hearts of men and women everywhere.

America will be a lonely land without him. But America will always be a better Nation—stronger, safer, more conscious of its heritage, more certain of its destiny—because Ike was with us when America needed him.

In this sad hour, Mrs. Johnson and I join with people the world over in expressing to Mrs. Eisenhower and her family our profound sympathy.

# Eulogy Delivered by the President

# RICHARD M. NIXON

## at the Capitol Rotunda During the State Funeral of Former President

# DWIGHT DAVID EISENHOWER

Mrs. Eisenhower, Your Excellencies, friends of Dwight David Eisenhower in America and throughout the world:

We gather today in mourning, but also in gratitude.

We mourn Dwight Eisenhower's death, but we are grateful for his life.

We gather, also, conscious of the fact that in paying tribute to Dwight Eisenhower, we celebrate greatness. When we think of his place in history, we think, inevitably, of the other giants of those days of World War II and we think of the qualities of greatness and what his were that made his unique among all.

Once, perhaps without intending to do so, he, himself, put his finger on it. It was 1945, shortly after V-Day, at a ceremony in London's historic Guild Hall. The triumphant Supreme Commander of the Allied Forces in Europe was officially given the Freedom of the City of London.

In an eloquent address that day, Dwight Eisenhower said, "I come from the heart of America."

Perhaps no one sentence could better sum up what Dwight Eisenhower meant to a whole generation of Americans. He did come from the heart of America, not only from its geographical heart, but from its spiritual heart.

He exemplified what millions of parents hoped that their sons would be—strong, courageous, honest and compassionate.

And with his own great qualities of heart, he personified the best in America.

It is, I think, a special tribute to Dwight Eisenhower that despite all of his honors, despite all of his great deeds and his triumphs, we find ourselves today thinking, first, not of his deeds but of his character. It was the character of the man, not what he did, but what he was that so captured the trust and faith and affection of his own people and of the people of the world.

Dwight Eisenhower touched something fundamental in America which only a man of immense force of mind and spirit could have brought so vibrantly alive. He was a product of America's soil and of its ideals, driven by a compulsion to do right and to do well; a man of deep faith who believed in God and trusted in His will; a man who truly loved his country and for whom the words "freedom" and "democracy" were not cliches, but they were living truths.

I know Mrs. Eisenhower would permit me to share with you the last words he spoke to her on the day he died. He said, "I have always loved my wife. I have always loved my children. I have always loved my grandchildren. And I have always loved my country." That was Dwight Eisenhower.

He was a man who gave enormously of himself. His way of relaxing from the intense pressures of office or command was to do something else intensely, whether as a fierce competitor on the golf course or executing one of those hauntingly beautiful paintings that he did with such meticulous care. But even more than this, he gave enormously of himself to people. People loved Dwight Eisenhower. But the other side of this coin was that he loved people.

He had the great leader's capacity to bring out the best in people. He had the great humanist's capacity to inspire people, to cheer them, to give them lift.

I remember, for example, just a few months ago when I asked all of the members of the Cabinet to go out and call on him. Each of them returned with wonder and admiration and said, "You know, I went out there to cheer him up and instead I found he cheered me up."

His great love of people was rooted in his faith. He had a deep faith in the goodness of God and in the essential goodness of man as a creature of God.

This feeling toward people had another side. In the political world, strong passions are the norm and all too often these turn toward personal vindictiveness. People often disagreed with Dwight Eisenhower, but almost nobody ever hated him.

And this, I think, was because he, himself, was a man who did not know how to hate.

Oh, he could be aroused by a cause, but he could not hate a person. He could disagree strongly, even passionately, but never personally.

When people disagreed with him, he never thought of them as enemies. He simply thought, "Well, they don't agree with me."

I remember time after time, when critics of one sort or another were misrepresenting him or reviling him, he would sit back in his chair and with that wonderful half-smile and half-frown, he would say, "I am puzzled by those fellows." And he was genuinely puzzled by frenzy and by hate because he was incapable of it himself. He could never quite understand it in others.

The last time I saw him that was what he talked about. He was puzzled by the hatreds he had seen in our times. And he said the thing the world needs most today is understanding and an ability to see the other person's point of view and not to hate him because he disagrees.

That was Dwight Eisenhower.

And yet, of course, he was more than all of that. He had a side more evident to those of us who worked with him than to the rest of the world. He was a strong man. He was shrewd. He was decisive.

Time and again I have seen him make decisions that probably made the difference between war and peace for America and the world.

That was always when he was at his best. No matter how heated the arguments were, he was always then the coolest man in the room.

Dwight Eisenhower was that rarest of men—an authentic hero.

War brings the names of many men into the headlines and of those some few become national or even international heroes. But as the years then pass, their fame goes down.

But not so with Dwight Eisenhower. As the years passed, his stature grew: Commander of the mightiest expeditionary force ever assembled; receiver of the surrender of the German Armies in World War II; President of Columbia University; Supreme Commander of NATO; 34th President of the United States. The honors, the offices were there in abundance. Every trust that the American people had it in their power to bestow, he was given.

And, yet, he always retained a saving humility. His was the humility not of fear but of confidence. We walked with the great of the world, and he knew the greater human.

His was the humility of man before God and before the truth. His was the humility of a man too proud to be arrogant.

The pursuit of peace was uppermost in his mind when he ran for the Presidency. And it was uppermost in his conduct of that Office. And it is a tribute to his skill and determination that not since the 1930's has the Nation enjoyed so long a period of peace, both at home and abroad, as the one that began in 1953 and continued through his Presidency.

As Commander of the mightiest allied force ever assembled he was the right man at the right place at the right time.

And as President once again, he was the right man at the right place and at the right time.

He restored calm to a divided Nation. He gave Americans a new measure of self-respect. He invested his Office with dignity and respect and trust. He made Americans proud of their President, proud of their country, proud of themselves.

And if we in America were proud of Dwight Eisenhower, it was partly because he made us proud of America.

He came from the heart of America. And he gave expression to the heart of America and he touched the hearts of the world.

Many leaders are known and respected outside their own countries. Very few are loved outside their own countries. Dwight Eisenhower was one of those few. He was probably loved by more people in more parts of the world than any President America has ever had.

He captured the deepest feelings of free men everywhere. The principles he believed in, the ideals he stood for, these were bigger than his own country.

Perhaps he himself put it best again in that Guild Hall speech in 1945. He said then, "Kinship among nations is not determined in such measurements as proximity, size and age. Rather, we should turn to those inner things, call them what you will, I mean those intangibles that are the real treasures that free men possess, to preserve his freedom of worship, his equality before the law, his liberty to speak and act as he sees fit, subject only to provisions that he not trespass upon similar rights of others.

"A Londoner will fight and so will a citizen of Abilene. When we consider these things, then the Valley of the Thames draws closer to the farms of Kansas and the plains of Texas."

Some men are considered great because they lead great armies or they lead powerful nations. For eight years now, Dwight Eisenhower has neither commanded an army nor led a nation. And, yet, he remained through his final days the world's most admired and respected man, truly the first citizen of the world.

As we marvel at this, it leads us once again to ponder the mysteries of greatness. Dwight Eisenhower's greatness derived not from his office, but from his character, from a unique moral force that transcended national boundaries, even as his own deep concern for humanity transcended national boundaries.

His life reminds us that there is a moral force in this world more powerful than the might of arms or the wealth of nations. This man who led the most powerful armies that the world has ever seen, this man who led the most powerful Nation in the world, this essentially good and gentle and kind man, that moral force was his greatest.

For a quarter of a century, to the very end of his life, Dwight Eisenhower exercised a moral authority without parallel in America and in the world. And America and the world is better because of it.

And so today we render our final salute. It is a fond salute to a man we loved and cherished. It is a grateful salute to a man whose whole extraordinary life was consecrated to service. It is a profoundly respectful salute to a man larger than life who by any standard was one of the giants of our time.

Each of us here will have a special memory of Dwight Eisenhower.

I can see him now standing erect, straight, proud and tall, 16 years ago as he took the oath of office as the thirty-fourth President of the United States of America.

We salute Dwight David Eisenhower standing there in our memories, first in war, first in peace, and wherever freedom is cherished, first in the hearts of his fellow men.

## Benediction by The Rev. Edward L. R. Elson, D.D.
## Capitol Rotunda Funeral Service for President Eisenhower
## Sunday, March 30, 1969

Unto God's most gracious care and protection, we commit you.

The Lord bless you and keep you.

The Lord make His face to shine upon you and be gracious unto you, the Lord lift up His countenance upon you and give you peace, now and evermore.

And now may the God of peace who brought again from the dead our Lord Jesus Christ, that great Shepherd of the sheep, through the blood of the everlasting covenant, make you perfect in every good work, to do His will, working in you that which is well pleasing in His sight, through Jesus Christ our Lord to whom be glory for ever and ever. *Amen.*

## Funeral Service for the Honorable
# DWIGHT DAVID EISENHOWER
## (1890–1969)

## Monday, March Thirty-first, A.D. 1969
## Four-thirty O'Clock in the Afternoon

## Washington Cathedral, Washington, D.C.

ORGAN PRELUDE

Chorale-Prelude, "Schmücke dich, o liebe Seele" — *Johann Sebastian Bach*
Chorale-Prelude, "O Welt, ich muss dich lassen" — *Johannes Brahms*

*The Ministers, meeting the body, and going before it, will escort it to the place of honor in the Crossing of the Cathedral, while the people stand and the choir sings:*

THE PALMS — *J. Fauré*

O'er all the way green palms and blossoms gay
Are strewn this day in festal preparation,
Where Jesus comes to wipe our tears away,
E'en now the throng to welcome him prepare.

Join all and sing, his Name declare,
Let ev'ry voice resound with acclamation,
Hosanna! Praised be the Lord,
Bless him who cometh to bring us salvation.

His word goes forth and peoples by its might
Once more regain freedom from degradation,
Humanity doth give to each his right,
While those in darkness find restored the light.
*Refrain*

Sing and rejoice, O blest Jerusalem,
Of all thy sons sing the emancipation,
Through boundless love the Christ of Bethlehem
Brings faith and hope to thee for evermore.
*Refrain*

THE OPENING SENTENCES

*The Dean of the Cathedral will then offer the following prayer:*

Remember thy servant Dwight David, O Lord, according to the favour which thou bearest unto thy people, and grant that, increasing in knowledge and love of thee, he may go from strength to strength, in the life of perfect service, in thy heavenly kingdom; through Jesus Christ our Lord, who liveth and reigneth with thee and the Holy Ghost ever, one God, world without end. *Amen.*

*Minister and People:*

OUR FATHER, who art in heaven, Hallowed be thy Name. Thy kingdom come, Thy will be done, On earth as it is in heaven. Give us this day our daily bread. And forgive us our trespasses, as we forgive those who trespass against us. And lead us not into temptation, but deliver us from evil. For thine is the kingdom, and the power, and the glory for ever and ever. *Amen.*

HYMN (*sung by all, standing*)

A mighty fortress is our God,
A bulwark never failing;
Our helper he amid the flood
Of mortal ills prevailing:
For still our ancient foe
Doth seek to work us woe;
His craft and power are great,
And, armed with cruel hate,
On earth is not his equal!

Did we in our own strength confide,
Our striving would be losing;
Were not the right man on our side,
The man of God's own choosing:
Dost ask who that may be?
Christ Jesus, it is he;
Lord Sabaoth his Name,
From age to age the same,
And he must win the battle.

*Martin Luther, 1529*

PSALMS 46 and 121 (*read responsively*) *Led by the minister of the National Presbyterian Church*

God is our refuge and strength, a very present help in trouble.

*Therefore will we not fear, though the earth be removed, and though the mountains be carried into the midst of the sea;*

Though the waters thereof roar and be troubled,

*Though the mountains shake with the swelling thereof.*

There is a river, the streams whereof make glad the city of God,

*The holy place of the tabernacles of the Most High.*

God is in the midst of her; she shall not be moved:

*Good will help her, and that right early.*

The nations raged, the kingdoms were moved: he uttered his voice, the earth melted.

*The Lord of hosts is with us; the God of Jacob is our refuge,*

Come, behold the works of the Lord,

*What desolations he hath made in the earth.*

He maketh wars to cease unto the end of the earth;

*He breaketh the bow, and cutteth the spear in sunder; he burneth the chariots in the fire.*

Be still, and know that I am God: I will be exalted among the nations, I will be exalted in the earth.

*The Lord of hosts is with us; the God of Jacob is our refuge.*

I will lift up mine eyes unto the hills: from whence shall my help come?

*My help cometh from the Lord, who made heaven and earth.*

He will not suffer thy foot to be moved: he that keepeth thee will not slumber.

*Behold, he that keepeth Israel will neither slumber nor sleep.*

The Lord is thy keeper: the Lord is thy shade upon thy right hand.

*The sun shall not smite thee by day, nor the moon by night.*

The Lord will preserve thee from all evil: he will preserve thy soul.

*The Lord will preserve thy going out and thy coming in from this time forth, and even for evermore.*

Glory be to the Father, and to the Son, and to the Holy Ghost;

*As it was in the beginning, is now, and ever shall be, world without end. Amen.*

THE APOSTLES' CREED (*said by all*)

I BELIEVE in God the Father Almighty, Maker of heaven and earth: And in Jesus Christ his only Son, our Lord; who was conceived by the Holy Ghost, born of the Virgin Mary, suffered under Pontius Pilate, was crucified, dead, and buried; he descended into hell; the third day he rose again from the dead; he ascended into heaven, and sitteth on the right hand of God the Father Almighty; from thence he shall come to judge the quick and the dead.

I believe in the Holy Ghost; the holy Catholic Church; the communion of saints; the forgiveness of sins; the resurrection of the body; and the life everlasting. *Amen.*

THE READING OF THE SCRIPTURES (*people seated*)

*"Hear the reading of God's word, being excerpts from the Letters of Paul, the Apostle, and the words of our Lord Jesus Christ."*

II TIMOTHY 4: 6–7

6 ". . . the time of my departure is at hand.
7 I have fought a good fight, I have finished my course, I have kept the faith:

ROMANS 8: 14, 35, 37–39

14 For as many as are led by the Spirit of God, they are the sons of God.
35 Who shall separate us from the love of Christ? shall tribulation, or distress, or persecution, or famine, or nakedness, or peril, or sword?
37 Nay, in all these things we are more than conquerors through him that loved us.
38 For I am persuaded, that neither death, nor life, nor angels, nor principalities, nor powers, nor things present, nor things to come,
39 Nor height, nor depth, nor any other creature, shall be able to separate us from the love of God, which is in Christ Jesus our Lord.

I THESSALONIANS 4: 13, 14, 18

13 But I would not have you to be ignorant, brethren, concerning them which are asleep, that ye sorrow not, even as others which have no hope.

14 For if we believe that Jesus died and rose again, even so them also which sleep in Jesus will God bring with him.

18 Wherefore comfort one another with these words.

II CORINTHIANS 4: 5

5 For we know that if our earthly house of this tabernacle were dissolved, we have a building of God, an house not made with hands, eternal in the heavens.

I CORINTHIANS 13: 9–13

9 For we know in part, and we prophesy in part.

10 But when that which is perfect is come, then that which is in part shall be done away.

11 When I was a child, I spake as a child, I understood as a child, I thought as a child: but when I became a man, I put away childish things.

12 For now we see through a glass, darkly; but then face to face: now I know in part; but then shall I know even as also I am known.

13 And now abideth faith, hope, charity, these three; but the greatest of these is charity.

I CORINTHIANS 15: 57, 58

57 Thanks be to God, which giveth us the victory through our Lord Jesus Christ.

58 Therefore, my beloved brethren, be ye steadfast, unmoveable, always abounding in the work of the Lord, forasmuch as ye know that your labour is not in vain in the Lord.

EPHESIANS 6: 10–18

10 Finally, my brethren, be strong in the Lord, and in the power of his might.

11 Put on the whole armour of God, that ye may be able to stand against the wiles of the devil.

12 For we wrestle not against flesh and blood, but against principalities, against powers, against the rulers of the darkness of this world, against spiritual wickedness in high places.

13 Wherefore take unto you the whole armour of God, that ye may be able to withstand in the evil day, and having done all, to stand.

14 Stand therefore, having your loins gird about with truth, and having on the breastplate of righteousness;

15 And your feet shod with the preparation of the gospel of peace;

16 Above all, taking the shield of faith, wherewith you shall be able to quench all the fiery darts of the wicked.

17 And take the helmet of salvation, and the sword of the Spirit, which is the word of God:

18 Praying always with all prayer and supplication in the Spirit.

Hear the words of our Lord Jesus Christ:

MATTHEW 5: 3, 4, 8, 9

3 Blessed are the poor in spirit: for theirs is the kingdom of heaven.
4 Blessed are they that mourn: for they shall be comforted.
8 Blessed are the pure in heart: for they shall see God.
9 Blessed are the peacemakers: for they shall be called the children of God.

JOHN 14 (adapted from the Presbyterian Book of Common Worship)

Jesus said: "Let not your heart be troubled: ye believe in God, believe also in Me. In My Father's house are many dwelling places: if it were not so, I would have told you. I go to prepare a place for you. And if I go and prepare a place for you, I will come again, and receive you unto Myself; that where I am, there ye may be also. And whither I go ye know, and the way ye know. I am the way, the truth, and the life: no man cometh unto the Father, but by Me.

"These things have I spoken unto you, being yet present with you. But the Comforter, which is the Holy Spirit, whom the Father will send in My name, He shall teach you all things, and bring all things to your remembrance, whatsoever I have said unto you. Peace I leave with you, My peace I give unto you; not as the world giveth, give I unto you. Let not your heart be troubled, neither let it be afraid."

*The congregation will remain seated while* Psalm 23 *is sung by the Cathedral choir to the words and music of the Scottish Psalter.*

The Lord's my Shepherd, I'll not want;
He makes me down to lie
In pastures green; he leadeth me
The quiet waters by.

My soul he doth restore again;
And me to walk doth make
Within the paths of righteousness,
E'en for his own Name's sake.

Yea, though I walk in death's dark vale,
Yet will I fear none ill;
For thou art with me; and thy rod
And staff me comfort still.

My table thou has furnished
In presence of my foes;
My head thou dost with oil anoint,
And my cup overflows.

Goodness and mercy all my life
Shall surely follow me;
And in God's house forevermore
My dwelling place shall be. *Amen.*

MEMORIAL AND PASTORAL PRAYERS

Almighty God, Father of mercies and Giver of all comfort, deal graciously, we pray Thee, with all those who mourn this day, that casting every care on Thee, they may know the consolation of Thy love, the healing of Thy grace, and the companionship of Thy presence. Through Jesus Christ our Lord.

Eternal Father, in whom we live and move and have our being, draw us close to Thee and let Thy light and joy fill our souls as we offer unto Thee the praise and thanksgiving of our hearts; for the mystery and wonder of life here and hereafter. We thank Thee that deep in the human heart is an unquenchable trust that life does not end with death, that the Father who made us will care for us beyond the bounds of vision even as He has cared for us in this earthy pilgrimage. We praise Thy name that our hope has been so wondrously confirmed in the life, the words and resurrection of our Lord Jesus Christ.

We give Thee thanks for all the sacred memories and hallowed recollections which cluster about this hour.

We thank Thee for Thy servant Dwight David. For his goodly heritage, his godly parents, his boyhood home and early training, and for his beloved companion of the years. We thank Thee for the nobility of his manhood, the integrity of his person, the hospitality of his mind and magnanimity of his spirit; for his steadfastness under provocation, for his gifts of reconciliation, for his kindness and his firmness, for his compassion and mercy, for his warm friendship, his transparent spirituality, his patience in suffering, and for all that endeared him to the multitudes of mankind. Especially do we thank Thee for his Christian testimony, for the depth and durability of his faith, for his constant witness to the spiritual basis of our common life, for his steadfastness in seeking to know and to do Thy will, and for his daily walk with Thee.

We thank Thee too for all the human graces with which Thou didst endow him—for his sheer joy in living, for his infectious humor, his zeal as sportsman and competitor, his love of beauty and his efforts to express it on canvas and in words, for his love of family and for the sanctity of his home.

O God, in whose sovereign will is the destiny of men and nations, who art a God of history and beyond history, we give Thee special thanks for the magnitude of his public service—for his military prowess in defense of freedom; for his leadership in winning and in conserving the peace; for his high service as President of the Republic. We give Thee thanks for his vast labors transcending all parties and factions, encompassing all men and nations, for his high vision of the better world toward which all men of good will strive, and for his devotion to that higher kingdom, the ruler of which is God and the law of which is love.

O Eternal Father, suffer us not to miss the glory of this hour. May a new spirit arise in us this day. Give us eyes to see and hearts to feel the undaunted courage, the invincible faith, the unconquerable love of Thy servant, Dwight David, that we may be true as he was true, loyal as he was loyal; that we may henceforth be good enough and great enough for our times. Through Jesus Christ our Lord. Amen.

And now, O Father, who doest all things well, with thankful hearts that Thou has given him to us for a season, we give Thy servant, Dwight David, back to Thy tender care, until the shadows flee away, and the brighter day dawns, when the visible and invisible are as one in Thy higher kingdom. Through Jesus Christ our Lord. *Amen.*

BENEDICTION by the Bishop of Washington

Unto God's gracious mercy and protection we commit Dwight David. The Lord bless him and keep him. The Lord make his face to shine upon him, and be gracious unto him. The Lord lift up his countenance upon him, and give him peace, both now and evermore.

And now may the God of peace, who brought again from the dead our Lord Jesus Christ, the great Shepherd of the sheep, through the blood of the everlasting covenant; Make you perfect in every Good work to do His will, working in you that which is well pleasing in his sight; through Jesus Christ, to whom be glory for ever and ever. *Amen.*

HYMN (*sung by all, standing*)

Onward, Christian soldiers,
Marching as to war,
With the cross of Jesus
Going on before!
Christ, the royal Master,
Leads against the foe;
Forward into battle,
See, his banners go.

Onward, Christian soldiers,
Marching as to war,
With the cross of Jesus
Going on before!

Like a mighty army
Moves the Church of God;
Brothers, we are treading
Where the saints have trod;
We are not divided,
All one body we,
One in hope and doctrine,
One in charity.
*Refrain*

Onward, then, ye people,
Join our happy throng,
Blend with ours your voices
In the triumph song;
Glory, laud, and honor
Unto Christ the King;
This through countless ages
Men and angels sing.
*Refrain*
*Amen.*

*During the singing of the hymn the Ministers and Honorary Pallbearers take their places around the body and at the end of the hymn they escort it to the North Entrance while the United States Marine Band, the President's Own, plays* "Army Blue."

HONORS TO THE PRESIDENT played by the Marine Band.

*As the body is carried down the steps of the Cathedral the Marine Band will play "Lead, Kindly Light."*

*The congregation leaves to the tolling of the Bourdon Bell.*

## OFFICIATING CLERGY

The Very Reverend Francis B. Sayre, Jr.
*Dean of Washington Cathedral*

The Reverend Edward L. R. Elson
*Minister, National Presbyterian Church*

The Right Reverend William F. Creighton
*Bishop of Washington*

Choir of the Washington Cathedral
Paul Callaway, organist

## Funeral Service for

# GENERAL OF THE ARMY

## and 34th President of the United States of America

# DWIGHT DAVID EISENHOWER

## Abilene, Kansas
## Wednesday, April 2, 1969
### 10:30 a.m.

*Parts of the service conducted by:*

Rev. Robert A. MacAskill, D.D., Pastor, The Presbyterian Church, Gettysburg, Pennsylvania

Call to Worship:

"Our help is in the name of the Lord, who made heaven and earth and in Jesus Christ who said: "I am the Resurrection and the Life, he that believeth in Me, though he were dead, yet shall he live: and whosoever liveth and believeth in Me shall never die."

Prayer:

Eternal God, our Heavenly Father, who lovest us with an everlasting love, and can turn the shadow of death into the morning: Help us now to wait upon Thee with reverent and believing hearts. In the silence of this hour speak to us of eternal things, that through patience and comfort of the Scriptures we may have hope, and be lifted above our darkness and distress into the light and peace of Thy presence, through Jesus Christ our Lord . . . who taught us when we pray to say:

"Our Father, who art in Heaven; Hallowed be Thy name. Thy kingdom come. Thy will be done; On earth as it is in heaven. Give us this day our daily bread. And forgive us our debts; As we forgive our debtors. And lead us not into temptation; But deliver us from evil; For Thine is the kingdom, and the power, and the glory, for ever. Amen.

Scripture Reading:

"Let not your heart be troubled; ye believe in God, believe also in me. In my Father's house are many mansions: if it were not so, I would have told you. I go to prepare a place for you. And if I go and prepare a place for you, I will come again, and receive you unto myself; that where I am, there ye may be also." John 14: 1–3.

The Text:

"For I am now ready to be offered and the time of my departure is at hand. I have fought a good fight, I have finished my course, I have kept the faith: henceforth there is laid up for me a crown of righteousness, which the Lord, the righteous judge, shall give me at that day: and not to me only, but unto all them also that love his appearing." II Timothy 4: 6–8.

The Meditation:

In thinking about a text and an outline for my remarks on this occasion, there comes to my mind the words of scripture which I have just read. For they seem appropriate and applicable as we consider the life and service of General Dwight D. Eisenhower.

"I have fought a good fight"

By training and temperament General Eisenhower prepared himself for awesome responsibilities as a soldier and statesman. He was aware of the destruction and futility of war and tyranny and this gave him an even greater determination for peace and freedom. In a sense his military training and leadership prepared him for the role of President. Always guided by a sense of reasonableness, he did much to keep a balance between military and peaceful pursuits.

In his farewell address as President to the American people, January 17, 1961, he said: "In the councils of government we must guard against the acquisition of unwarranted processes. We should take nothing for granted. Only an alert and knowledgeable citizenry can compel the proper meshing of the large industrial and military machinery of defense with our peaceful methods and goals, so that security and liberty may prosper together."

His preparation for life and service contained a strategy whether it be a military offensive or a peaceful proposal. He believed in having the facts at hand, receiving good counsel, and proceeding in a resolute and determined course of action.

One of the significant decisions and proposals of his administration was the Atoms for Peace program, offered the United Nations American uranium for peaceful uses by "havenot" countries.

In his concluding remarks of the First Inaugural Address he said: "We are not the helpless prisoners of history; we had to be willing to accept whatever sacrifices might be required—for the people that values its privileges above its principles soon loses both. "The peace we seek is more than the stilling of guns, easing the sorrow of war. More than escape from death, it is a way of life. More than a haven for the weary, it is a hope for the brave."

All of this required a strategy, a struggle and a sacrifice in fighting a good fight!

"I have finished my course"

In General Eisenhower's long and useful life he labored unceasingly for the things that make for peace with justice—a familiar phrase of his. No matter what he set out to do, whether in a game of golf, or a military strategy or proposed legislation, he always had a definite goal and objective in view. This gave him a tenacity of purpose, a singleness of mind, and a determination to follow through.

The course which started in Abilene some 78 years ago was destined to unfold from the grassroots of this American heartland to the far reaches of the world. In traveling this path, General Eisenhower had a firm reliance on divine guidance, deeply imbedded in the heritage of God fearing parents who imparted this wisdom and love unto their children. In making his way through life, he followed a course that was anchored in the eternal purposes of God as expressed in the words of a favorite Psalm—121 "I lift up my eyes to the hills. From whence does my help come? My help comes from the Lord, who made heaven and earth. The Lord will keep your going out and your coming in from this time forth and for evermore." With this assurance and confidence he finished the course!

"I have kept the faith"

This was an expression of his life that impressed those who knew him. He had a vibrant faith in God, his fellowmen and his country. He said, "We had to proclaim our faith. It was our faith in the deathless dignity of man. And the faith we hold belongs, not to us alone but to the free of the world—the grower of rice in Burma and the planter of wheat in Iowa, the shepherd in southern Italy and the mountaineer in the Andes. It confers a common dignity upon the French soldier who dies in Indochina, the British soldier killed in Malaya, the American life given in Korea."

He spoke of a faith in the beneficence of the Almighty. To him "faith was the substance of things hoped for, the evidence of things not seen."

In a recent article he expressed his faith in the young people of our land when he said: "The world will soon be yours to do with as you can. I would urge you to approach your task with boldness and the hope and the joy of challenge in your hearts—and with dedication to freedom and human dignity. For this is the only route to peace with justice. Good luck, then, and may the Lord go with you. I, for one, believe in you!"

Here then, was the simple, straight-forward, uncomplicated faith of a world leader. He not so much articulated a faith as he acted upon it. His faith in God, gave him a humility and a high regard for human life. It caused him to be dedicated to the preservation and perpetuation of such a way of life.

Because of this faith he was liberated from provincialism and little things and given a world vision and concern for all men. He believed in the words of a favorite hymn: "Faith of our Fathers living still, in spite of fire, dungeon and sword."

As has been said of Lincoln, can now be said of Dwight Eisenhower, "He belongs to the ages." For his spirit and influence are an expression of the American ideal of "liberty and justice for all." President Nixon stated it well in his message on Sunday: "He was known not so much for what he did as for what he was—it was the character of the man." His example of character, integrity, humility and dedication is indeed a rich legacy and will give us inspiration to resist the forces of tyranny and help us to usher in a new day of brotherhood and good will to the glory of God and the welfare of mankind.

In this confidence we commit him to the care and keeping of a merciful and loving God, sustained in the power and hope of Him who said: "Well done thou good and faithful servant, enter into the joy of thy Lord." *Amen.*

The Prayer:

We give thanks to Thee O God for this, Thy servant, Dwight David Eisenhower, recalling all in him that made others love him. We bless Thee for the good and gracious influence in his home and training, for all that ministered to his best life. We thank Thee for the goodness and truth that have passed from his life into the lives of others, and have made the world richer for his presence.

Grant us, we beseech Thee, the comfort of Thy presence, and the ministry of Thy Holy Spirit. Renew within us the gifts of faith, patience, and enduring love. Help us to walk amid the things of this world with eyes ever open to the beauty and glory of the eternal, that so, among the sundry and manifold changes of this life, our hearts may surely there be fixed where true joys are to be found; through Jesus Christ our Lord. *Amen.*

The Benediction:

The God of peace, that brought again from the dead our Lord Jesus, that great Shepherd of the sheep, through the blood of the everlasting covenant, make you perfect in every good work to do His will, working in you that which is well-pleasing in His sight; and may the grace of the Lord Jesus Christ, and the love of God, and the communion of the Holy Spirit, be with you, and with those you love, in this time of bereavement and forever more. *Amen.*

## Burial Service for
# GENERAL DWIGHT DAVID EISENHOWER
## in the Place of Meditation
## Eisenhower Center, Abilene, Kansas
## April 2, 1969

## Conducted by
## Chaplain (Maj. Gen.) Luther D. Miller, USA, Ret.
## Former Chief of Army Chaplains

All that the Father giveth me shall come to me; and him that cometh to me I will in no wise cast out.

He that raised up Jesus from the dead will also quicken our mortal bodies, by his Spirit that dwelleth in us.

Wherefore my heart is glad, and my glory rejoiceth: my flesh also shall rest in hope. Thou shalt show me the path of life; in thy presence is the fulness of joy, and at thy right hand there is pleasure for evermore.

O God, the Father of our Lord, Jesus Christ, vouchsafe we beseech Thee to bless this grave to be the peaceful resting place of the body of thy servant, through the same, thy blessed Son, who is the resurrection and the life, and who liveth and reigneth with Thee and the Holy Spirit, one God, world without end. *Amen.*

Unto Almighty God we commend the soul of our comrade departed, and we commit his body to the ground; earth to earth, ashes to ashes, dust to dust; in sure and certain hope of the Resurrection unto eternal life, through our Lord Jesus Christ; at whose coming in glorious majesty to judge the world, the earth and sea shall give up their dead; and the corruptible bodies of those who sleep in him shall be changed, and made like unto his own glorious body; according to the mighty working whereby he is able to subdue all things unto himself.

I heard a voice from heaven, saying unto me, Write, From henceforth blessed are the dead who die in the Lord: even so saith the Spirit; for they rest from their labours.

The Lord be with you.
And with thy spirit.

Let us pray.

Lord, have mercy upon us.
Christ, have mercy upon us.
Lord, have mercy upon us.

O God, whose mercies cannot be numbered; Accept our prayers on behalf of the soul of thy servant departed, and grant him an entrance into the land of light and joy, in the fellowship of thy saints; through Jesus Christ our Lord. *Amen.*

Remember thy servant, Dwight Eisenhower, O Lord, according to the favor which Thou bearest unto thy people, and grant that, increasing in knowledge and love of Thee, he may go from strength to strength in the life of perfect service in thy heavenly kingdom, through Jesus Christ our Lord, who liveth and reigneth with Thee and the Holy Ghost, ever one God, world without end. *Amen.*

Almighty and everlasting God, before whom stand the living and the dead, we praise and bless thy holy name for the good examples of those, thy servants who, having finished their course here on earth, now rest from their labors. Especially do we remember at this time our departed comrade, Dwight Eisenhower. We thank Thee for the memories which gather about this great life, his unending devotion and tireless efforts on behalf of our nation and the military forces. Help us to prize highly and to guard carefully the gifts which such loyalty and devotion to duty have passed on to us. Grant that we may be true as he was true; that we may be loyal as he was loyal; and that we may serve our country and our God all the days of our lives and leave the world better as he did for having lived in it, through Jesus Christ our Lord. *Amen.*

In memory of a great soldier, Dwight Eisenhower, O Lord, God of hosts, may we his comrades gird ourselves to finish the work he began, that thy peace may come to all our troubled world. Make us aware, we beseech Thee, of the responsibility that rests upon us to teach the world that righteousness alone exalteth a nation. Make us willing to seek moral objectives together, that in united action our nation may be as resolute for righteousness and peace as she has been for war, through Jesus Christ our Lord. *Amen.*

Heavenly Father, though all our sympathy goes out to these our dear friends, we know that sympathy cannot bind up broken hearts. Only Thou canst do that. We ask Thee now to perform that gracious and healing ministry. Help them who walked by Dwight Eisenhower's side—help them in this hour of grief and parting to rededicate themselves to Thee in a way that shall bring their troubled hearts thy promised joy and peace. We make this intercession through Jesus Christ our Lord. *Amen.*

The God of peace, who brought again from the dead our Lord Jesus Christ, the great Shepherd of the sheep, through the blood of the everlasting covenant; Make you perfect in every good work to do his will, work in you that which is well pleasing in his sight; through Jesus Christ, to whom be glory for ever and ever. *Amen.*

21 Gun Salute

The march of another soldier is ended. His battles are all fought and his victories all won and he lies down to rest awhile, awaiting the bugle's call.

Unto God's gracious mercy and protection we commend you, Old Friend. May the Lord bless you and keep you. May the Lord make his face to shine upon you and be gracious unto you. May the Lord lift up his countenance upon you and give you peace, both now and evermore. *Amen.*

Volley

Taps

Band

## Memorial Service for
## The Honorable
# DWIGHT DAVID EISENHOWER
## Abilene, Kansas
## April 2, 1969

## Dean W. Miller, Minister of the Palm Desert Community Presbyterian Church Palm Desert, California

Scripture Readings:

I will lift up mine eyes unto the hills,
From whence cometh my help.
My help cometh from the Lord,
Which made heaven and earth.
He will not suffer thy foot to be moved:
He that keepth thee will not slumber.
Behold, He that keepeth Israel
Shall neither slumber nor sleep.
The Lord is thy keeper:
The Lord is thy shade upon thy right hand.
The sun shall not smite thee by day,
Nor the moon by night.
The Lord shall preserve thee from all evil:
He shall preserve thy soul.
The Lord shall preserve thy going out and thy coming in
From this time forth, and even for evermore.

—*Psalm 121*

The Lord is my Shepherd; I shall not want.
He maketh me to lie down in green pastures:
He leadeth me beside the still waters.
He restoreth my soul:
He leadeth me in the paths of righteousness for His name's sake.
Yea, though I walk through the valley of the shadow of death,
I will fear no evil: for Thou art with me;
Thy rod and Thy staff they comfort me.
Thou preparest a table before me in the presence of mine enemies:
Thou anointest my head with oil;
My cup runneth over.
Surely goodness and mercy shall follow me all the days of my life:
And I will dwell in the house of the Lord for ever.

—*Psalm 23*

Dwight David Eisenhower was held in esteem as the First Citizen of the World, but he was first a citizen of Abilene, Kansas. Mrs. Eisenhower said that although he traveled the world, he always thought of and loved his town of Abilene.

Here he spent his boyhood days, and here his character was formed and shaped in the Eisenhower family. Because of his Kansas heritage it is most fitting that he be laid to rest near his family home.

President Nixon quoted the General as saying once, "I come from the heart of America," and so it is to the heart of America General Eisenhower has returned today.

I would speak also of a companion-soldier, Mamie Doud Eisenhower. Mrs. Eisenhower graciously shared her husband with the world, but he belonged uniquely to her in the relationship of marriage. During fifty-three years of marriage she fulfilled, with unusual fidelity and devotion, her wedding vows: "To be thy loving and faithful wife; in plenty and in want; in joy and in sorrow; in sickness and in health; as long as we both shall live."

In a day when wedding vows are often taken lightly, Mrs. Eisenhower stands as a symbol of the beauty and holiness of marriage.

In Micah we read:

"He has showed you, O man, what is good;
and what does the Lord require of you
but to do justice, and to love kindness,
and to walk humbly with your God?"

Dwight David Eisenhower, in his long life of service to God and man, fulfilled this threefold prophetic requirement: that of justice in the daily relationships of life, kindness to one's fellows, and walking humbly before God.

In an interview in Palm Desert, California, the General expressed these convictions:

Some day, he firmly believed, he would stand before his God; for his personal faith told him there is a life ahead. And of this, too, he was convinced: that the same Lord who was with him on Malta, and during those anxious early hours of D-Day when he headed the mightiest invasion in history, will stand with him at the beginning of the greatest adventure of his career . . . entrance into eternal life.

"Well done, good and faithful servant, enter into the joy of your Master."

Let us pray:

"Father of all mercies and God of all comfort, who hast brought life and immortality to light through our Lord Jesus Christ, we thank Thee that 'Life is ever Lord of death, and love can never lose its own.'

"We praise Thee for the inspiration of Christian friendships; especially do we thank Thee for Thy servant, Dwight David Eisenhower, whose memory we are here to honor.

"For the gentleness of his character, the breadth of his sympathies, the power of his convictions, his genius for friendship, his patriotism as a citizen, his high honor as a man, and for his devotion to Christ and his church—we give Thee thanks.

"Give especially to those who most intimately mourn his going, wide margins of comfort around their spiritual need and deep wells to draw their consolation from.

"Now that for a time we have parted, be beseech Thee to bless the family circle that is severed, and the comrades who are bereft. As Thou hast given them this new tie to bind them to the world unseen, so grant unto them that where their treasure is, there, may their hearts be also.

"Once more we stand upon the shore of the sea and bid farewell to a ship that loses itself over the rim of the world. O God, give fair voyaging and safe harbor! And as we stand upon this hither shore and bid farewell, grant us faith to hear the voices which on yonder shore cry, 'Welcome!' and 'All hail!'

"And unto Thee shall be the glory forever, world without end." *Amen.*

# General Eisenhower's Membership in the National Presbyterian Church

In preparing for his first Inauguration, General Dwight David Eisenhower asked the Rev. Dr. Edward L. R. Elson, pastor of The National Presbyterian Church, to conduct a private pre-Inaugural service of dedication in the Church on the morning of January 20, 1953. The President invited only the Vice President, members of the Cabinet, members of the White House staff, officials of the Inaugural Committee, and their families to share in this service—a total of 181 persons. Following the 20-minute service, the President-elect went to his suite in the Statler-Hilton Hotel, sat down at a table, and on a yellow pad wrote a brief prayer with which he began his first Inaugural address. The spirit of the man and the language of the prayer profoundly moved people everywhere when he said, "Give us, we pray, the power to discern clearly right from wrong and allow all our words and actions to be governed thereby and by the laws of this land."

President Eisenhower had long considered completing his identification with the Church as an active communicant member of a particular congregation. The matter was discussed with Dr. Elson on several occasions prior to his Inauguration and several notes were exchanged between the minister and the nation's new leader. On February 1, 1953, the President and Mrs. Eisenhower were received into full communicant membership of The National Presbyterian Church. They appeared before the Session of the Church in the room off the N Street entrance of the old church. Having been a member of the Presbyterian Church from childhood, Mrs. Eisenhower was received on reaffirmation of faith from her Denver church. It not being the practice of President Eisenhower's parents' church to baptize infants, the President therefore made his personal profession of faith and received Christian baptism, kneeling on the prie-dieu provided for that purpose. At the service which followed, President and Mrs. Eisenhower received Holy Communion for the first time as members of this congregation and were publicly acknowledged as two members of a class of fifty new church members.

During the eight years which followed, President and Mrs. Eisenhower were unfailingly present at church service and they entered wholly into the life of the congregation.

President Eisenhower gave personal leadership in developing the new National Presbyterian Church and Center. While President he enlisted the support of Presbyterian laymen and he personally contributed to the project. It is fitting that the Chapel of the Presidents be dedicated to him.

# Memorial Services

IN THE

# Senate of the United States

IN EULOGY OF

# Dwight David Eisenhower

# In the Senate of the United States

*MARCH 31, 1969*

PRAYER

The Reverend Edward L. R. Elson, D.D., Chaplain of the Senate. On the day of his first inauguration, January 20, 1953, President Dwight David Eisenhower attended a brief pre-inaugural church service in the National Presbyterian Church, after which he went to his rooms and wrote a prayer of his own. Several hours later, in front of this Capitol Building, when he began his inaugural address, he asked everyone to join him as he offered his own prayer. In the words of his prayer, let us pray today:

"Almighty God, as we stand here at this moment, my future associates in the executive branch of the Government join me in beseeching that Thou will make full and complete our dedication to the service of the people in this throng and their fellow citizens everywhere.

"Give us, we pray, the power to discern clearly right from wrong and allow all our words and actions to be governed thereby and by the laws of this land.

"Especially we pray that our concern shall be for all the people, regardless of station, race, or calling. May cooperation be permitted and be the mutual aim of those who, under the concept of our Constitution, hold to differing political beliefs—so that all may work for the good of our beloved country and for Thy glory. Amen."

*Mr. Mansfield.* Mr. President, I ask unanimous consent to have printed in the RECORD the transcript of the proceedings of the informal meeting of Senators in connection with the funeral ceremonies for the former President of the United States, Dwight David Eisenhower, held in the Senate Chamber yesterday, Sunday, March 30, 1969.

*The Vice President.* Without objection, it is so ordered.

*Mr. Dirksen.* Mr. President, I ask unanimous consent also to have printed in the RECORD the eulogy delivered by the President of the United States and the benediction by the Reverend Edward L. R. Elson, Chaplain of the Senate, at the memorial service on yesterday.

*The Vice President.* Without objection, it is so ordered.

The transcript of the proceedings, the eulogy, and the benediction were ordered to be printed in the RECORD, as follows:

IN THE SENATE CHAMBER, SUNDAY, MARCH 30, 1969

An informal meeting of Senators, called by the majority leader, the Senator from Montana (Mr. MANSFIELD), and the minority leader, the Senator from Illinois (Mr. DIRKSEN), was held at 3:30 p.m. in connection with arrangements for the funeral ceremonies for the former President of the United States, Dwight David Eisenhower.

The meeting was called to order by the Senator from Louisiana (Mr. ELLENDER), as Presiding Officer.

FUNERAL SERVICES

*Mr. Mansfield.* Mr. President, this is an informal meeting of the Senate, and I wish to make the following announcement on behalf of the distinguished minority leader and myself:

Funeral services for the late President at the Washington National Cathedral will be held tomorrow at 4:30 p.m.

Buses will depart under escort from First Street NE., between the Senate Office Buildings, at 3:30 p.m. and return immediately after the services. Those going in private cars are advised to enter the cathedral grounds from Woodley Road and proceed to the north transept entrance.

Tickets for the services for Senators and wives will be delivered by the Sergeant at Arms. Members of the Senate delegation are scheduled to be seated in the cathedral at 4:15 p.m.

*Mr. Dirksen.* Mr. President, we were in some doubt as to whether an official delegation from the House and Senate should attend the funeral at Abilene, Kans. At the last minute, however, it developed that it was not desired to have the formal attendance of a House delegation, and therefore those concerned were not particularly happy about having a Senate delegation.

There are two reasons for that. There will be an outdoor service on the Eisenhower Library steps. Then a private service will take place in the little chapel. The chapel holds 50 persons. The service will be brief. So the idea of sending a delegation was discouraged. Therefore, there will not be a delegation from the House or the Senate. That, however, does not preclude any individual Member of the Senate who desires to do so from attending the funeral. Moreover, I am advised that Senators probably will not find any accommodations in Abilene, because military personnel from all over the country are already there.

*Mr. Mansfield.* I should think it would be most appropriate for the Senators from Kansas to go, if they desire to do so, because the funeral will take place in their State, and it is personally important to them.

*Mr. Pearson.* My colleague from Kansas, Mr. Dole, and I intend to go.

*Mr. Mansfield.* Mr. President, as previously ordered, the Senate will meet at 12 o'clock noon tomorrow.

I now move that this informal meeting of Members of the Senate be adjourned. I suggest that the distinguished Senators from Kansas both meet directly behind the President pro tempore of the Senate.

The motion was agreed to; and (at 4 o'clock and 3 minutes p.m.) the informal meeting of the Senate was adjourned.

The Senate proceeded in a body to the rotunda and the bier of the former President of the United States, Dwight David Eisenhower, headed by the President pro tempore of the Senate (Mr. Russell); the Senators from Kansas (Mr. Pearson and Mr. Dole); the majority leader (Mr. Mansfield); and the minority leader (Mr. Dirksen).

## President Nixon's Eulogy to General Eisenhower

We gather today in mourning but also in gratitude. We mourn Dwight Eisenhower's death, but we are grateful for his life. We gather also conscious of the fact that in paying tribute to Dwight Eisenhower we celebrate greatness. When we think of his place in history, we think inevitably of those other giants of World War II. And we think of the qualities of greatness and what his were that made his unique among all.

Once, perhaps without intending to do so, he himself put his finger on it. It was 1945 shortly after V–E Day at a ceremony in London's historic Guildhall. The triumphant Supreme Commander of the Allied Forces in Europe was officially given the freedom of the city of London. In an eloquent address that day, Dwight Eisenhower said:

> I come from the heart of America.

Perhaps no one sentence could better sum up what Dwight Eisenhower meant to a whole generation of Americans.

He did come from the heart of America, not only from the geographical heart but from its spiritual heart. He exemplified what millions of parents hoped that their sons would be—strong and courageous and honest and compassionate. And with his own great qualities of heart, he personified the best in America. It is, I think, a special tribute to Dwight Eisenhower that despite all of his honors, despite all of his great deeds and triumphs, we find ourselves today speaking first not of his deeds but of his character.

It was the character of the man—not what he

did, but what he was—that so captured the trust and faith and affection of his own people and of the people of the world. Dwight Eisenhower touched something fundamental in America, which only a man of immense force of mind and spirit could have brought so vibrantly alive. He was a product of America's soil and of its ideals, driven by a compulsion to do right and to do well. A man of deep faith who believed in God and trusted in His will. A man who truly loved his country and for whom words like "freedom" and "democracy" were not cliches. But they were living truths. I know Mrs. Eisenhower would permit me to share with you the last words he spoke of her on the day he died. He said:

> I've always loved my wife, I've always loved my children, I've always loved my grandchildren and I've always loved my country.

That was Dwight Eisenhower.

### A MAN WHO GAVE ENORMOUSLY

He was a man who gave enormously. His way of relaxing from the intense pressures of office or command was to do something else intensely, whether as a fierce competitor on the golf course or executing one of those hauntingly beautiful paintings that he did with such meticulous care.

But even more than this, he gave enormously of himself to people.

People loved Dwight Eisenhower. But the other side of this coin was that he loved people. He had the great leader's capacity to bring out the best in people. He had the great humanist's capacity to inspire people, to cheer them, to give them lift. I remember, for example, just a few months ago when I asked all of the members of the Cabinet to go out and call on him, each of them returned with wonder and admiration and said, "You know, I went out there to cheer him up and instead I found he cheered me up."

His great love of people was rooted in his faith. He had a deep faith in the goodness of God and in the essential goodness of man as a creature of God. This feeling toward people had another side.

In the political world, strong passions are the norm. And all too often these turn toward personal vindictiveness. People often disagreed with Dwight Eisenhower but almost nobody ever hated him. And this I think was because he himself was a man who did not know how to hate. Oh, he could be aroused by a cause. But he could not hate a person. He could disagree strongly, even passionately, but never personally. When people disagreed with him, he never thought of them as enemies. He simply thought, "Well, they don't agree with me." I remember time after time when critics of one sort or another were misrepresenting him or reviling him, he would sit back in his chair with that wonderful half-smile and half-frown, he would say, "I'm puzzled by those fellows." And he was genuinely puzzled by frenzy and by hate and because he was incapable of it himself, he could never understand it in others.

The last time I saw him, that was what he talked about. He was puzzled by the hatred he had seen in our times. And he said the thing the world needs most today is understanding, an ability to see the other person's point of view. And not to hate him because he disagrees. That was Dwight Eisenhower.

And yet, of course, he was more than all that. He had a side more evident to those of us who worked with him than to the rest of the world. He was a strong man, he was shrewd, he was decisive. Time and again, I have seen him make decisions that probably made the difference between war and peace for America and the world. That was always when he was at his best. No matter how heated the arguments were, he was always then the coolest man in the room.

Dwight Eisenhower was that rarest of men, an authentic hero. Wars bring the names of many men into the headlines and of those some few become national or even international heroes. But as the years then pass, their fame goes down. But not so with Dwight Eisenhower. As the years passed, his stature grew. Commander of the mightiest expeditionary force ever assembled, receiver of the surrender of the German armies of World War II, president of Columbia University, supreme commander of NATO, 34th President of the United States, the honors and offices were there in abundance, every trust that the American people had it in their power to bestow he was given.

And yet he always retained a saving humility. His was the humility not of fear but of confidence. He walked with the great of the world and he knew that the great was human. His was the humility of man before God and before the truth. His was the humility of a man too proud to be arrogant.

The pursuit of peace was uppermost of his mind when he ran for the Presidency and it was uppermost in his conduct of that office. And it is a tribute to his skill and determination that not since the 1930's has the Nation enjoyed so long a period of peace, both at home and abroad, as the one that began in 1953 and continued through his Presidency. As commander of the mightiest allied force ever assembled, he was the right man at the right place at the right time. And as President, once again he was the right man at the right place at the right time. He restored calm to a divided Nation. He gave Americans a new measure of self-respect. He invested his office with dignity and respect and trust. He made Americans proud of their President, proud of their country, proud of themselves.

And if we in America were proud of Dwight Eisenhower, it was partly because he made us proud of America. He came from the heart of America and he gave expression of the heart of America and he touched the hearts of the world. Many leaders are known and respected outside their own country. Very few are loved outside their own country. Dwight Eisenhower was one of those few.

### CAPTURED DEEPEST FEELINGS

He was probably loved by more people in more parts of the world than any President America has ever had. He captured the deepest feelings of free men everywhere. The principles he believed in, the ideals he stood for, these were bigger than his own country. Perhaps he himself put it best again in that Guildhall speech in 1945. He said then:

> Kinship among nations is not determined in such measurements as proximity, size and age. Rather, we should turn to those inner things, call them what you will, I mean those intangibles that are the treasures that free men possess. To preserve his freedom of worship, his equality before the law, his liberty to speak and act as he sees fit, subject only to provisions that he not trespass upon similar rights of others, a Londoner will fight—and so will a citizen of Abilene. When we consider these things, then the valley of the Thames draws closer to the farms of Kansas and the plains of Texas.

Some men are considered great because they lead great armies, or they lead powerful nations. For 8 years now Dwight Eisenhower has neither commanded an army nor led a nation. And yet he remained to his final days the world's most admired and respected man, truly the first citizen of the world. As we marvel at this, it leads us once again to ponder the mysteries of greatness. Dwight Eisenhower's greatness derived not from his office but from his character, from a unique moral force that transcended national boundaries even as his own deep concern for humanity transcended national boundaries.

### HIS LIFE REMINDS US

His life reminds us that there is a moral force in this world more powerful than the might of arms or the wealth of nations. This man who led the most powerful armies that the world has ever seen; this man who led the most powerful nation in the world; this essentially good, and gentle, and kind man; that moral force was his greatness. For a quarter of a century to the very end of his life Dwight Eisenhower exercised a moral authority without parallel in America and in the world. An America and the world are better because of it.

And so today we render our final salute. It is a fond salute to a man we love and cherish. It is a grateful salute to a man whose whole extraordinary life was consecrated to service. It is a profoundly respectful salute to a man larger than life, who by any standards was one of the giants of our times. Each of us here will have a special memory of Dwight Eisenhower. I can see him now standing erect, straight, proud, and tall 16 years ago as he took the oath of office as the 34th President of the United States of America.

We salute Dwight David Eisenhower standing there in our memory—first in war, first in peace, and wherever freedom is cherished, first in the hearts of his fellow men.

### BENEDICTION

The Reverend Edward L. R. Elson, Chaplain of the U.S. Senate. Unto God's most gracious care and protection, we commit you.

The Lord bless you and keep you.

The Lord make His face to shine upon you and be gracious unto you, the Lord lift up His countenance upon you and give you peace, now and evermore.

And now may the God of peace who brought

again from the dead our Lord Jesus Christ, that great Shepherd of the sheep, through the blood of the everlasting covenant, make you perfect in every good work, to do His will, working in you that which is well pleasing in His sight, through Jesus Christ our Lord to whom be glory for ever and ever. Amen.

(This marks the end of the proceedings, of Sunday, March 30, 1969.)

*Mr. Mansfield.* Mr. President, I send to the desk a resolution and ask unanimous consent for its immediate consideration.

*The Vice President.* The resolution will be stated.

The legislative clerk read as follows:

S. Res. 174

*Resolved*, That the Sergeant at Arms of the Senate is hereby authorized and directed to purchase a floral wreath to be placed by the catafalque bearing the remains of former President of the United States and General of the Army of the United States, Dwight David Eisenhower, while lying in state in the rotunda of the Capitol of the United States, the expenses of which shall be paid from the contingent fund of the Senate.

*The Vice President.* Is there objection to the present consideration of the resolution?

There being no objection, the resolution (S. 174) was considered and unanimously agreed to.

*The Vice President.* The Chair lays before the Senate the message from the President of the United States on the death of Dwight David Eisenhower which will be read and laid on the table.

The legislative clerk read as follows:

*To the Congress of the United States:*

It is my sad duty to inform you officially of the death of Dwight David Eisenhower, the thirty-fourth President of the United States.

We have lost a great leader, a great friend and a great man. I know there are many members of the Congress who had the privilege of serving under his military leadership, and who later, during his eight years, as President, shared with him in the building of a better America. He had a profound respect for the traditions, the institutions and the instruments of our nation. He leaves to the Congress and to all Americans the spirit of patriotism and statesmanship beyond party which marked his entire career. As we grieve at his death, we all will recall that spirit, which can guide and sustain us in our tasks ahead. He has been an inspiration to us all, and ours is a better government because he walked among us.

Richard Nixon.

The White House, *March 28, 1969.*

A message from the House of Representatives by Mr. Bartlett, one of its reading clerks, communicated to the Senate the intelligence of the death of General of the Army Dwight David Eisenhower, beloved former President of the United States of America. The message, ordered to be laid on the table, is as follows:

H. Res. 351

*Resolved,* That the House of Representatives has learned with profound regret and sorrow of the death of General of the Army Dwight David Eisenhower, beloved former President of the United States of America.

*Resolved,* That in recognition of the many virtues, public and private, of the illustrious soldier and statesman, and as a mark of respect to one who has held such eminent public stations, the Speaker shall appoint a committee of the House to join with such Members of the Senate as may be designated, to attend the funeral services of the former President.

*Resolved,* That the House tenders its deep sympathy to the members of the family of the former President in their sad bereavement.

*Resolved,* That the Sergeant at Arms of the House be authorized and directed to take such steps as may be necessary for carrying out the provisions of these resolutions, and that the necessary expenses in connection therewith be paid out of the contingent fund of the House.

*Resolved,* That the Clerk communicate these resolutions to the Senate and transmit a copy of the same to the family of the deceased.

*Resolved,* That as a further mark of respect to the memory of the former President, this House do now adjourn.

*Mr. Pearson.* Mr. President, on behalf of myself and the distinguished junior Senator from Kansas (Mr. Dole), I send to the desk Senate Resolution 175 and ask unanimous consent for its immediate consideration.

*The Vice President.* The resolution will be stated.

The legislative clerk read as follows:

S. Res. 175

*Resolved,* That the Senate has heard with profound sorrow and deep regret the announcement of the death of Dwight David Eisenhower, a former President of the United States and General of the Army of the United States.

*Resolved,* That as a token of honor to his illustrious statesmanship, his leadership in national and world affairs, his distinguished public service to his nation, and as a mark of respect to one who has held such eminent public station in life, the Senate hereby expresses its deep sensibility of the loss the nation has sustained by his death, and its sympathy with the family in their bereavement.

*Resolved,* That the two Senators from Kansas be appointed by the President of the Senate to attend the funeral of the deceased, to be held at Abilene, Kansas.

*Resolved,* That the Secretary of the Senate transmit these resolutions to the House of Representatives and transmit a copy thereof to the family of the deceased.

*Resolved,* That as a further mark of respect to the memory of the deceased the Senate do now adjourn.

*The Vice President.* Is there objection to the present consideration of the resolution?

There being no objection, the Senate proceeded to consider the resolution.

## Hon. James B. Pearson

OF KANSAS

Mr. President, when the inevitable and expected word came, I believe that all of us thought of the life rather than the death of Dwight David Eisenhower.

As a soldier, as a President, and as a citizen, he constantly occupied a great place. Solomon said, "The place showeth the man." And the great places that Eisenhower held, by offer of a free people, did indeed show the man. It revealed that he understood that the high ground of command was useless unless it represented the power to do good. The places he held persuaded him that progress was essential and that good thoughts are no more than good dreams unless action follows.

As a soldier, he believed in peace.

As a President, he gave confidence and stability and a calmness to our people to the end that our acts were brighter and our institutions stronger. Somehow, Eisenhower, befuddled by the world of politics, found strength and truth that the career practitioners of government never learn nor understand.

And now, in his last years as a citizen, he served as an example of what is great in our people and good in our time. One example we might find of greatest comfort is that he was proof once again that in a free society difficult events and hard circumstances will produce the right man at the right time.

Abraham Lincoln once said:

> If I went West, I think I would go to Kansas.

Ike now goes west to Kansas, from whence he came, and to the rewards that God assures all mankind.

## Hon. Robert J. Dole

OF KANSAS

Mr. President, today the world mourns Dwight David Eisenhower, and while there is a sense of profound loss, there is not despair. After a full life of service, his memory is unquestionably forever secure in the affections of his fellow men everywhere. He was truly a leader of men and of nations in war and in peace.

His dreams as a boy in Abilene, Kans., could never have envisioned the heights he was to scale in his lifetime. From a family of humble origins in the heartland of America, General Eisenhower rose to command successfully the largest military force ever assembled.

The honesty and sincerity so characteristic of this man throughout his life can be traced to the spiritual heritage of his ancestors and strong guidance from his mother. His broad grin and good humor that reflected these qualities made him a popular idol and were part of his magic. Wherever seen throughout the world, people reacted to the special qualities exuded by this man. Winston Churchill understood these qualities and once commented that Ike "was a great commander, who not only can lead an army, but can stir men's hearts."

The contributions made by General Eisenhower are legend. His success in time of war marked him as a great leader of men. Thereafter his unparalleled success in politics underscored the respect and confidence he enjoyed in America.

It is only natural that those of us from Kansas have always exhibited special pride in General Eisenhower, for as President Nixon so eloquently stated yesterday, General Eisenhower "did come from the heart of America—the geographical and spiritual heart."

General Eisenhower once said:

> I come from the people, the ordinary people.

Kansans are proud to be termed ordinary people and especially proud and honored that the people from whence he came were Kansas people.

His great triumphs and deeds were always marked by the extra dimensions of his personality, his character, and his humanity.

On behalf of all Kansans, I proudly salute

General Eisenhower as we pause to commemorate his greatness.

## Hon. Hugh Scott

OF PENNSYLVANIA

Mr. President, I ask unanimous consent to have printed in the RECORD a list of 23 accomplishments which former President Eisenhower thought were most significant in his term, and also a prayer for a friend which President Eisenhower read at Morningside Heights, N.Y., on the morning of his election day which I had prepared for him the night before.

There being no objection, the material was ordered to be printed in the RECORD, as follows:

A PRAYER FOR A FRIEND

(BY HUGH SCOTT)

Dear God, in all things Thy will be done. If it please Thee that Thou shalt give to us the victory, help him to judge that which is surely good, to turn aside from all unworthiness.

Help him to share and to hold that faith shown bright in the eyes of the little children along the many places of his going.

Help him to follow after the ways that lead to peace, that by Thy grace the sounds of battle may be stilled, our sons returned to field or marketplace.

Help him, by high example, to bring our people together in friendly amity and tolerant accord that each may, in his own fashion, freely enjoy the fruits of a peaceful, happy land.

Help him, above all, O Lord, to be himself.

Amen.

(Prepared on election eve in November 1952 and read by General Eisenhower on the morning of election day while standing by the fireside mantel in his home in Morningside Heights in New York City.)

---

[From the Philadelphia Inquirer, Mar. 31, 1969]

EISENHOWER LISTED 23 TOP ACCOMPLISHMENTS IN 8 YEARS AS PRESIDENT

WASHINGTON, March 30.—In a heretofore unpublicized letter, Gen. Dwight D. Eisenhower listed the end of the Korean War, the first civil rights law in 80 years and 21 other events as principal accomplishments of his Administration.

And he wrote critically of those who take deportment and words rather than achievements as the measure of people in responsible positions.

The letter was written Oct. 18, 1966, from Eisenhower's Gettysburg, Pa., farm to James C. Hagerty, press secretary during the Eisenhower presidency.

Hagerty read it Sunday on television during coverage of memorial ceremonies for Gen. Eisenhower, who died Friday. Hagerty is an ABC executive.

In the letter, Eisenhower said: "A few days ago when asked for a list of accomplishments of the Republican Administration I dashed these off from the 'top of my head' along with a few comments."

The list:

Statehood of Alaska and Hawaii.

Building of St. Lawrence Seaway.

End of Korean War thereafter no American killed in combat.

Largest reduction of taxes to that time.

First civil rights law in 80 years.

Prevention of Communistic efforts to dominate Iran, Guatemala, Lebanon, Taiwan, South Vietnam.

Reorganization of the Defense Department.

Initiation, and great progress in, most ambitious road program by any nation in all history.

Slowing up and practical elimination of inflation.

Initiation of space program with successful orbit in less than three years, starting from scratch.

Initiating a strong ballistic missile program.

Conceiving and building the Polaris program, with ships operating at sea within a single administration.

Starting federal Medical Care for the aged (Kerr-Mills).

Desegregation in Washington, D.C., and Armed Forces even without laws.

Fighting for responsible fiscal and financial policies throughout eight years.

Extension of OASI (Social Security) coverage to over 10 million persons.

Intelligent application of federal aid to education (Defense Education Bill).

Preservation, for the first time in American history, of adequate military establishment after cessation of war.

Using federal power to enforce orders of a federal court in Arkansas, with no loss of life (Little Rock school crisis).

Good will journeys to more than score of nations in Europe, Asia, Africa, South Africa and in the Pacific.

Establishment of the Department of Health, Education and Welfare.

Initiation of plan for social progress in Latin America after obtaining necessary authorization from Congress for $500 million—later called Alliance for Progress.

Atoms for Peace proposal.

## Hon. Everett McKinley Dirksen

OF ILLINOIS

Mr. President, to all that is mortal comes the day of dissolution. What comfort there is in the fact that to the moment when the shadow of death hovered over him, he was lucid, peaceful, and ready. What counts now is the lesson of his life.

We refer to Washington as the Father of our

Country. Eisenhower was a father to the country. He came at a time when concern and ferment were everywhere. He came when an uneasy Nation needed him. In his touch was that magic balm to dissipate fear, to restore confidence, and to set the Nation on the high road again.

What words or what phrase best describes his impact on the people? I would have to say from my friendship with him that it was the "wholesome touch." Perhaps there are times when a Nation needs brilliance in diplomacy, skill in administration, in-depth background on legislative needs. But there are also times when a Nation needs an abiding father with the wholesome approach of a national leader, and this is precisely what he brought when it was needed.

Years ago, a Senator said to me:

If there were no third-term limit, Eisenhower could be elected and reelected as long as he lived, because people believe in him.

To that I replied:

And because he believes in people.

Prior to World War II, he might have been considered just another among many officers in the U.S. Army. But there was a difference. He did his homework and he did it well. And when the time came to find a grand captain for the vast and serious task which confronted the world, he was ready. The military hierarchy, whose task it was to find an outstanding planner and tactician, made no mistake.

First, he became the commander in chief of the U.S. forces in Europe. Later he became commander in chief of the allied forces in Africa. Later he became supreme commander of the Allied Expeditionary Forces.

It was all done with so little personal publicity. It was done without propaganda. It was not glory but victory that he sought.

How comparatively little we heard about his rescue of Africa from British disaster. How little we heard about his healing touch in dissipating the fear and gloom in Britain after the tragic retreat to Dunkirk. Only when he mounted the grand assault from the beaches of Normandy did we hear much of him. Eleven months later the enemy surrendered.

I was privileged to be present at the Thanksgiving service in Rheims, France. It was the day after victory. I saw him there. But I also saw something else—humble people, kneeling in church, expressing their gratitude for victory and their appreciation for his service and leadership.

It was not so strange that a grateful people in this land should turn to him in time of peace for guidance and leadership. They felt that one who could meet the challenge of Hitler could also meet the challenges and complexities of the postwar period. So from supreme commander he became President and Commander in Chief of the Armed Forces of the United States. It was not so much some vast, undisclosed, administrative talent which endeared him to the people, but the rightness of his outlook, his humane views, his compassionate heart, and his dedication to the cause of peace.

In his day, many things were contrived to serve the cause of continuing peace. The North Atlantic Treaty Organization came into being. The U.S. Information Agency was created. The Southeast Asia Treaty Organization was ratified. An International Finance Corporation was created. An International Atomic Energy Agency was approved. A U.S. Development Loan Fund was established. A mutual security pact with Japan was consummated. There were many others—all of them designed to serve the cause of peace.

As this effort to serve the cause of peace and understanding continued, he was always mindful of the inescapable fact that to give effective leadership to the free world we ourselves must always be strong and secure. There were many things to attest that fact.

The first nuclear submarine was approved. The U.S. Air Force Academy was established. The National Aeronautics and Space Administration was created. The Defense Reorganization Act came into being. The National Defense Education Act was consummated. These and others were designed to maintain a military posture which would command respect.

But even as he sought to serve the cause of peace and security, he was equally mindful of the needs of the Nation at home. The Department of Health, Education, and Welfare was established, the better to coordinate the services of the Federal Government in this field. Social security benefits were broadened. The research and assistance program on air pollution was enacted. The minimum wage increase was approved. The Interstate Highway Act came into being. The basic Civil Rights Act—the first in more than 80 years—was consummated. There were so many others, including medical care for the aged, small business investment, poultry products inspection, library service, water facilities, the disposal of surplus agricultural commodities, return to the States of their rights to submerged lands, the Korean GI bill of rights, and the Great Plains program.

This—all this—is a monument to the universality of mind and heart and spirit of one who in our time achieved greatness without losing his humility, who was loyally served because he was esteemed, and who found a place deep in the throbbing hearts of Americans and the world because they loved him.

## Hon. Mike Mansfield

OF MONTANA

Mr. President, I ask unanimous consent to have printed in the RECORD a telegram received from the Honorable Luis M. Farias, President, Gran Commission of the Congress of the United Mexican States.

There being no objection, the telegram was ordered to be printed in the RECORD, as follows:

GRAN COMMISSION OF THE CONGRESS OF THE UNITED MEXICAN STATES

*Mexico City, Mexico, March 29, 1969.*

Senator MIKE MANSFIELD,
*Majority Leader, U.S. Senate, Capitol Hill, Washington, D.C.*

DEAR MIKE: Once more I must address you in mourning. A great American has died leaving a feeling of emptiness. Courageous in war, firm in his handling of public affairs, full of warmth in personal relations. Dwight D. Eisenhower left many friends in all corners of the world. To my country he always showed his fondness. Please accept my condolences.

HON. LUIS M. FARIAS,
*President.*

Mr. President, we were a nation at war; Dwight David Eisenhower, general, did much to end it.

We were of an Atlantic community on the verge of a second great war; Dwight David Eisenhower, Supreme Commander, NATO, did much to prevent it.

We were a people torn by political dissension and ideological confusion; Dwight D. Eisenhower, President, did much to calm it.

We were of a world divided by ideology into hostile camps; Dwight D. Eisenhower, statesman, threw across the chasm the lines of human contact.

This man entered into the service of his country as a young lieutenant of the armies; he left its service as President of the United States. Until his death, his counsel remained at the call of his successors; it was sought, in turn, by President Kennedy, President Johnson, and President Nixon.

Why is it that the trust which he had from friends in his earliest years enlarged into a trust of countless millions in this country and throughout the world? Was it because Dwight D. Eisenhower was a friendly man, warm with the strengths and weaknesses of his humanity? Was it because he was a wise man with a folk wisdom of rural America, enriched by an everwidening experience in the affairs of the Nation and the world? Was it because he was a dependable man, with a determined but dogmatic-free dedication to his duties, his country, and the ideals of freedom?

It was for all these reasons and more that Dwight D. Eisenhower was trusted. He was trusted, in the end, because he was the personification of a trusted America. He incarnated America's revulsion with the Nazi-racism of his era and America's compassion for all those who suffered under its ruthless political-militarism. He expressed America's simple hope for a world of peace and order. His smile spoke vividly of America's friendship for all peoples.

The era which he personified is gone; Dwight D. Eisenhower is gone. Yet, they are not gone. They are tied together—the man and his times. Together, they are woven into the Nation's continuing effort to give full meaning to the Constitution's promise for all citizens. Together, they are forever a part of the world's search for a peaceful order of life for all peoples.

Dwight D. Eisenhower, 1890–1969, boy from Abilene, soldier, general, President, and before all else, decent American.

## Hon. Jacob K. Javits

OF NEW YORK

Mr. President, I rise today to pay tribute to Gen. Dwight D. Eisenhower whom I knew well before he had achieved the rank of general and long before he sought the Presidency. I met him when he was G–5 at the Pentagon in 1941, when I first came to Washington and became a civilian aide to the Chief of the Chemical Warfare Service.

I had occasion to see the general in that service before Pearl Harbor and then had occasion to serve under him when he was in command in the European Theater both in the United Kingdom and in Algiers, North Africa.

After the war, I had the privilege, I think, of being among the first to suggest that he should seek the Presidency in 1948. I then joined with 18 or 19 other Members of the House, at the end of 1951, in urging him to stand for the Presidency as the nominee of the Republican Party. Then, of course, I had the great privilege of working for his election in 1952 and in running with him in 1956 when I first sought election to the Senate from New York.

Over the years I have seen a great deal of General Eisenhower. I saw him, of course, while he was President. Thereafter, as he gradually withdrew from activities, I saw him again in Palm Springs, Calif., and at Gettysburg, Pa.

Dwight D. Eisenhower was one of America's really genuine heroes in the eyes of its people. As so many have said—and as President Nixon said so beautifully yesterday—he was a man of tremendous warmth and sentiment, a very personable man, one with a great sense of humor, deep feeling, and passionate conviction. He could get very angry, but anger never controlled his actions. He could be the warmest, the dearest, the most special human being on earth. Just to see him with Mamie in his later years would make anyone understand that.

I heard stories from a wide range of individuals—from the generals who served under him, like Al Gruenther, and the dressmakers who served Mamie, like those in New York—which proved that to them he was, uniformly, the greatest human being.

Our Nation and the world have lost a great leader in war and a great champion of peace. For Dwight D. Eisenhower was that rare military captain who genuinely renounced the very calling which put him among the historic great.

Dwight David Eisenhower was one of the greatest friends the people of the world ever had. A commanding personality, he inspired trust and confidence through his warmth, compassion, and simple lack of pretension. These unique qualities of leadership enabled him to bring together the clashing interests of many nations into the greatest wartime alliance in Western civilization. He, as much as any man in history, represented the aspirations of free people the world over to defeat tyranny and maintain peace through the collective strength of the free.

Mr. President, the evaluations of history are always interesting, especially for one, like myself, who has lived with a man—as so many others have—like Dwight D. Eisenhower. I had the rather interesting opportunity to try that out. The New York Times' Sunday Magazine, some years ago, published an interesting and informative piece evaluating Presidents, and where they stood in the hierarchy of greatness in the eyes of their countrymen. They did not rate President Eisenhower very high. They put others ahead of him.

I protested that. The general got a great kick out of my protest. The New York Times printed my letter in which I stated that I thought he was a great President. Mr. President, I ask unanimous consent that that letter be inserted in the RECORD at the conclusion of my remarks.

Mr. President, greatness consists not only of great achievements—and I think it is only fair to say that Dwight Eisenhower's greatest achievement was in leading the forces of victory in World War II—but also lies in the good sense and the wit, even the brilliance, not to do some things, to keep the Nation from doing them.

I think that General Eisenhower could just as easily have gotten into the Vietnam trap as his successors, but he did not. I think that it was just as hard to make peace in Korea as it will prove to be in Vietnam; but he managed to carry it off. It took a very long time to do so. It posed great difficulties.

Dwight D. Eisenhower was the first President of my party since 1932 after 20 years out of power. It would have been possible for President Eisenhower to pursue a negative course. The party had been in opposition for a very long time, under a conservative, perhaps an isolationist influence. He did not pursue that course. On the contrary.

Although I had many differences with him, especially in the field of civil rights and economics, he brought the Republican Party into the mainstream of modern American political thought. Even in such areas as health, it is too often forgotten that President Eisenhower's administration produced the first medical care plan which had really seriously been put before Congress. It was defeated in the other body, where I was serving at that time; but, nonetheless, President Eisenhower's administration produced it. And so with a whole host of other developments. The Republican tradition on civil rights was extended by the first breakthrough on civil rights legislation since Reconstruction days, desegregation in the District of Columbia, and the will to use Federal troops in order to sustain Federal safeguards for the individual American.

But above all, President Eisenhower made his greatest contribution in foreign policy, confirming and extending America's role as a world power concerned with the development of free societies everywhere, but ever cautious to avoid precipitating a conflict in such troubled areas as Berlin and Vietnam. As historian Henry Steele Commager has written:

> History will accord Eisenhower a major part of the credit for the generosity and maturity with which the United States accepted and discharged her obligations during the Fifties; it will accord him credit for preventing the Republican Party—and perhaps the country—from going down the dusty road to a sterile isolationism at a crucial moment in history.

Thus, Mr. President, I rise to join the leadership and my colleagues in paying tribute to a great, a warm, and a happy American.

Interestingly enough, because of his temperament, his tremendous optimism, and his unflagging will to live, I think that he will be an inspiration to our youth, in spite of their changing and rather restless character. Those of us who remember him as the immensely popular wartime commander and peacetime Chief Executive will always think of him as a great champion of peace. He knew war well but renounced it. We all know of his "open skies" proposal and his goals in disarmament and arms control, and we hope that they will guide our own actions today.

For Mrs. Javits and myself I extend our warmest sympathies to Mamie Eisenhower, whom we both know, and to John and his children, whom the President loved so much. The comfort of that family is in the fact that Dwight Eisenhower was a man who kept the light of faith in America's traditions and institutions more brightly and inspiringly lit than any other man in modern history. He will always remain a beautiful, inspiring, warm figure for that reason, as well as a most pleasant memory in my heart and the hearts of a whole host of Americans who, like myself, had the privilege of warm personal contact with him.

EXHIBIT I

EISENHOWER GREAT

To the EDITOR:

With reference to your article by Arthur M. Schlesinger, "Our Presidents: A Rating by 75 Historians" (July 29), I have no desire to quarrel with such an eminent group but I found their evaluation of Dwight D. Eisenhower as an "average" President extraordinary.

Perhaps Professor Schlesinger did, too, for he found it necessary to at least offer a defense for their surprising evaluation: "* * * Eisenhower, the most recent, and consequently, the hardest of the Presidents to evaluate. * * *"

I believe that as history is evaluated in the perspective of time even this same group of historians would come to agree that President Eisenhower deserves the label of "great" for his achievements in the cause of peace (Korea, United Nations, Middle East, etc.); for his impact on the course of the Republican Party (decisively putting it on the road in favor of a reasonable Government role in the country's welfare and preventing a resurgence of isolationism); and for giving the nation an unparalleled sense of moral dedication and unity when it was most needed.

JACOB K. JAVITS,
*U.S. Senate.*

WASHINGTON, D.C.

## Hon. Charles H. Percy

OF ILLINOIS

Mr. President, Dwight David Eisenhower was a good man. A military strategist, a statesman, leader of his political party, a humanitarian, an educator—all of these accomplishments marked his fruitful life. But ask the average citizen of the world how he would describe Dwight David Eisenhower in a few words and chances are he would simply say: "He was a good man."

How many leaders of men would qualify for such a description? He achieved great power without ever really grasping for it. He was disappointed when friends disagreed with him but he never personalized opposition. His temper flared on occasion, but his aim was only to assure excellence.

The "man from Abilene" probably was liked by a broader cross section of Americans than any other public figure of his times and this in fact served as the basis of his wide appeal. It was his inner spiritual force that caused his outward radiation of goodness and charm and gained him acceptance at home and abroad as a man of profound good will. He always preferred to conciliate opposing points of view rather than to demand strict obedience to his orders. And his manifest sincerity disarmed even those who opposed him.

As a friend of both generals and captains of industry, he left as his legacy a warning of the dangers inherent in the military-industrial complex. As a military man, he desired above all else and worked without cessation for one goal—a lasting peace in his time.

In fact, the choice of every means, the foundation of every decision made by Dwight Eisenhower during his long service to our country, has been a judgment whether the cause of peace would thereby be served. Several years ago, looking back on his career, Dwight Eisenhower said that he regarded the greatest achievement in which he had participated to have been the defeat of Nazi Germany only 11 months after the Normandy invasion and an 8-year Presidency without war. Typically, he felt his greatest disappointment was our inability to bring about a lasting accord with the Soviet Union, for he had hoped the years of his Presidency would bring us to a place where we could say that a just and permanent peace was in sight.

The affection for him knows no boundaries among men. His appeal is universal and his lifetime of service to his fellow man had some impact on virtually every person on the face of the globe.

Dwight David Eisenhower marched through the history of his times with other great men—Franklin D. Roosevelt, Harry S. Truman, Sir Winston Churchill, George C. Marshall, Douglas MacArthur, Charles de Gaulle, and all of the others in the world's capitals and on its battlefields. And his warmth as a man, let alone his military and diplomatic skills, was the equal of any of his contemporaries and superior to most.

Let us not forget on this day what Dwight Eisenhower said to us at the end of his 8 years in the White House:

> To all of the peoples of the world I once more give expression to America's prayerful and continuing aspiration. We pray that peoples of all faiths, all races, all nations may have their great human needs satisfied; that those now denied opportunity shall come to enjoy it to the full; that all who yearn for freedom may experience its spiritual blessings; that all who are insensitive to the needs of others will learn charity; that the scourges of poverty, disease, and ignorance will be made to disappear from the earth; and that, in the goodness of time, all peoples will come to live together in a peace guaranteed by the binding force of mutual respect and love.

Today, leaders of the world have come to Washington to pay tribute to our 34th President. We are grateful for their display of affection and high regard for this truly great man. But the eulogy that would have meant most to him, however, would not come from such great figures, but from that citizen of the world whose simple but profound tribute today would be: "Dwight David Eisenhower was a good man."

Just before he died, Dwight Eisenhower said that he had always loved his wife, his children, his grandchildren, and his country.

I should like to express the deepest sorrow to Mamie Eisenhower, who had stood by his side for so many years, and who, in recent months, had borne the greatest part of the burden of the Nation and the world as the general's health failed. Her accomplishments, her dignity, and her greatness in what she had contributed to him through his lifetime should never be underestimated.

A very special relationship also existed between Dwight Eisenhower and his brother Milton. Often, during the course of his Presidency, he told me that Milton Eisenhower should have really been President. That showed the respect he had for his brother, to whom he turned many times for guidance and judgment.

Though he had a great respect for all the members of his family, there was a very special affection between Dwight Eisenhower and his brother Milton. I think every Member of this body would recognize the wonderful relationship those two men had.

So I extend particularly to my friend Milton Eisenhower my deep sorrow, but also a sense of gratitude in knowing how much he had been able to contribute to his brother.

On this day, when we join with his family in

mourning their loss, we can say that his family, his friends, and his country will always love Dwight Eisenhower.

## Hon. John Sparkman

OF ALABAMA

Mr. President, I join Senators in paying tribute to Dwight David Eisenhower. I first met General Eisenhower during the maneuvers in the Carolinas in the days before we became involved in the Second World War. Then I visited his headquarters in Belgium during the war. I visited him in Paris when he was in command of the newly established NATO forces. And, of course, I knew him here at home.

Dwight D. Eisenhower was an unusual person. To my way of thinking, he is one of the really great men of America. He had unusually great achievements in the military service, both as commanding officer of the Allied forces during the great crusade in Europe—a successful crusade, a crusade that was a victory not only for our country but for many of the countries that had been overrun and for many of the countries that had little hope of ever attaining freedom—and as Chief of Staff of the Army, after his assignment was over in the expeditions in Europe.

Then he became commander of the first NATO forces in Europe; and I think to him must go a great deal of credit for welding together the forces of the different countries participating in NATO.

Finally in that connection, I saw General Montgomery, on television, make a short statement in which he paid tribute to General Eisenhower. In spite of the differences that they sometimes had and the difficulties that they encountered in working together, he paid high tribute to General Eisenhower for the masterly job that he did in welding together the forces of the various countries in the Allied effort during World War II.

I was impressed by a statement that I heard made on TV last night when the representative of the Tunisian Government came to the microphones at Dulles Airport. He said that Tunis and all Tunisians were grateful to President Eisenhower because he had brought freedom to their country; and he said that, as a matter of fact, every freedom-loving person in the world owed a debt of gratitude to Dwight D. Eisenhower, because he had opened up so many countries that had little hope prior thereto.

President Eisenhower, after completing his service as head of the NATO forces, became President of the United States. I have said, in answer to questions put to me with reference to the 1952 campaign, that I felt that President Eisenhower was destined almost from the time he was nominated to be elected President, and that I believed it was because of the great, warm place that he had in the hearts of Americans, particularly the parents of American boys whom he had commanded in the crusade in Europe.

President Nixon yesterday, in paying his eulogy to President Eisenhower, referred to something that was first said of President Washington—and, you know, when we think of the two, there are many similarities that can be drawn. He said that Dwight D. Eisenhower occupied the unusual place of being first in war, first in peace, and first in the hearts of the freedom-loving people all over the world for whom he had done so much.

I think that was a very fitting statement regarding President Eisenhower. I join with those who say that he was a man of great kindness, gentleness, and firmness in his convictions. He was a man of big heart, whom the American people came to love and whom, with hearts full of gratitude, they will always remember.

## Hon. John J. Williams

OF DELAWARE

Mr. President, I join my fellow Senators in paying my respects to General Eisenhower and to the members of his family.

Volumes have been and will continue to be written about the achievements of this great American, Dwight David Eisenhower, but if it were all to be summed up in just a few words it would be to say: "General Eisenhower was a good man, a man of integrity, a man dedicated to the cause of peace, and one who took great pride in serving his country and his fellow man."

With his passing, free men everywhere have lost a good friend, but we can take comfort in the knowledge that our country and the world are better places in which to live as the result of his life.

## Hon. Edward M. Kennedy

OF MASSACHUSETTS

Mr. President, it is a very solemn occasion we observe today, as the Nation prepares to bury one of the outstanding citizens of this century, General of the Army Dwight David Eisenhower. It is fitting that every one of us pay tribute to him; for in thinking back over his remarkable life and reflecting upon his personal qualities, there is much we can learn as well as admire.

I believe that the words of a distinguished Senator from Massachusetts, Henry Cabot Lodge, Sr., spoken about Theodore Roosevelt, can be said as well of Dwight Eisenhower:

> He was a great patriot, a great man; above all a great American. His country was the ruling mastering passion of his life from the beginning even unto the end.

General Eisenhower first became known to the American people when he was named Supreme Allied Commander in the European Theater in World War II. For those any younger than myself it is almost impossible to re-create the tension and the drama of those days. World War II was perhaps the last time when the unity of this Nation was complete and the private interests of our citizens subordinate to an overriding national cause. Many of us lost brothers, sons, and fathers in that war. But no one had any doubt about why these sacrifices had to be made. As the ships set out across the English channel, bearing with them the hopes of a free civilization; and as the President of the United States raised a simple prayer for their success to Almighty God, the Nation knew that the responsibility for developing and coordinating and seeing through what still stands as the most massive and difficult military operation in the history of the world, was in the hands of one man—Dwight Eisenhower.

What he did in those years made him a hero to all Americans and a liberator to many of the nations of the world. This gave him the overriding respect and popularity that allowed him to be a force for peace and world leadership.

General Eisenhower was a career soldier. He embodied the best qualities of the military as those qualities are expressed in the motto of the West Point he loved so much—in the words "duty, honor, country."

It is said that Americans neglect their military in times of peace and rush for its protection in time of danger. Watching the change from what the Armed Forces were in 1939 to what they became in 1942, General Eisenhower could certainly see merit in that view. But he believed—and he made it very clear in his actions and statements as President—that the Armed Forces, just as the executive and legislative branches of the Government, are servants of the people and that their preparations and activities must stay within the confines of public policy, even if that policy later turns out to be wrong. This is their duty to their country and it is what distinguishes a nation directed by its people from a people directed by their state.

As President of the United States for 8 years, General Eisenhower made significant accomplishments. He was the American President who negotiated an end to a war without insisting on capitulation. He made the first approaches toward a reduction of tension between the United States and the Soviet Union through his atoms-for-peace proposal. He created the first program for economic aid to Latin America. On major foreign policy decisions, like the reaction to the French defeat in Indochina and the military action in Suez, he exercised a wholesome restraint on our use of power.

Here at home he was the first President forced to use the power of the Federal Government to enforce the law of the land on equal opportunity in education and he was instrumental in bringing about the acceptance by all political parties of the most basic domestic reforms accomplished since 1933. But in many ways his major accomplishment was that he helped to unify the United States and helped to calm it after a period of intense domestic conflict and bitterness. He led us through a useful period of tranquillity in which we prepared for new assaults upon our country's problems.

Many look back upon the Eisenhower years as a period of calm that will never again be with us. Perhaps, as Abraham Lincoln said:

> The dogmas of the quiet past are not adequate for the stormy present.

But certainly the qualities of personality that Dwight Eisenhower had—which had so much to do with his success—his religious faith, his humility and his candor, his ability to bring men together—certainly these examples can help us in the stormy present. And as Ralph Waldo Emerson said of Abraham Lincoln:

> His heart was as great as the world, there was no room in it to hold the memory of the wrongs.

And of course, Dwight Eisenhower's great personal courage in the face of declining health in the last few years stands as a great testimony to all his personal qualities—all of his courage.

It is in reflecting on these qualities, as well as on his life, that every American, on this solemn day of memory and prayer, can draw strength and hope from the life and example of Dwight David Eisenhower for the future.

## Hon. Howard H. Baker, Jr.

OF TENNESSEE

Mr. President, today I sadly join the millions of mourners throughout the world who are paying tribute to the memory of Dwight D. Eisenhower.

From out of the volumes that have been written and from the new comments that are sure to be made, one single thread in the life of Dwight Eisenhower seems to me to have endured beyond all the other outstanding characteristics of this great man: That was his continuing contribution to world peace.

Many men have sought this elusive goal, but few have added so much to this massive effort that has consumed the talents and energies of so many over the ages.

I hope these remarks are free of vanity or are not too highly personalized—they are meant to be neither—when I point out that my generation is uniquely a product of the Eisenhower age.

I entered the Navy in World War II at the age of 17, in the midst of General Eisenhower's preparations for ultimate victory in Europe. I returned from the service to enter law school in the midst of the Korean war. Then followed his election to the Presidency and the end of the Korean hostilities.

My beginning years as a practicing lawyer were during the stability of the Eisenhower administration, and the focus of much of my effort and attention since coming to the U.S. Senate has been an effort to implement the Eisenhower-Strauss plan for a series of nuclear desalting plants to reach the root causes of conflict in the strife-torn Middle East.

I recall with pride and satisfaction my conversations with the former President Eisenhower, at his office at Gettysburg, about the philosophy and form of his grand proposal for the Middle East and his counsel and advice on measures calculated to bring about its implementation.

My store of experience and knowledge is richer, as is the country's and the world's, for the talents and the time of Dwight David Eisenhower.

Mr. President, I extend my heartfelt sympathy and condolences to Mrs. Eisenhower and her family on my own behalf, on behalf of my wife, and on behalf of my mother, who served in Congress and was a friend of the Eisenhower family.

## Hon. Harry F. Byrd, Jr.

OF VIRGINIA

Mr. President, Dwight David Eisenhower's great strength as a leader was that the people had confidence in him.

He was trusted by the people of the United States as few men ever have been.

Virginia lays claim to a special relationship to Dwight Eisenhower. His mother, Ida Stover, was born and reared in Augusta County, about 10 miles south of Harrisonburg. It is interesting to note in passing that Abraham Lincoln's father was born about 10 miles north of Harrisonburg, in Rockingham County.

Ida Stover was born 107 years ago in a small white frame farm house near Fort Defiance, Augusta County. She lived the first 21 years of her life in that area. It was after the death of her parents that she went West and was one of the first women admitted to Lane College, LeCompton, Kans. It was there that she met David Eisenhower, the general's father.

General Eisenhower was proud of his mother having been a Virginian. Addressing the Virginia Legislature in 1946, he opened his brief remarks with these words:

> It is one of the high honors of my life to return to a joint meeting of the Legislature of the State in which my mother was born and reared.

Virginians responded with affection to Dwight David Eisenhower. He was enormously popular in our State.

In the summer of 1948, the Democratic State convention called on General Eisenhower to seek the Democratic nomination for President—and the State convention pledged to the general its delegates' support at the Democratic National Convention to be held in Philadelphia.

Four years later, when Dwight Eisenhower was the presidential nominee of the Republican Party, he carried Virginia handily, and 4 years later increased his majority.

While he became the supreme commander of the greatest army in the history of the world and later President of the United States, the most powerful position in the world, he remained to the end the same approachable, lovable "Ike."

Freeman Gosden, a native of Richmond, Va., who reached fame and fortune in California and was a neighbor and constant companion to General Eisenhower in Palm Springs, Calif., during recent years, gave me last night this interesting insight into the late President.

The former President, said Mr. Gosden, liked to shop in the supermarkets. Frequently he would gather his golfing companions, Mr. Gosden, Mr. George Allen, and sometimes Mr. Randolph Scott—who has many family connections in Jefferson County, W. Va.—and would go to the local market to buy groceries. He would pick out a cart, push it himself, make his purchases and instruct the butcher how to cut the beef. When he would be recognized and spoken to, he always would take off his hat with a bow to the lady speaking to him.

Yes; Dwight David Eisenhower walked with kings, but he never lost the common touch.

On Saturday, March 29, 1969, the Richmond Times-Dispatch published an editorial captioned: "Dwight David Eisenhower: A Greatly Beloved Leader." It was written by the longtime editor of the Times-Dispatch, now retired, Virginius Dabney.

It is so beautifully written, and it captures so well the spirit of our late President, that I ask unanimous consent that it be printed in the RECORD.

There being no objection, the editorial was ordered to be printed in the RECORD, as follows:

DWIGHT DAVID EISENHOWER: A GREATLY BELOVED LEADER

The world's most beloved man is dead. DWIGHT D. EISENHOWER was not the most brilliant man of his time or the most erudite or the most widely read. But he had a personality which inspired affection throughout the globe. Wherever he went in the years after World War II, cries of "Ike" resounded on every hand, and signs bearing the words "We Like IKE" were widely displayed.

It was the affection and trust which he inspired, no less than the admiration, which made him an unbeatable Republican candidate for president in 1952 and 1956. The Democrats had been in power for 20 years, and they seemed destined to stay there for 20 more when GENERAL EISENHOWER was persuaded to become a candidate.

His two terms gave the country a period of stability and orderly progress, free from wars and riots, which were in happy contrast to the hectic era in which we find ourselves today. So-called intellectuals were never happier than when ridiculing PRESIDENT EISENHOWER—for his sometimes confused sentences at press conferences, his fondness for golf, and so on. But he gave the United States a welcome interlude from hopelessly unbalanced budgets and colossal and continuing deficit spending, from grafting "five percenters" and other chiselers, from perpetual catering to this or that bloc of voters.

HE CRUSHED HITLER

GENERAL EISENHOWER'S career in World War II made him one of the great military figures in American annals. His role as supreme commander of Allied forces in Europe imposed upon him the duty of deciding when to invade HITLER'S "Festung Europa," in the face of German mines, bombs, shells, and machine guns.

Storms along the English Channel in early June 1944, made the invasion potentially disastrous. But GENERAL EISENHOWER got all the expert advice he could from every quarter, and then he alone decided, despite the obvious risks, to send the vast Allied armada through the channel fogs against the heavily fortified coast of Normandy on the early morning of June 6. The rest, the saying goes, is history.

EISENHOWER was a world figure after the war, and both political parties wanted him to run for the presidency. After much pressure from numerous directions, he finally consented—primarily as a public duty. He had taken practically no part in politics up to that time. He decided to join the Republican party and to let his name be placed in nomination at the Republican National Convention of 1952. Once he got the nomination, he was unbeatable for two terms.

DWIGHT D. EISENHOWER was a "good" man, in the best sense of the word. His face bespoke honesty and integrity, and he looked you in the eye when he talked to you. His flashing smile was of well-nigh incredible dimensions, and lit up a room like a giant electric bulb.

He was never stuffy, never impressed with his own importance. He was considerate of the feelings of others, no matter how humble they might be. The latter trait is illustrated in an episode which occurred during "IKE'S" presidency, at a dinner in the grand ballroom of the Statler Hotel in Washington.

A GENEROUS GESTURE

As the waiters were removing the dishes, one ill-fated waiter dropped an entire tray within a few feet of MR. EISENHOWER at the speakers table. The tray hit the floor with a noise that sounded like an exploding bomb. Secret Service men leaped from behind potted palms, and the poor waiter stood there amid the debris, looking as though the end of the world had come.

"IKE" reached into his pocket, took out a couple of bills, and pressed them into the waiter's hand. Nobody saw him do it except the lady who was seated next him. It was a generous and characteristic gesture.

The jibes at PRESIDENT EISENHOWER because he played golf fairly frequently were entirely uncalled for. Other Presidents have been similarly careful of their health, and they had to be, in order not to break themselves down.

In a conversation in 1947, when he was Army Chief of Staff, he revealed that whereas the bursitis in his left shoulder was much better, he had developed an arthritic condition in both forearms. The doctors had told him, he said, that if he didn't use them actively, the arms would atrophy.

So he said he had just taken golfing lessons in Florida from "JOE" KIRKWOOD, the professional, and added: "As soon as the weather opens up it'll be nine holes a day, or at least twice a week."

He did not seem alarmed over the prospect that his forearms might atrophy, and as matters turned out, they never did, presumably because he followed the advice of his doctors and played golf regularly from that time on.

The facts as to his arthritic forearms have never been published before, as far as we are aware. Why he did not make them known, and thereby avoid much unfair criticism is a mystery. We reveal them now in justice to GENERAL EISENHOWER.

Statistics showed that he was not absent from his office any more than PRESIDENT JOHN F. KENNEDY, for example, if as much. Yet he was sneered at regularly and over the years because of his fondness for golf.

HE KNEW U.S. HISTORY

As for the charge that MR. EISENHOWER seldom read anything, he was more widely read than he got credit for. One expects a president of the United States to be well acquainted with American history, and especially with the administrations of predecessors in office. But when "IKE" was Army Chief of Staff, soon after World War II, with no thought of becoming president, he was nevertheless well versed in the history of the men who had occupied the White House. This was obvious to persons who talked with him informally at the time.

Virginia lays claim to a special relationship to DWIGHT EISENHOWER, since his mother, Ida Stover, was born and grew up in Augusta County. Ida Stover's birth on May 1, 1862, took place in a small white frame farmhouse at the bottom of a hill near a creek in the area of Fort Defiance, 10 miles from Staunton. She lived there or nearby for the first 21 years of her life.

Ida Stover went West after the death of her parents, and was one of the first women admitted to Lane College, Lecompton, Kans. It was there that she met David Eisenhower, to whom she was later married. They moved to Texas, and seven sons were born to them. Dwight David was the most eminent, but each of the six who lived to manhood made his mark.

Many Virginians were not aware that DWIGHT EISENHOWER's mother was a Virginian until 1946, when the General came to Richmond as aide to Winston Churchill, who addressed the Virginia General Assembly. Mr. Churchill made the principal address, but "IKE" almost stole the show with a brief talk made in response to repeated cries from the audience that he say something.

HIS VIRGINIA MOTHER

"Ladies and gentlemen," said GENERAL EISENHOWER in opening his impromptu remarks, "it is one of the high honors of my life to return to a joint meeting of the legislature of the state in which my mother was born and reared." A few other equally simple and sincere sentences followed. The talk made as deep an impression as the more formal address of Mr. Churchill.

DWIGHT EISENHOWER's early days in Denison, Tex., and Abilene, Kans., where his mother and father strove to rear and educate their six sons, influenced his future life for the better. The parents had difficulty making ends meet. The father was a railroad mechanic, a creamery worker, etc. The boys had to find jobs, help with the family chores, and so on. They came up the hard way, but they made it.

DWIGHT DAVID EISENHOWER became not only supreme commander of Allied forces in Europe in World War II, but president of the United States. None of these honors "went to his head" or caused him to "lose the common touch." He remained to the end, the same approachable, lovable "Ike," the man whom millions looked up to, and who left an indelible mark on American and world history.

## Hon. Jack Miller

OF IOWA

Mr. President, the Nation has lost a great and dearly beloved citizen—one whose death seems to have taken a piece from each of our hearts. History will record that the people of the United States—of all political faiths—respected and trusted him more than any President of recent memory. He and his good wife and family maintained dignity, wholesomeness, and understanding in the White House and wherever they went.

Perhaps the most memorable day in my life occurred on May 13, 1965, when I spent an entire day with this great man. We flew out from Gettysburg together to Grinnell, Iowa, where he spent the day at Grinnell College, visiting the classrooms and answering questions, and capping it with a fine address to the entire student body that evening. He made similar campus visits on several occasions in his later years, because he had a deep affection for young people and wished to do what he could to help them face the responsibilities of good citizenship which would soon be theirs.

Our country is the better for what will be known as the Eisenhower years—years which have now ended but which should inspire all of us to be better citizens.

It will be written that we not only "liked Ike, but that we loved him."

## Hon. Albert Gore
OF TENNESSEE

Mr. President, teeming and uncounted millions of people, not only in the United States, but also throughout the world have a sense of genuine loss in the passing of the 34th President of the United States, Dwight David Eisenhower.

As I have listened to the tributes being paid to President Eisenhower in the Senate today, I have found wholehearted agreement with the eloquent references, made to his greatness in war, his ennobling characteristics as a domestic leader, and his qualities of character.

By what strange circumstances do men rise to possess great leadership, great trust, and great affection in the hearts of their countrymen? One cannot prescribe a set formula. Life is not that simple. Political fortunes are not so achieved. It is, rather, by a strange and fortuitous combination of qualities, circumstances, and character.

President Eisenhower possessed qualities which endeared him to people. It was said eloquently by the senior Senator from Illinois (Mr. DIRKSEN) today that Dwight David Eisenhower was a father to the country. I think he did have a father image to the country. But he also had a big brother image. He also had an image of companionship and friendship.

If it would not be termed disrespectful, I would say he had the image of a jolly good fellow. He was a forthright man—nothing devious, deceptive, or dissembling about Mr. Eisenhower. People instinctively trusted him and identified themselves with the admirable attributes he exemplified.

Possibly, historians will not characterize him as an activist President, but I think it should be noted that he brought to the White House a conception of staff performance and a willingness and an ability to select good men, to vest confidence in those men, and to delegate to those men genuine responsibility. Perhaps more than any other President of his time, he institutionalized the office of the Presidency. Throughout his term he had keen disappointments but also notable successes. It would take a book adequately to treat with this man.

Permit me to close, Mr. President, by saying that in my opinion he was one of the most beloved Americans of all time.

## Hon. George Murphy
OF CALIFORNIA

Mr. President, I should like to take this opportunity to join with my colleagues in expressing my great grief at the passing of our beloved friend, great general, and great President.

In periods of deep grief, such as we are experiencing today, we mortals are often inclined to compensate for our sorrow by allowing our thoughts to revert to happier times.

Like many of my fellow Americans, I, too, have found much needed consolation in the personal memories I associate with our former President's halcyon days.

In particular, I have found a measure of solace in reminiscing about the particularly cheerful periods when I had the privilege of serving him during the inaugural ceremonies for the newly elected President in 1952 and again for the reelected President 4 years later—the Lincoln Birthday celebrations, the closed-circuit dinners, the informal gatherings at the White House. Those were the happier days, and I shall always cherish them as being among the most enjoyable moments of my life.

I recall a luncheon at Palm Springs, where the host at the luncheon was General Eisenhower. Also present was the son of a former President, Herbert Hoover, Jr.

A group of 10 friends met for lunch to decide whether I should become a candidate for the Senate or not.

One of my friends at the luncheon pointed out, "You have never run for office before. You'll have no chance."

General Eisenhower, pointing to Herbert Hoover, Jr., said, "His father had never run for elective office, and I had never run for elective office. We both got elected President of the United States. Therefore, that should be no objection. Now, what's the next order of business?"

I am pleased to say that it was on that day I decided to become a candidate.

I mention these things today because my recollections, I think, are typical of the reactions of people from San Diego to Bangor, and from Seattle to Miami, all of whom felt a rare and inspiring closeness with this understanding and compassionate man.

For each of us, General Eisenhower was something special—something deeply and intensely personal.

In my case, as I have said, I like to think of those happier inaugural days, especially in 1952.

At the same time, I cannot help remember that those were also days in which we were engaged in a long, bloody war in Korea, and we were weary of the long casualty lists and the apparent failure of our efforts to obtain a timely, just, honorable peace.

These days we sometimes hear people say, "Beware of the judgment of military men." I would remind them that this was a man whose life was dedicated to the military, and who brought us more peace than any other man during my lifetime.

On the domestic scene, there was the restless uncertainty that always accompanies wartime stresses and tensions.

If ever in our history there was a need for a man of heroic principles and inflexible strength, it was in those bleak days of late 1952 and early 1953; and we, as a nation, turned to the man we had just elected as our President to provide us with the leadership and example we so sorely needed.

History has long since written the formal record of his foreign and domestic successes.

But somehow the factual accounts of the archives seem today to be strangely out of place, cold and insufficient.

For example, we remember mainly in this hour how "I like Ike" was transformed from a political slogan into a personal expression of the national spirit—a spirit based on trust, hope, and integrity.

We remember, too, the Eisenhower years of peace, but within our souls we recognize that the legacy of that era is not only a devotion to the cause of peace, but also, and just as important, a national dedication to the principle that international tranquillity must be accompanied by honor and justice.

In addition, we remember the important domestic progress of the Eisenhower years. But once again the official transcripts fail to tell the entire story; for what we have today, which is even more important than the laws and precedents themselves, is a renewed conviction that social advances must be based on the dignity of the individual rather than the enhancement of the State.

Yes, the most enduring record of General Eisenhower's greatness has been indelibly inscribed, not only in our tomes and records, but also in our hearts and souls and minds, for all time.

For each of us, it is a most personal heritage.

For the Nation as a whole, it is a priceless gift, for he reminded us as no other man has ever done that the State is only as strong as the individuals who compose it.

This was a great, beloved, courageous, kind man.

May he enjoy that special peace reserved for the soldier who has fought the gallant fight and returned to his rightful home.

I extend my sincere sympathy to Mrs. Eisenhower and the entire family in this period of national grief. This is a sad day for our Nation, but it should be a day of rejoicing, because once again we have sent a man to history in whom we can all take great pride.

## Hon. Robert C. Byrd

OF WEST VIRGINIA

Mr. President, as I recall Dwight David Eisenhower, I can best recall special qualities of him, as a man, which I believe were basic to his greatness as a world leader.

One of these was his ability to inspire others to have confidence in him and to respect him as a man of integrity and a true disciple of peace, both in his own time and in future time, for the people of his Nation and of the world. Another very great quality of his—his inner strength—made it possible for him to marshal his inner resources to meet the demands upon his thoughts and his physical self, so often heavily placed upon him.

As supreme commander of the Allied Expeditionary Force in World War II, as president of Columbia University, and ultimately as Chief Executive of the United States, Dwight David Eisenhower believed in peace throughout the world; and in his leadership in the interests of peace, he became, as he has been often titled, "truly a citizen of the world."

Although a professional soldier, an expert in the direction of armies, he by his nature was first and foremost a humanitarian devoted to the well-being of his fellow man.

This attitude, so basic to his character, was demonstrated in March 1945, just before American Forces crossed the Rhine.

On the particular occasion about which the anecdote has been told and retold, General Eisenhower noted a young soldier who appeared worried and despondent. He approached him and asked, "How are you feeling, son?"

"General," came back the answer, "I'm awful nervous. I was wounded 2 months ago and just got back from the hospital yesterday. I don't feel so good," said the soldier.

"Well," said Eisenhower, "You and I are a good pair, because I am nervous, too. Maybe if we just walk along together to the river we will be good for each other."

This humility, this common bond with those who served under him, was to endear him to millions, and was to become one of the most widely recognized attributes of this very great soldier and dedicated public servant.

Yet although Dwight Eisenhower had great compassion for others, his own character allowed him no self-pity. When he was only 16, this self-discipline was to serve him well. Blood poisoning developed in his left leg and, as it spread, doctors urged amputation, saying that it was his leg or his life. But this future great leader of men and nations, from the depth of his own inborn discipline, refused to have the operation and through his determination and faith was able to walk out of his room on two healthy legs just 3 weeks later.

This same inner strength was exhibited time and again during World War II, when his decisions were responsible for the success of campaigns against the Germans.

It was exhibited when President Eisenhower, in pursuit of peace, flew to Paris for the North Atlantic Council meeting after having suffered a stroke only days before. Although this determined gesture could very probably have brought on another siege of illness, Eisenhower ignored the possible consequences, shouldered his burdens, and applied decisive and imaginative leadership to the critical affairs of state at that period.

Yet Eisenhower was never known, apparently, to be overly imbued with his personal importance. It is said that he approached his tasks as president of Columbia University in a vein of humility and some anxiety as to his ability to do a job so very different from that to which he had devoted his long military career. Having accepted the appointment because of his conviction that he could do a great service for the youth of America through the advancement of education, he nonetheless felt concerned as to his ability to do justice to his new tasks.

At one time, it is reported that this early anxiety which he had felt was mentioned to him after a reception at one of Columbia's affiliated colleges. A professor confided:

> You know, General, when we heard you were coming here, some of the faculty were downright scared of you.

General Eisenhower is reported to have replied:

> The faculty would have been reassured to know I was scared to death of them.

It is a matter of history now that General Eisenhower, unsure though he might have been about his new position, nonetheless turned in a good performance. He has been credited with being a superb administrator who supported orderly academic freedom and campus democracy.

I have on occasions during recent months thought that had General Eisenhower been president of Columbia University during these times of student unrest, current on our Nation's campuses and universities, he would have set a tone of self-discipline and responsible leadership which might well have provided a model for similar behavior in our Nation's academic councils.

Eisenhower is gone. Myriad legends about him will be told and retold. The Eisenhower legend will last as long as our country does—a country which is better and nobler for his having lived, and served, and died as an American.

## Hon. Milton R. Young
OF NORTH DAKOTA

Mr. President, Gen. Dwight D. Eisenhower's passing has saddened the hearts of all Americans. As a general, he occupied one of the most important military assignments in the history of the Nation, that of commander of all Allied European forces in World War II. His superb handling of this difficult assignment made him a hero to people everywhere.

As President of the United States, he had a way about him that commanded the respect and admiration of people in every walk of life. No President was more loved and respected than he. He will go down in history as one of our greatest Presidents.

It was when he was President that I came to know Dwight Eisenhower best. As one of the Republican leadership of the Senate, I met with him quite often on important national and international matters. It was always a great inspiration to meet with him.

Dwight Eisenhower had a way about him that in the eyes of most people he could do no wrong. There was a reason for this. Besides having a wonderful personality, he was a very honest and courageous man who had natural good judgment and good sense. It was these qualities that people all over the world recognized and appreciated.

Because of the great respect and esteem the American people had for him, he was probably the only President in our history who could have been elected on either the Republican or the Democratic ticket.

It was a great tribute to him that his popularity, and the esteem in which people everywhere held him, continued long after he left public office and until his death.

He will be remembered through history as a beloved, great leader of a great nation. This is a sad day for all of us. I extend my deepest sympathy to Mrs. Eisenhower and all of his wonderful family.

## Hon. Margaret Chase Smith
OF MAINE

Mr. President, Dwight D. Eisenhower, the foremost military leader of his time, had many great attributes. But his greatest achievement was peace. He was a five-star general; yet he accomplished more peace in his 8 years as President than did his civilian predecessors and successors at the White House.

He was a man of peace. He was a leader of peace. He was an achiever of peace. What greater achievement can any mortal being have given to his fellow human beings.

It was on this note of peace that my association with him first started. He asked me in August 1952, to write an article for the Woman's Home Companion on why he should be elected President. I did, and in it stressed his desire and capability for peace.

He made other requests of me. I granted every request he made. The only one I now regret and feel that I made a mistake on was when he called me from Camp David and asked me to vote for the Dixon-Yates contract and said that my vote would mean a great deal to him personally.

I am sure that I cast many votes that displeased him. It has been widely reported that two of my votes greatly disappointed and displeased him. But he never expressed his displeasure to me and did not contact me either before or after those two votes.

Such was a measure of this man of peace who refrained from giving vent to his feelings concerning those who disappointed him and those who attacked him.

This morning on the NBC–TV "Today" program, William Monroe observed that while George Washington could not tell a lie about cutting down the cherry tree, Dwight Eisenhower would not tell a lie about the U–2 spy plane flying over Russia.

His honesty in this crisis brought down on his head the sharpest political attacks ever made on him. Some persons apparently felt that at long last he had made a serious political error that could be greatly politically exploited.

There were those who charged Dwight D. Eisenhower with being senile, lazy, and having disgraced the United States in this matter; and there were those who publicized such charges and represented them as documentation of the thinking of the people at the grassroots.

Dwight D. Eisenhower never defended himself against such slurs. He never replied in kind.

Yet there were those critics who charged that

he was unduly sensitive to criticism—that he was hypersensitive. If he was, he never displayed such hypersensitivity.

But he was sensitive—and I am proud that he was—because that very sensitivity made him the thoughtful, responsive, and warm human being that he was.

Last September and October I was a fellow patient in ward 8 at the Walter Reed Army Medical Center with him. Through the attending doctors and nurses we kept informed on each other's respective progress and exchanged messages of cheer and encouragement.

On his birthday I gave him some of the new super solid state golf balls to symbolize my confidence that he would recover enough to return to his favorite pastime. He gave me some of his birthday cake.

During these 2 months it was my privilege to get to know Mrs. Eisenhower better. Very thoughtfully she would stop by my room to cheer me. We had some most enjoyable conversations, and in getting to know her better I could certainly have a greater appreciation of the saying that behind every great man there is a woman.

I came to know Mamie Eisenhower for the great woman that she is. I saw her, day by day, maintain her constant and dedicated vigil. I saw her maintain an undaunted courage and cheerfulness that lifted the spirit of the entire ward 8. I know that her spirit and her kindness helped to accelerate my own mending and recovery.

Dwight D. Eisenhower's will to live was a medical marvel—almost a medical miracle. But I am sure that one reason his brave, but weakening, heart wondrously rallied so many times was that his devoted wife at his bedside gave so much of her own heart to him to help carry the necessary strength of heart for recovery.

Yes, Dwight D. Eisenhower was a man of peace. He planned and fought for peace. He lived for peace. And he died in peace—in the peace of the mind that he had not only fought the good fight for peace but that few mortals had ever achieved as much peace for as many people as he did.

## Hon. George D. Aiken
OF VERMONT

Mr. President, the great things a President does are repeated a thousand times over after his death but I have always felt that it was the everyday things of life and the attention paid to smaller matters which characterize a man.

President Eisenhower's deeds which affected the Nation and the world will be repeated for generations to come and his praises will be sung by all people and all nations, so I would like to recite a few small events which I believe portrayed his character as much as the invasion of Germany, as much as the end of World War II, or the 8-years of peace and progress for which his administration is so well remembered.

It was after the war and before he became a candidate for President that I was driving along the road in northern Vermont with my radio tuned to the Canadian Broadcasting System.

General Eisenhower was making a speech, as I recall, in Toronto.

Where he made it does not matter, but what he said has remained in my mind ever since.

He said in effect that his greatest ambition in life was to put men in his line of work out of business.

After he was elected President and had been inaugurated, I wrote him a note which said in effect that I would not attempt to tell him how to run the Government of the United States, but that I would be available if I could help him at any time.

I did not call at the White House very often, and then only when matters of importance required the President's attention.

At the time he took office, the agricultural attachés of our embassies abroad were used largely as guides for very important persons visiting those countries.

Some of them knew very little about agriculture and were not expected to.

Representative Hope, of Kansas, chairman of the House Committee on Agriculture, and I called on the President one morning to tell him that a change should be made in this system.

He listened to us and without hesitation called the State Department and stated that from then on he wanted the agricultural attachés to have the same standing as the military attachés, in foreign countries.

Since that time they have been among our most effective representatives abroad.

At another time a serious agricultural problem arose. At this time, I cannot even remember when the problem was, but I do remember well the circumstances. It was Saturday noon when I learned of it, and action had to be taken before 9 o'clock Monday morning. The Secretary of Agriculture had gone to the mountains to spend a weekend.

Ordinarily, one would not have expected to find top officials at the White House or even in Washington on Saturday afternoon.

I took a chance and called the White House. The President responded almost immediately. I told him the problem.

He said, in characteristic fashion, "I will look after it myself."

Secretary Benson was called back from his weekend vacation and the problem was solved by 8 o'clock Monday morning.

On only one occasion did I see President Eisenhower lose his poise.

At that time he literally went through the ceiling expressing his opinion of the war contractors who were currently exerting great pressure upon the Defense Department.

By his actions at that time he clearly expressed himself as believing human life to be of greater value than war contracts.

These are some of the incidents which characterize the man Dwight Eisenhower.

The pages of history will not record them, but to me they were of marked significance.

## Hon. Edmund S. Muskie

OF MAINE

Mr. President, for more than a quarter of a century, Dwight Eisenhower has been a familiar and well-loved name in American homes and in distant lands around the globe.

It is a name associated with historic events and historic achievements; with great leadership; with the skills which led us to victory in war; and with a deep-seated urge to lead mankind toward peace.

Above all, however, he was a man and a human being whose quality and character made a deep and lasting impact upon each of us.

To those of us who served in World War II, he was more than a superlative military leader. He was a man whose warmth, simplicity, and sturdiness were reassuring, inspiring, and comforting.

To all of us, his postwar leadership in Europe, as the first commander of NATO, represented an appropriate conversion of his talent for leadership from war to his unceasing search for peace.

It was understandable and inevitable, notwithstanding the frustration of his political opposition, that he should be called to the Presidency.

And again, in the 8 years of his Presidency, it was the quality of the man which we remember most—his capacity to inspire the trust and confidence of his people.

It was because his countrymen believed him to be a good man that they entrusted him with leadership and responded to it.

And it is thus that we will remember him—a good man who loved his countrymen and who was loved by them.

## Hon. Mark O. Hatfield

OF OREGON

Mr. President, we shall long remember Dwight David Eisenhower as a soldier whose victories won the peace; as a President whose abilities brought confidence in a time of increasing fear; and as a man whose entire life was characterized by integrity, courage, and, above all, faith. We have all shared in the warmth of his personality and in the depth of his spirit. In a time of growing impersonalization, he brought to the Office of President a personal vitality and singular devotion which were a constant source of inspiration for all Americans. Just 17 years ago, General Eisenhower spoke to the Republican National Convention and the Nation in words which are a fitting tribute to his own life as well as a guideline for our future.

He said:

> None of us—
>
> has known of a time that has placed a higher premium on statesmanship—on courage, competence, and leadership—on solid commonsense, on willingness to subordinate self to the general good.

And so it was with Ike.

During his service as supreme commander of the Allied Forces during World War II, our servicemen, including myself, discovered in the general a continual source of reassurance and confidence. We placed our faith in Eisenhower—faith in his judgment, faith in his wisdom, and faith in his courage.

In the years following that war, America found itself wandering, doubting, and unsure of its future. Destiny called Dwight Eisenhower again; it called him because he was worthy of the people's faith. Our Nation knew that Eisenhower as President would bring wise, calm leadership and reassurance during that crucial decade. The accomplishments of those years are often overlooked with the rapidly increasing pace of change in our world. But let us recall that it was President Eisenhower who ended the Korean war; promoted desegregation in our Armed Forces; won passage of the first civil rights bill in 80 years; enforced the orders of the Federal courts to desegregate our school system; established the Department of Health, Education, and Welfare; initiated efforts to encourage social progress in Latin America; and proposed the Atoms for Peace program to the U.N.

Yet the true contribution of Dwight Eisenhower is to be found not in these significant accomplishments of administration, but in his qualities of character.

The faith that the people of our land placed in President Eisenhower was matched by his faith in the people of the world. In his good will trips throughout the globe, President Eisenhower conveyed the warmth and openness of the American people to the citizens of the world community. His originating of the people-to-people programs demonstrated his belief that the bond of mankind can overcome the barriers of nation, race, and ideology.

In his farewell address to the Nation in January of 1961, President Eisenhower demonstrated wisdom and foresight which must be carefully pondered by our Nation today. As an academic leader and former president of Columbia University, it was President Eisenhower who cautioned us about the threat to academic freedom posed by the Government's growing involvement in university research. As our greatest military leader of the century, it was President Eisenhower who first warned against the alarming growth and influence of our defense industry.

But again, let us remember Dwight Eisenhower as a man of faith. The citizens of our Nation found him worthy of their faith, and he constantly demonstrated his faith in his fellowmen. But these qualities were rooted in a far more fundamental commitment. Dwight Eisenhower placed a quiet, confident, and firm faith in God. It was Eisenhower's spirit which we shall remember. His personal devotion and trust in his Creator is his greatest and most lasting quality.

Today the general lies in the Capitol as thousands pass by to pay their tribute. On January 20, 1953, Dwight Eisenhower was also at the Capitol. He rose to give his inaugural address. Before he began, he asked for the privilege of offering his own personal prayer. Let us always remember him standing there and steadfastly praying these words:

> Almighty God, as we stand here at this moment my future associates in the Executive branch of Government join me in beseeching that Thou will make full and complete our dedication to the service of the people in this throng, and their fellow citizens everywhere.
>
> Give us, we pray, the power to discern clearly right from wrong, and allow all our words and actions to be governed thereby, and by the laws of this land. Especially we pray that our concern shall be for all the people regardless of station, race or calling.
>
> May cooperation be permitted and be the mutual aim of those who, under the concepts of our Constitution, hold to differing political faiths; so that all may work for the good of our beloved country and Thy glory. Amen.

## Hon. James B. Allen
OF ALABAMA

Mr. President, the Nation mourns the passing of President Dwight David Eisenhower.

Today I speak for myself as an American, as an individual citizen, and as a Representative in this august body of the State of Alabama and her people.

The people loved, admired, and respected President Eisenhower. They had confidence in him. They trusted him. They felt that they knew him; that he was their friend; that he stood for all that was best for them and their country.

They felt that to him a public office was truly a public trust.

He was a man above partisanship; above sectionalism. He was a man from the people, a man of the people, a man for the people—all of the people.

Let us all profit by the example that he set, by the high road that he followed throughout life.

Of him it can truly be said—in the words of Rudyard Kipling in setting some of the attributes of a real man—he could "walk with kings, nor lose the common touch."

Americans and the free world are poorer because of his passing, but richer because of his life among us.

On behalf of the people of Alabama and of Mrs. Allen and myself, I extend heartfelt sympathy to Mrs. Eisenhower and the Eisenhower family.

## Hon. Strom Thurmond

OF SOUTH CAROLINA

Mr. President, General Eisenhower will long be remembered for many things. His long and distinguished career as a soldier and as a statesman leaves a legacy of noteworthy accomplishments. In my judgment, however, one quality of General Eisenhower's stood out. That quality was his ability to win the affection of people—both of those who knew him and of the public. "I like Ike" was more than a political slogan. It summed up the warmth and respect which people had for General Eisenhower and which was his greatest strength.

In political life all men aspire to a certain degree of popularity. It is, of course, a prerequisite to even limited success in service in government, but General Eisenhower's popularity was more significant and deeper than that which comes to most political figures. It characterized his distinguished military career. During World War II, I served in the First Army in Europe under General Eisenhower. There is no question that he was held in great esteem by the soldiers and that this was a tremendous asset to him. Later when I served as national president of the Reserve Officers Association, I had the privilege of having a number of conferences with President Eisenhower at the White House. He was courteous, friendly, and helpful. From his own personal experience he realized the importance of the Reserves to the Nation. During World War II, 98 percent of the Army and 85 percent of the Navy consisted of citizen soldiers. He favored the Reserve program because he knew firsthand of its importance to the Nation.

Mr. President, the popularity which General Eisenhower enjoyed was important to the Nation when he served as President. The personal qualities of General Eisenhower—his warmth, his dignity, his integrity, and the response these qualities inspired in the public—were of great importance in unifying the American people. The personal bitterness and abusive language which unfortunately have become more a part of political life in the last few years, were largely absent during Dwight Eisenhower's tenure as President, and much of this must be due to the kind of man that President Eisenhower was. His political enemies might disagree with him but nevertheless they liked him.

Mr. President, more than any other American in the 20th century, General Eisenhower commanded the affection and respect of all the people of the United States. All of us are saddened by the passing of this brave soldier, great statesman, and renowned world figure. All through his career he was supported, fortified, and encouraged by his lovely wife, Mamie Eisenhower, who was an inspiration to him—in every activity in which he engaged. My sympathy is with Mrs. Eisenhower and the other members of the family in this time of sorrow. I know that they are comforted by the knowledge that President Eisenhower gave so much of himself to his God, his country, and his fellow man.

## Hon. Ralph Yarborough

OF TEXAS

Mr. President, Dwight David Eisenhower was a general at war, but a man of peace. He was a man who worked to end wars and to prevent wars.

Dwight D. Eisenhower, after World War II, sought the world to follow the Biblical injunction to beat swords into plowshares and spears into pruninghooks. After World War II, he followed the advice of Isaiah, "Nation shall not lift up sword against nation, neither shall they learn war any more."

Though he admonished this, it fell to Eisenhower to lead a great army in the biggest war in the history of mankind. History records the great battles of World War II won under the leadership of Eisenhower in the crusade in Europe. People have recorded in their hearts the memory of Eisenhower, the supreme commander of Allied forces in Europe, taking time to visit the men who would do the fighting, just before the invasion forces started to France, and of his visits to them across Europe as the lines of battle advanced. It was this humaneness that set him apart and above the average man. It was evident to all who knew Eisenhower as a soldier, that his quest was peace, not military victories only.

It was my privilege and honor and duty to serve under Gen. Dwight D. Eisenhower in the crusade in Europe. I as a staff officer of the 97th Infantry Division in that war, serving in several different armies and corps, as we were transferred from sector to sector of the fighting front, ending up on V–E Day on the road to Pilsen, in Czechoslovakia. All who served in the vast Allied armies in the crusade in Europe for the freedom of mankind felt the impact of the Eisenhower personality. Perhaps the greatest of all of his accomplishments was his ability to get men of different nations and languages to work harmoniously together in a common cause. As one admirer said:

> Eisenhower knew how to work with people and he knew how to get people to work together.

He had the knack of tact, to hold divergent forces together and to keep them working together.

The author John Gunther visited General Eisenhower in France in 1951, when Eisenhower was head of supreme headquarters, Allied Powers in Europe. Gunther came from that meeting and wrote, not of great war plans, but of Eisenhower the man, saying:

> He has been a soldier all his life, but believes in peace. He does not stand for war, but for defense against war.

Eisenhower achieved a great victory in Europe in World War II. He later went back to Europe to build forces which would preserve peace, preserve it without fighting.

As a newly elected President, Eisenhower brought about a settlement of a shooting war in Korea.

Through all of this, moments of great strain and moments of great triumph, Eisenhower remained a man of the people.

He never forgot or ignored his birthplace in Texas or his home in Kansas where he grew to manhood. It was this tie to the heartland of America which kept President Eisenhower first in the esteem of his countrymen. People instinctively liked General Eisenhower. All were touched by his ready smile.

It was this fondness which people felt for Eisenhower which has made his death such a sad, personal event for the people of this country. People admired him for his achievements, but they loved him for himself.

No man could ask for a greater tribute than the love and esteem the people of this country have for Dwight David Eisenhower.

The love of his fellow man is the tribute to Eisenhower, the man. The peace he won and preserved is the tribute to President Eisenhower, the soldier-statesman.

The Bible says, "Blessed are the peacemakers; for they shall be called the children of God." While his critics were screaming for a war with China, and accusing him of a no-win policy, Eisenhower had the judgment, the wisdom, the humaneness, the greatness to save America and the world from a long, bloody war in Asia. For this, the American people should and will love him always.

## Hon. Clifford P. Case

OF NEW JERSEY

Mr. President, I think that all of us at this time, for reasons that run very deep, are saddened by the death of General Eisenhower. However, it seems to me that the overriding fact that comes to the minds of all of us when we think about the life of President Eisenhower is the strange and providential way in which man seems to be called by our country and by the world for leadership when he is desperately needed.

This has been true throughout the history of our country, and throughout the history of the world—else, probably mankind would not have survived as long as it has.

If ever the world needed a leader, if ever our country in its history needed a leader, it was at the time we discovered how to destroy all mankind, including ourselves.

I do not believe anyone could have come to the helm of government in the United States more profoundly qualified for leadership in the transition from what we might call the world of innocence to a world in which man's survival lay in his own hands and better fulfill the role which was demanded of him than General Eisenhower.

He was not a deeply intellectual man, and he was often derided by sophisticates as an amiable buffoon, which only goes to prove how inadequate sophisticates are in dealing with the great problems of the world and of society.

President Eisenhower had a kind of intuitive sense of what was necessary in the gravest matters that put him uniquely into a position of world leadership as well as, of course, the leadership of our country. He articulated and made it acceptable to the people of this country and, I think, of the world, too, that atomic war could no longer be tolerated, that confrontation between the great powers in the direct sense would no longer be possible, that that sort of war was unthinkable.

He sensed this, and he made it stick. It is now accepted doctrine. And men have found that they can live in such a world.

We will always be blessed with the guidance which he gave us on that issue which, I think, was the greatest contribution any man could possibly have given any nation or the world.

It is for this intuitive understanding of what human respect required and his ability to make that understanding common property that I think he will go down in history.

We are lucky in our time to have found the leader that our time required.

## Hon. Richard B. Russell

OF GEORGIA

Mr. President, the death of Dwight D. Eisenhower has removed from this earthly scene a man who possessed to an unprecedented degree the love and confidence of the American people and the respect of the entire world. His services as President have been greatly underrated and with the passing time his stature will loom larger and larger among the 37 who have served in that position.

The confidence of the average citizen in Dwight Eisenhower should renew the hopes of every American for the future of our country. His faith in the patriotism and judgment of our people in the mass was probably greater than that of any President since Jefferson. He sought and held our highest political office without being a politician. His sincerity and integrity were so transparent that he did not find it necessary to come up with a new program every day in the effort to buy the good will and support of some special group.

Being human, he made mistakes and, being too trusting, he was at times betrayed by those whom he had trusted. But his great decency and honesty shone through the miasma of demagoguery and promises of "something for nothing" which mark politicians of this period and were completely comprehended by the vast majority of our people.

It was my high privilege to know President Eisenhower personally over a long span of years. I admired him as a man and was grateful for his friendship. I share the sorrow that is common to all who knew him and worked with him, and I extend my deepest sympathy to his family.

## Hon. Norris Cotton

OF NEW HAMPSHIRE

Mr. President, my first memory of General Eisenhower was when as a member of a subcommittee of the Committee on Appropriations of the House of Representatives, I visited NATO headquarters in 1951. We were briefed by him over a period of days. I returned from Paris convinced that the Nation needed him as its President. I was one of the 19 Members of the House who joined in a letter asking him to return and be a candidate. After he consented, I became one of the delegates from New Hampshire pledged to his cause.

It was my privilege to serve, first in the House and then in the Senate, during those 8 years when nations that had long before learned the firmness of his purpose and felt the magic of his name remained at peace. No American boy perished under gunfire anywhere in the world.

Like President Nixon, my most vivid memory of General Eisenhower is his first inauguration. In my scrapbook, where I keep the utterances I have heard and will never forget, are the words he spoke that day:

> The peace we seek signifies more than stilling the guns, easing the sorrow of war. More than an escape from death, it is a way of life. More than a haven for the weary, it is a hope for the brave.

> This is the hope that beckons us onward in this century of trial. This is the work that awaits us all to be done with bravery, with charity—and with a prayer to Almighty God.

He was a great soldier, but a far greater apostle of peace.

Now he is at peace. May peace come to the country he loved and led.

## Hon. John O. Pastore
OF RHODE ISLAND

Mr. President, a great man moves on to immortality as Dwight David Eisenhower passes from history's living page.

From a life crowded with service for others, he will be remembered under many names—President, general, educator, author, family man, and by the universal and affectionate title of "Ike."

This seems to personify the humble and democratic heart of a man who walked with kings.

I would turn back the pages of time to December 8, 1953, for an Eisenhower date and deed I shall always remember.

On that day President Eisenhower gave an astonished General Assembly of the United Nations his proposal of "atoms for peace." He assured them that the United States would join with all interested nations—including Communist Russia—in cooperative research into the peaceful uses of atomic energy.

Out of this proposal came the International Atomic Energy Agency within whose framework we have studied and striven for effective nuclear restraints.

Dwight Eisenhower—a man of highest military stature, a man of deepest humanity—was essentially a man of peace.

A worried world sought his counsel.

His judgment will be missed.

## Hon. Gordon Allott
OF COLORADO

Mr. President, the last battle for a great general has ended and our Nation has suffered the loss. All of us, young and old, mourn the passing of General Eisenhower.

He stood for so much that has made America what it is today: dedication, public service, military bravery, commonsense, and devotion to God and country.

Like all men of his stature, his service to his Nation is appreciated more today than it was while he occupied the important positions of responsibility which filled his lifespan. History will appreciate Ike even more.

I knew him well, and with all who served with him in government I respected him and his principles, just as he respected the principles which made America great.

That he lived as long as he did is a final tribute to his spirit for life. Many a weaker man would have given up long ago. Ike was a fighter and he fought until the end.

While his passing was not unexpected, it nevertheless is a trial to all those who knew and loved him. Welda and I join the whole Nation in extending our deepest sympathy to his wife, Mamie, and the whole Eisenhower family.

## Hon. Jennings Randolph
OF WEST VIRGINIA

Mr. President, shortly after the passing of Dwight David Eisenhower on Friday, March 28, I issued the following statement:

> Former President Dwight Eisenhower was a soldier and statesman who served our Republic in war and in peace.
>
> Americans admired the general for his fortitude and faith.
>
> I recall his personal and official kindness and consideration during the years I was in the Senate during his administration.

## Hon. Karl E. Mundt
OF SOUTH DAKOTA

Mr. President, yesterday afternoon the President of the United States shared with the world the moving last words of Dwight Eisenhower as spoken to his wife on the day he died:

> I've always loved my wife, I've always loved my children. I've always loved my grandchildren and I've always loved my country.

Less than two dozen words are contained in those brief sentences.

But what immense sweep these words have, for they tell us all that we need ever know about the man and what he has meant to this country and what the people of this country—all humanity, in fact—meant to him.

Virtually every trust of leadership that could be demanded of a man was given him.

And because of that victorious leadership in war, bringing us victory and peace, and his successfully ending yet another war in far-off Korea—virtually every honor that could be bestowed upon Dwight Eisenhower was his.

We knew him as the general who directed the greatest military operation of all time in bringing to defeat the forces of oppression and tyranny which had enveloped Europe.

We knew him as the supreme commander of NATO who brought the Western nations together again as the impenetrable shield to prevent another massive, destructive war.

We knew him as the President who brought an end to another war in Korea and then kept the peace—an era of peace longer than any this Nation has known for three decades.

But we all knew—and the world knew—Dwight Eisenhower best as "Ike."

And those last words of Dwight Eisenhower—telling of his great love—define for us more clearly than all of the books written about him, all of the articles devoted to his life, and all of the eulogies spoken of him, why "Ike" will remain in the hearts of Americans a hero for all time.

When Dr. Billy Graham learned of the death of General Eisenhower, he described the former President as the greatest American since Abraham Lincoln.

I think Dr. Graham has captured in his description exactly the sentiments felt by the citizens of this country, as well as those of free peoples everywhere, who believe Dwight Eisenhower personified the American ideal of the love of liberty which has stood continually as a beacon to the oppressed and a barrier to the oppressor.

Mr. President, those of us who have had the honor to serve in one capacity or another with Dwight Eisenhower have been privileged beyond expectation. I shall always cherish my days in the House of Representatives and in the Senate in which I had the opportunity to be a member of those committees which conferred with him during his years of military service, and during those years in which he served as our President.

Mr. President, Mrs. Mundt joins with me today in extending our sympathies to the family of Dwight Eisenhower, the great man, who, as President Nixon said, came from both the geographical and the spiritual heart of America.

Because of him, truly, we are the richer in spirit.

## Hon. John L. McClellan

OF ARKANSAS

Mr. President, when I learned that General Eisenhower had passed on, Mrs. McClellan and I promptly dispatched a wire to Mrs. Eisenhower extending to her and members of the family our deepest sympathy and prayerful expression that they would be comforted and sustained in this time of their greatest bereavement. Some excerpts from that message of condolence can be appropriately repeated in my remarks today.

I stated to her that "General Eisenhower was a patriotic, courageous, and valiant soldier who led the mighty forces of the free world to victory over aggression and conquest" in World War II. I also said that "he was a statesman of understanding, patience, and wisdom who brought calmness and hope to a troubled world." And that "the exemplary and forceful qualities of leadership that he provided as President instilled confidence and inspired peoples and nations to exert greater and more dedicated efforts in the cause of peace and tranquillity among nations."

I further emphasized that he "earned and received the respect and esteem of the American people and was admired and beloved by them to a degree unexcelled by any other great leader or President of this generation."

Mr. President, his passing is a great loss to humanity. He contributed much to the social and cultural progress of our people and steered the ship of state, when he was at the helm, in the direction of a higher civilization and a better and safer world. These sentiments I record with deepest sincerity and out of a reverent respect and esteem for him as a man, as a citizen, and as one of America's greatest leaders of our time and generation.

## Hon. Len B. Jordan

OF IDAHO

Mr. President, because of his long and grave illness the news of General Eisenhower's death comes as no surprise. Even so, the acute sense of loss is not lessened for the respect he had is universal.

The world has lost a great soldier and statesman, our Nation has lost a beloved leader, and all of us have lost a wise counselor and friend.

The life of General Eisenhower is a splendid example of American achievement. Perhaps only in America can a boy, born of humble, God-fearing parents, rise to such heights of leadership in war and in peace.

I shall always prize my personal contacts with him, starting with the kickoff of his 1952 presidential campaign from the capitol steps in Boise when I was Governor. On his invitation I came to Washington, D.C., to be Chairman of the International Joint Commission and to work in related problems in natural resources.

He has made a great contribution to the world he served in time of crisis, and to the country he loved with such fervor and served with utmost dedication. He will be remembered, not only for his record which speaks for itself, but for the fact that for all his work with national and world leaders, and the tremendous power he wielded over the course of history, he still kept the humility and the common touch and the sense of humor of the smalltown boy from Kansas.

## Hon. William Proxmire

OF WISCONSIN

Mr. President, no American in this century inspired in people all over the world the love and trust General Eisenhower inspired. He was a good and gentle man, a man of peace and compassion, a man of monumental integrity and honesty.

Ike had a genius for unifying disparate personalities into a working and effective team. This was his great strength as commander of the largest military force in history, a force which liberated half a continent from the Nazi tyranny. It was one of his great strengths as President.

He brought to the White House a dignity and a sense of honor that elevated the Presidency in the eyes of the people.

He had nothing but scorn for those public men who engaged in demagoguery and character assassination.

Ike did not regard the Presidency as a bully pulpit. He did not believe the President should dominate the other coequal branches of the Government in making national policy. Many disagreed with that view. But one must pay it high respect.

The man who led allied forces against the blackest example of one-man rule in modern history surely had ample reason to mistrust the concentration of political power in the hands of one individual.

President Eisenhower's warning against the influence of the military-industrial complex in his farewell address as President was never more relevant than it is today as we are about to move ahead with expensive new weapons systems.

"I like Ike" was not merely a narrow party slogan. It was, to the end, the sentiment of a nation.

## Hon. Barry M. Goldwater

OF ARIZONA

Mr. President, standing in the rotunda of the Capitol yesterday as President Nixon eulogized former President Eisenhower, the thought came to me that while many men who had served our country well and with valor had gone to rest with the flag draped over their coffins, very few had so richly deserved and won that honor as had General Eisenhower. The flag means more to us because of him, and our country will forever be better through the great example he set of devotion to it and love for it.

## Hon. Thomas J. Dodd

OF CONNECTICUT

Mr. President, a great leader of the American people has passed away, and the Nation is in mourning. Our hearts go out in sympathy to his beloved widow and family.

I was privileged to serve in both the House of Representatives and the Senate during his term as President. I shall always remember his unfailing courtesy, consideration, and kindness.

Great men are able to rise to distinguished positions within a certain field or a certain career. But it is the extraordinary man who achieves comparable greatness in more than one realm. The late Gen. Dwight David Eisenhower was such a man.

General Eisenhower was a military genius of the first order. His thoughts and actions were characterized by discipline, decisiveness, and deep courage.

As President, General Eisenhower helped the American people to maintain a sense of balance and to view events in proper perspective. He fostered among us a spirit of security and hope.

Our grief at the death of General Eisenhower is magnified by the knowledge that we shall not soon see his like again. He represented an America for which we feel nostalgia, an America where our values were clear and there was no compromising with one's duty to one's country.

## Hon. Peter H. Dominick

OF COLORADO

Mr. President, our Nation mourns the loss of a great soldier, statesman, and President. I feel the deep personal loss of a good friend with the death of former President Eisenhower. To the very last day of his life he was a symbol of strength and honor for the people of the United States and the world.

General Eisenhower was a frequent visitor to our State of Colorado and often said he considered it his second home. I first met Ike in 1951, when he was president of Columbia University. He was a guest in our Colorado home in 1954 and 1956. He was one of the major reasons that I first entered politics back in the early fifties.

Our thoughts are with Mrs. Eisenhower, who has always shown such courage during the many episodes of illness endured by the general over the past several years.

## Hon. Claiborne Pell

OF RHODE ISLAND

Mr. President, if ever there was a man who epitomized the word "good," who possessed the quality of goodness to an infinite degree, it was Dwight David Eisenhower. He was a man of peace who proved himself unsurpassed in war. He was a man of gentleness who lived a life of high adventure. He was a gentle man who bested some of the most bestial fighters of our century. He was a simple man whose goodness, kindness, and humility helped him overcome obstacles and achieve his objectives. His services to our country as soldier and leader of armies, as president of a great university, as a man of inspiration, and as President of the United States were all of the highest order.

Most important, he was a man of truth, incapable of duplicity. Our country and our world trusted him. Finally, he was a man of wisdom and vision, whose farewell words as President, warning us of the dangers of the industrial-military complex, should be heeded by the Nation that now mourns the passing of this great and good man.

## Hon. Roman L. Hruska

OF NEBRASKA

Mr. President, in the death of General Eisenhower, the world has lost one of its towering figures, one whom history will regard among the truly great.

Born and raised against a humble, midwestern background, this remarkable man led the forces of freedom to victory in a great world war and, at the end of that career, answered a further call to serve his country in its highest office. Again, he demonstrated an inspired ability to unify and to lead the Nation at a particularly critical time in its history. As we look back on the 8 years of his administration we recognize the great stability, firmness, and progress which marked that time.

Even after he had laid down the burdens of the Presidency, he continued to play a constructive and effective role as a true elder statesman, spurning petty partisan considerations and concerning himself only with the welfare of the country he loved and served so long and so well.

It is amazing that one generation could produce both an Eisenhower and a Churchill, two mighty and beloved leaders who will be revered as long as men prize freedom.

## Hon. Abraham Ribicoff

OF CONNECTICUT

Mr. President, we mourn today the loss of Dwight David Eisenhower. We mourn his passing, and we remember his contributions to this world.

He was a leader—a man who led great armies to victory in the Second World War. Because he knew the horrors of war, he worked unceasingly for peace. Few men have left a more significant imprint on the 20th century.

In his lifetime, he won high office and held imposing titles—General of the Armies—president of a great university—President of the United States. But our memories of Dwight Eisenhower are not related to pomp and ceremony. We remember him as a warm, outgoing person—a man of character, integrity, and good will.

He battled in the arena of politics—and won. And he won more than the Presidency. He won the affection and respect of the American people.

Now he is gone, and we will miss him. But his words and deeds will live on in our history and influence our Nation for generations to come.

## Hon. Paul J. Fannin

OF ARIZONA

Mr. President, the Nation, and indeed all of the free world, mourns the death of Dwight D. Eisenhower. His absence will be lamented not only by free men everywhere but also by those who long to be free, for Dwight Eisenhower epitomized the fight for freedom in all aspects of his life.

From a Kansas farm boy to Supreme Allied Commander in Europe to President of the United States, Dwight David Eisenhower symbolized all that is good about America. His life bounded all elements of the American ideal and wrapped them in reality.

Now we are all much poorer because he is gone.

To say that he was a great American is inadequate.

To say he was a great statesman lacks completeness.

To outline his accomplishments in war and peace as a protector of the free world ignores the foundations for domestic progress he laid here at home.

It remains for history to indelibly inscribe upon the tables of time the unique and continuing contributions made by Dwight Eisenhower, not only through his public service but by his private example of integrity, courage, and devotion to duty.

Though we grieve over his death and sorrow at his passing, our lives are enriched by the record of the life he lived in service to his fellow man, his nation, and his God.

## Hon. Walter F. Mondale

OF MINNESOTA

Mr. President, Dwight David Eisenhower is gone, and Americans everywhere mourn his passing.

What he did is engraved in the national consciousness: at Normandy; at Bastogne; on the Elbe; in 8 years as one of the most beloved Presidents with which the Nation has been blessed.

I would speak of Dwight Eisenhower the man, for, in many ways, what he was, was even more important than his deeds, great though they were.

He was a uniquely American product: A soldier who had seen the face of war, and who turned his country away from it. He was perhaps the most beloved man of this time, yet a man who never lost his humility.

We asked of him perhaps more than we should ask of any man. It was his decision, and his alone, that determined the life or death of hundreds of thousands of American men on that June 6 D-Day more than two decades ago. It was his decision, more than once in his 8 years in the White House, that meant the difference between peace and war.

A small incident, unknown at the time, illumines his character. On the eve of D-Day, when the greatest invasion force in man's history moved toward Omaha, Juneau, and the other beaches of Normandy, Dwight Eisenhower, in the loneliness of his command post, wrote two communiques. In the first he foretold a great victory for American arms. In the second—should that happen—he wrote of a bloody defeat, and in the communique he wrote that the defeat was his alone, that he had made the decision, that the blame was his alone.

He was, above all, a good man, in the best sense of that most overused word. We knew that he was, and we gave him our love; he gave to us his all.

## Hon. John Sherman Cooper
### OF KENTUCKY

Mr. President, I do not believe I can add anything to the tributes which have been paid to Dwight David Eisenhower. Certainly nothing can be added to the record of his life.

I can only voice my own appreciation of his life, and for having known him and having served under him in the Army of the United States in Europe in 1944 and 1945, as Ambassador of the United States to India and Nepal by his appointment, and as a Member of the U.S. Senate when he was President.

Although I am sure these following articles have been placed in the Record by other Senators, I feel that they, added to the magnificent eulogy by President Nixon, have expressed the admiration and the affection of the American people.

I ask unanimous consent that the editorial published by the New York Times on Sunday, March 30, and the article by Mr. Arthur Krock published by the Times on Saturday, March 29, be printed in the Record following my remarks.

I emphasize President Eisenhower's initiative toward ending the cold war, and toward the achievement of peace. I quote the last two paragraphs of an editorial in the New York Times of March 31, entitled "Guests at the Funeral":

> The passage of time has only added importance to the beginnings toward ending the cold war that were made when Eisenhower and Khrushchev met in Geneva in 1955 and then in this country in 1959. Their meetings broke the ice of the Stalinist era and—despite the U–2 flareup in 1960—helped pave the way for the limited but important progress that has been made this decade.
>
> The world leaders at this funeral of a soldier for peace could render him no more significant tribute than to advance the spirit of reconciliation he set in motion.

Finally, I take the liberty of using that part of the eulogy of President Nixon when he quoted the last words of President Eisenhower to Mrs. Eisenhower:

> I've always loved my wife. I've always loved my children. I've always loved my grandchildren. And I've always loved my country.

To Mrs. Eisenhower, who shared his trials and triumphs and who contributed to his life, we offer our admiration and sympathy.

We shall miss him.

[From the New York Times, Mar. 30, 1969]

There being no objection, the editorial and article were ordered to be printed in the Record, as follows:

#### A Peacemaker Remembered

On this day of national mourning for Dwight Eisenhower, there is everywhere a sense of loss but not of tragedy. It is a time of sorrow but not of desolation, of nostalgia but not of despair. After a full, active life of service to his nation and mankind he died rich in honors and secure in the affections of his countrymen.

In war, he had known moments such as the North African invasion and the Normandy D-Day when daring and high resolve were rewarded. In peace, he had labored with patience and insight for better international relationships and helped bring about a significant change in the cold war. As party leader and President he was no stranger to controversy. Like all men he had some failures of understanding and made some mistakes of judgment, but he left the White House after eight years still retaining the confidence of the nation.

Even in the last year of his life when pain and distress were often his unwelcome companions, he had also occasions for satisfaction—the political party of his choice restored to power, a political protege elected to the White House, a grandson married. As with the lives of General George C. Marshall, his close military colleague, and Winston Churchill, his great wartime ally, there is about Eisenhower's life a sense of fulfillment, of missions accomplished.

He played a historic military role in a warlike age but it is as a peacemaker he will be remembered. He had a sure instinct for popular sentiment. In a television talk in 1959 with British Prime Minister Harold Macmillan, President Eisenhower said, "I think that people want peace so much that one of these days governments had better get out of their way and let them have it."

Tendered a dinner in his honor by New York City in June 1945, he early defined the philosophy that guided his peace-keeping efforts: "I believe we should be strong, but we should be tolerant. We should be ready to defend our rights but we should be considerate and recognize the rights of the other man."

His tolerance, his fairmindedness, his ability to put himself in the other man's shoes and see the problem from another viewpoint won the confidence of his fellow Americans, ignited the hopes of his contemporaries and earned the respect of his adversaries. Regardless of provocation and pressure, he never lost sight of his essential goal. He overruled military advisers and refused to intervene in French Indo-China in 1954. He broke with the nation's oldest allies, France and Britain, to oppose the Suez invasion of 1956. He incurred the political risks of inviting Premier Khrushchev for a tour of this country in 1959 and did not lose faith in eventual Soviet-American accommodation despite the Premier's tirades at the unsuccessful Paris summit conference in 1960. His farewell message to the American people upon leaving the White House the following year was a warning against the power of the military-industrial complex.

"He is great who is what he is from nature, and who never reminds us of others," Emerson wrote in his Essay on Great Men. Eisenhower met this definition. As a famous general, he was as unlike Napoleon or Wellington in his personal style as any man could be, and just as dissimilar to his American predecessors of past wars—Washington, Jackson, Grant, Pershing. He was unique.

Yet, from another vantage point, Eisenhower could, like Lincoln, say that he was a common man but God must like common people because he makes so many of them. "Ike" looked like everybody's grandfather. In his simple tastes, plain dress and easy manner, he could have been an obscure country doctor or another Midwestern businessman. Of his generation, he was the typical American writ large, and so countless millions whom he had never met could think of him as a neighbor and a friend. Born in Texas, reared in Kansas, educated in New York, on duty at Army posts across the country, and retiring at last to a farm in Pennsylvania, Dwight Eisenhower belonged to all Americans. They honor him today, neighbor, friend, peacemaker.

[From the New York Times, Mar. 29, 1969]

TOPICS: "AN UNCOMPLICATED MAN"

(By Arthur Krock)

WASHINGTON, March 28.—"To mold, to balance and to integrate" the forces contending, designedly or inherently, to undermine "the principles of our democratic system"—this was the lifetime mission of Dwight D. Eisenhower as he saw and practiced it. In many conversations with him before, during and after his Presidency, his sense of this mission invariably emerged. So it was wholly in character that his fixed dedication dominated Eisenhower's Farewell Presidential Address to the American people on the night of Jan. 17, 1961.

A BASIC DOCUMENT

To schoolboys the best-known examples of state papers in this particular field are Washington's Farewell Address and the peroration of Lincoln's Second Inaugural. Indeed, they are the only ones with which schoolboys are familiar. But as time recedes into eternity from the day of Eisenhower's death on March 28, 1969, the extraordinary combination in his Farewell stress on his lifetime principle, and foresight of the threat to which it was being increasingly exposed, will establish this document also as fundamental to the basic education of Americans.

He cited two forces in particular as comprising the threat to "the very structure of our society": A military-industrial complex and a "scientific-technological élite," both born of another new threat. And this he described as "a hostile ideology—global in scope, atheistic in character, ruthless in purpose and insidious in method." In other words, the Bolshevist design to impose Communism by force throughout the world.

CARICATURE REFUTED

If there were room here for additional extracts, they could only serve to support the point I am seeking to make. It is, that not only does Eisenhower's Farewell reflect and maintain the purpose which guided him as President, as soldier and as a private person: the Address refutes the caricature drawn of Eisenhower by variously motivated critics as a chief magistrate who let his subordinates do the governing because he had no original ideas, no passion for the advancement of humanity and a distaste for mental concentration on the problems confronting the President as steward of the nation.

But the refutation of this appraisal has much more material to produce than the Eisenhower speech of Jan. 17, 1961. The records of the crisis meetings of the National Security Council, 1963–61, are now under seal at Camp Ritchie, Maryland. When these papers are released for publication they will, according to a common judgment expressed to me by participants in the discussions, reveal that the President:

Made all the final decisions; firmly and fully enforced them; that his reliance on the staff system stopped at the deciding line; that his grasp of complex issues was profound; and that his expositions of his own views were both forceful and clear.

SOURCE OF POPULARITY

But, since a large part of the public incessantly read the contrary in the press, and heard it on the air and in the political arena, what were the sources of a popular sentiment that, the political professionals generally agreed, would have elected Eisenhower to a third term if he had been legally eligible—and willing?

He has been a victorious American commander of the largest armies ever assembled. But victory in war, even a war that preserved the Union, did not save Grant from the political obloquy in which his Presidency ended. And Washington left the Presidency amid a rising tide of malice and slander.

GOOD AND UNSELFISH

The sources of Eisenhower's unbroken hold on the American people were probably that few could see, hear or talk with him and not come away with the conviction that here was a good man, an uncomplicated man, unselfish in his patriotism—the kind of man who has risen from simple beginnings to the possession of great power without impairment of integrity.

This certainly was my feeling in conversations, intimate and otherwise, in Paris, in the Pentagon, at the White House and thereafter. And, aside from the foresight, perception and passion for the traditional concept of "the democratic system" in the Farewell Address,

Eisenhower was the kind of President the nation wanted in his time, a time that may come again.

(NOTE.—Through all the years of the Eisenhower Presidency, Arthur Krock wrote the "In The Nation" column in The Times.)

## Hon. J. Caleb Boggs
OF DELAWARE

Mr. President, death has taken from us Dwight David Eisenhower who dominated the middle of the 20th century as a soldier, statesman, and humanitarian.

We all are diminished by the loss.

My deepest sympathies go to Mrs. Eisenhower and their wonderful family.

People throughout the world had great faith and confidence in General and President Eisenhower. And he, in turn, had great faith in the goodness of man and in the simple virtues.

In 1952, before his election, he put some of the tenets of his faith down on paper, and I believe they have great relevance for us here today. He said:

> If each of us in his own mind would dwell upon the simple virtues—integrity, courage, self-confidence, and unshakeable belief in the Bible—would not some of our problems tend to simplify themselves?
>
> Would not we, after having done our best with them be content to leave the rest with the Almighty? I think it is possible that a contemplation, a study, a belief, in those simple virtues would help us mightily.

General Eisenhower's great faith in this country and its people was reciprocated fully by the people.

My personal faith in this great man springs from the dark days of World War II when I served under him in Europe. I recall we had absolute confidence in his command leadership. But he was more than a military leader. He was beloved by the men in the ranks to whom his infectious grin and willingness to consider their problems symbolized a great moral leader.

It was my privilege to get to know the general better in later years. In 1952 and 1956 I campaigned for him as I was running for Governor of Delaware. His visits to our State were memorable occasions to me.

He frequently held briefing sessions for the Governors in those day, and it was my privilege as Governor of the First State to be seated at his side. He was always well prepared at those sessions and brisk in matters of business. But he also liked to talk about his golf game and tell of the pleasure he found in doing his own cooking.

President Eisenhower's years of prominence served his country well. He answered every call—to the military, to education, to his Nation's highest office—but, above all, to his fellow man.

It may well be said, as Louisa May Alcott wrote:

> For such as he there is no death;
> His life the eternal life commands;
> Above man's aims his nature rose.
> The wisdom of a just content
> Made one small spot a continent,
> And tuned to poetry Life's prose.

## Hon. John G. Tower
OF TEXAS

Mr. President, it will be many, many years before the Nation is again blessed with a man such as Dwight David Eisenhower. Many others have chronicled his historic achievements, which were very great indeed, and I can add little to that. The thing that I best recollect about the general, however, is his strong sense of humanism and his dedication to the morality that has pervaded the American people and made them able to endure all the hardships that befall a great nation.

Soldier, statesman, writer that he was, I believe that he will be best remembered in the history of our Nation as the guiding light for America during years of peril and an inspiration to us all in rebuilding the world and leading it from devastation to unprecedented growth. The general lived as he died, always fighting against overwhelming odds and seeking out the best of all possible solutions.

The years 1952–60 are already looked back upon in nostalgic terms for our Nation. During that time, we were a nation unified for a common purpose, seeking a common goal, hand in hand. The Eisenhower years were a Periclean age when we were recovering from nearly 12 years of warfare and international strife. The leadership provided during those years enabled us to bind up our wounds, rebuild much of the world, and chart a course for growth unknown before in the world.

As easy as it is to heap praise upon someone

with General Eisenhower's stature, I am certain that he would want to be remembered as a man of the people, an American Cincinattus, who heeded the call of his Nation when it needed him even at the risk of great personal sacrifice. When the former President suffered his first heart attack which brought him so close to death some 14 years ago, it would have been easy for him to have retired from public life, which was the advice of many physicians. However, in the true Eisenhowerian sense, he put his personal considerations aside to serve his country that he loved so dearly.

Mr. Eisenhower spoke often of his country and the people who comprised it during his colorful and spiritually rewarding service to his nation, but I believe that one of his most poignant statements came from him just after he had assumed his Presidential office in 1953 and was proceeding on his work. When he spoke, he captured what must be considered as one of the finest thoughts on the essence of what is America. As always with the general, it was short, simple, and to the heart of the matter:

> But never let us forget that the deep things that are America are the soul and the spirit. The Statue of Liberty is not tired, and not because it is made of bronze. It is because no matter what happens, here the individual is dignified because he is created in the image of God. Let us never forget it.

## Hon. William B. Saxbe

OF OHIO

Mr. President, Dwight David Eisenhower was a man for all seasons and all peoples. America has lost a great patriot and a great leader. The sadness of this time is even deeper because America has also lost a great man.

This soldier-statesman, a man of peace and love of country, was a fighter to the end. He was a marvelous fighter who lived like a general and died like a general.

Yet even in war, Mr. Eisenhower was a messiah of peace. On a 20th-century day of apprehension, June 6, 1944, for example, he messaged the people of Western Europe while Allied troops were storming ashore in Normandy:

> This landing is part of the concerted United Nations plan for the liberation of Europe, made in conjunction with our great Russian allies . . . I call upon all who love freedom to stand with us now. Together we shall achieve victory.

In all of my personal contacts with Mr. Eisenhower, I was always impressed with his outgoing, warm personality and attitude. Even when he ascended to the two highest positions of his twin careers—General of the Army and President of the United States—this plain-talking man from Abilene never lost the humility and touch that bonded him to his people. Perhaps his greatest appeal, in fact, rested in the way even the most humble of Americans was able to identify with the man we all called "Ike."

Mr. Eisenhower's view of humility may have been best expressed late in World War II, in an address at Guildhall, London. He said that day:

> Humility must always be the portion of any man who receives acclaim earned in the blood of his followers and the sacrifices of his friend.

Dwight David Eisenhower, our 34th President, was born October 14, 1890, in Denison, Tex. He was the third son of David and Ida Elizabeth Stover Eisenhower. A year later the family moved to Abilene, Kans., where the young "Ike" earned both academic and scholastic honors at Abilene High School. Eisenhower entered West Point in July 1911, where, 4 years later, he was commissioned a second lieutenant in the Infantry and assigned to Fort Sam Houston, Tex.

It was there that he met Mamie Geneva Doud, a gentle lady who would spend the next 52 years at his side. They were married July 1, 1916, at Denver, Colo.

General Eisenhower's military career is known today to nearly all Americans: It spanned two world wars and a number of lesser crises in our history. His ability as a master planner and tactician were quickly recognized by his superiors.

The general was named commander in chief of Allied forces in North Africa in 1942, and directed the successful campaigns in Africa, Sicily, and Italy.

Later, he was named supreme commander of all Allied Forces in Europe and directed the "great invasion" that eventually brought the enemy to his knees.

I do not intend to recount Mr. Eisenhower's political career here, except to note that he was elected President in November 1952, and took office January 20, 1953. He was reelected President in 1956.

It was typical of Mr. Eisenhower that, for a man who spent more than half of his life in the uniform of a warrior, he was always a highly religious and devout man. Shortly after World War II, when he had directed the most awesome military machine ever assembled, Mr. Eisenhower was asked about his religious beliefs. He replied:

> I am the most intensely religious man I know. Nobody goes through six years of war without faith.

His inner beliefs were perhaps best expressed for all time in a message to the American people in 1953. He said:

> The things that make us proud to be Americans are of the soul and spirit. They are not the jewels we wear, or the furs we buy, the house we live in, the standard of living, even, that we have. All these things are wonderful to the esthetic and to the physical senses.
>
> But never let us forget that the deep things that are America are the soul and the spirit. The Statue of Liberty is not tired, and not because it is made of bronze. It is because no matter what happens, here the individual is dignified because he is created in the image of his God . . .

That was Dwight David Eisenhower.

## Hon. Charles McC. Mathias, Jr.

OF MARYLAND

Mr. President, millions of words, in many languages, have been written and spoken in tribute to Dwight David Eisenhower through the years and over this sad weekend. As heads of state, prominent men and women, and ordinary citizens have expressed their admiration and respect for General Eisenhower, one remarkable theme has been that of simple, universal affection for this extraordinary man.

Americans can say of Dwight Eisenhower, more than of any other man, that he was their friend. Those of us who had the privilege of knowing him only share in a richer sense this conviction that he was a genuinely warm and sincerely dedicated human being.

It was this human quality that gave an extra dimension to General Eisenhower's dramatic career as a soldier. He directed the greatest Allied Expeditionary Force in history, and in the course to that victory he was able to shape a grand alliance of free men which reached and endured far beyond the formal accords of governments.

It was this human quality that gave the Eisenhower Presidency its emphasis on peace and on humane concerns, an emphasis which met a deep national need, steadied the country, and brought the free world to new, lasting confidence and energy.

It was this human quality that produced the great sense of friendship and regard for Dwight Eisenhower which we have witnessed among those far too young to have served in World War II or voted in the national elections of the 1950's.

It was this human quality which made him, as President Nixon stated in his moving eulogy of yesterday, "an authentic hero"—not only recognized for his heroic deeds, but loved for his authentic faith and personal commitment.

To some, General Eisenhower's death marks the further disappearance of those grand figures and historic leaders who made the free world a reality. To many, his death has brought a sadness and nostalgia for a somehow simpler world in which there were great men who could lead peoples in great causes, live rich and full lives, and pass on peacefully.

Yet, in the respectful quietness of national mourning, we have all felt a return to those qualities of humanity and decency which are at the heart of America. We have felt a sense of community which, although evoked by sorrow, gives us hope.

Dwight David Eisenhower is mourned and will be remembered above all else because he had a vision of a world in which men would be guided by their higher ideals, a world in which the selfishness and folly of nations would be submerged in the greater desire and willingness of people to act together in the cause of peace and freedom. It is this vision, grounded in faith and infused with compassion, which will be his legacy and should be our guide.

## Hon. Richard S. Schweiker

OF PENNSYLVANIA

Mr. President, many words have been spoken and written in the hours since Gen. Dwight D. Eisenhower lost his gallant fight for life on Friday, even though words are inadequate to express America's loss of a great man. His dedication to freedom and his service to his country as a soldier and as a statesman to maintain that freedom have been widely praised. His strength of character, which in turn gave moral strength to millions of Americans for two decades, has been widely honored.

I should like to add a short personal tribute to General Eisenhower, as one who was honored to have known him as a friend and adviser. I am particularly moved to be able to make my tribute in this historic Senate Chamber, because it was General Eisenhower's early support and encouragement over a year and a half ago, that contributed to my decision to become a candidate for the U.S. Senate seat I presently hold.

General Eisenhower lived in, and loved, Gettysburg, Pa., and we in turn, from Pennsylvania, gained the honor of calling him a neighbor. He brought the same high sense of personal honor and integrity to his activities in Pennsylvania, as he did to the affairs of state as President of the United States. He brought the same love of his fellow man to the town of Gettysburg, as he did across the world, in the many stirring trips as President we still remember.

As a general, he united allied countries to wage a fight against oppression. As President, he united our country in an unprecedented time of peace and prosperity, to improve the lot of all mankind. As a man, he represented the highest qualities of what has made America great, and he served his country long and selflessly to make it great. I can think of no better eulogy than to recount his life of service, and his love of humanity, and the inspiring example that his life provided for us all.

We have lost a great leader, and the Eisenhower family has lost a great man. He was, is, and will be one of America's most beloved Presidents.

## Hon. Ted Stevens

OF ALASKA

Mr. President, for a large portion of my life, Dwight David Eisenhower was my Commander in Chief, in peace and in war. Today, millions of Americans feel, as we do, the sense of loss that comes from losing not only a leader, but a friend.

No President in our memories has so firm a place in the hearts of our Nation. Fathers fought under his command, and their sons grew up to know him as a man of peace. All Americans mourn him today. But it is mourning that covers a deep sense of gratitude. America is a better place for his having been here; Americans know this and are thankful for it. He led his countrymen through some of the most difficult years the United States has ever known—and he led them later to peace, strength, and prosperity at home and abroad.

President Eisenhower held a special place in the hearts of Alaskans, over and above that which exists so completely throughout the country. For it was under his administration that Alaska became our 49th State. It was with President Eisenhower's support that Alaskans were granted the full rights and privileges of American citizenship. In a speech in Denver in 1950, recognizing the unjustness of territorial status, he said:

> Quick admission of Alaska and Hawaii to statehood will show the world that America practices what it preaches.

For our 34th President, statehood for Alaska was a matter of simple justice. And in January 1959, this hope of equality for Alaska became a reality with his proclamation of January 3, 1959, that Alaska was a fullfledged member of the Union. In a very real sense he was a "50-star" general—for he was the first President to serve as the leader of our Union of 50 States. Alaskans mourn his passing with special sorrow. He gave us so much; indeed, without Dwight David Eisenhower, I doubt seriously whether many of us would be here today.

A nation should always mourn the passing of a leader. But many of us today not only mourn; we grieve the passing of an era. It seems only a short time ago that, as supreme commander, Gen. Dwight Eisenhower's firm voice commanded the Allied Armies in Europe; and an even shorter time ago that he steered this great country through crisis and change. He conceived of Atoms for Peace and started the process by which we shall achieve our ageless dream of reaching the stars. His strengths, ideals, and accomplishments will be landmarks for use and all Americans in times to come.

Mr. President, as Dwight D. Eisenhower gave unstintingly to America, America in return gave him its love and respect. He had many honors, the love of his country, and the respect of the world. But when he listed the accomplishments of his administration, statehood for Alaska and Hawaii appeared first on the long list of achievements of the Nation under his leadership.

To Alaskans, he was a man who matched our mountains—a man who stood above the crowd, a man firm in purpose, devout in his heart, and true to the ideals he espoused.

Dwight Eisenhower loved his country—he served it well.

He would ask no greater epitaph than that.

## Hon. Hiram L. Fong

OF HAWAII

Mr. President, I am deeply grieved by the death of our beloved leader Dwight David Eisenhower. Hoping against hope, I had prayed that this gallant soldier would once again conquer physical adversity.

There is no question that America has lost one of its greatest heroes—a brilliant general, a skilled statesman, an outstanding leader.

We—and the world—will sorely miss one of our foremost citizens, a man of upright convictions who throughout his entire life was a force for goodness and justice for all mankind.

It is sad indeed that his wise counsel is lost to us particularly at a time when the winds of dissension tear at the fabric of our civilization and moral confusion corrodes a growing segment of society. We need so much his calm and reasoned counsel and his dignity and faith and inspiration.

His passing is a real loss, not only to the American people but to peoples in far-flung lands around the globe, who recall his magnificent record in ending war and in building peace.

Millions of Americans remember General Eisenhower in his capacity as World War II commander in chief of the Allied Forces in Europe, and their gratitude to him for his leadership is personal.

Millions of Americans remember his strength and ability as supreme commander of the North Atlantic Treaty Organization, which served to keep the hard-won peace in Europe after World War II.

Millions recall his tenure as president of Columbia University, a magnificent institution of higher education, to which he imparted great prestige and honor.

Millions of Americans lived during the 8 years of his Presidency, and they know from personal experience the peace and tranquillity and progress of the years 1953 through 1960—and their gratitude to him is personal.

Other millions are too young to remember most of the deeds and the accomplishments of Dwight David Eisenhower in his long life of service to the American people and to freedom-loving people everywhere. They only know from history books of his wartime record and his performance as 34th President of the United States.

In these eulogies, we hope to recall and convey as best we can something of the greatness and the goodness of Dwight Eisenhower and to preserve for posterity the fundamental precepts for which he stood.

Trained as a soldier, he left military service after reaching the pinnacle of success to enter civilian life, where he also reached the pinnacle of success—success measured not alone by his winning two terms as President of the greatest Nation on earth, but success measured by his ability to keep the peace.

A soldier of war became one of America's greatest peacemakers. Surely his skill at maintaining peace is one of the greatest monuments to his memory.

Others will chronicle the triumphs, the milestones, and the contributions of Dwight Eisenhower to his country and to the world. Today I should like to emphasize his major achievements as two-term President of the United States—"major" as he himself assessed his tenure in office. For his own evaluation of his record reveals, better than my words can do, his sense of values and his concern and compassion for people.

Called upon in October 1966 to defend his record as President, General Eisenhower enumerated 23 accomplishments.

We see Dwight Eisenhower's passionate devotion to peace in these achievements on his list:

End of the Korean war—thereafter no American killed in combat while he was President.

Good will journeys to more than a score of nations in Europe, Asia, Africa, South Africa, and in the Pacific.

Prevention of Communist efforts to dominate Iran, Guatemala, Lebanon, Formosa, South Vietnam.

Atoms-for-peace program.

Preservation for the first time in American history of adequate military establishment after cessation of war.

Initiating a strong ballistic missile program.

31-935 O—70——3

Conceiving and building the Polaris program, with submarines operating at sea within a single administration.

Reorganization of the Defense Department.

Initiation of a plan for social progress in Latin America after obtaining necessary authorization from Congress for $500 million.

We see Dwight Eisenhower's compassion for people in these accomplishments on his list:

Intelligent application of Federal aid to education—National Defense Education Act.

Extension of social security old-age and survivors insurance to over 10 million persons.

Starting Federal medical care for the aged—Kerr-Mills program.

Establishment of the Department of Health, Education, and Welfare.

We see Dwight Eisenhower's firm adherence to Government's obligation to maintain a sound currency and monetary system in the following achievements he listed:

Slowing up and practical elimination of inflation.

Largest reduction in taxes to that time.

Fighting for responsible fiscal and financial policies throughout 8 years.

We see Dwight Eisenhower's awareness of the need for resource development and technological progress in the following achievements on his list:

Building of the St. Lawrence Seaway.

Initiation of the Nation's space program with successful orbits in less than 3 years, starting from scratch.

Initiation of, and great progress in, the most ambitious road program by any nation in all history.

We see Dwight Eisenhower's deep passion for justice, fairplay, and equal rights in these accomplishments on his list:

The first civil rights law in 80 years.

Using Federal power to enforce orders of a Federal court in Arkansas, with no loss of life.

Desegregation in Washington, D.C., and in the Armed Forces by administrative action.

And last, but not least, statehood for Alaska and Hawaii.

It is significant that Dwight Eisenhower mentioned statehood first in his listing. But I mention it last because I want to say a few words about Dwight Eisenhower's vital role in statehood.

We of Hawaii owe a special debt of gratitude to him, for he made it possible for Hawaii to become a State of the Union, a status for which we had struggled for more than half a century.

As President he was an ardent champion of statehood for Hawaii. In his state of the Union message on January 5, 1956, President Eisenhower spoke of "one particular challenge" confronting Americans. He said:

> In the Hawaiian Islands, East meets West. To the Islands, Asia and Europe and the Western Hemisphere, all the continents, have contributed their peoples and their cultures to display a unique example of a community that is a successful laboratory in human brotherhood.
>
> Statehood, supported by the repeatedly expressed desire of the islands' people and by our traditions, would be a shining example of the American way to the entire earth. Consequently, I urgently request this Congress to grant statehood for Hawaii.

Never before had any Chief Executive called for statehood for Hawaii with such enthusiasm or urgency. Within 4 years, the issue was resolved on the side of justice and fairplay.

Congress passed the Hawaii statehood bill in March 1959, and President Eisenhower promptly signed it into law. It was a glorious victory in Hawaii's struggle for equal rights that began more than a half a century earlier.

The long and arduous campaign for statehood came to a final end on August 21, 1959, when President Eisenhower signed a proclamation which declared, in part, that "admission of the State of Hawaii into the Union on equal footing with the other States of the Union is now accomplished.

I remember so clearly the day Dwight Eisenhower invited me, one of Hawaii's first two U.S. Senators, to the White House to accept the first 50-star flag representing the addition of Hawaii to the Union. Ike's pleasure and pride in Hawaii statehood were genuinely evident, and we all realized a wonderful new chapter in our Nation's history was beginning.

So, on this 10th anniversary of statehood, the people of Hawaii salute Dwight Eisenhower with a grateful "Thank you" and with the warmest aloha from our hearts. We are indeed deeply touched that he listed statehood for Hawaii as one of the great achievements of his Presidency.

Just as Hawaii has special reason to be grateful to Dwight Eisenhower, so billions of freedom-loving human beings on this planet have good reason for gratitude. As an outstanding and victorious soldier, he captured the affection and respect of his countrymen and of the peoples saved and liberated through his brilliant leadership.

And as a soldier of peace in the decades following, he increased their affection and respect. Dwight Eisenhower became the most popular President since George Washington and, although he had been out of public office for 9 years, he remained the most admired man in the world to his final days.

As President Nixon so aptly said yesterday in his moving eulogy, Dwight Eisenhower "was probably loved by more people in more parts of the world than any President America has ever had."

When future generations of America ask "Why was this so?" we want them to know the qualities of mind and spirit that so endeared Dwight Eisenhower to his fellow man.

He personified the essential goodness and greatness of the American Nation and the American people. He came from humble beginnings and he was taught to revere God, to love his country, and to honor his fellow man.

He was taught to distinguish right from wrong and to persevere in behalf of what is right.

Raised in the heartland of America, among plain, God-loving, dignified people, Dwight Eisenhower personified those enduring qualities that are universally admired and respected—gentle kindness, inherent decency, human compassion, unquestioned honesty, integrity, courage, strength in adversity, self-respect, humble confidence, and unfailing faith in God and in men, the children of God.

These but barely sketch the true dimensions of this giant among men. Ordinary standards and ordinary words inadequately measure the extraordinary man that Dwight Eisenhower was.

Perhaps the simplest and best way to describe the stature of Dwight Eisenhower is to say that he was a man who loved people and his love was so all embracing that billions of human beings here and abroad reciprocated.

In many lands, among many races, and in many tongues, the feeling is, and for years has been, expressed in the same way: "I like Ike." No higher tribute can be paid the memory of Dwight Eisenhower.

My wife Ellyn joins me in extending our deepest sympathy to Mrs. Eisenhower, John Eisenhower, and all the members of the Eisenhower family. We shall always cherish the memory of their beloved "Ike."

## Hon. Charles E. Goodell

OF NEW YORK

Mr. President, today this Nation mourns not only a former President and general, but a man.

It is a cliche to say that Dwight David Eisenhower was admired; how much more fitting to his memory it is to say "we like Ike."

It might be worth noting in passing that all the political slogans in American history—"Fifty-four forty or fight," "Tippecanoe and Tyler too," "Back to normalcy," "Chicken in every pot," and many many others were slogans about an issue or about a man and an issue. "I like Ike" was the only slogan that expressed America's feeling about a man.

There is a deeper reason for this mass affection than the fact of his military genius or his infectious grin.

I think President Nixon put his finger on it when he said in yesterday's eulogy:

> We find ourselves, thinking today, not of his deeds, but of his character.

I think that no finer tribute to Ike can be made than that we resolve today to rededicate ourselves, not only as a people but as individuals, to the basic values that went to make up that character.

Ethics, morality, courage, integrity, honor, decency, faith.

Dwight David Eisenhower possessed and used these simple homely virtues each day of his life.

We would do well to reassess our outlook on what these values mean in our society today.

We have, to all too great extent, relinquished much of our self-control as well as our public control. There has been a loss of resolve, a lessening of the built-in deterrents that are such an essential part of the human psyche.

We have become a nation of people that is increasingly more permissive and increasingly less prohibitive in its critique of the scene in which we are involved.

Our sense of proportion seems to have undergone a not too subtle erosion.

It is my earnest belief that the basis of decent

human conduct is still to be found in the fabric of the Ten Commandments and the Sermon on the Mount.

Today, unfortunately, it has become somewhat "square" to refer to the values of the spirit—and yet there is not one of us, who deep in his heart does not desire for his children that they grow up with a deep sense of spiritual value.

Let us therefore on this day of sadness, pause to reflect and to make use of the lesson of Ike's career and how he conducted himself personally.

Let us each in our hearts resolve to be unafraid and unashamed to proclaim that the quiet dignity of good character is a virtue to be praised rather than to be ridiculed as "out of date."

And let us see to it—each of us—that we never let this concept die, that we follow the words of the passage from Deuteronomy that say:

> And these words which I command thee this day, shall be upon thy heart. Thou shalt teach them diligently unto thy children and shalt speak of them when thou sittest in thy house, when thou walkest by the way, and when thou liest down and when thou rises up . . . that ye may remember and do all my Commandments and be holy unto your God.

Dwight Eisenhower was "holy unto his God." People realized this; it was an unspoken understanding.

In the words of President Nixon:

> We are grateful for the life of Dwight David Eisenhower. He truly came from the heart of America.

*The Presiding Officer.* The question is on agreeing to the resolution, which will be stated.

The legislative clerk read the resolution as follows:

S. Res. 175

*Resolved,* That the Senate has heard with profound sorrow and deep regret the announcement of the death of Dwight David Eisenhower, a former President of the United States and General of the Army of the United States.

*Resolved,* That as a token of honor to his illustrious statesmanship, his leadership in national and world affairs, his distinguished public service to his nation, and as a mark of respect to one who has held such eminent public station in life, the Senate hereby expresses its deep sensibility of the loss the nation has sustained by his death, and its sympathy with the family in their bereavement.

*Resolved,* That the two Senators from Kansas be appointed by the President of the Senate to attend the funeral of the deceased, to be held at Abilene, Kansas.

*Resolved,* That the Secretary of the Senate transmit these resolutions to the House of Representatives and transmit a copy thereof to the family of the deceased.

*Resolved,* That as a further mark of respect to the memory of the deceased the Senate do now adjourn.

The resolution (S. Res. 175) was unanimously agreed to.

*The Presiding Officer.* In accordance with the provisions of Senate Resolution 175, under the order previously entered, and as a further mark of respect to the memory of the deceased former President of the United States, Dwight David Eisenhower, the Senate will now adjourn.

Accordingly (at 2 o'clock p.m.), the Senate adjourned until tomorrow, Tuesday, April 1, 1969, at 12 o'clock meridian.

# Memorial Tributes

IN THE

# Senate of the United States

IN EULOGY OF

# Dwight David Eisenhower

# Memorial Tributes in the Senate

## *OF THE UNITED STATES*

## Hon. Everett McKinley Dirksen

OF ILLINOIS

Mr. President, I ask unanimous consent to have printed in the RECORD the text of the funeral service for the Honorable Dwight David Eisenhower at Washington Cathedral, on Monday, March 31, 1969, together with the scriptural selections by the Reverend Dr. Edward L. R. Elson, Chaplain of the Senate.

There being no objection, the material was ordered to be printed in the RECORD, as follows:

FUNERAL SERVICE FOR THE HONORABLE DWIGHT DAVID EISENHOWER, 1890–1969, MARCH 31, 1969, 4:30 O'CLOCK IN THE AFTERNOON, WASHINGTON CATHEDRAL, WASHINGTON, D.C.

THE ORDER OF SERVICE

Organ prelude:

Chorale-Prelude, "Schmücke dich, o liebe Seele", *Johann Sebastian Bach;* Chorale-Prelude, "O Welt, ich muss dich lassen", *Johannes Brahms.*

*The Ministers, meeting the body, and going before it, will escort it to the place of honor in the Crossing of the Cathedral, while the people stand and the choir sings:*

"The Palms" by *J. Fauré:*

"O'er all the way green palms and blossoms gay
Are strewn this day in festal preparation,
Where Jesus comes to wipe our tears away,
E'en now the throng to welcome him prepare.

"Join all and sing, his Name declare,
Let ev'ry voice resound with acclamation,
Hosanna! Praised be the Lord,
Bless him who cometh to bring us salvation.

"His word goes forth and peoples by its might
Once more regain freedom from degradation,
Humanity doth give to each his right,
While those in darkness find restored the light.

*"Refrain*

"Sing and rejoice, O blest Jerusalem,
Of all thy sons sing the emancipation,
Through boundless love the Christ of Bethlehem
Brings faith and hope to thee for evermore.

*"Refrain."*

The opening sentences.

*The Dean of the Cathedral will then offer the following prayer:* "Remember Thy servant Dwight David, O Lord, according to the favour which Thou bearest unto Thy people, and grant that, increasing in knowledge and love of Thee, he may go from strength to strength, in the life of perfect service, in Thy heavenly kingdom; through Jesus Christ our Lord, who liveth and reigneth with Thee and the Holy Ghost ever, one God, world without end. *Amen.*"

*Minister and People:* "Our Father, who art in heaven, hallowed be Thy name, Thy kingdom come, Thy will be done, on earth as it is in heaven; give us this day our daily bread, and forgive us our trespasses, as we forgive those who trespass against us, and lead us not into temptation, but deliver us from evil, for thine is the kingdom, and the power, and the glory for ever and ever. *Amen.*"

Hymn (*sung by all, standing*):

"A mighty fortress is our God,
A bulwark never failing;
Our helper he amid the flood
Of mortal ills prevailing:
For still our ancient foe
Doth seek to work us woe;
His craft and power are great,
And, armed with cruel hate,
On earth is not his equal!

"Did we in our own strength confide,
Our striving would be losing;
Were not the right man on our side,
The man of God's own choosing:
Dost ask who that may be?
Christ Jesus, it is he;
Lord Sabaoth his Name,
From age to age the same,
And he must win the battle."

*Martin Luther, 1529.*

Psalms 46 and 121 (*read responsively*) *Led by the minister of the National Presbyterian Church:*

"God is our refuge and strength, a very present help in trouble.

*"Therefore will we not fear, though the earth be removed, and though the mountains be carried into the midst of the sea;*

"Though the waters thereof roar and be troubled.

*"Though the mountains shake with the swelling thereof.*

"There is a river, the streams whereof make glad the city of God,

*"The holy place of the tabernacles of the Most High."*

"God is in the midst of her; she shall not be moved:

*"God will help her, and that right early.*

"The nations raged, the kingdoms were moved: he uttered his voice, the earth melted.

*"The Lord of hosts is with us; the God of Jacob is our refuge.*

"Come, behold the works of the Lord,

*"What desolations he hath made in the earth.*

"He maketh wars to cease until the end of the earth;

*"He breaketh the bow, and cutteth the spear in sunder; he burneth the chariots in the fire.*

"Be still, and know that I am God: I will be exalted among the nations, I will be exalted in the earth.

*"The Lord of hosts is with us; the God of Jacob is our refuge.*

"I will lift up mine eyes unto the hills: from whence shall my help come?

*"My help cometh from the Lord, who made heaven and earth.*

"He will not suffer thy foot to be moved: he that keepeth thee will not slumber.

*"Behold, he that keepeth Israel will neither slumber nor sleep.*

"The Lord is thy keeper: the Lord is thy shade upon thy right hand.

*"The sun shall not smite thee by day, nor the moon by night.*

"The Lord will preserve thee from all evil: he will preserve thy soul.

*"The Lord will preserve thy going out and thy coming in from this time forth, and even for evermore.*

"Glory be to the Father, and to the Son, and to the Holy Ghost;

*"As it was in the beginning, is now, and ever shall be, world without end. Amen."*

"The Apostles' Creed" (*said by all*): "I believe in God the Father Almighty, Maker of heaven and earth: And in Jesus Christ his only son, our Lord; who was conceived by the Holy Ghost, born of the Virgin Mary, suffered under Pontius Pilate, was crucified, dead, and buried; he descended into hell; the third day he rose again from the dead, he ascended into heaven, and sitteth on the right hand of God the Father Almighty; from thence he shall come to judge the quick and the dead.

"I believe in the Holy Ghost; the holy Catholic Church; the communion of saints; the forgiveness of sins; the resurrection of the body; and the life everlasting. *Amen."*

THE READING OF THE SCRIPTURES (PEOPLE SEATED)

*The congregation will remain seated while* Psalm 23 *is sung by the Cathedral choir to the words and music of the Scottish Psalter.*

"The Lord's my Shepherd, I'll not want;
He makes me down to lie
In pastures green; he leadeth me
The quiet waters by.

"My soul he doth restore again;
And me to walk doth make
Within the paths of righteousness,
E'en for his own Name's sake.

"Yea, though I walk in death's dark vale,
Yet will I fear none ill;
For thou are with me; and thy rod
And staff me comfort still.

"My table thou hast furnished
In presence of my foes;
My head thou dost with oil anoint,
And my cup overflows.

"Goodness and mercy all my life
Shall surely follow me;
And in God's house forevermore
My dwelling place shall be. *Amen."*

Memorial and pastoral prayers.

Benediction by the Bishop of Washington: "Unto God's gracious mercy and protection we commit Dwight David. The Lord bless him and keep him. The Lord make His face to shine upon him, and be gracious unto him. The Lord lift up His countenance upon him, and give him peace, both now and evermore.

"And now may the God of peace, who brought again from the dead our Lord Jesus Christ, the great Shepherd of the sheep, through the blood of the everlasting covenant; make you perfect in every good work to do His will, working in you that which is well pleasing in His sight; through Jesus Christ, to whom be glory for ever and ever. *Amen."*

Hymn (*sung by all, standing*):

"Onward, Christian soldiers,
Marching as to war,
With the cross of Jesus
Going on before!
Christ, the royal Master,
Leads against the foe;
Forward into battle,
See, his banners go.

"Onward, Christian soldiers,
Marching as to war,
With the cross of Jesus
Going on before!

"Like a mighty army
Moves the Church of God;
Brothers, we are treading
Where the saints have trod;
We are not divided,
All one body we,

One in hope and doctrine,
One in charity.

*"Refrain."*

"Onward, then, ye people,
Join our happy throng,
Blend with ours your voices
In the triumph song;
Glory, laud, and honor
Unto Christ the King;
This through countless ages
Men and angels sing.

*"Refrain Amen."*

*During the singing of the hymn the Minister and Honorary Pallbearers take their places around the body and at the end of the hymn they escort it to the North Entrance while the United States Marine Band, the President's Own, plays "Army Blue."*

Honors to the President played by the Marine Band.

*As the body is carried down the steps of the Cathedral the Marine Band will play "Lead, Kindly Light."*

*The congregation leaves to the tolling of the Bourdon Bell.*

OFFICIATING CLERGY

The Reverend Edward L. R. Elson, Minister, National Presbyterian Church.

The Very Reverend Francis B. Sayre, Jr. Dean of Washington Cathedral.

The Right Reverend William F. Creighton, Bishop of Washington.

Choir of the Washington Cathedral, Paul Callaway, organist.

---

SCRIPTURE SELECTIONS READ BY THE REVEREND DR. EDWARD L. R. ELSON, MINISTER, THE NATIONAL PRESBYTERIAN CHURCH, AT THE FUNERAL SERVICE OF PRESIDENT DWIGHT DAVID EISENHOWER, MARCH 31, 1969

Hear the reading of God's word, being excerpts from the Letters of Paul, the Apostle, and the words of our Lord Jesus Christ.

II Timothy 4: 6 and 7: ". . . the time of my departure is at hand." "I have fought a good fight, I have finished my course, I have kept the faith."

Romans 8: 14, 35, 37 to 39: "For as many as are led by the Spirit of God, they are the sons of God." "Who shall separate us from the love of Christ? shall tribulation, or distress, or persecution, or famine, or nakedness, or peril, or sword?" "Nay, in all these things we are more than conquerors through him that loved us." "For I am persuaded, that neither death, nor life, nor angels, nor principalities, nor powers, nor things present, nor things to come," "Nor height, nor depth, nor any other creature, shall be able to separate us from the love of God, which is in Christ Jesus our Lord."

I Thessalonians 4: 13, 14, and 18: "But I would not have you to be ignorant, brethren, concerning them which are asleep, that ye sorrow not, even as others which have no hope." "For if we believe that Jesus died and rose again, even so them also which sleep in Jesus will God bring with him." "Wherefore comfort one another with these words."

II Corinthians 4: 5: "For we know that if our earthly house of this tabernacle were dissolved, we have a building of God, an house not made with hands, eternal in the heavens."

I Corinthians 13: 9 to 13: "For we know in part, and we prophesy in part." "But when that which is perfect is come, then that which is in part shall be done away." "When I was a child, I spake as a child, I understood as a child, I thought as a child: but when I became a man, I put away childish things." "For now we see through a glass, darkly; but then face to face: now I know in part; but then shall I know even as also I am known." "And now abideth faith, hope, charity, these three; but the greatest of these is charity."

I Corinthians 15: 57 and 58: "Thanks be to God, which giveth us the victory through our Lord Jesus Christ." "Therefore, by beloved brethren, be ye steadfast, unmoveable, always abounding in the work of the Lord, forasmuch as ye know that your labour is not in vain in the Lord."

Ephesians 6: 10 to 18: "Finally, my brethren, be strong in the Lord, and in the power of his might." "Put on the whole armour of God, that ye may be able to stand against the wiles of the devil." "For we wrestle not against flesh and blood, but against principalities, against powers, against the rulers of the darkness of this world, against spiritual wickedness in high places." "Wherefore take unto you the whole armour of God, that ye may be able to withstand in the evil day, and having done all, to stand." "Stand therefore, having your loins girt about with truth, and having on the breastplate of righteousness, "And your feet shod with the preparation of the gospel of peace;" "Above all, taking the shield of faith, wherewith ye shall be able to quench all the fiery darts of the wicked." "And take the helmet of salvation, and the sword of the Spirit, which is the word of God: "Praying always with all prayer and supplication in the Spirit."

Hear the words of our Lord Jesus Christ:

Matthew 5: 3, 4, 8, 9: "Blessed are the poor in spirit: for theirs is the kingdom of heaven." "Blessed are they that mourn: for they shall be comforted." "Blessed are the pure in heart: for they shall see God." "Blessed are the peacemakers: for they shall be called the children of God."

John 14 (adapted from the Presbyterian Book of Common Worship): "Jesus said: 'Let not your heart be troubled: ye believe in God, believe also in Me. In My Father's house are many dwelling places: if it were not so, I would have told you. I go to prepare a place for you. And if I go and prepare a place for you, I will come again, and receive you unto Myself; that where I am, there ye may be also. And whither I go ye know, and the way we know. I am the way, the truth, and the life: no man cometh unto the Father but by Me.

'These things have I spoken unto you, being yet present with you. But the Comforter, which is the Holy Spirit, whom the Father will send in My name, He shall teach you all things, and bring all things to your remembrance, whatsoever I have said unto you. Peace I leave with you, My peace I give unto you; not as the world giveth, give I unto you. Let not your heart be troubled, neither let it be afraid.' "

Prayers by the Reverend Dr. Edward L. R. Elson, Minister, the National Presbyterian Church, at the Funeral Service of President Dwight David Eisenhower, March 31, 1969

Almighty God, Father of mercies and Giver of all comfort, deal graciously, we pray Thee, with all those who mourn this day, that casting every care on Thee, they may know the consolation of Thy love, the healing of Thy grace, and the companionship of Thy presence. Through Jesus Christ our Lord.

Eternal Father, in whom we live and move and have our being, draw us close to Thee and let Thy light and joy fill our souls as we offer unto Thee the praise and thanksgiving of our hearts; for the mystery and wonder of life here and hereafter. We thank Thee that deep in the human heart is an unquenchable trust that life does not end with death, that the Father who made us will care for us beyond the bounds of vision even as He has cared for us in this earthly pilgrimage. We praise Thy name that our hope has been so wondrously confirmed in the life, the words and resurrection of our Lord Jesus Christ.

We give Thee thanks for all the sacred memories and hallowed recollections which cluster this hour.

We thank Thee for Thy servant Dwight David. For his goodly heritage, his godly parents, his boyhood home and early training, and for his beloved companion of the years. We thank Thee for the nobility of his manhood, the integrity of his person, the hospitality of his mind and magnanimity of his spirit; for his steadfastness under provocation, for his gifts of reconciliation, for his kindness and his firmness, for his compassion and mercy, for his warm friendship, his transparent spirituality, his patience in suffering, and for all that endeared him to the multitudes of mankind. Especially do we thank Thee for his Christian testimony, for the depth and durability of his faith, for his constant witness to the spiritual basis of our common life, for his steadfastness in seeking to know and to do Thy will, and for his daily walk with Thee.

We thank Thee too for all the human graces with which Thou didst endow him—for his sheer joy in living, for his infectious humor, his zeal as sportsman and competitor, his love of beauty and his efforts to express it on canvas and in words, for his love of family and for the sanctity of his home.

O God, in whose sovereign will is the destiny of men and nations, who art a God of history and beyond history, we give Thee special thanks for the magnitude of his public service—for his military prowess in defense of freedom; for his leadership in winning and in conserving the peace; for his high service as President of the Republic. We give Thee thanks for his vast labors transcending all parties and faction, encompassing all men and nations, for his high vision of the better world toward which all men of good will strive, and for his devotion to that higher kingdom, the ruler of which is God and the law of which is love.

O Eternal Father, suffer us not to miss the glory of this hour. May a new spirit arise in us this day. Give us eyes to see and hearts to feel the undaunted courage, the invincible faith, the unconquerable love of Thy servant, Dwight David, that we may be true as he was true, loyal as he was loyal; that we may henceforth be good enough and great enough for our times. Through Jesus Christ our Lord. Amen.

And now, O Father, who doest all things well, with thankful hearts that Thou has given him to us for a season, we give Thy servant, Dwight David, back to Thy tender care, until the shadows flee away, and the brighter day dawns, when the visible and invisible are as one in Thy higher kingdom. Through Jesus Christ our Lord, Amen.

## Hon. Gale W. McGee

OF WYOMING

Mr. President, America again pauses to pay tribute to one of its great leaders. Dwight David Eisenhower, General of the Army, Supreme Commander of Allied Forces in Europe during World War II, 34th President of the United States, and a man beloved of all of us, is dead. We mourn his passing, but we are encouraged and inspired by the example of lifelong service he has given us.

"Ike" Eisenhower, Mr. President, embodied much of what is the spirit of America, becoming for a generation of Americans a symbol. Though many of us were cast as opponents in the political scheme which is the great strength of our country, the whole world knows that we all liked Ike. Largely this is because it was so apparent that Ike liked us. He liked all men. He was a soldier always, but a soldier in the cause of peace, a crusader. He has left our heritage richer.

As always, Mr. President, Ike gave us inspiration even in his final days. His indomitable spirit fought against the ravages of disease and his spirits remained high to the end. Through that final struggle, also, his devoted wife Mamie and son John, as well as other members of his family, bore their burdens with strength and courage. I know all Americans have compassion for them. We all assuredly share their bereavement.

Mr. President, I ask unanimous consent that, as part of this tribute to General Eisenhower, the comments of my hometown newspaper, the Laramie Daily Boomerang, and of the Wyoming Eagle be printed in the Record.

There being no objection, the items were ordered to be printed in the Record, as follows:

[From the Laramie (Wyo.) Daily Boomerang, Mar. 29, 1969]

A SALUTE TO AN AMERICAN

Dwight D. Eisenhower is dead.

Perhaps nothing is more symbolic of the Eisenhower spirit than the fight he waged against a losing cause for nearly one year. Throughout that time "Ike," as most people will remember him, fought back time and time again to overcome each current crisis. The spell of crisis after crisis finally proved to be too much.

A nation, its people and the people around the world mourn his death. Most probably we were aware after the series of heart attacks last year that the former President and supreme commander of allied forces very likely would never leave the hospital again.

History will judge Mr. Eisenhower on two counts. He will be judged as a general on the first of these, and here he should go down in history as one of the greatest. It will take time for judgment on his role as President but he came to the Republican party as a candidate when the Republican party was seriously in danger of becoming non-existent and when it had no candidate who could really lead it to victory.

Since Eisenhower's announcement that he would run for office, the party managed to come back to the point that the two-party system was no longer in danger of becoming a thing of the past.

Loss of Eisenhower's wisdom on things military and as leader of the Republican party are going to be felt strongly. He became an image of great things in America and that image will remain.

Eisenhower, the man, is dead. His spirit and his courage will ever be on the American scene. The country and the world are certainly better for his having been present to deal with the problems and needs of both.

---

[From the Cheyenne (Wyo.) Morning Eagle, Mar. 29, 1969]

MILLIONS MOURN

The United States and much of the world are mourning the death of former President Dwight D. Eisenhower today.

General Eisenhower wrote an important chapter in history—and occupied a special place in the hearts of millions.

He was a symbol of courage and dedication.

A great many Americans are remembering General Eisenhower today as the great and widely respected leader of allied forces in Africa and Western Europe during World War II.

With his familiar Ike smile, he had the trust, confidence and respect of millions in the armed services as well as outside. He had the special qualities that made him a great military leader under the most difficult circumstances, involving the armed forces of more than one nation.

At the close of World War II he was perhaps the most popular man in all America.

Political leaders of the United States may remember just how unpolitical Ike was during the years immediately following the war.

During this period, he was constantly confronted by ardent admirers who wanted to push him for political office.

He once asked, in exasperation: "How many times does a fellow have to say 'no?' "

In May 1948, he retired as chief of staff and a month later became president of Columbia university.

He was called back to the Pentagon for temporary service as chairman of the Joint Chiefs of Staff, to help get the service unification program going. In December 1950, he was sent to Paris to be supreme commander of the new North Atlantic Treaty Organization (NATO).

He continued to be the center of speculation as a possible candidate for President, although few, indeed, really knew whether he was a Republican or Democrat. It was recalled that President Franklin D. Roosevelt had named him—then a relative unknown outside of military circles—as supreme commander of allied forces for the invasion of Africa.

Gov. Thomas E. Dewey of New York, twice defeated GOP presidential candidate, and others were backing an "Ike for President" move on the Republican side.

It wasn't until Jan. 7, 1952, the year of the election, that Eisenhower finally proclaimed himself a Republican and said he would be a candidate for President if he "got a clear-cut call to political duty."

The very popular general, of course, was elected President in the 1952 general election—by a landslide.

Four years later, in 1956, he was reelected by an even bigger majority.

General Eisenhower continued to demonstrate his courage, strength and determination to the end.

He waged a tremendous battle against illness dating back to his first heart attack in 1955. He had been in Walter Reed Army Medical Center almost a year, with a string of four heart attacks, surgery and pneumonia in February, and congestive heart failure earlier this month.

He died at 10:25 yesterday morning (MST) at the age of 78.

And, today, millions are remembering . . .

## Hon. Marlow W. Cook

OF KENTUCKY

Mr. President, as a young county executive of 36 I was invited to attend a meeting at Gettysburg, Pa., on the farm of former President Dwight D. Eisenhower. One of my most prized possessions is a picture taken of the two of us while I was there.

It was my privilege to be a precinct worker in 1952 when we worked so hard for the election of the great general. Probably more individuals than at any other time in history got out and worked for the man who had led us once before as Commander of Allied Forces during World War II. It was, in fact, an easy task to labor for such a hero whose accomplishments all Americans felt so much a part of.

Mr. President, knowing that immortality is no part of mortal man, I can only say that to be a Member of this body and be privileged to have my remarks be a part of history as a tribute to our former President is an honor which defies explanation. To have been a part in some small way in having had such a man as President of our country for 8 years shall always be a cherished part of my political endeavors.

This was a man the Republicans wanted in 1952, not because he was a party man, but because he could salvage a two-party system that some apparently had little concern to salvage. For those of us in our middle twenties he was to be the one man who could pull the Republican Party kicking and screaming into the 20th century. This he did, and for this we shall be forever grateful—not just as a party but as a nation.

To meet him was to know a kind man. To hear him was to listen to an honest man. No such words as "credibility gap" could have been uttered by the most contrary newswriter in those 8 years. Security was President Eisenhower. Confidence was President Eisenhower. And the abiding faith of this man reflected itself in a people who saw no dishonor or disrespect in referring to their President as "Ike" anywhere in the world. He was a man we all knew intimately in the true tradition of America.

He said during an interview at Gettysburg that he wanted to take worn-out land and through hard work and revitalization leave it far better land when he died. Through his efforts he has done for America that same job of revitalization and has indeed left for us a far better land.

## Hon. Herman E. Talmadge

OF GEORGIA

Mr. President, all the Nation and the world mourn the loss of Dwight David Eisenhower, whom history will remember as one of the truly great Americans of all times. General Eisenhower served his country with distinction in time of war and peace. He directed the course of this Nation and our allies to victory over tyranny in a time when the freedom and dignity of man were put to its most severe test. His courage and devotion to duty earned him the eternal gratitude of his fellow countrymen and all the people of Europe.

As President of the United States, Eisenhower was again called to lead our Nation and the free world through war against totalitarianism, and to guide our people through economic and social crisis.

He was a great general. He was a fine man and one of the most popular Presidents in American history. He will be sorely missed.

## Hon. Wallace F. Bennett

OF UTAH

Mr. President, a little bit of each of us died last Friday when General Eisenhower passed away at Walter Reed Hospital. A little bit of each of us will be buried on Wednesday when Ike is laid to rest in his boyhood town of Abilene, Kans.

To offer eulogy to a man of General Eisenhower's stature is in many ways difficult and perhaps futile. A spoken word with but few exceptions will not outlive a lifetime of greatness, deeds, and service. Few will remember what is said of President Eisenhower during this time of mourning. Almost no one who knew him or who will study his life will forget his deeds and lifetime of service. General Eisenhower was the epitome of modesty. He had almost no concern for the image which he made and this indeed is a rare trait at a time when image is often considered more important than performance. As the Supreme Allied Commander in Europe, General Eisenhower commanded the largest war machine ever created. To assemble it was difficult, but to land it successfully on the coast of France at Omaha and Utah beaches was perhaps asking too much. Yet General Eisenhower succeeded, and we will always remember that success. But what if the Normandy landings had failed? Prior to D-Day Ike had prepared a statement personally assuming all responsibility for the failure, should it come. Mr. President, I submit that like the men he commanded, uncommon courage was a common virtue to the Supreme Commander.

He conducted the Presidency of the United

States with a rare and honorable dignity. He acted and formulated his policies in a way that he believed best for the American people and the world. It was a refreshing 8 years when candor, honesty, and decency each had a fountainhead at the White House. The most severe test of any man's performance is the test of time, and General Eisenhower is passing that test remarkably well. He will be buried in Abilene adjudged by most as a great President and in retrospect the people of America and the people of the world have come to appreciate that fact.

It can be safely said of the man who left his hometown to attend West Point that, wherever he went, greatness pursued him. He was indeed the antithesis of the fact that most men seek greatness. In the life of Dwight Eisenhower, greatness sought the man. Certainly General Eisenhower proved perhaps more than any man in American history that simplicity and greatness are not incompatible.

Wrapped up in President Eisenhower were all of the virtues that made and still make America great. He understood and lived, as few men have, the concept of duty. He believed in and practiced honor. There were no pomp and pretense in him because simplicity was as much a part of him as was his contagious smile. President Eisenhower had also mastered the first and great Commandment of the New Testament, which was so beautifully pointed out by President Nixon on Sunday. One of the greatest tributes that can be given to any man is to say that he hated no one. He could disagree, but that disagreement was with ideas, with policies, and with thoughts.

I was also very impressed by the comments of President Nixon when he said that "Mr. Eisenhower was the right man at the right time in the right place." Not since the Civil War has the Nation been so confused, so torn, and so divided in its national life. The virtues that made this country great are undergoing criticism and reevaluation. I cannot help thinking that with the passing of this great American, we can pause in this crisis and reexamine his life and by so doing rediscover and hopefully rededicate ourselves to the principles of national greatness. We truly need in America a rededication and a new determination to live by the principles for which President Eisenhower stood.

To the people of Utah, Ike was a special man. In the 1952 and 1956 elections they gave him an overwhelming majority. They loved him and respected him. They knew they had a friend in Washington when he fought for and helped win the battle for the Upper Colorado River project. I speak for all of our citizens when I say that he will be long remembered and forever respected.

One cannot bid farewell to General Eisenhower, nor pay a truly fitting tribute to him without expressing appreciation, love, and respect for the courageous and wonderful lady that stood by him throughout his years of public service. One can probably never measure nor really know the sustaining power and influence that Mrs. Eisenhower had on her husband. She understood and knew him better than anyone else and we can only say that her role as wife and companion is deeply appreciated by all Americans. She invokes in my mind the Scripture from the Book of Ruth where if she did not say it in words, she performed it in deeds. Whither he went she went, and her people and his people and his causes were hers. We offer to Mamie Eisenhower at this time our love, our respect, and our deepest sympathies.

In closing, may I repeat once again a thought from President Nixon's eulogy: not since the time of George Washington has this Nation been able to say about a President or any public figure that he was first in war, first in peace, and first in the hearts of his countrymen. But perhaps the greatest tributes that will ever be paid Gen. Dwight D. Eisenhower are the silent ones, or those unspoken or unwritten, in which mothers and fathers throughout America and the world are saying to their sons, or perhaps even silently wishing in their hearts, that they hope they might grow up to be like Ike.

I ask unanimous consent that editorials from leading Utah newspapers praising General Eisenhower be printed in the RECORD.

There being no objection, the editorials were ordered to be printed in the RECORD, as follows:

[From the Deseret (Utah) News, Mar. 28, 1969]

WHY AMERICANS WILL ALWAYS LIKE IKE

As a sorrowing nation mourns the passing of one of its greatest and most beloved leaders there is little to be said about Dwight David Eisenhower that has not only been said before, but repeated frequently.

From his early years as a Kansas farmboy to his rise

from an obscure lieutenant to become Supreme Commander of the allied forces that smashed Hitler's "Fortress Europe" from his stint as President of Columbia University to his accomplishments as the first Republican President of the United States in twenty years and his public service after leaving the White House the life of "Ike" Eisenhower has been thoroughly chronicled as for few others.

No words can add or detract from his accomplishments or the honor bestowed upon him all over the world, nor can words enhance the love or ease the sadness that his countrymen feel at his demise.

As Americans reflect upon the life and works of this remarkable soldier, statesman, and leader, they would do well to ask why he won the admiration, but also the respect of so many people in all walks of life.

Was it because Dwight David Eisenhower was a fatherly figure to the entire country—firm but kind? Was it because he had the "common touch" being a man of simple tastes? Was it because he genuinely liked people—and they responded in kind? Was it because of his undeniable sincerity as a man of peace? Was it clean cut integrity?

No doubt these and many other well known aspects of Dwight Eisenhower's personality help explain his amazingly widespreaded and enduring popularity.

But there is one facet of his character that has been generally neglected which speaks volumes about the man. It is a facet that was touched on in a thumbnail sketch written two years ago by Bryce N. Harlow, one of Eisenhower's closest aides during his eight years in the White House who observed:

"Take the attributes you consider the most admirable in the people you know, put them in a mixer and you'll come up with the Eisenhower blend."

He is vitality and power and force—yet he is profoundly sensitive to the needs and feelings of others. He dominates the people around him—yet eagerly solicits and advises and readily acknowledges error. He has great dignity and reserve reflecting a quarter century of command and association with world leaders—yet he transforms instantly in "Ike of Kansas" with the school boy grin radiating amiability and warmth and a friendliness of a cocker spaniel.

He had had the adulation of people all over the world for two decades and more—yet is humble to the point of being self-effacing. He detests the personal pronoun and has scratched out hundreds of I's from speechcrafts. Many of his political speeches have ended up almost sterile because of his dislike of blowing his own horn.

During all of his White House days, he forbade the use of the word *"my"* before the *cabinet* insisting that the prestigious institution should always be called "the cabinet."

One of his favorite admonitions is "always consider your job important, never yourself." In 1942 in North Africa General Marshall asked him what is the most important attribute of a leader, his answer was "selflessness."

Whatever history records of Dwight D. Eisenhower's accomplishments as a soldier and statesman, the record will not be complete without his accomplishments as a man and the inspiration he provided by helping Americans live better lives of service and devotion to their country.

---

[From the Salt Lake (Utah) Tribune, Mar. 29, 1969]

### A Man for His Times

Often in this fortunate country's history the right man has come forth in times of national need. Former President Dwight D. Eisenhower was such a man.
man and the inspiration he provided by helping Ameri-
to plan, then execute, the invasion of Hitler's Fortress

During World War II he rose from relative obscurity to plan, then execute, the invasion of Hitler's Fortress Europe. In 1952 when Americans were frustrated and bogged down in a seemingly fruitless and unwanted war in Korea, he agreed to seek the presidency if given "a clear call to political duty." Republican leaders saw to it that the call was forthcoming and Gen. Eisenhower, then serving as supreme commander of the new North Atlantic Treaty Organization forces, answered without further hesitation.

Americans of all political persuasions turned to the former general in hope that his international prestige could restore and preserve peace and bring on the good life. To a remarkable degree these hopes were realized. The eight Eisenhower years, though frayed at times by tense international incidents, were in the overall, good ones.

His death Friday at the age of 78 will be mourned as one mourns the passing of a kindly relative who saw the family through troubled times in other years that now seem almost placid by comparison.

Though he was coaxed into politics, and never practiced that art in the usual fashion. Gen. Eisenhower was nevertheless reluctant to cut political ties after stepping down. He continued active in Republican affairs and spoke out frequently in criticism—and sometimes support—of the Kennedy and Johnson administration that followed. He took a hand in reknitting the Republican Party which strayed from his more liberal concepts and came to disaster in the Goldwater debate of 1964. His last public utterance was addressed to the party, revitalized and then meeting in convention in Miami Beach last August.

History has yet to pronounce its verdict on Eisenhower the general or on Eisenhower the President. Criticisms of both roles have been made by knowledgeable persons of high repute and these must be weighed. But Eisenhower of the infectious grin and fatherly aura must be audited in the abstract.

His greatness lay in his ability to instill in millions of people here and abroad the feeling that the world's mightiest power was in responsible hands and that all was well. Though hampered by illness and pressed by mounting crises that eventually eroded some confidence in his leadership, Dwight Eisenhower made good that trust. The America he handed over to John F. Kennedy was by no means perfect, but it had been calmed and rested and made ready to withstand the upheavals that have visited it since.

## Hon. John O. Pastore
OF RHODE ISLAND

Mr. President, supplementary to the remarks that I made on the floor of the Senate yesterday in tribute to our beloved former President, Dwight David Eisenhower, I ask unanimous consent to print in the RECORD at this point of my remarks a very lovely poem written by Virginia Louise Doris, of Rhode Island, on the occasion of President Eisenhower's second inauguration.

It exemplifies in beautiful language the spirit that this great soldier-hero brought to the Nation as a gallant and revered statesman.

There being no objection, the poem was ordered to be printed in the RECORD, as follows:

WARRIOR

*(In honor of President Eisenhower's inauguration, January 20, 1957)*

Stalwart breed, of freedom's dream,
A force imbedded far beyond
The blast of martial drum, bears in
Arms, a birth of manly strength.

Pattern, formed in bone of youth,
Springing to excessive courage
By his vision of country, fair and
Green; the American vista.

Sound the bugle, with its golden
Victory, for the heritage we share
Is proud, in its invincible plan,
Fulfilled by exacting balance.

The conqueror's blood flows fast, and
Heady, through a brave heart;
Never faltering at burden of duty,
Nor trembling in affairs of state.

Wisdom, matched by knowledge, and
Justice, is his role as he scans,
With sleepless orbit, the flux of tensions,
In this liberty-loving nation.

Salute, each citizen, our Leader!
March in solid affirmation, along
The adventurous road of future; spirit
Aflame, this hour, in our soldier's honor!

VIRGINIA LOUISE DORIS.

## Hon. Alan Bible
OF NEVADA

Mr. President, I wish to add my own thoughts to the eloquent expressions of respect and admiration that already have been offered to the memory of General Eisenhower in this Chamber, across the land, and throughout the capitals of the free world.

Few Americans have ever served their Nation with the devotion and dedication of Dwight David Eisenhower. From the time of his early boyhood in Kansas, he was totally committed to the perpetuation of the American ideal.

He was born to command. As a young second lieutenant leading a company, as a general leading the mightiest army in all history, and as a President leading a great people he was destined to shape the course of human events.

We admired him for his strength and wisdom and we loved him for his warm good humor and modesty. He embodied the highest of human virtues.

Few of us will ever forget the final words he spoke to his wife on the day of his passing:

> I have always loved my wife. I have always loved my children. I have always loved my grandchildren. I have always loved my country.

Mr. President, that tender expression may well prove the most enduring memorial to a man who revered everything decent and noble because, instinctively, he was a warm and gentle human being with an infinite capacity for love.

The enormity of his contribution to the American people and to all the free nations of the earth can never be adequately measured. Perhaps it is enough to say that we are immeasurably in his debt, just as our children and their children and countless generations to come will be in his debt. Soldier, statesman, patriot—he left his imprint on the ages.

## Hon. Ernest F. Hollings
OF SOUTH CAROLINA

Mr. President, with the death of General Eisenhower, the Nation loses one of the great heroes and genuine leaders this century has produced. As a military leader, he provided direction when the free world demanded a calm and deliberate leadership. As President, he produced a stability which every American yearns for today. General Eisenhower truly put country before self and, in so doing, left a great legacy for those who direct this Nation today.

As Supreme Commander of the Allied Expeditionary Forces in World War II, as president of

Columbia University, and as President of the United States, Dwight David Eisenhower exhibited an unequaled sense of duty that has been forever inscribed in our history and in the hearts of millions throughout the world. His record of public service will stand as an inspiration for those who believe in character and government. We shall all be better for the life of dedication he led.

## Hon. B. Everett Jordan

OF NORTH CAROLINA

Mr. President, I share with a grateful nation and the entire free world a deep feeling of grief and loss in the death of Gen. Dwight D. Eisenhower, in every sense a great and gallant leader in war and a distinguished and revered President in the years of peace which he did so much to win.

As one privileged to serve in the Senate during the closing years of his administration, I came to know and respect him for his warm humanity, his insight and perception of people and problems, and his unswerving dedication to his country and its welfare.

Although we were of different political parties, I found myself during those years in frequent agreement with his policies and proposals primarily because they seemed so attuned to American traditions, ideals, and goals on which the country had been founded and which had brought it to its position of world leadership.

One of the things most often said about General Eisenhower by those seeking to detract was that he lacked political skill. This may in a sense be true, but I think it was one of the greatest sources of his strength rather than a weakness in his armor.

I think it was the very fact that he was not regarded as a master politician that best explains the trust, belief, and loyalty which he inspired not only among his fellow countrymen but in much of the rest of the world.

The "I Like Ike" slogan which served as the trademark of his campaigns was not just a catchy phrase. It was true to a degree seldom matched in the history of electioneering.

People did, indeed, like Ike. They liked him for his honesty, his courage, his integrity, his humanity and his simplicity.

They liked—even loved—him through two terms in office and the more than 8 years which ensued after he left the White House and there was more than ample proof of that in the outpouring of a world's genuine sorrow in his passing.

The general once told a London audience that "I am from the heart of America."

And whatever other verdict history may render, it will say that is where he remains enshrined.

## Hon. Howard W. Cannon

OF NEVADA

Mr. President, the United States mourns the death of Dwight David Eisenhower—soldier, statesman, patriot.

This selfless person, devoted to the common cause of humanity, to his country, to his family, was truly a man among men. I was proud to have known him and to serve with him as an officer under his command in World War II and to be a Member of the Senate in 1959 and 1960, during his second term of office as President of the United States.

As a man who had never lost his capacity to lead, he was an inspiration to me in my efforts to serve my country and represent my fellow citizens of the State of Nevada.

The respect and affection which Dwight Eisenhower enjoyed among all men reflected the deep faith in his candor, his integrity, his simplicity, his natural dignity, and the warmth of his personality.

Our Nation will not forget his service to his country and to the free world. He will be long and gratefully remembered.

## Hon. Gaylord Nelson

OF WISCONSIN

Mr. President, the Nation grieves at the loss of one of its truly great statesmen and leaders, Dwight David Eisenhower.

General Eisenhower was a man of peace and personal charm, a man who embodied the most noble and honorable qualities of the American character. His warmth as an individual and his ability as a statesman have left a profound mark of appreciation on the memories of all those at home and abroad who knew and loved him.

Our Nation is indebted to the generosity of his spirit. He gave of himself in selfless manner as he led this country with its allies through the dark struggle against the forces of Nazi tyranny. General Eisenhower was both competent and compassionate as a military commander. He moved decisively toward ending the conflict and destruction of war, yet never lost sight of the personal needs and sorrows of those men who fought under him. He carried within him the burden of every soldier who suffered death and hardship on the battlefield.

General Eisenhower was a man of international stature. He sought the interests of all men, above and beyond the personal devices and desires of the few. He looked forward with anticipation to the day when peace and tranquillity would be a permanent reality fostered by the counsel of those who had learned from the bitter lessons of the past.

Retaining a constant distaste for war, and having had a first-hand knowledge of its cost, he warned against the growing influence of the institutions of war, lest they purchase the future of the world at the expense of human civilization.

We pay tribute to Dwight Eisenhower for the unswerving loyalty and commitment he had to his country. He served us all well, remaining cheerful to the end, calling forth in us the best that we could give.

As President his popularity attested to the trust and love which the American people gratefully afforded him.

America and the world are better for having known Dwight Eisenhower. His presence will be greatly missed. Yet his memory will never diminish.

As a Nation, we strive to honor him by living those qualities of life which to Dwight Eisenhower were his creed and his manner.

## Hon. Quentin W. Burdick

OF NORTH DAKOTA

Mr. President, one of America's greatest sons has returned to the plains of the Midwest, having concluded a lifetime of service to his country. Dwight David Eisenhower, General of the Army, 34th President of the United States, one of the most beloved men in America, is laid to rest in the heartland of the Nation he served and led.

Future historians will write what his deeds and accomplishments meant to the world. We of this generation were too close to the many events he helped shape. His leadership of the diverse elements in the Allied armies against the common aggressor brought victory in the largest war in history. His later leadership as President brought us through a difficult time of readjustment. He ended a bloody war in Asia, he made the first stand for civil rights when the order of our Highest Court was ignored. Now the work for his fellowmen is done and Dwight David Eisenhower has returned to the native Kansas he loved.

Not only does every American feel a personal loss at his passing, but the whole world mourns the death of this good man. His name and good works will live in history.

## Hon. Fred R. Harris

OF OKLAHOMA

Mr. President, in the past few days I think all of us have come to realize more fully just how much our 34th President, Dwight David Eisenhower, was respected and revered by the people of this Nation, and for that matter, the peoples of all nations. America is mourning the death of one of its most distinguished citizens and one of its best loved Presidents. Thousands came to pay their last respects—to join in a final salute—to this gallant soldier whose leadership in time of war and later in quest of a lasting peace has had great impact on our Democracy. The tragedy of President Eisenhower's death has touched many nations, for he was really a citizen of the world.

Born in Texas and reared in Kansas, he was a neighbor in a very real sense of the State of Oklahoma and to Oklahomans. He visited with us a number of times, always friendly, courteous, and helpful, and we shared the pride in his achievements.

The bravery and unfailing good humor that he displayed in his last days was a reflection of the great courage and dedication that marked his entire life.

Dwight Eisenhower was trusted and respected by his fellow men because he was decent and upright and honorable, and because he trusted and respected his fellow men. We will miss him deeply.

## Hon. Ralph Yarborough

OF TEXAS

Mr. President, yesterday we heard many fine tributes by Members of the Senate to Dwight David Eisenhower. Today, I would like to add to those tributes with the words of the editorial writers of some of the newspapers in Texas.

President Eisenhower was born in Texas, at Denison, Tex., on October 14, 1890. He was the first person born in Texas ever to be President of this Nation. It was in Texas that President Eisenhower met Mamie Geneva Doud, who was later to become Mrs. Dwight Eisenhower, First Lady of America.

Texans have felt especially close to the Eisenhowers through the years. Because of the close ties of Texas with Dwight Eisenhower, I think it appropriate that the tributes to that great general of peace include these remarks from newspapers in Texas. I add these in addition to my personal tribute to President Eisenhower on the floor of the Senate yesterday.

I ask unanimous consent that the following editorials be printed at this point in the RECORD: "Ike Was a Leader Who Inspired Trust," Fort Worth Star Telegram of March 29; "General Ike One of Best Loved and Most Selfless of Americans," San Antonio Express and News of March 29; "Dwight D. Eisenhower," Dallas Morning News of March 29; "Dwight David Eisenhower," Beaumont Enterprise of March 29; "Eisenhower," San Antonio Light of March 29; "Dwight D. Eisenhower," Houston Chronicle of March 29, and "He Served Our Nation Ably in War and Peace," the Houston Post, March 29.

There being no objection, the editorials were ordered to be printed in the RECORD, as follows:

[From the Fort Worth (Tex.) Star-Telegram, Mar. 29, 1969]

### IKE WAS A LEADER WHO INSPIRED TRUST

Dwight D. Eisenhower was the kind of man who inspired America's trust, whether at peace or at war. This was because Ike carried with him, into the White House as upon the Normandy beachhead, the sort of personal integrity and character that built confidence into those whom he led.

It was this force of character that brought him out of the ranks—for 25 years he failed to rise above lieutenant colonel—to lead the great World War II Crusade in Europe. At West Point, where his first love was athletics, he ranked 61st in grades and 95th in conduct among 163 fellow classmen. Never mind that; when the free world needed a leader, he was there.

Mr. Eisenhower viewed war with the abhorrence of a man who had seen it firsthand, yet he thought it could be avoided only if the United States remained mighty both militarily and economically. When he became President in 1953, he said in his first inaugural address that the nation's goal must be peace with honor. There must be no appeasement, he warned, for a "soldier's pack is not so heavy a burden as a prisoner's chain."

As we look back now upon those presidential years, they might appear to be extraordinarily tranquil, almost an idyllic interlude between the great conflagrations of world war and those of society's crises of the 1960s. Yet the Eisenhower years were beset with issues that stirred the nation: The alarms during his first administration over Communist infiltration into government and, later, the historic beginnings of true racial integration, Sputnik's smashing psychological and propaganda victory for the Soviets, the paralyzing U-2 spy plane incident, crises at the Suez Canal, in Lebanon, Matsu and Quemoy, the severing of diplomatic relations with Castro's Cuba.

Problems enough for any President, they were, and not even Ike's famous grin or his spirit of optimism could hide his deep concern over America's future and that of the world.

Although Mr. Eisenhower came very close to being a consensus President, he had his detractors. There were those who differed with his concepts of security in a nuclear age. Others complained about his aloofness from the rough-and-tumble of politics, or his sometimes rambling syntax, or even his brave efforts to break 80 on the golf course.

Yet few figures in American public life have commanded the love and respect that were showered upon Mr. Eisenhower. It was almost impossible to dislike him as a man, or to question his unyielding desire to do what was right. He gave of himself unstintingly to build a more peaceful and decent world, and for his own country he nurtured a love that will remain a model through the years.

"There is nothing wrong with America that faith, love of freedom, intelligence and the energy of her citizens cannot cure," Mr. Eisenhower declared.

There could be no more fitting an epitaph.

[From the San Antonio (Tex.) Express and News, Mar. 29, 1969]

### GENERAL IKE ONE OF BEST LOVED AND MOST SELFLESS OF AMERICANS

The remarkable career of Dwight D. Eisenhower, Texas-born, Kansas-reared farm boy who became supreme commander of allied armies in World War II and president of the United States, ended with courage and that fairly typified his life.

The general survived the dangers of modern war, the pressures of the presidency, the attacks of disease when it seemed probable that he couldn't. History will record him as a candid and unusual citizen. His candor brought professional diplomats down in scorn upon him at times. Some critics say he was an inept president. Jokes about his hours on the golf course were legion.

The truth is that he presided over the nation at a time when the country was sick of war, afraid of aggressive communism and riding a tidal wave of prosperity. He tried to reverse the trend toward more-powerful central government and he tried to make the staff system of the Army work in the White House. Whatever failures there were in each effort were due to historical and traditional momentum in society and government that greater politicians than he failed to master.

Gen. Eisenhower was held in special regard in San Antonio. He began his career here and he met Mamie here. He also started his rapid rise to the top of his military service here, as chief of staff of Gen. Walter Krueger's Third Army.

He had the happy warrior look but he never acquired the reputation for being a willing warrior. He was a civilized man, one of the most-loved of his era and a gallant soldier-citizen.

[From the Dallas (Tex.) Morning News, Mar. 29, 1969]

### Dwight D. Eisenhower

Of all his virtues, the word stability best describes the nature and contribution of Dwight David Eisenhower, military leader and 34th president of the United States. He died as he had lived, tenacious but firm and calm in time of crisis.

Few in our history have stepped forward even once as the man of the hour. But twice the time and the circumstances converged upon this native son of Texas.

A grim, resolute but troubled free world, engulfed in the uncertainties of global conflict, turned to Gen. Eisenhower for leadership. That overwide mouth pulled to one side in determination, he led the crusade that was to salvage from bombed-out rubble a Europe with new leases on freedom and self-confidence.

In 1952 a nation reeling from "corruption, communism and Korea" sought him out once again. America did more than just like Ike, it loved him as an older brother. The broad grin promised that things would turn out all right despite the mistakes of the moment. His lack of polish, by professional political standards, marked him as a man of the people.

Most of all, the nation in that worrisome hour longed for the stability born of battlefield judgment and command decision. It craved a leader who would station himself at the front gate and defend the family against one and all—a counselor whose unembroidered advice was steeped in experience.

Not long ago Eisenhower gazed back into what for him was the recent past and told his old running mate, Richard Nixon, that 1968 resembled 1952. "The people of this country genuinely want a change. They're tired of the way the Democrats have been running the government. I think they want the Republicans to have a chance at things now."

When Eisenhower, the military victor, was called upon to be Eisenhower, the political savior, the nation was dizzy from the New Deal, the Fair Deal and their legislative binges. The voters wanted a breather—a time to sit down and assess what had come to pass.

The activists, who see legislation as the one and only cure-all, impatiently labeled Eisenhower a do-nothing president. The label is patently ridiculous.

Eisenhower's service as president is best symbolized by the painting which hangs in many a doctor's office. The dim light is casting long shadows. The young patient lies gravely ill, and the doctor sits at bedside, ostensibly doing nothing.

But to view this picture is to believe instinctively that the patient will recover. The strong hand extended in comfort can be all-conquering therapy.

Eisenhower sat up with America, and when morning dawned health had prevailed over sickness. Inner strength had triumphed over fatigue.

Stability is strength. Stability was Eisenhower.

[From the Beaumont (Tex.) Enterprise, Mar. 29, 1969]

### Dwight David Eisenhower

Soldier, statesman, president, paragon of homely virtues . . .

Above all, Dwight David Eisenhowr was a designer and defender of freedom: For all the people in his own broad and beloved land and for human souls everywhere who seek self-determination and vow vengeance upon the despot's heel.

No man in modern time has been a greater scourge of political systems and military machines that ravage the God-given rights of others.

As supreme commander of the Allied invasion forces in Europe in World War II, he met and licked the Nazi legions on many a bloody battlefield. As supreme commander of the Atlantic pact forces after the war, he became a symbol of worldwide resistance to the expansion of communism, Hitler's successor in infamy and oppression.

Then as president of the United States for eight years, he held firm, in policies and practices, to the conviction that national weakness is an invitation to enslavement, that eternal vigilance is only an exercise in common sense, that freedom is insured only for a people willing to defend it with their lives.

The good general's last advice for his country came in the form of an address to last year's Republican National Convention in which he warned that communism hasn't changed its spots, that at this very moment its technicians of totalitarianism are mapping new assaults on American ideals and influence around the globe.

In his last days, the old warrior harbored the fear that his country would become party to a Vietnam agreement amounting, in his words, to "camouflaged surrender." He reminded that many of the years of his life had been spent in resisting such scoundrels as those we now oppose in Southeast Asia.

Eisenhower sought with equal passion paths of peace and understanding between nations. He was an internationalist in the fullest sense, gave strong support to the United Nations, and recognized the urgency of measures aimed at easing the awesome threat to civilization inherent in the nuclear arms race.

But to the general's way of thinking, appeasement became, in the final analysis, an instrument of war and further oppression, not independence and understanding and mutual respect.

Eisenhower was not without loyalty to the Republican Party. Still, he never was quite comfortable in the role of the partisan. He found especially irritating the pettiness, piddling personality clashes, and favor seeking that are built-in party patterns.

The same nonpartisan feeling was reflected by the American people. From the beginning of his political venture, he was looked upon as a leader peculiarly above partisanship.

The image of elder statesman was bestowed naturally and affectionately soon after he left the White House.

His love of country—and countrymen—was uninhibited and uncomplicated. To him, there never could be as much wrong with this nation as was right with it. He was an old-fashioned patriot in an age of almost traumatic change.

But the deep divisions in our society sorely wounded the general's spirit, especially the growing disrespect for law and order. Living hard by the Gettysburg battlefields, he had a constant reminder of the most tragic fruit of division in American history.

Texans' affection for Eisenhower was mixed with deep pride, for he was a native of this state. It will be recalled that in both his races for the presidency he carried Texas handily.

This newspaper joins the nation and the Free World in a fond farewell to a great man and a great friend.

It won't be the same without Ike.

---

[From the San Antonio (Tex.) Light, Mar. 29, 1969]

### Eisenhower

It can truly be said that he gave his life to his beloved country—and was beloved in return. His death is a personal thing, bringing sadness into every home.

Few thought of him as "Gen." Eisenhower, or "President" Eisenhower, or "Mr." Eisenhower. To his shining credit as a human being, the people thought of him simply as "Ike," a nickname in which he took satisfaction.

Only a few of the greatest men are ever genuinely humble, but it glowed in the warmth of his unaffected and infectious smile as it glowed in these revealing words he once spoke:

"Humility must always be the portion of any man who receives acclaim earned in the blood of his followers and the sacrifices of his friends."

Those words were uttered in 1945 at the glorious climax of a long career as a professional warrior. The former West Point cadet had just achieved victory as commander of the greatest amalgamation of military forces ever mustered in the world.

Thus it was never the role of hero or leader which gave satisfaction to Dwight David Eisenhower. To him the most important thing in life was to do one's duty in accordance with one's principles and to the best of one's abilities.

The people sensed and responded to this, electing him to a second term in the White House although he would have preferred to retire to the Gettysburg farm which he and Mrs. Eisenhower had lovingly established as their first permanent home.

As President he labored unceasingly for the peace and world stability he had sought to assure on the battlefields of Europe. His disappointments were profound, thanks to Communist hostility, but steady and patient persistence in his chosen course avoided open conflict for eight years while shoring up the strength and unity of the free world.

At home, meanwhile, he gave his devotion and energies to further the constitutional system in which he so passionately believed. A whole new era of justice for the underprivileged was opened when he sent troops to Little Rock, Ark., to enforce court-ordered school integration.

But this is not the place to enumerate the manifold achievements of a man who, even in retirement and plagued by repeated heart attacks, continued to serve his country and his political party with the valued and trusted advice of an elder statesman.

Instead this is the place to give thanks for the towering example set by the devotion of Dwight David Eisenhower, a great American and a great human being—and to mourn his loss.

It would be wrong to call his death a tragedy. He had a long and richly useful life and he lived it with grace. Our sorrow is in having to say goodbye to such a good, true friend.

---

[From the Houston (Tex.) Chronicle, Mar. 29, 1969]

### Dwight D. Eisenhower

Soldier, educator, author, President, peacemaker, great American. These are the roles that Dwight D. Eisenhower lived with honor and distinction.

Almost a decade has passed since he left the White House and moved out of the world spotlight. It was 24 years ago that he retired as a five-star general from the Army. Inevitably, his moments of crisis and triumph have dimmed in the public mind. But one thing stands out as clear as ever: Gen. Eisenhower was one of the most beloved and trusted men of his time.

Had he not been elevated to the presidency, he still would have left his mark on history. As supreme commander of the World War II Allied Expeditionary Forces, he commanded the greatest land-air-naval invasion force the world has ever known.

First, in North Africa, then in Sicily and Italy, and finally in Europe he displayed the planning ability and the strategic daring which ultimately destroyed a powerful German Army.

Friend and foe alike hailed his military genius. He was a stern commander, but even the enemy respected him. To his own troops he was Ike, perhaps the most civilian-minded professional soldier this nation has ever produced.

He was trained as a military man, but he hated war, and as President he dedicated himself to the promotion of world peace and friendship under freedom.

Both political parties sought him as a presidential candidate. At first he wasn't interested. He had a soldier's disdain for politics. As a soldier he didn't vote and he did not affiliate with any political organization.

In the White House he remained aloof from partisan politics as best he could. Party affairs bored him, to the dismay of his fellow Republicans and to the delight of the American people who tend to share that view.

As President, he declined to assume the strong presidential role of his predecessors. He relegated much of the foreign responsibilities to John Foster Dulles, his trusted secretary of state. On the domestic side, leaders of the Democratically controlled Congress—such as Senate Majority Leader Lyndon Johnson—assumed important leadership responsibilities.

Critics said Ike abdicated too much responsibility. Yet he remained true to his own idea of the presidency. He declined to project himself into many public issues because he felt the federal government was assuming too large a share of national decision-making.

Arguments over that aspect of his leadership will continue for years to come. In retrospect, he perhaps was a product of the nation's needs. His White House years followed a great war and all the turbulence and agony that goes with war; before that a great depression which produced the New Deal reforms of Franklin Roosevelt.

The nation needed a man like Eisenhower in the 50s. His was not a time of dynamic leadership but rather of surcease and stability. The whole free world looked to Eisenhower for confidence, for he was a man the whole world respected and trusted.

Perhaps his greatest political achievement was in bringing the Republican Party up to date. He was a moderate Republican himself, and he forced a stubborn GOP to accept the achievements of the New Deal, then he pulled the party toward the broad middle ground where it remains today.

Here in the South, it will be remembered that President Eisenhower in 1957 ordered federal troops into Little Rock, Ark., to enforce a court-ordered plan of school integration. It was the first such use of federal power since the days of Reconstruction. "Mob rule," he said, "cannot be allowed to override the decisions of the courts."

It was Eisenhower, the soldier-statesman, who brought peace in Korea after three harsh years of war.

It was Eisenhower, the peacemaker, who used his farewell address to warn of the potentially dangerous influence on the nation of the burgeoning industrial-military complex. That farewell warning rivals in wisdom the farewell address of the first President, George Washington, to whom President Eisenhower has often and aptly been compared.

Gen. Eisenhower will not go down in history as the greatest among Presidents. Rather, he will be remembered as the greatest among Americans: A man beloved by first his troops and then his countrymen, whose honesty, integrity, dedication and good will were never questioned.

---

[From the Houston (Tex.) Post, Mar. 29, 1969]

### He Served Our Nation Ably in War and Peace

They called him Ike.

American war hero, 34th President of the United States, historian, private citizen whose retirement from public life was never quite complete, all these things he was, but to the man on the street he was Ike.

And of all the accomplishments of this remarkable man, his greatest was probably the place he won in the hearts of the American people.

A man trained in war, he dedicated his public life to the pursuit of reason. Frequently under intense criticism, he always sought to find a way to talk, to discuss, to reason. He believed intensely that the strength of America was in its historic refusal to go to the easy way of extreme measures. And the people understood this, and so responded in great numbers to the man Dwight David Eisenhower.

His life was like a blueprint for an American success story.

He was born on Oct. 14, 1890 in Denison, Texas, the first President to be born in Texas. He was about a year old when his parents moved to Abilene, Kansas. His boyhood was typical of the youth of his time and place. He tended garden, took care of the chickens, sold eggs, milked the cow, delivered chickens and vegetables, did odd jobs, helped his father.

He became a soldier almost by chance. His first choice was Annapolis, but he discovered he would be past the age limit of 20 when the term started.

Instead, he went to West Point, and the course of American history was changed.

Graduating 61st in a class of 164 in 1915, he began a historic military career. It would be years, however, before the focus of world attention would turn toward the soldier named Ike.

In the Louisiana maneuvers of 1941, Ike was singled out for his tactical brilliance. Thus began a series of Army assignments that would lead a heretofore obscure officer to a five-star generalcy and supreme command of the great "Crusade in Europe."

The story of that crusade is well known.

Ike's personality helped forge the victory.

He possessed unexampled powers to weld diverse forces, and at times, in the handling of individualistic and temperamental commanders, he needed them to their fullest.

The Germans regarded his ability as a fighting commander highly. One German general was later to say that the German general staff regarded him as the greatest general of the war, because of his able planning, his daring and the extent of his authority.

"He took great gambles, as in Africa and later on the French beaches, but he won and that justified his daring," the former enemy said.

With the war won, Ike hoped to retire to the peace of a quiet life. Presidential offers were dangled before him, but they were spurned.

After the war, he served as president of Columbia University, and then was called back into the service of his country by President Truman to become commander of the North Atlantic Treaty Organization forces.

In 1952, he yielded to the constant calls that he turn to politics. In a dramatic return to the United States, he campaigned and won the Republican presidential nomination. He went on to serve two terms as President, both times winning by overwhelming majorities.

On Jan. 20, 1953, at the age of 62, he became the 34th President of the United States, the first Republican to occupy the White House in 20 years.

If there is any single way to describe the Eisenhower presidency it is in the phrase "peace with honor." (He was later to name the second part of the history of his presidential years "Waging Peace.")

Ike served in tense times, with the threat of nuclear disaster ever present. The Korean War ended in his term. Josef Stalin died, and a new regime emerged in Moscow. The Geneva summit of 1955 eased world tensions, but later they were heightened in the U–2 affair.

On the home front, Ike was deeply committed to governmental fiscal responsibility.

The two themes—peace and prosperity—brought reelection in 1956 by the greatest popular vote ever recorded, despite recurring worries about his health.

He worked hard at molding a united GOP around his philosophy of "Modern Republicanism." He was, however, disappointed when Richard Nixon failed in his bid to succeed him. He continued to urge unity within the party. In retirement, his advice was constantly sought by his two Democratic successors, Presidents Kennedy and Johnson.

Unity and its strength meant much to Ike.

Later, reminiscing on his term as President, he was to say, "When I came to the presidency, the country was rather in an unhappy state. There was bitterness and there was quarreling and so on . . . I tried to create an atmosphere of greater serenity and mutual confidence, and I think that it . . . was noticeable over those eight years that that was brought about . . ."

His legacy to the American people was his life of service and his realization of the importance of peace, justice and mutual confidence.

## Hon. Edward W. Brooke

OF MASSACHUSETTS

Mr. President, nothing can be added to what has already been said and felt by the people of this Nation and the world on the death of our great President and wartime leader, Dwight David Eisenhower.

The world mourns his death, at the same time that it marvels at the fullness of his life. For President Eisenhower truly exemplified the best that is America, and was, in the eloquent words and drawing of the incomparable Herblock, a "50-star general." He will be sorely missed; but what is more, he will be remembered with the love and gratitude of all men.

## Hon. Spessard L. Holland

OF FLORIDA

Mr. President, there is little that anyone can say to add to the many statements already made in the CONGRESSIONAL RECORD about the Nation's warm affection for the late General Dwight David Eisenhower. Each of us has many nostalgic personal memories about him. I have many such memories, some of them reflected in prized pictures on the wall of my office—some in cherished books on my bookself—some simply fond recollections.

His fame as a great national and world leader, the five-star general who, as Supreme Commander of the Allied Forces, led them to victory in Europe, and the 8-year President who brought back to our Nation relative serenity and greater confidence in our National Government, will always live in the annals of our Nation and in the lasting memories of our people. I have decided that the best contribution that I can make on this sad occasion is to insert in the RECORD three of the dozens of highly complimentary editorials which have appeared in Florida newspapers, which reflect, I am sure, the true feelings of most of our Florida people. I ask, therefore, that there be incorporated in the RECORD as part of my remarks the following editorials written by talented, knowledgeable, and patriotic editorialists.

First. I ask that an editorial from the Jacksonville, Fla., Times-Union of March 29 entitled "Dwight David Eisenhower" may appear in the RECORD as part of my remarks.

Second. I ask that an editorial from the Orlando Sentinel dated March 29 entitled "A Love Affair Ends" may appear in the RECORD as part of my remarks.

Third. I ask that an editorial from the St. Petersburg Times of March 29, entitled "An

American's American," may appear in the RECORD as part of my remarks.

Mrs. Holland and I share the grief of Mrs. Eisenhower and other members of their family at this sad time and express to them our deep and affectionate sympathy.

There being no objection, the editorials were ordered to be printed in the RECORD, as follows:

[From the Jacksonville (Fla.) Times-Union, Mar. 29, 1969]

DWIGHT DAVID EISENHOWER

Dwight David Eisenhower, gallant to the end, was a man uniquely suited to his times and to the roles which life called upon him to fill.

The family into which he was born in 1890 was to become an outstanding example of the American dream—that of achieving success from humble beginnings through diligence and hard work. His parents were religious, hard working and poor and their six sons were called upon to work hard in their early years doing farm chores and odd jobs. All became successful in later life.

For Dwight David Eisenhower, the path to the White House was through a military career. He entered The U.S. Military Academy at West Point through an appointment achieved by competitive examination.

There followed a long period of slow but steady advancement toward his two early ambitions: to become a colonel before he retired and to have the command of troops.

It was not until after he had passed the age of 50 that he achieved either but then advancement, command and recognition came with lightning swiftness.

A temporary colonel in 1941, he was to become in slightly more than three years Commander of Supreme Headquarters, Allied Headquarters in Europe and achieve the highest military rank as a General of the Army and a year later he became Army Chief of Staff.

To be the architect of victory in Europe during World War II would have left an enduring place in history for General Eisenhower but his nation was to call upon him to play an even larger role.

His mother's comment on his success in World War II was to be prophetic of even greater things. "I knew we would win," she said, "for Dwight always got what he went after."

He went after the presidency of the United States of America and won overwhelmingly in 1952 and again in 1956.

Especially in these days of division at home and war abroad, his presidential terms evoke nostalgia for happier years.

During his retirement, President Eisenhower summed up the feeling himself when he said: "When I came to the presidency, the country was rather in an unhappy state. There was bitterness and there was quarreling and so on . . . I tried to create an atmosphere of greater serenity and mutual confidence, and I think that it . . . was noticeable over those eight years that that was brought about."

It was noticeable as was the truth of his statement that during his eight years, the nation was strong, prosperous and there were no wars.

We leave to historians and those with better credentials, the assessment of his greatness and his place in history.

Perhaps the reaction of the individuals in this nation on the occasion of his passing will never be recorded in the history books but it is the finest tribute that can be paid to the man himself.

The people of the nation which he served so well did not merely admire or respect him. They felt comfortable with him. They liked Ike. And they will miss him.

[From the Orlando (Fla.) Sentinel, Mar. 29, 1969]

A LOVE AFFAIR ENDS

Dwight David Eisenhower has been a leader among us for so long the world will be not the same without him.

Unlike the martyred Kennedys, with us so briefly they seemed to flash like meteors across the political skies, we have known Ike in war and in peace; in the prime and vigor of his life and in its sunset years.

Throughout his distinguished career in the military and in government, he enjoyed a rare rapport with the American people. His popularity never dimmed.

There were, to be sure, critics of his military and presidential regimes but, when viewed in the light of the vilification heaped upon other leaders, they were mild and almost academic.

"I like Ike" was the slogan of his first presidential campaign and the American people did and they never stopped. No other national or international political figure enjoyed the sustained love and affection we conferred upon him.

He made a graceful transition from commander in chief of the largest and most powerful military force the world has ever assembled to eight years as president of the United States.

They were years which seem, in retrospect, tranquil.

His election as President continued an American tradition which began with George Washington, that of the all conquering military hero becoming the civilian leader when the battles stopped.

The battle of life itself has now stopped for Dwight Eisenhower, 34th president, and the nation which knew and loved and followed him mourns.

Yet it is mourning of a more gentle nature than that which has racked this nation in recent months for there is the knowledge that this was a life fully lived, a promise realized, a greatness fulfilled.

And however history will judge Eisenhower the soldier and the President, it must write him as a great patriot, a giant in his time.

[From the St. Petersburg (Fla.) Times, Mar. 29, 1969]

AN AMERICAN'S AMERICAN

In life Dwight David Eisenhower achieved the pinnacles in what are certainly three of the most important walks of modern American life: the military, the educational and the political.

Yet in his death, Eisenhower probably will be best remembered and most mourned for a fourth, and more personal achievement. More than any other political leader of our time, he won the deep affection of his fellow countrymen of both parties, and of all walks of life.

With his amiable personality, his infectious grin, his dignity of bearing when dignity was demanded, his deep devotion to duty to his country, his brilliance and drive as a military leader, his love for sports and—yes—his sudden flares of temper, he was the very personification of many Americans' concept of what an American leader should be.

Although the policies and record of his administration were subject to partisan attack, it was a curiously impersonal sort of attack which rarely was directed at him as an individual. The stature of his personality was exemplified by the fact that all of his successors, Presidents Kennedy, Johnson and Nixon, freely consulted him in times of crisis and his counsel and cooperation were always freely given.

It has been said by his intimates that Eisenhower never felt completely at ease in the presidency; that in politics he was out of his natural element. As a military leader, he was accustomed to restricting himself to major decisions of strategy and allowing his field commanders to choose the tactics for achieving the strategic goals. And that was the way he ran his administration.

He continued intact all of the major social and economic reforms of the Roosevelt and Truman administrations, despite strong pressure from some of his closest supporters to abandon them. His most far-reaching domestic decision was the appointment of Chief Justice Earl Warren.

In history, Dwight David Eisenhower will go down as one of the great military leaders of modern warfare. But when the somber cortege escorts the caisson bearing his coffin to his final resting place, when the traditional volleys are fired across his grave, he will be mourned and loved through the Western World as a leader who also was a warm and intensely human man.

## Hon. Frank Church
OF IDAHO

Mr. President, I shall remember Dwight David Eisenhower as a general who brought war to an end and as a President who kept the peace.

What more could be asked of a man in service to his country? What more could be given?

For the misadventures he avoided, for the interventions he refused to undertake, for the foreign wars he decided not to fight, I shall remember this President as one who possessed the wisdom to temper power with restraint.

## Hon. Jennings Randolph
OF WEST VIRGINIA

Mr. President, the world has been made poorer in recent days by the passing of Dwight Eisenhower.

So much has been said about General Eisenhower that it is difficult to speak of him without being repetitious, for such was the character of the man that he inspired warm affection and genuinely felt tributes.

Former President Eisenhower was a unique individual, particularly in this tormented age in which we live. His life was the embodiment of the virtues which we were taught in school as comprising the American character and which today seem too often to have been forgotten. He was a reminder that there is yet a place for honesty, virtue, hard work, good cheer, and simple faith. He proved that these values are compatible with our complex and troubled civilization of the late 20th century.

The continuing esteem in which he was held after his Presidency and the outpouring of feeling which we have witnessed since his death are proof that the American people, and people everywhere, yearn for an orderly and peaceful existence, not necessarily for a return to an earlier day.

Dwight Eisenhower's record as soldier, educator, and President can and will be debated for years. But the enduring memory of the man will rest not on what battles were won or what laws were passed under his guidance so much as on his ability to unite, inspire, and calm those who looked to him for leadership.

This was the true and unquestioned genius of Dwight Eisenhower.

## Hon. Harold E. Hughes
OF IOWA

Mr. President, yesterday our Nation buried a great leader.

The flags are still at half-mast, but there is a strange sense of unreality about it all.

All Americans felt so close to President Eisenhower for so long, it is difficult to believe he is gone.

Of course, he is not gone in the real sense. His place in history and in the hearts of Americans is secure for all time.

We remember his brave leadership—his great contributions to his country in war and peace.

But we also remember his quick smile, his lack of pretense, his warm compassion, his special quality as a person.

He was a great leader, but above all he was a man of decency and good will.

He will be keenly missed, and our deepest sympathies are with Mrs. Eisenhower and the family.

But he will be remembered always as the prototype of the man of good will by people of all creeds and stations, the world over.

## Hon. Frank Church
OF IDAHO

Mr. President, for the past week our Nation has paid tribute to Dwight David Eisenhower—a man who led his Nation in war and guided it along the paths of peace; a man of arms whose greatest concern was their elimination.

On January 17, 1961, President Eisenhower delivered to the American people his farewell address. The words he spoke at that time represent a confluence of the ideas he so deeply felt both as general and President. They are even more meaningful today than they were at the time they were spoken for, I fear, we have been derelict in heeding them.

Many agree that President Eisenhower's farewell address was his greatest gift to the American people. With that thought in mind, I ask unanimous consent that it be republished in the Record.

There being no objection, the address was ordered to be printed in the Record, as follows:

Farewell Radio and Television Address to the American People, January 17, 1961

(Delivered from the President's Office at 8:30 p.m.)

*My fellow Americans:* Three days from now, after half a century in the service of our country, I shall lay down the responsibilities of office as, in traditional and solemn ceremony, the authority of the Presidency is vested in my successor.

This evening I come to you with a message of leave-taking and farewell, and to share a few final thoughts with you, my countrymen.

Like every other citizen, I wish the new President, and all who will labor with him, Godspeed. I pray that the coming years will be blessed with peace and prosperity for all.

Our people expect their President and the Congress to find essential agreement on issues of great moment, the wise resolution of which will better shape the future of the Nation.

My own relations with the Congress, which began on a remote and tenuous basis when, long ago, a member of the Senate appointed me to West Point, have since ranged to the intimate during the war and immediate postwar period, and, finally, to the mutually interdependent during these past eight years.

In this final relationship, the Congress and the Administration have, on most vital issues, cooperated well, to serve the national good rather than mere partisanship, and so have assured that the business of the Nation should go forward. So, my official relationship with the Congress ends in a feeling, on my part, of gratitude that we have been able to do so much together.

II

We now stand ten years past the midpoint of a century that has witnessed four major wars among great nations. Three of these involved our own country. Despite these holocausts America is today the strongest, the most influential and most productive nation in the world. Understandably proud of this pre-eminence, we yet realize that America's leadership and prestige depend, not merely upon our unmatched material progress, riches and military strength, but on how we use our power in the interests of world peace and human betterment.

III

Throughout America's adventure in free government, our basic purposes have been to keep the peace; to foster progress in human achievement, and to enhance liberty, dignity and integrity among people and among nations. To strive for less would be unworthy of a free and religious people. Any failure traceable to arrogance, or our lack of comprehension or readiness to sacrifice would inflict upon us grevious hurt both at home and abroad.

Progress toward these noble goals is persistently threatened by the conflict now engulfing the world. It commands our whole attention, absorbs our very beings. We face a hostile ideology—global in scope, atheistic in character, ruthless in purpose, and insidious in method. Unhappily the danger it poses promises to be of indefinite duration. To meet it successfully, there is called for, not so much the emotional and transitory sacrifices of crisis, but rather those which enable us to carry forward steadily, surely, and without complaint the burdens of a prolonged and complex struggle—with liberty the stake. Only thus shall we remain, despite every provocation, on our charted course toward permanent peace and human betterment.

Crises there will continue to be. In meeting them, whether foreign or domestic, great or small, there is a recurring temptation to feel that some spectacular and costly action could become the miraculous solution to all current difficulties. A huge increase in newer elements of our defense; development of unrealistic programs to cure every ill in agriculture; a dramatic expansion in basic and applied research—these and many other possibilities, each possibly promising in itself, may be suggested as the only way to the road we wish to travel.

But each proposal must be weighed in the light of a broader consideration: the need to maintain balance in and among national programs—balance between the private and the public economy, balance between cost and hoped for advantage—balance between the clearly necessary and the comfortably desirable; balance between our essential requirements as a nation and the duties imposed by the nation upon the individual; balance between actions of the moment and the national welfare of the future. Good judgment seeks balance and progress; lack of it eventually finds imbalance and frustration.

The record of many decades stands as proof that our people and their government have, in the main, understood these truths and have responded to them well, in the face of stress and threat. But threats, new in kind or degree, constantly arise. I mention two only.

IV

A vital element in keeping the peace is our military establishment. Our arms must be mighty, ready for instant action, so that no potential aggressor may be tempted to risk his own destruction.

Our military organization today bears little relation to that known by any of my predecessors in peacetime, or indeed by the fighting men of World War II or Korea.

Until the latest of our world conflicts, the United States had no armament industry. American makers of plowshares could, with time and as required, make swords as well. But now we can no longer risk emergency improvisation of national defense; we have been compelled to create a permanent armaments industry of vast proportions. Added to this, three and a half million men and women are directly engaged in the defense establishment. We annually spend on military security more than the net income of all United States corporations.

This conjunction of an immense military establishment and a large arms industry is new in the American experience. The total influence—economic, political, even spiritual—is felt in every city, every State house, every office of the Federal government. We recognize the imperative need for this development. Yet me must not fail to comprehend its grave implications. Our toil, resources and livelihood are all involved; so is the very structure of our society.

In the councils of government, we must guard against the acquisition of unwarranted influence, whether sought or unsought, by the military-industrial complex. This potential for the disastrous rise of misplaced power exists and will persist.

We must never let the weight of this combination endanger our liberties or democratic processes. We should take nothing for granted. Only an alert and knowledgeable citizenry can compel the proper meshing of the huge industrial and military machinery of defense with our peaceful methods and goals, so that security and liberty may prosper together.

Akin to, and largely responsible for the sweeping changes in our industrial-military posture, has been the technological revolution during recent decades.

In this revolution, research has become central; it also becomes more formalized, complex, and costly. A steadily increasing share is conducted for, by, or at the direction of, the Federal government.

Today, the solitary inventor, tinkering in his shop, has been overshadowed by task forces of scientists in laboratories and testing fields. In the same fashion, the free university, historically the fountainhead of free ideas and scientific discovery, has experienced a revolution in the conduct of research. Partly because of the huge costs involved, a government contract becomes virtually a substitute for intellectual curiosity. For every old blackboard there are now hundreds of new electronic computers.

The prospect of domination of the nation's scholars by Federal employment, project allocations, and the power of money is ever present—and is gravely to be regarded.

Yet, in holding scientific research and discovery in respect, as we should, we must also be alert to the equal and opposite danger that public policy could itself become the captive of a scientific-technological elite.

It is the task of statesmanship to mold, to balance, and to integrate these and other forces, new and old, within the principles of our democratic system—ever aiming toward the supreme goals of our free society.

V

Another factor in maintaining balance involves the element of time. As we peer into society's future, we—you and I, and our government—must avoid the impulse to live only for today, plundering, for our own ease and convenience, the precious resources of tomorrow. We cannot mortgage the material assets of our grandchildren without risking the loss also of their political and spiritual heritage. We want democracy to survive for all generations to come, not to become the insolvent phantom of tomorrow.

VI

Down the long lane of the history yet to be written America knows that this world of ours, ever growing smaller, must avoid becoming a community of dreadful fear and hate, and be, instead, a proud confederation of mutual trust and respect.

Such a confederation must be one of equals. The weakest must come to the conference table with the same confidence as do we, protected as we are by our moral, economic, and military strength. The table, though scarred by many past frustrations, cannot be abandoned for the certain agony of the battlefield.

Disarmament, with mutual honor and confidence, is a continuing imperative. Together we must learn how to compose differences, not with arms, but with intellect and decent purpose. Because this need is so sharp and apparent I confess that I lay down my official responsibilities in this field with a definite sense of disappointment. As one who has witnessed the horror and the lingering sadness of war—as one who knows that another war could utterly destroy this civilization which has been so slowly and painfully built over thousands of years—I wish I could say tonight that a lasting peace is in sight.

Happily, I can say that war has been avoided. Steady progress toward our ultimate goal has been made. But, so much remains to be done. As a private citizen, I shall never cease to do what little I can to help the world advance along that road.

VII

So—in this my last good night to you as your President—I thank you for the many opportunities you have given me for public service in war and peace. I trust that in that service you find some things worthy; as for the rest of it, I know you will find ways to improve performance in the future.

You and I—my fellow citizens—need to be strong in our faith that all nations, under God, will reach the goal of peace with justice. May we be ever unswerving in devotion to principle, confident but humble with power, diligent in pursuit of the Nation's great goals.

To all the peoples of the world, I once more give expression to America's prayerful and continuing aspiration:

We pray that peoples of all faiths, all races, all nations, may have their great human needs satisfied; that those now denied opportunity shall come to enjoy it to the full; that all who yearn for freedom may experience its spiritual blessings; that those who have freedom will understand, also, its heavy responsibilities; that all who are insensitive to the needs of others will learn charity; that the scourges of poverty, disease and ignorance will be made to disappear from the earth, and that, in the goodness of time, all peoples will come to live together in a peace guaranteed by the binding force of mutual respect and love.

## Hon. Carl T. Curtis

OF NEBRASKA

Mr. President, historians, gifted writers, heads of government, and others have said and will continue to say many fine things about General Eisenhower. General Eisenhower merits all of these praises. I cannot attempt to compete with what others have so well said about this distinguished soldier, President, and citizen.

Mr. President, I speak, however, as a Senator from Nebraska to have the Record show the high esteem, the great affection, and the profound respect that the people of the State of Nebraska had for our 34th President.

For many years writers who are qualified in the field of military strategy will find a rich source of material in studying the career of Gen. Dwight David Eisenhower. He was a soldier and a leader of men who now has taken his place with the greatest of men down through the recorded period of history.

When General Eisenhower was serving as President of the United States I thought that he was a good, wise, and just head of our Government. Somehow the qualities and accomplishments that are of real value grow as time goes on. While always a supporter of President Eisenhower, my high appraisal, my respect, and my admiration for his performance in the Office of President increased as years pass. One of the tests of greatness is that it stands the test of time. President Eisenhower was not merely another President, whose memory will fade with the years. His record as President stands out with greater brightness every passing day.

When a problem was presented to President Eisenhower, the whole world knew that it would be approached honestly, forthrightly, and intelligently. People everywhere knew that the problem would be considered in the light of the historic, religious, political and economic traditions of our country. They knew that the problem would be viewed by a man whose vast storehouse of knowledge and experience did not cause him to lose the viewpoint and the hopes and aspirations of the every-day American.

The people trusted President Eisenhower. There was nothing mean or small about him. He made a great President because he followed great principles.

Mr. President, the country is fortunate that General Eisenhower was permitted to live beyond his years of public service. It meant that the Nation had the opportunity to know and observe a man who represented the highest and best in citizenship. Not only was he a senior military officer and a senior political leader, but in retirement he was a senior citizen representing the highest and best and providing the noblest example for all mankind.

Mr. President, one of the able poetic writers of our day, Miss Mattie Richards Tyler, of Washington, D.C., has set forth her thoughts, which I consider as appropriate to close my remarks. I ask unanimous consent that her poem be printed in the RECORD.

There being no objection, the poem was ordered to be printed in the RECORD, as follows:

LAST MARCH OF OUR FIVE-STAR GENERAL, PRESIDENT DWIGHT DAVID EISENHOWER, MARCH 28, 1969

(By Mattie Richards Tyler)

The streets of Washington are lined with crowds . . .
Our Flag, half-staff, proclaims the Nation's sorrow;
But planes and dreams still soar above the clouds,
And he would bid us bravely face tomorrow.
Our Ike, America's loved president,
Is dead! Because he lived and passed our way,
The world is richer for his life—well spent.
"One Nation, under God," [1] we march today.

He lies in state beneath the Capitol dome . . .
Triumphantly, our General met life's test.
Play on, O Service Bands, as he heads home—
This great American who gave his best.
While Stars and Stripes, unfurled, salute the sky,
We grasp his Torch of Faith as he goes by!

[1] Pledge of Allegiance

## Hon. Clifford P. Hansen

OF WYOMING

Mr. President, a great leader has passed. The entire free world mourns the death of President Eisenhower. He met the highest challenges of the 20th century, as a soldier and as a statesman. He served his people of the United States, on the battlefields of the world and in the White House.

As a general, he mourned the loss of comrades in arms who fell before the guns of the enemy. He survived World War II to carry on their quest for world peace. As President, he was praised as the "peacemaker." President Eisenhower was instrumental in bringing about a halt to the bloodshed in Korea.

His firm and positive decisions in the Middle East and other areas of the world, backed by a readiness to support words with deeds, kept the United States from war during the 8 years he served in the White House.

Yet, President Eisenhower, of modest origin in Abilene, Kans., was a practical and realistic man. He did not view the world through rose-colored glasses, and he had no illusions as to the ever-present threat to the freedom of the United States. We may recall words from his speech to the city of London on July 12, 1945:

As long as there are sovereign nations possessing great power, war is inevitable.

Let us not forget this warning from General Eisenhower. And while we search for the road to peace, let us ever be mindful of the security of the United States of America and ascertain that no nation can lull us to sleep—that no nation will become more powerful than the United States.

Mr. Eisenhower's presence and counsel will be sorely missed by this country and the world. The words of those of us who have joined in paying tribute to him today certainly can do nothing to ease this loss. But we know that General Eisenhower has joined his troops, and that they welcome him into their heroic ranks.

## Hon. Harrison A. Williams, Jr.

OF NEW JERSEY

Mr. President, Dwight David Eisenhower now takes his place in history—a victorious general, a man who knew power and used it wisely, a great and good leader of the American people.

In war, he cemented the allies into the world's greatest invasion and provided the firm, resourceful, inspirational guidance that brought the evil forces of Nazi Germany to destruction and set Western Europe free.

In peace, he drew his fellow countrymen in respect and admiration of his achievements. It has been truly said that he was an authentic national hero. When an admiring and grateful nation rewarded him with the White House, he gave us 8 years of calm, marked by peaceful progress and unmarred by upheaval at home or overseas.

His distinguished service as a military man and as President, engraved on the hearts of his countrymen the depth of character—a man of sincerity and wisdom, moderate and conciliatory in guiding his administration, but always inflexible in his devotion to right.

We mourn his passing. He served his country with courage and devotion. He was one of America's finest sons.

## Hon. William B. Spong, Jr.

OF VIRGINIA

Mr. President, from the time Dwight David Eisenhower came to prominence during World War II, he was a symbol of integrity, sincerity, and warmth to the Americans he led in war and peace. Tributes paid here in Washington last Sunday and Monday and the final rites yesterday in Abilene, Kans., attest to the warm affection in which he was held.

Virginians feel a particular sense of loss because of General Eisenhower's family ties to our State. His mother, Ida Stover, was born and raised in Augusta County in the Shenandoah Valley. He was warmly received on his visits to Virginia, and spoke with pride of his mother having been a Virginian.

While General Eisenhower's tangible accomplishments as a military leader and statesman were visible to all, his contributions as a public servant far transcended the holding of a command, or an office. His legacy to the American people was the depth of his spirit, his unassuming manner and, most of all, his ability to instill in the people a sense of confidence and assurance.

Mr. President, I ask unanimous consent that editorials of tribute from Virginia newspapers—the Norfolk and Portsmouth Ledger-Star of March 28, the Virginian-Pilot of March 29, and the Roanoke Times of March 29—be printed in the RECORD.

There being no objection, the editorials were ordered to be printed in the RECORD, as follows:

[From the Norfolk and Portsmouth (Va.) Ledger-Star, Mar. 28, 1969]

### DWIGHT DAVID EISENHOWER

The old gentleman whose syntax overwhelmed the purists is now no longer with us and the Crusade for Europe that started him on the road to immortality is something that happened a quarter century ago, an event whose significance is reduced by the dust of time and the fact that it is three wars back.

We mention Dwight Eisenhower's syntax for a particular purpose; for while it represented one of the points many chuckled about, it represented also one of the general's greatest strengths. People, upon hearing him on the air waves or in person, in reading his press conferences and spontaneous talks reported precisely as they occurred, felt a great empathy for the man. He, too, could make mistakes in the language—just as they.

He defeated for the Presidency one of the great purists of the language, Adlai Stevenson, a man of polish and erudition; an intellectual who know his own faults and had his own doubts. Mr. Stevenson ran well, as we remember his campaign, but the people decided that the old general, the kind-faced, lovable father-figure of a man, was what they preferred. So overwhelmingly did the people prefer the general that it was just as though he had no opponent.

There are those who think of the Eisenhower years as years of the fallow fields, when America stood still. To a point, that is true; but it is also true that America needed to stand still for a time. America had had 12 years of Mr. Roosevelt's manipulations and eight of Mr. Truman's policies, and all they could see from 1941 to 1952 was war, trouble, and war.

We liked Ike because he promised something different; he really didn't believe that America's role was to make over the world, and he promised to end the war in Korea. He did, and despite the missionary urging of his Secretary of State, Mr. Dulles, to go the brink of war in pursuit of policies, President Eisenhower kept us out of war. The fact is that the Korean War ended early in Eisenhower's first term and no others were started.

Since his departure from the White House, the record shows that 33,000 Americans have lost their lives in Vietnam—a place in which he did not become involved beyond the small involvement inherited from Mr. Truman. When President Kennedy was sworn in we had fewer than 1,000 advisers in Vietnam.

The movers and shakers criticized the Eisenhower years also because they seemed to produce no change of consequence in American directions. But the seeds of great change were being sowed at Little Rock and in the space race we now are leading. And now the stirrings and upheavals in the cities' inner cores and upon the nation's campuses are upon us in such great measure that no one knows where these things will all come out.

Except that as the eight years of Eisenhower take on the kind patina of history it may well seem to many that the general's hand guided the country through the happiest and most peaceful years in their memory.

And that, though we tend to forget it, is one of the chief reasons this government was established.

---

[From the Virginian-Pilot, Mar. 29, 1969]

### EISENHOWER THE UNIFIER

Dwight D. Eisenhower will be remembered as a unifier in war and peace. He harnessed diverse temperaments of Allied generals during World War II, when he was Supreme Allied Commander. In 1950 as NATO's first European commander he led in integrating joint defense forces of the West to resist pressures from the East. With a distaste for "government by factions and fractions," he achieved a high degree of harmony in America during two terms as President. And he tried to unify the United States and the Soviet Union in a quest for peace.

Early in World War II Winston Churchill marveled at the way General Eisenhower not only allowed but encouraged his chief of staff, Bedell Smith, to disagree—and then won him to a decision as completely as if General Smith had got his own way. Later, the Allied Commander practiced the same persuasiveness on the Prime Minister in allaying doubts in the invasion of Normandy.

After helping liberate and rearm Western Europe, he was persuaded to run for President. He was alarmed, he said later, by a drift toward Federal paternalism on the domestic scene and signs of isolationism similar to the wave that followed World War I. To a land tense and tired, he brought an era of good feeling. "We are just happier," the President said after his first term. "We are just a happier nation." The air of calm persisted despite one crisis after another—Korea, Formosa, Indochina, Hungary, the Suez Canal—during which he traveled 325,000 miles, endured three major illnesses, and became the oldest President in office. After threading his way through the Formosa trouble in 1955, he remarked, "The hard way is to have the courage to be patient."

The wish of the American voters coincided with his own instinct to keep to the middle way between extremists. He also moved the Republican Party nearer the center. If he disdained patronage and fence-mending and called himself a political novice, he showed a sure touch in advancing his career. But then, after all, the GOP rode his coat-tails and even made inroads in the South. (Five GOP Congressional seats in Virginia are largely an Eisenhower legacy.)

No other American in this century has been as widely beloved and trusted. The electorate had an unshakable faith in his decency and judgment. Columnists might deride his wondrous syntax; the voters understood. Some of his circumlocution was artful. "Far better to stumble or speak guardedly than to move ahead smoothly and risk imperiling the country," he said.

Out of office he wrote four volumes of reminiscences fully as readable as anything produced by most of the critics of his style.

His sense of duty was such that during his first illness he drew satisfaction from the thought that he couldn't have picked a better date for a heart attack—the economy was booming, Congress was out of session, no world crisis was pending.

If he was a horse for work, he was equally zealous at hunting, fishing, golfing, and bridge. (Vivid in the memory is an interview after a particularly good bag of quail. When you go out after a long lapse of time, explained the President, you revert to the first simple motions you learned as a boy.)

Like every man in office, he experienced controversy. At the height of Virginia's fling at Massive Resistance, he fell into such sharp disfavor with the State's leader that none of them turned out to welcome him on a visit to Stratford, Lee's birthplace.

But when the President left that Westmoreland County mansion at the close of the tour, he chuckled in surprise at the sight of 1,500 persons gathered on the far lawn. He waved, and smiled, rather abashedly; and with that, the crescent broke and came running toward him, a fringe of children on the front of the wave. As they reached him, he leaned down, caught a child in his hands, raised her over his head—and that was the photograph that rebuked churlish officials next morning: a child looking down and laughing at the beaming face of the President of the United States.

The people liked Ike.

---

[From the Roanoke (Va.) Times, Mar. 29, 1969]

DWIGHT EISENHOWER: NATIONAL HERO, EFFECTIVE LEADER IN WAR AND PEACE

Dwight Eisenhower was an authentic hero, a soldier-president whose rock-like integrity, personal magnetism and infectious grin won him the votes of 35 million Americans and the lasting respect of all his fellow countrymen.

"I Like Ike" was more than a catchy campaign slogan. It accurately described a national mood, first in the Forties, when as allied commander in Europe, Gen. Eisenhower directed the invasions of North Africa, Sicily and the Italian mainland, the cross-Channel invasion of France and ultimately the defeat of the German armies beyond the Rhine; in the Fifties, when as 34th President, Ike put unity of country above partisan politics, provided steady, undramatic leadership that helped quiet the nation's post-Korea neuroses, and kept the peace in the face of continuing Cold War tensions and nuclear deadlock; in the Sixties, during which he was titular Republican leader, a loyal supporter of Kennedy-Johnson foreign policy and a tenacious battler against the ravages of old age.

Mr. Eisenhower ran the presidency with a light yet steady hand. He early settled on a policy of peaceful co-existence with the opposition-controlled Congress, narrowly defined his own powers, at times de-emphasized the role of the federal government and shunned for too long such national problems as McCarthyism and school integration. In the latter years of his eight-year term, he properly assumed a more activist role as chief executive.

His critics invariably characterize the Eisenhower years as a time of drift and indifference, a time when the nation was doing nothing to prepare for the school revolution that inevitably was to follow. But these critics do an injustice to Ike, for his low-key leadership was desperately needed by a country still trying to recover from the discord and frustration of the Korean stalemate, the paranoid fear of an imagined internal Communist threat, and the corruption of certain Truman Administration officials.

When Eisenhower was tested by crisis, he did not falter. Whether in putting down Gov. Faubus' expedient defiance of federal court orders integrating the Little Rock schools or in showing the flag in the face of Communist threats in Lebanon and the Formosa Straits, he displayed the necessary firmness.

He did not devise an enlightened fiscal and monetary policy to spur the greater economic growth that clearly was needed to deflate Nikita Khrushchev's tiresome boasts that the Soviet Union would bury the U.S., but neither had any President before him.

He did not commit the U.S. to space exploration until Sputnik shook the nation from its lethargy, but moved swiftly to get the U.S. into space once the Soviet challenge was laid down.

He did not saddle the country with a binge of social-welfare legislation, yet he began a prudent expansion of the central government's role in education, civil rights and other activities that the Republican party's dominant congressional leadership had too long ignored.

A war hero, and life-long military man, Mr. Eisenhower nonetheless was emphatic in insisting on subordination of the military to civil power. Significantly, he was one of the first to recognize the threat posed by the Cold War's "conjunction of an immense military establishment and a large arms industry." Neither an isolationist nor a mindless appeaser, he stressed the imperative need for strong national defense. Still he had the vision to speak out, shortly before he left the White House, of the "unwarranted influence" being gained by an arms industry-military complex. A decade later, the nation only now is coming to realize the full import of that warning.

President Eisenhower wrongly permitted his strong-willed secretary of state, John Foster Dulles, to commit the U.S. to cover most of the globe as a peacekeeper. But he vetoed a U.S. military rescue of the French colonialists in Vietnam. He questioned whether the nation should rely solely on weapons for its security. He laid the groundwork (despite Hungary and the U-2 blow-up) for an eventual U.S.-Soviet detente. He called the lack of disarmament progress in the Fifties his "greatest disappointment." And he once declared, "Every gun that is made, every warship launched, every rocket fired signifies, in the final sense, a theft from those who hunger and are not fed, those who are cold and are not clothed."

Historian Charles L. Mee, Jr., has called Ike's first campaign for the presidency "less a contest than a prolonged triumphal parade." In truth, his whole life was a triumphal parade. He remained to his death the nation's most admired citizen, even more so in his final days when a dogged will to live kept him alive and alert long after ordinary men would have given up the fight.

Ike was probably the last soldier-president. In the nuclear age no wars can be won, no military heroes can emerge. He grasped the new realities of nuclear deadlock; as speech writer Arthur Larson reminds us in a recent book, Dwight Eisenhower waged peace for eight years with the same effective leadership and impressive results as he waged against Hitler's Third Reich, and closed out the statemated war in Korea. More could not have been asked of him, and a saddened nation today speaks with a single voice in mourning his death.

## Hon. Karl E. Mundt

OF SOUTH DAKOTA

Mr. President, Ray McHugh, chief of the Washington bureau of the Copley News Service, in a recent column, reflected on the funeral ceremonies for, and tributes to, former President Dwight Eisenhower.

Mr. McHugh's column, beautifully written, has captured the essence of what I believe most of us have felt during the days of the ceremonies and those which followed.

I am pleased to bring it to the attention of the Senate because of the fine tribute it is to General Eisenhower, but more so because it gives an added sense of meaning to the events of early April in which all Americans were in one way or another participants.

I ask unanimous consent that this excellent article be printed in the RECORD.

There being no objection, the article was ordered to be printed in the RECORD, as follows:

TRIBUTE—NATIONAL—INTERPRETIVE

(By Ray McHugh, chief, Washington Bureau, Copley News Service)

WASHINGTON.—The last echoes of the cannon and the bugles have faded away; the tributes are ended; but the American people may discover that in death, Gen. Dwight D. Eisenhower performed one last service for them that could overshadow all his victories in war, all his achievements in peace.

The last five days have seen a "coming together" of Americans in salute to a man who has been called "the all-American president," "the 50-star general," "the most beloved American of the 20th century."

Out of the death of Gen. Eisenhower and the sad, but majestic pageantry of his final rites here in Abilene, Kans., have come some powerful reminders about the roots of America.

As men looked back on Gen. Eisenhower's years of high military command and on his presidency, it was inevitable that they should comment on the order that marked those years—even the war years.

As they looked back even further, into the general's own origins, it was inevitable that they should comment on his simple, protestant heritage, his firm belief in the West Point creed of "duty, honor, country"; his uncomplicated character that disdained political maneuvering, rejected the waste of hatred and reflected until the very end his faith in his country and the principles on which it was built.

It will be a long time before American history books forget his last words to his wife Mamie:

"I've always loved my wife.

"I've always loved my children.

"I've always loved my grandchildren.

"I've always loved my country."

The outpouring of genuine affection and respect for the old soldier must have surprised those in Washington who have delighted for almost a decade in pointing to his 1953–1961 presidency as a "do-nothing" period.

Many younger political figures dismissed the simple, open Eisenhower style as an anachronism. His principles no longer fit the changing times and mood of the nation, they said.

They must wonder today if times and moods have really changed that much, or if they have been listening only to strident minorities.

For the nation, too, Gen. Eisenhower's death brought a kind of reawakening. An increasingly secular citizenry suddenly paused, looked at its television screens, and seemed drawn back to the "God of our Fathers," the apt title of one of Gen. Eisenhower's favorite hymns.

"Onward, Christian Soldiers" had the ring of a call to duty and "Army Blue" was a reminder that old loyalties are not to be forgotten.

It has been easy for some Washington observers to disregard the relative order and quiet of the Eisenhower years as a post-war "interlude" and to blame the disorder and tension of the 1960s on the release of suppressed frustrations and the encouragement of intellectual ferment.

In the dignity of the last five days, both arguments seemed to collapse.

Gen. Eisenhower brought more to the national scene than a contagious grin. He brought a strength of purpose and a conviction in America. Perhaps even his closest friends did not grasp the full measure of that strength until this week.

In death he reminded millions not only of his achievements, but of their own achievements, their own origins and the origins of their country. Each act in the funeral drama—a program he had personally approved three years ago—seemed to emphasize these origins.

The change that came over the nation was almost visible in the lines that honored the 34th President as he lay in repose at the National Cathedral, then in state at the Capitol.

In those first hours Saturday the lines were made up largely of the middle aged and older Americans who remembered Gen. Eisenhower fondly as a great wartime commander and as a President who kept the peace. There were few young people or children. Few negroes.

But in the final hours at the Capitol Tuesday, at the railroad stations along the 1,300 mile ride home to Kansas and in the streets of Abilene Wednesday, youth and people of all races joined the tribute.

It was as if this man many could not even remember had in death awakened a pride of country, a new awareness of God, a selflessness that too many had forgotten.

For the first time in a long time, Americans had a good look at themselves and liked what they saw. Gen. Eisenhower was so typical of America that each in his own way could see a bit of himself in the soldier-president.

## Hon. Joseph D. Tydings

OF MARYLAND

Mr. President, of only one other citizen in the history of the Republic could it be said "First in war; first in peace; first in the hearts of his countrymen." This memorial to the Father of our Country applies as well to its 34th President, whose passing we now mourn.

His nation's hero in war, its leader in peace, beloved by his fellow citizens and the citizens of the world, Dwight David Eisenhower epitomized the vigor, conviction, discipline, and integrity which are the foundation stones of our country.

He was an American. He was a great American of his era. And even in retirement he enriched our national life with his summons to the fundamental values in the American heritage.

We will miss him. But his life will not be honored if we simply recall his virtue as some relic of our national past. We must, instead, live as he would have lived: tolerant of the views and failings of others, but relentlessly demanding in the energy, honesty and vigor with which we pursue our own life and work.

So let us honor our departed leader. Let us be proud to have been his countrymen.

## Hon. Birch Bayh

OF INDIANA

Mr. President, General Eisenhower served America as military leader, as President, as citizen. At all times, in all positions, he was a man utterly dedicated to the welfare of this Nation.

His interest in his country did not diminish when he left public office. As a private citizen he had a sustaining concern for the United States.

It was Eisenhower the citizen who came to Washington in 1964 to give his support to help in the adoption of the 25th amendment, the Presidential successful and disability amendment.

It was Eisenhower the citizen who at that time stated the creed he practiced, both as general and as President:

> We do believe that all of us, of all parties and all levels of government, have as our first thought and concern, the United States of America.
>
> And, if we do that, I think all of the other problems kind of recede in their immediacy, their urgency, and in their, you might say, crisis-type of complexion and they become resolvable by people of good will—that is, good Americans.

He believed in the American people, and they in him. To use the words of Dag Hammerskjold:

> He had been granted a faith which required no confirmation—a contact with reality, light and intense like the touch of a loved hand; a union in self-surrender without self-destruction where his heart was lucid and his mind loving.

Duty, honor, country, the code of West Point, became his personal commitment. He led America, both in war and in peace, and earned her love and respect forever.

America is greatly saddened by his loss.

## Hon. Everett McKinley Dirksen

OF ILLINOIS

Mr. President, on Monday of this week, April 14, some 5,000 women began the 17th annual Republican Women's Conference, convening at the Sheraton Park Hotel here in Washington, D.C. At the super gala that night one of the first items on the program was a beautiful tribute paid to our former President and Commander in Chief, Dwight David Eisenhower, by a distinguished Member of the House of Representatives, Mrs. CHARLOTTE T. REID, of Illinois. Through the years and especially during the past weeks, respect, appreciation, love, and compassion have been poured on General Eisenhower, but I believe you will join me in feeling that no finer and more appropriate tribute has been paid than the one so elegantly expressed by Mrs. REID.

I ask unanimous consent that the tribute be printed in the RECORD.

There being no objection, the tribute was ordered to be printed in the RECORD, as follows:

SUPER GALA—REPUBLICAN WOMEN'S CONFERENCE, WASHINGTON, D.C., APRIL 14, 1969

It was just two weeks ago tonight—as dusk settled over the Capitol, that official Washington said a final farewell to perhaps the best-loved American of this century. The slow-paced cortege, with its caisson bearing the simple G.I. coffin, followed by the riderless horse, symbol of the fallen hero—had come to a halt. The solemn processions of the State Funeral had reached Union Station. The last echoes of the cannon and bugles had faded away. Now Dwight David Eisenhower was going home to Abilene for the last time—home to his chosen resting place in the heartland of America from whence he had come.

For three days, Heads of State and Ministers—great men and women from every part of the world—had come to mourn with citizens from all walks of life—of all races and religions—at the somber Lincoln Catafalque in the hushed vastness of the Capitol Rotunda—and to raise their voices in the triumphant words of "Onward Christian Soldiers" and "God of Our Fathers" in the majesty of the Washington Cathedral. And as the funeral train began its long and lonely journey across mountain and plain, river and farm, an entire Nation stood at attention in final salute—hat in hand, and for most of us a lump in the throat. Yes, in death just as so often in life, Dwight David Eisenhower had once again touched his people deeply.

Each of us here tonight will always have a special memory of General Eisenhower—and each his own personal tribute to one who so joyously took the journey of life, who took it with vision and foresight, and with all the courage and determination at his command.

His deeds were great and many, and historians will so record them. They will tell of Eisenhower the soldier, whose devotion to his country was the motivation of a lifetime in its service—Eisenhower, the Commander of the mightiest expeditionary force ever assembled in the cause of freedom—and Eisenhower, the General, receiving the surrender of the Hitler armies in World War II.

They will tell, also, of Eisenhower the educator, as President of Columbia University—one of the Nation's great centers of learning and culture.

They will tell of Eisenhower, the crusader for world peace and international understanding and brotherhood while Supreme Commander of NATO.

And they will tell of Eisenhower, our 34th President, with his magnetic grin, who brought to the Nation a welcome period of peace and order—and a strength of purpose and conviction in America.

Yes, every trust we Americans had in our power to bestow was freely given him. It was bestowed because he reflected in his own life and personality the best traditions of a free people—and our Nation's faith and hope. We admired his courage of mind and heart, his strength of character, his idealism, his devotion to his family, his belief in the worth of his fellow man, his simplicity, his understanding warmth, and his candor. Everyone "liked Ike"—for most seemed to see in him and his homely virtues some small reflection of themselves. He was so typical of America that each in his own way could see a bit of himself in the soldier-President.

And even in death, I think that General Dwight D. Eisenhower performed one last service which must not go unheeded. Sad though it has been, this period of mourning—with all its memories of the simple heritage of this man from Abilene who brought such inspiration to so many—of his belief in the creed of "duty, honor, country"—of his devotion to the principles on which this Republic was built—of the peace and tranquillity which characterized his years in the White House—all this has reminded millions not only of the achievements of a great fellow American, but of our own achievements as well. It has reminded us of our own priceless heritage and the hard fought origins of our country.

And as he faded quietly away—as old soldiers are said to do—he left with each of us who kept vigil with him a little of his pride in America, a little of his awareness of God, and a little of his responsibility to mankind.

May the Lord bless his memory—and may the Lord give to each of us the strength and courage to carry on those ideals and goals which he lived in life and which were his legacy in death.

Yes—America and the world like Ike. There can be no finer tribute!

## Hon. Margaret Chase Smith

OF MAINE

Mr. President, for myself and on behalf of my colleague from Maine (Mr. MUSKIE), I ask unanimous consent to have printed in the RECORD a joint resolution of the Legislature of Maine in memoriam of Gen. Dwight David Eisenhower, 34th President of the United States of America.

There being no objection, the joint resolution was ordered to be printed in the RECORD, as follows:

IN MEMORIAM

Whereas, we are deeply grieved by the death of General Dwight David Eisenhower the thirty-fourth President of the United States of America and truly a great American; and

Whereas, the spirit of his firm but compassionate leadership shall forever remain in the hearts of all peace-loving people throughout the world; and

Whereas, his every act reflected an inspiring sense of enduring devotion to duty, to honor and to country long to be cherished by all free men; and

Whereas, in his passing, not only the people of this State, but a nation of states and a world of nations, have suffered, as history will record, an irreparable loss; now, therefore, be it

Resolved, the House of Representatives concurring, that the Legislature stand and tender a moment of silent prayer and upon adjourning this day, it do so out of respect to the memory of our beloved General Dwight D. Eisenhower; and be it further

Resolved, that a copy of this joint resolution, suitably engrossed, be transmitted to the family of the deceased.

In Senate Chamber, read and adopted, ordered sent forthwith, April 1, 1969.

Sent Down For Concurrence.

JERROLD B. SPEERS,
*Secretary.*

House of Representatives, read and adopted, April 1, 1969.

In concurrence.

BERTHA W. JOHNSON,
*Clerk.*

## Hon. Winston L. Prouty

OF VERMONT

Mr. President, "Dwight David Eisenhower": The name evokes the title "President" and rank of "general" and at once something more, something simpler. For to his time and his people, he was simply "Ike," in a word, a most likable man.

We marched with "the general" across North Africa, then on to Sicily and Italy. We embarked with him on the "great crusade" that began on the beaches of Normandy and ended in that schoolhouse in Rheims.

We followed him eagerly, for he was a brilliant stategist and something more. He had that ability to weld together the greatest alliance of armies the world has ever seen. He was able to sustain victory with modesty, extend a hand and grin to the troops. "My name's Eisenhower" was all he said.

After the war, Sir Winston Churchill was to call him "the great and humble soldier." Great he was, and more. He was an authentic hero, and the Nation embraced him while he shunned heroics.

He was able to evade the early "Draft Ike" boomlets that sprung up around the country, but a large body of Americans were persistent—they wanted "Ike."

In the winter of 1952, I joined with a number of Republican colleagues in the House of Representatives in urging General Eisenhower to return from Europe and seek our party's nomination for the Presidency. As a freshman Representative, I was flattered to be included in this entreaty.

Ike answered our urgings in a letter dated March 10, 1952. I shall never forget his reply. It showed the two characteristics that were the mark of his greatness: candor and humility. At once he pointed to what he considered to be the lack of a popular call for his candidacy and his obligations to SHAPE; but he qualified this latter point humbly:

> Of course, I am not indispensable to the success of NATO and SHAPE—even if at one time many may have thought me so. If I were, then I should actually be to some extent a failure, for one of my primary objectives here has been the development of an organization that can carry on despite any loss of personnel—from the Supreme Commander through all the levels of the staff. With the help of devoted and able associates, that sort of organization has been perfected. I firmly believe that, should I walk out of this headquarters tomorrow, the mission would be carried on by competent hands—carried on successfully.

I admired General Eisenhower's modesty and sense of duty, but I disagreed with his conclusion. He humbly overlooked his irreplaceable contribution which was his extraordinary ability to understand others' viewpoints, to work in harmony with them, and to bring their divergent opinions together.

As his unparalleled cohesive talents were needed in wartime, they were needed during the early cold war years in Europe. Likewise and perhaps to an even greater extent, they were needed at home.

He reexamined his March 10 position and returned, and what we now refer to as "the Eisenhower years" began.

He was a soldier, yet he dedicated his Presidency to seeing, in his words, "people in my profession permanently put out of a job." He ended the war in Korea and waged peace for the 8 years of his incumbency.

"The Eisenhower years" are only a decade past, yet they seem even further removed. Now they seem a simple time, yet our nostalgia is deceptive.

It is now fashionable to dismiss "the Eisenhower years" as merely a period of consolidation, but this ignores the crises and conflicts, programs, and progress which marked the era.

What we seem to remember most at this time is the fact that the challenges of those years were met with the reassurance that President Eisenhower brought to the Nation, the feeling that Eisenhower was in the White House and all was well with the world.

We placed our faith in him and he sustained it, and the world seemed so much simpler as long as he was with us.

Now, therefore, the parting is difficult, because what he was is as important as what he did.

Farewell, General; goodbye, Mr. President. You served us well and gave us much, and we asked so much of you.

## Hon. Lee Metcalf
OF MONTANA

Mr. President, Dwight D. Eisenhower was a great man. The very mention of his name evokes emotions in the heart of every American. Men who were in the European Theater in World War II remember him as the commander in chief who led the Allied forces to victory. Those who are especially identified with the years from 1953 to 1961 remember him as a distinguished President of the United States. There are those who identify with his earlier years, or with his presidency of Columbia University. But everyone who thinks of Dwight D. Eisenhower thinks of a man of humility, yet a man of stature, a great leader but not a demander, a man who was a peer in his own time, yet a man who was a friend of all.

I was fortunate in being a part of the organization in London that General Eisenhower led while preparing for the Normandy invasion. As a very junior officer I knew of the admiration and respect he elicited from all ranks. His ability to mediate between the prima donnas of his command and his ability to obtain the utmost from his associates were facets of his character that made all ranks his friend.

I came to Congress in the first year of President Eisenhower's administration and was a part of the legislative branch while he led the executive department. He was always understanding, ever considerate. He brought to the civilian administration the feeling that he had for his troops under his military command. He wanted to improve the status of the people he governed; while he recognized that they were going to be subjected to risks and dangers, he wanted to minimize those risks and dangers.

He was a great general, a distinguished president, an admirable citizen; but more, he was a mighty American in all the connotations of that term. The world will miss him and all of us who were associated with him regret his death, but even after our memory is faded and gone this man will be remembered as a statesman of grandeur and dignity.

## Hon. Robert P. Griffin
OF MICHIGAN

Mr. President, an article published in the April issue of Reader's Digest contains this passage:

> Well, I for one refuse to become pessimistic about America's future. Granted the storm signals are up, I believe nevertheless that as a people we have the good sense to place patriotism and human understanding above the arrogance of prejudice—that we can solve peacefully the problems that beset us. I believe that we will do so through our traditional reliance upon the philosophy of moderation—or Government by Common Sense.

Those words of faith and confidence were written, shortly before his last illness, by the most admired, the most beloved American of this century—Dwight David Eisenhower.

The United States and the world are much

better places in which to live today because of the dedicated life and services of Dwight David Eisenhower.

Military strategist, educator, and statesman, General Eisenhower was all of these—and much more. In the hearts and minds of people everywhere, he was a soldier who hated war and fought unceasingly for peace. His quest for peace was as intense during the 8 important years when he occupied the White House as it was during wartime when he commanded the most powerful armies in history.

Unwavering in his faith in America and the future, he was the very symbol of the Nation's spirit. In his state of the Union message on January 5, 1956, he said:

> Our resources are too many, our principles too dynamic, our purpose too worthy and the issues at stake too immense for us to entertain doubt or fear. . . .

In the twilight years of his life, General Eisenhower wrote that his greatest regret, when leaving the White House, was that he had not achieved greater success in reducing world hostility and making progress toward global disarmament.

Then he added:

> But though, in this, I suffered my greatest disappointment, it has not destroyed my faith that in the next generation, the next century, the next millenium these things will come to pass.

If and when world peace and order does come, it will be due, in no small measure, to the inspiring, dedicated efforts of Dwight David Eisenhower and his devotion to the principles of freedom with justice for all.

In this century there have been other great statesmen and other great soldiers, but Dwight David Eisenhower had no peer in the hearts of the people. He was a most exceptional man.

Perhaps that feeling is summed up best in what started out to be only a political slogan. In time, the slogan—"I like Ike"—became a phrase of affection heard around the world.

The wisdom and counsel of Dwight David Eisenhower will be sorely missed. But his lifetime of service to the world and the country he loved so much will remain as a monument of inspiration for all.

## Hon. Everett McKinley Dirksen

OF ILLINOIS

Mr. President, Dr. Amado M. Yuzon, president and chairman of the United Poets Laureate International, Quezon City, Philippines, was a great admirer of the late President Eisenhower. The late President's great friendship for the Filipino people inspired Dr. Yuzon to write a sonnet about our late beloved President. It is entitled "Eisenhower—Sonnet on His Death." I ask unanimous consent that it be printed in the RECORD.

There being no objection, the sonnet was ordered to be printed in the RECORD, as follows:

EISENHOWER—SONNET ON HIS DEATH

(By Amado M. Yuzon)

Like Washington, he was the war-and-peace
Titan of Presidents all—as a whole;
While Lincoln emancipated the black race,
He led the hosts of freedom in his days
And freed all Europe from the Nazi rule.
Unlike the Jacksons and the McKinleys
Who had pushed far and wide the nation's border,
He flew the flag with nothing to increase
But the empire of human liberties
In yet the greatest, costliest world disorder.
Now he is dead—the soldier, President,
And may his God rest him in peace sublime. . . .
Leaving behind as deathless monument
Democracy—this monarch of his time!

QUEZON CITY, PHILIPPINES, *April 3, 1969.*

## Hon. Milton R. Young

OF NORTH DAKOTA

Mr. President, the late Dwight D. Eisenhower was revered not only by our people who knew him so well, but by people all over the world.

Mr. President, a friend of mine has sent me the address delivered by the Rev. Erwin R. Ruklic, pastor of the International Church of Bangkok, Thailand, during a memorial service honoring General Eisenhower. The service was attended by a number of ambassadors from the various embassies in Bangkok and a large number of leaders from the Thai Government. The American community in Bangkok was also well represented.

Mr. President, I ask unanimous consent that the address be printed in the Record.

There being no objection, the address was ordered to be printed in the Record, as follows:

Dwight David Eisenhower: A Meditation

(An address by the Rev. Erwin R. Ruklic, pastor, at the Memorial Service in the International Church of Bangkok, Thailand, on March 31, 1969; United States Ambassador Leonard Unger presided)

Dwight D. Eisenhower—soldier; statesman; university president; national hero; world leader.

These are the facts of the soldier of war who became a crusader for peace.

When we recall his name we remember the common touch of his humanity.

His grin and nickname—Ike were the trademarks of a humble but human figure of mankind.

The qualities that revealed the stature of the man will will long be remembered:

"His virtue was modesty.

"His character was honesty.

"His life was service.

"His leadership was trusted."

Though he began his career as a soldier he finished his life as a civilian—the President of the United States.

The highest honor came to him without solicitation or desire.

He did not covet the life of a politician; it was the politicians who needed him.

And the people of his country paid him the highest compliment—not once but twice—by electing him as their President with the largest margin of votes.

His nation gave him the blessing of trust, confidence and encouragement.

He brought the country together at a time when it needed to be strengthened and sustained.

The American people enjoyed a climate of unity because he gave them his unqualified trust.

His immense influence for public morality, personal integrity, and civic responsibility was the beach head of his presidential office.

He gave himself unselfishly and unreservedly to this highest office of public service.

And whenever he made his periodic treks to the greens, the American public was ever so happy to see their President relax.

And in the mood of jest, one quipster remarked: "I'm not sure whether Ike is a full time President and a Part time golfer, or a Full time golfer and a Part time President."

However, none of his constituents criticized him on taking leave for a long weekend.

They loved him the more for it.

Few other Presidents had so caught the imagination of the people as this man.

Deeply concerned about world peace, he visited 31 countries during his presidency in an effort to strengthen and stabilize the nations around the world.

The words of an earlier President, Thomas Jefferson, so aptly described him:

"When a man assumes a public trust, he should consider himself as public property."

Indeed, this man—was the people's President.

For the greatness of the man was in the goodness of the man.

And the strength of the man was in the character of the man.

Nothing can surpass the qualities of integrity and honesty; commitment and compassion—for these outlast and outshine all others.

Few people remember that it was not until after he entered the White House that he made one of the most important decisions of his life.

For the first time in his life he became a Christian and united with the Church. He always made it a practice to nurture his faith and put his faith to work.

He took it upon himself to worship with others and made it a regular habit to do so wherever his duties took him: in the nation's capital or Augusta, Ga.; in the United States or in his travels abroad.

In his book, Waging Peace: The White House Years, he tells this personal account of his visit to Rome:

Having worshipped at St. Paul's Episcopal Church, he went to make a scheduled call on the Pope—John 23rd. Pope John, bright and active at the age of 78, had the vivacity and zest of a young man.

They had met years before when both served in Paris: Their conversation included reminiscences, observations of the cold war; some hope for the future, and cheerful banter about their respective careers and present positions.

"You were a general and became President," said Pope John jokingly, "and I was a sergeant and became Pope."

The people's President met the people's Pope.

A nation has lost a warrior—a warrior for truth and justice; humanity and peace.

A world mourns his passing and pays tribute to a greatness that is rooted in goodness; a life that reflects its Creator; and a death that knows not the end but marches forward valiantly and triumphantly in the name of the Master, Jesus Christ, his Lord and his Saviour.

Dwight David Eisenhower.

# Memorial Tributes

IN THE

# House of Representatives of the United States

IN EULOGY OF

# Dwight David Eisenhower

# In the House of Representatives of the United States

*MARCH 31, 1969*

PRAYER

The Chaplain, Rev. Edward G. Latch, D.D., offered the following prayer:

*Yea, though I walk through the valley of the shadow of death, I will fear no evil: for Thou art with me.*—Psalm 23: 4.

Almighty and Eternal God, the comforter of Thy children and the strength of those who put their trust in Thee, we assemble this day with sorrow in our hearts at the passing of General of the Army Dwight David Eisenhower, our beloved 34th President. Even in the sadness of farewell we think fondly of him who walked so worthily in our midst and who served so well as the leader of our country.

We mourn his passing because he reflected in his own personality the tradition of a free people and revealed in his life the shrine of our Nation's faith and hope.

We thank Thee for him, for his courage of mind and heart, for his strength of character, for his desire to do what he firmly believed to be right and for his devotion to his family and to his country. Certainly our United States is a better nation—stronger and freer—because he lived and led us in war and in peace.

So we honor the memory of this great and good man, "who more than self his country loved," and in so doing we dedicate ourselves anew to Thee and to our Nation in the global struggle between democracy and dictatorship.

Comfort the family with Thy sustaining spirit and strengthen them for these hours and for the days to come. Keep them and us, steady and strong, this day and forever more. Amen.

*The Speaker* laid before the House the following message from the President of the United States:

*To the Congress of the United States:*

It is my sad duty to inform you officially of the death of Dwight David Eisenhower, the thirty-fourth President of the United States.

We have lost a great leader, a great friend and a great man. I know there are many members of the Congress who had the privilege of serving under his military leadership, and who later, during his eight years as President, shared with him in the building of a better America. He had a profound respect for the traditions, the institutions and the instruments of our nation. He leaves to the Congress and to all Americans the spirit of patriotism and statesmanship beyond party which marked his entire career. As we grieve at his death, we all will recall that spirit, which can guide and sustain us in our tasks ahead. He has been an inspiration to us all, and ours is a better government because he walked among us.

RICHARD NIXON.

THE WHITE HOUSE, *March 28, 1969.*

*The Speaker.* The gentleman from Pennsylvania (Mr. MORGAN) will assume the chair.

*The Speaker pro tempore* (Mr. MORGAN). The Chair recognizes the gentleman from Massachusetts, the distinguished Speaker of the House.

*Mr. McCormack.* Mr. Speaker, I ask unanimous consent to insert at this point in the RECORD the eulogy delivered on President Eisenhower yesterday in the rotunda by President Nixon.

*The Speaker pro tempore.* Is there objection to the request of the gentleman from Massachusetts?

There was no objection.

PRESIDENT'S EULOGY TO EISENHOWER AT RITES IN CAPITOL'S ROTUNDA

Mrs. Eisenhower, your excellencies, friends of Dwight David Eisenhower in America and throughout the world.

We gather today in mourning but also in gratitude. We mourn Dwight Eisenhower's death. But we are grateful for his life.

We gather also conscious of the fact that, in paying tribute to Dwight Eisenhower, we celebrate greatness. When we think of his place in history, we think inevitably of the other giants of those days of World War II.

And we think of the qualities of greatness and what his were that made his unique among all.

Once, perhaps without intending to do so, he himself put his finger on it.

It was 1945, shortly after VE Day at a ceremony in London's historic Guildhall. The triumphant Supreme Commander of the Allied Forces in Europe was officially given the freedom of the city of London.

In an eloquent address that day, Dwight Eisenhower said:

"I come from the heart of America."

MEANING FOR AMERICANS

Perhaps no one sentence could better sum up what Dwight Eisenhower meant to a whole generation of Americans. He did come from the heart of America, not only from its geographical heart but from its spiritual heart. He exemplified what millions of parents hoped that their sons would be—strong and courageous and honest and compassionate.

And with his own great qualities of heart, he personified the best in America. It is, I think, a special tribute to Dwight Eisenhower that, despite all of his great deeds and his triumphs, we find ourselves today thinking first, not of his deeds, but of his character.

It was the character of the man—not what he did, but what he was—that so captured the trust and faith and affection of his own people and of the people of the world.

Dwight Eisenhower touched something fundamental in America which only a man of immense force of mind and spirit could have brought so vibrantly alive. He was a product of America's soil, and of its ideals, driven by a compulsion to do right and to do well, a man of deep faith who believed in God and trusted in his will, a man who truly loved his country and for whom words like freedom and democracy were not cliches—but they were living truths.

I know Mrs. Eisenhower would permit me to share with you the last words he spoke to her on the day he died.

LAST WORDS QUOTED

He said, "I've always loved my wife. I've always loved my children. I've always loved my grandchildren. And I have always loved my country." That was Dwight Eisenhower.

He was a man who gave enormously of himself. His way of relaxing from the intense pressures of office or command was to do something else intensely—whether as a fierce competitor on the golf course or executing one of those hauntingly beautiful paintings that he did with such meticulous care.

People loved Dwight Eisenhower. But the other side of this coin was that he loved people. He had the great leader's capacity to bring out the best in people. He had the great humanist's capacity to inspire people, to cheer them, to give them lift. I remember for example, just a few months ago when I asked all of the members of the Cabinet to go out and call on him. And each of them returned with wonder and admiration and said, "You know, I went out there to cheer him up and instead I found he cheered me up."

His great love of people was rooted in his faith. He had a deep faith in the goodness of God and in the essential goodness of man as a creature of God. This feeling toward people had another side. In the political world strong passions are the norm. And all too often these turn toward personal vindictiveness. People often disagreed with Dwight Eisenhower, but almost nobody ever hated him. And this, I think, was because he himself was a man who did not know how to hate. Oh, he could be aroused by a cause—but he could not hate a person. He could disagree strongly, even passionately, but never personally.

When people disagreed with him, he never thought of them as enemies. He simply thought, they don't agree with me.

I remember, time after time, when critics of one sort or another were misrepresenting him or reviling him, he would sit back in his chair, and with that wonderful half-smile and half-frown, he'd say: "I'm puzzled by those fellows."

And he was genuinely puzzled by frenzy and by hate; because he was incapable of it himself, he couldn't ever quite understand it in others.

AN AUTHENTIC HERO

The last time I saw him that was what he talked about. He was puzzled by the hatreds he had seen in our times. And he said the thing the world needs most today is understanding, and ability to see the other person's point of view, and not to hate him because he disagrees. That was Dwight Eisenhower.

And, yet, of course, he was more than all that. He had a side more evident to those of us who worked with him than to the rest of the world. He was a strong man. He was shrewd. He was decisive. Time and again I have seen him make decisions that probably made the difference between war and peace for America and the world.

That was always when he was at his best.

No matter how heated the arguments were, he was always then the coolest man in the room. Dwight Eisenhower was that rarest of men—an authentic hero. Wars bring the names of many men into the headlines and of those some few become national or even international heroes, but as the years then pass their fame goes down.

#### STATURE CONTINUED TO GROW

But not so with Dwight Eisenhower. As the years passed his stature grew. Commander of the mightiest expeditionary force ever assembled, receiver of the surrender of the German armies in World War II, president of Columbia University, Supreme Commander of NATO, 34th President of the United States—the honors, the offices, were there in abundance. Every trust that the American people had it in their power to bestow, he was given.

And, yet, he always retained a saving humility.

His was the humility not of fear but of confidence. He walked with the great of the world and he knew that the great are human. His was the humility of a man too proud to be arrogant.

The pursuit of peace was uppermost in his mind when he ran for the Presidency, and it was uppermost in his conduct of that office.

And it is a tribute to his skill and determination that not since the 1930's has the nation enjoyed so long a period of peace both at home and abroad as the one that began in 1953 and continued through his Presidency.

As commander of the mightiest allied force ever assembled, he was the right man at the right place at the right time. And as President once again, he was the right man at the right place and at the right time.

He restored calm to a divided nation. He gave Americans a new measure of self-respect. He invested his office with dignity and respect and trust. He made Americans proud of their President, proud of their country, proud of themselves.

And if we in America were proud of Dwight Eisenhower it was partly because he made us proud of America. He came from the heart of America and he gave expression to the heart of America and he touched the hearts of the world.

Many leaders are known and respected outside their own countries. Very few are loved outside their own countries. Dwight Eisenhower was one of those few.

He was probably loved by more people in more parts of the world than any President America has ever had. He captured the deepest feelings of free men everywhere.

#### PRINCIPLES HE STOOD FOR

The principles he believed in, the ideals he stood for, these were bigger than his own country. Perhaps he himself put it best again in that Guidhall speech in 1945.

He said then:

"Kinship among nations is not determined in such measurements as proximity, size and age. Rather, we should turn to those inner things—call them what you will—I mean those intangibles that are the real treasures that free men possess. To preserve his freedom of worship, his equality before the law, his liberty to speak and act as he sees fit, subject only to provisions that he not trespass upon similar rights of others, a Londoner will fight and so will a citizen of Abilene.

"When we consider these things, then the valley of the Thames draws closer to the farms of Kansas and the plains of Texas."

Some men are considered great because they lead great armies, or they lead powerful nations. For eight years now, Dwight Eisenhower has neither commanded an army nor led a nation. And yet he remained through his final days the world's most admired and respected man, truly the first citizen of the world.

#### SOURCE OF HIS GREATNESS

As we marvel at this, it leads us again to ponder the mysteries of greatness. Dwight Eisenhower's greatness derived not from his office but from his character, from a unique moral force that transcended national boundaries, even as his own deep concern for humanity transcended national boundaries.

His life reminds us that there is a moral force in this world more powerful than the might of arms, or the wealth of nations. This man who led the most powerful armies that the world has ever seen; this man who led the most powerful nation in the world; this essentially good and gentle and kind man—that moral force was his greatness.

For a quarter of a century to the very end of his life, Dwight Eisenhower exercised a moral authority without parallel in America and in the world.

And America and the world is better because of him.

And, so, today we render our final salute. It is a fond salute to a man we loved and cherished. It is a grateful salute to a man whose whole extraordinary life was consecrated to service.

It is a profoundly respectful salute to a man larger than life who by any standard was one of the giants of our time.

Each of us here will have a special memory of Dwight Eisenhower.

I can see him now standing erect, straight, proud and tall 16 years ago as he took the oath of office as the 34th President of the United States of America.

We salute Dwight David Eisenhower standing there in our memories—first in war, first in peace and, wherever freedom is cherished, first in the hearts of his fellow men.

## Hon. John W. McCormack

OF MASSACHUSSETTS

Mr. Speaker, the sense of loss that afflicts this great Nation when a man who has occupied its Chief Magistracy passes to his eternal reward has a profound and touching effect upon us. In the death of Dwight David Eisenhower we see once again how deeply run the feelings of Americans, how fervently wells in their hearts a love of country, and how measureless is their fundamental respect for their greatest leaders. Has any monarch of the kingdoms of old, has any tyrant of the totalitarianisms of yesterday or of today, ever evoked by his demise the grief that has been experienced by all of us at President Eisenhower's passing?

The forebears of the man who was to lead the most massive invasion in the history of the world left Germany because of religious persecution. They settled during the eighties of the 18th century, in Pennsylvania. General Eisenhower's grandfather migrated to Kansas in 1878, and in Kansas the young American who was to be his country's 34th President grew to manhood. He was graduated from the U.S. Military Academy in 1915 and pursued one of the most distinguished military careers in this country's history. He led the invasion of north Africa and the invasion of Europe, both with stunning success. His overwhelming personal popularity among his admiring countrymen brought him to the Presidency for two terms.

His life is an example for all Americans, particularly of the younger generation to follow.

The policies that he followed as President of the United States were enunciated forcefully and unambiguously in his first state of the Union message of February 2, 1953, and never once did he waver from them. Down the long years those words of his return to our recollections as an apotheosis of the man, the soldier, the statesman, the humanitarian, the leader in peace and war, the President whom we have lost in death:

> As our heart summons our strength, our wisdom must direct it. There is, in world affairs, a steady course to be followed between an assertion of strength that is truculent and a confession of helplessness that is cowardly. There is, in our affairs at home, a middle way between untrammeled freedom of the individual and the demands for the welfare of the whole nation. This way must avoid government by bureaucracy as carefully as it avoids neglect of the helpless. In every area of political action, free men must think before they can expect to win. In this spirit must we live and labor: confident of our strength, compassionate in our heart, clear in our mind. In this spirit, let us together turn to the great tasks before us.

In the sunset of his years, this great American has recounted for us how, as a West Point plebe, he experienced a sudden sense of pride in his country's flag and commenced the lifetime of devotion to its causes that made him one of the bright and shining heroes of our national life.

The plebes assembled toward evening of that long-ago day of June 14, 1911, and, as a member of that group whom we knew best has told us:

> With the American flag floating majestically above us, we were sworn in as cadets of the U.S. Military Academy. It was an impressive ceremony. As I looked up at our national colors and swore my allegiance, I realized humbly that now I belonged to the flag. It is a moment I have never forgotten.

Dwight David Eisenhower's devotion to his country was the motivation of a lifetime in its service. His belief in his country's ideals led him to its Presidency. His belief in the worth of his fellow man, his religious idealism, his unaffected ways, his natural leadership, his magnetic smile, his stanch courage, endeared him to his countrymen who always had a special place for him in their affections. That special place, now vacant, is full of sorrow.

On March 29, 1969, I sent the following telegram:

MRS. DWIGHT DAVID EISENHOWER,
*Washington, D.C.*

DEAR MRS. EISENHOWER: In the passing of your beloved and distinguished husband, the Nation has lost one of its most outstanding statesmen and military leaders who served his country with sound judgment and courage in peace and in war. Your dear husband will always occupy a foremost position in American and in world history. For myself personally and as Speaker of the U.S. House of Representatives and for the Members thereof I extend to you and your beloved ones our deep sympathy in your bereavement.

JOHN W. MCCORMACK,
*Speaker, U.S. House of Representatives.*

We are all deeply touched. Not only the country but the world stops and pauses to pay tribute to one who took the journey of life, one who took it with vision and foresight, and who took it with courage and determination. This was a man of indomitable will, a man of extraordinary courage, who always kept foremost in his mind the flag of our country and as he referred to it on past occasions, everything that our flag stands for. He has taken the journey into the great beyond, but the memory of Dwight David Eisenhower as citizen, soldier, statesman, and as a human being with great love for his fellow men will always live in the minds of men and women everywhere, particularly those who want to be free under their own law.

Again, for myself and all of my colleagues, and

for Mrs. McCormack, I extend to Mrs. Eisenhower and her loved ones my deep sympathy in their great loss and sorrow.

## Hon. Gerald R. Ford

OF MICHIGAN

Mr. Speaker, the tributes that already have been given in memory of Dwight David Eisenhower have been so heartfelt and so moving that it is difficult to say more. This was my feeling after hearing President Nixon's eulogy in the rotunda on Sunday. I feel the same way now after hearing the fine and kind words of our beloved Speaker.

There is, however, one aspect of the late President's remarkable character on which I would like to comment. It is the great interest he had and the warm confidence he showed in America's young people. As commander of allied forces in World War II, he had led hundreds of thousands of young men in battle; he knew what they could do and the dedication and sacrifice of which youth is capable, so it is no wonder that he believed in them as he did. Because he had seen firsthand the sacrifices of youth and the struggle for peace he had no doubts about the youth of the past nor those of the coming generation. He was not dismayed by the ill-advised activities of the small minority among our youth because he knew the overwhelming majority were as dedicated to America as he himself. Frequently he called the youth of the past and particularly the youth of the future the finest generations of young Americans this Nation has ever produced.

It is curious that although he was older in years than any of our other Presidents when he left the White House, General Eisenhower was younger in spirit and attitude than many men half his age. He once observed that no man is truly a man who does not have something of a boy in him, and he never lost his competitive drive, his enthusiasm, and his great capacity for friendship.

One day, after the general had laid down the burdens of the Presidency, Mrs. Ford and I visited Gettysburg with our two oldest boys, Mike and Jack. I had arranged an appointment with the general because we wanted them to have an opportunity to shake hands with and see at close range this great American, but we had not expected in this courtesy call to take but a few minutes of his time. Instead, General Eisenhower kept us for almost 2 hours, detailing for our two sons the Battle of Gettysburg and recalling for them some of the fascinating highlights of his full career. He had a way with young people, and Mike and Jack were drawn to him because he never talked down to them and because he was so clearly interested in them and their opinions. I have often thought that if General Eisenhower had not become President, we would be eulogizing him for his great service on behalf of all mankind and for his leadership as a great university president or for some other conspicuous and dedicated service in the postwar years.

As President for 8 years, he was always mindful of the younger men in Government, always attentive to their views and conscious of his duty to bring them along the path of future service. He made the once ceremonial office of the Vice Presidency into an important adjunct of the Chief Executive, and those of us who were younger Members of Congress during his days in the White House will remember how closely he watched our performance and how sympathetically he considered our problems.

In recent years it was my privilege to serve with him on the national Republican coordinating committee, and there was no man of this group more faithful in attendance or more spirited in debate than the former President. Yet he never sought to dominate our discussion. What stands out in my mind most vividly with regard to General Eisenhower's contributions were the times when we on the committee were tempted by an excess of partisan zeal to swing a haymaker at the current occupant of the White House. In such circumstances the general would gently remind the rest of us:

> Well, gentlemen, if I were sitting in that chair I wouldn't like that one bit. Remember, he is the President of the United States.

It is the true measure of General Eisenhower's greatness that he cannot easily be compared with any of our other national heroes. He had the dignity and integrity of General Washington, but his beginnings were as humble as Lincoln's. His dedication to free government was as deep as Jefferson's and his vision of a world at peace as profound as Wilson's. But an authentic hero must be unique, and Dwight David Eisenhower was, above all, himself. Those who once complained he was no politician now know that this, being true to one's own best self, is the best politics of all.

Mrs. Ford and I express our deepest sympathy to Mrs. Eisenhower and the family. America has lost one of its greatest sons and all mankind one of its finest leaders.

## Hon. Carl Albert
OF OKLAHOMA

Mr. Speaker, when word reached us on Friday last that President Eisenhower had died I think my reaction must have been similar to that of just about every man, woman, and child in this country. I felt a sense of deep personal grief. I felt that someone close to me had gone. A strong pillar which for so long had helped to support the generation to which I belonged had been pulled down.

Now that his last days on earth have ended we see Dwight David Eisenhower in the total spectrum.

We see Eisenhower, the President—Eisenhower, the general—and Eisenhower, the man.

It is difficult at this point in history to assess the Eisenhower Presidency. In my opinion, given the perspective of time, Dwight D. Eisenhower as President will be rated much higher than many contemporary historians have seen fit to rate him in his lifetime. It is true that on the domestic front there were not spectacular new developments during the Eisenhower years comparable to those of the Roosevelt-Truman period before him, and the Kennedy-Johnson period after him. Nor can it be said that there were major changes in the broad outlines of President Truman's foreign policy. However, it must be said of President Eisenhower that he presided over the longest period of peace which our people have enjoyed since the late 1930's.

As a military leader General Eisenhower earned a unique place in the history of the Nation and in the history of warfare. It may be that other generals have been greater strategists and tacticians, more capable field commanders, but in the overpowering job of organizing, consolidating, and leading diverse interests and nationalities to sure and final victory against nazism, he stands in my opinion without peer in modern history.

From D-day to V–E Day he took personal responsibility and is entitled to personal credit for the success of every major decision.

It was General Eisenhower, the soldier, who, in the face of threatening weather reports, personally made the decision to cross the channel on June 6, 1944.

It was Eisenhower, the military leader, who shaped concerted and effective action from the work of many great field commanders of highly different views and talents.

It was Eisenhower, the statesman, who could win effective cooperation from the hands of all the Allied governments. His weapons were those of persuasion, patience and firmness.

With it all he had total assurance in his own competence and in his own authority.

Surely it can be said of Dwight Eisenhower, even more surely than Byron said of Napoleon, that "he was the Cincinnatus of the West."

It is to Eisenhower, the man, that we must turn to get a glimpse of the total impact of his life and character. Born on the Texas frontier, just 6 miles from Indian territory, reared on the plains of Kansas, midst pioneer environment, into a family of little wealth but high ideals, his rise to fame and power was as sure and certain as that of Abraham Lincoln. As Walt Whitman said of Lincoln, we can say of him: "One never sees that man without feeling that he is one to become personally attached to, for his combination of purest, heartiest tenderness and native western form of manliness."

Here was a man to whom people almost instinctly turned. Though patient and unassuming, he was uniformly succeessful in accomplishing every important job he ever undertook, and very important jobs, indeed, did he undertake: supreme Allied commander in Europe in World War II, Chief of Staff, Supreme Commander and organizer of NATO, and President of the United States. He had attributes of character and experience which engendered confidence in everyone who ever saw him.

First of all, he was likable. Everybody liked Ike. He was probably the most beloved President since Washington. In the second place, he was never a petty partisan. Although he was finally convinced that he could best serve his country by running for President on the Republican ticket, he seemed to abhor traditional party politics. In his splendid essay on the American Presidency Harold J. Laski pointed out in substance that the American people disliked extreme partisanship in their Presidents. Mr. Eisenhower was probably the least partisan President since George Washington. More significant than all those facts perhaps, is the fact that the American people, and indeed the people of all the world on both sides of the Iron Curtain, had confidence in the judgment and competence of General Eisenhower. From his broad experiences in war and in NATO, as a result of his unparalleled knowledge of military and political leaders around the world, General Eisenhower had developed a vast reserve of knowledge which gave him unique qualifications to make proper decisions when questions of war and peace were hanging in the balance. This, in my opinion, caused the American people to trust him, and it caused the leaders of every nation to respect him. This, it seems to me, was a most important factor in Eisenhower's Presidency and one that historians will have to take into account in assessing his total contributions to America and to the world.

Until the day he died, President Eisenhower was beloved across his native land. We still cherish and will long cherish his memory. He still lives in the hearts of his countrymen.

We in this Chamber now salute this great and noble man who sleeps today in honor and glory beneath the historic dome of this magnificent building within which we meet.

To Mrs. Eisenhower and her son and his family, the whole Nation extends its deepest sympathy as it mourns the loss of one of its greatest and noblest sons.

## Hon. Leslie C. Arends
OF ILLINOIS

Mr. Speaker, to all the wonderful words that have been said about former President and General Dwight David Eisenhower, I shall say, Amen.

Mr. Speaker, our Nation has lost its most beloved leader. I have lost a personal friend.

Not since Gen. George Washington has America known a servant of the people, both in war and in peace, more dedicated to his country than Gen. Dwight D. Eisenhower.

His leadership, and the deep sincerity of his devotion to the cause of freedom, engendered a faith in him among men everywhere and assures him a foremost place in history. His nobility of character and sincerity of purpose—that all men are born equal and endowed by their Maker with a right to be free—endeared him to the peoples of the world and earned for him their lasting gratitude.

He exemplified the finest qualities of America and of all Americans. His contribution to a better America and a better world was not solely on the field of battle nor in the councils of government, but also in the high quality of his moral leadership.

It is not we alone who mourn his loss. The humblest and the highest everywhere, around the globe, share our national grief.

He was a constant inspiration to me and to all of us who were privileged to work with him as our President.

For 8 years during his Presidency I was privileged to work closely with him. I looked forward to the weekly leadership meetings at the White House. However grave the matters discussed, he instilled in us confidence that what needs be done could be done. He was always understanding of different points of view and always objective as to what he hoped and desired to do legislatively. He sought to do only that which was in the best interests of our great country.

I was also privileged to play golf with him many, many times. Golf is a game he loved. It is often in a game, such as golf, that one gets to know his friend or adversary under the best and worst of circumstances, when one's skill and perseverance is being tested. He was a terrific competitor. He was one who always with every shot attempted to do his best. He played the game both hard and fair. And this is how he played the game of life, always fairly, with determination and purpose. For President Eisenhower I had the greatest respect, admiration, and love. He was one of the greatest men I have ever known. We are all the richer from having known him and for having had him as our leader.

Mrs. Arends joins me in extending our most sincere sympathy to his family.

## Hon. Hale Boggs
OF LOUISIANA

Mr. Speaker, I am honored to join my colleagues—and indeed the people of the world—in mourning the loss of a great American leader, Dwight David Eisenhower.

General Eisenhower once said, "I come from the heart of America." Today as we mourn his passing, I think it is appropriate to say that it is in the heart of America that his memory will forever reside.

For during his lifetime, General Eisenhower affirmed America—he was committed to our goals—and because of his devotion to our country, he rose from humble origins to her highest office.

Bismarck once observed that genuinely great men are known by three signs—generosity in the design, humanity in the execution, moderation in success. These, I believe, were the hallmarks of General Eisenhower's long and productive life.

The natural grief we feel on the loss of this great leader is, I think, tempered by our knowledge that few men live such long and accomplished lives.

In times of peace, in times of war—in all times of great national need—Dwight Eisenhower gave fully and generously of his rich resources of leadership. For his fellow man, he defended freedom, won victory, brought peace, and established security. No one, it would seem, could presume to do more.

He was, indeed, one of the great men of modern times, and I consider it one of the high honors of my life to have known him.

To his widow and his family, I join my colleagues in expressing our sorrow on his passing and our gratitude for having shared him with us.

## Hon. Chester L. Mize
OF KANSAS

Mr. Speaker, last Friday, March 28, 1969, Dwight David Eisenhower, General of the Army, the 34th President of the United States, loving husband and gentle father, the beloved leader of his people in war and peace, passed from this life.

His death saddens free men everywhere, for he did as much as any man to protect and perpetuate human freedom. He dedicated his entire life to it.

Dwight Eisenhower carried our burdens upon his strong, broad back. He was bigger than life, and he cared. His work for freedom was done willingly—eagerly—and done exceedingly well.

We pay tribute to his accomplishments today, and our tributes are fond tributes. The affection which Americans held for Ike was genuine, and the loss we suffer with his passing is the loss of a good friend. That is the most grievous loss that anyone can sustain.

### THE YEARS IN ABILENE

Eisenhower naturally liked people and respected them. He enjoyed the company of kings, of presidents, and prime ministers, and was at home with the lions of industry. He sought no less the companionship of students, farmers, workers, schoolteachers, small businessmen, and the troops. He gained strength from all of them.

In his youth, he knew no social stratification, no class distinction. No one was his "better"—no one was held in low esteem for want of proper heritage or current position. Each man had unique opportunity to prove himself, and each man deserved every success that came to him, for he had earned it.

That is the way it was in Abilene.

Abilene, at the turn of the century, was not a place for the habitually idle or frivolous. The unpaved, rutted, dusty streets, the hand-sawn lumber sidewalks, the sparse shops, the unrelenting challenge of the farms, and the wind-whipped outdoors in the dead of winter were enough to deter the faint of heart or weak of will from settling there.

Men came to Abilene for a decent chance to earn an honorable living, and most came with little more than a few chattels. The only avenue to achievement was bone-crushing hard work.

There were few charities and virtually no government programs of relief. No one was called to Abilene by special privilege, and practically no one was ever asked to leave. Men came there for better opportunity than they had ever known, and they stayed because that opportunity came to them if they worked.

Men were respected for what they did themselves, and the lessons of Eisenhower's youth were practical lessons.

Frugality, good commonsense, hard work, respect for knowledge, and attention to the teachings of the Bible were hallmarks of human dignity in Abilene those days.

In 1890, the year Dwight Eisenhower was born, the Populist movement was strong in the Midwest. Five Members of Congress and one U.S. Senator were elected from Kansas on the Populist ticket that year. The party achieved a clear majority in the lower house of the State legislature, and courthouses were well staffed with adherents to the cause.

Prevailing adverse economic conditions could not be squared with the abundance of rich Kansas farmland, the competence of the people, and their commitment to fair dealing and hard work.

Most Kansans fervently believed that low farm prices were unconscionable, that the railroads and bankers held too much power, and that foreclosures were unsufferable and had to be regulated for the protection of small businessmen and farmers.

By the time Eisenhower was a teenager, the political movement had waned. But the code of Populist idealism—reverence for work and respect for the people who did the work—was firmly established.

Those views that had swept Kansas like a prairie fire were widely debated during Eisenhower's youth—albeit with some restraint by that time—at the Chautauquas, the meeting halls, the husking bees, and no doubt at the creamery where he worked after school.

Walter T. K. Nugent, in his study of Kansas populism, gave this description of the prevalent notions of the time:

> The Populist belief consisted of a feeling that the United States was a different kind of political society from any that had ever existed before and therefore more worth preserving than any previous one. America was not just another nation-state but an embodiment of certain ideals. It was an embodiment of democratic republicanism: a society where the people rule, where the governed consent to their governors, where the rights of life, liberty and property are protected because this very protection is the object of their own self-government. It was the embodiment, too, of economic democracy: where resources wanted only honest labor to be translated into the reality of abundance, where opportunity was equal, where the distribution of the nation's wealth was equitable. It was the antithesis of Europe. . . . It was a place, in short, where the people rule for themselves and for the protection of their natural rights.

This, then, was the heritage which Dwight David Eisenhower carried with him to the U.S. Military Academy at West Point. His roots were firmly implanted in the nourishing earth that was Abilene. His parents were representative of the finest citizens of Abilene, and he was their own true son.

He never severed those early ties. The lessons he had learned in youth helped him achieve good works throughout his distinguished career of public service.

THE YEARS IN UNIFORM

From the time he boarded the train at Abilene bound for West Point until he resigned as Allied commander in Europe to seek the Presidency, Eisenhower was throughout an Army man. During 2 intervening years as president of Columbia University, he had been restive. President Truman's call for his return to active duty had been welcome.

He was an Army man in the finest tradition, and yet his style of command was somehow distinctive. Nobody ever dared wave at any other five-star general and shout, "Hi, there, Pal," yet everybody yelled, "Hi, there, Ike." He always grinned at them and waved back. Perhaps that was the difference.

Early in his "yearling" or sophomore year at West Point, he was revolted at the humiliation he had inflicted upon an unfortunate plebe and vowed to refrain from harshly reprimanding any other victim of West Point's indoctrination system. For his 3 remaining years at the Academy, he kept the resolution.

While a junior officer, Eisenhower preferred assignments with the troops rather than prized staff positions that carried certain promotion with them.

Throughout his military career, he had an almost mystical capacity to capture the affection of his subordinates—whether a platoon or an entire army—as well as their respect and allegiance. This affection, which he returned and appreciated, was perhaps not unusual for the man whose roots were so deeply imbedded in the mainstream of humanity.

He viewed that stream as many, many individuals, working together for a common goal. He never regarded a regiment or a republic as a "mass of people," but rather as a very special selection of unique and important individuals. No wonder his troops, and later his countrymen, were so unstinting and unswerving in their loyalty to him, their affection for him.

He, of all the professionals in the U.S. Army, was the logical choice to lead that force of citizen-soldiers, that force of workers and farmers and clerks and businessmen, that was to liberate Europe from the Nazis and the Prussian officer-elite.

Ike's men knew that he was one of them, for all his training and high professional skill. They loved him—they followed him. Together they conquered.

THE YEARS IN THE WHITE HOUSE

General Eisenhower came to the White House a popular man, and he left it a popular man. Through 8 years of difficult decisions, through successes and reversals, he held the confidence of those that had selected him for their leader.

He was a brilliant administrator at the White House, just as he had been in Europe. The people wanted a respite from the agonies of war in Europe and war in Korea. They wanted quiet efficiency. He gave it to them.

Americans are like other people—they genuinely want to have confidence in their President. Dwight David Eisenhower, the 34th President of the United States, provided a lifetime of leadership which inspired confidence.

No man will ever be called upon to render higher service to America—if she lasts 10,000 years.

## Hon. L. Mendel Rivers
OF SOUTH CAROLINA

Mr. Speaker, I associate myself with the noble sentiments of our beloved Speaker of the House. I would just like to observe about this great man Eisenhower a statement of Edwin Markham:

> When he fell in whirlwind, he went down
> As when a lordly cedar, green with boughs,
> Goes down with a great shout upon the hills,
> And leaves a lonesome place against the sky.

I doubt if we can think of one in the country who found as deep a place in the hearts and the love of America. He was truly a great man, a kindly man, a humble man.

## Hon. John P. Saylor
OF PENNSYLVANIA

Mr. Speaker, no finer tribute to the memory of our fallen leader can surpass the knowledge that whatever history says of his leadership—in war and peace—the people will affectionately remember him as "Ike."

He was never the textbook picture of the tough and austere military man; nor did he surround his presidency with the trappings of power as he could have. He was at heart a sincere, gregarious, and selfless public servant; and what he was at heart shown through to the American people. They knew that the man called "Ike" could be trusted implicitly.

The aura of power surrounded the man but it did not affect his presence. The feeling of command was there and yet no one could have divined to have been ordered. What sage could define the qualities of such leadership and charisma?

The country and the world will miss the man, but he left behind a memory of something more precious than a simple recall of his legion of accomplishments; he left us with a memory of an infectious smile.

The loss of that smile, with its ability to calm our fears, renew our strength, and uplift our spirits, is the greatest loss we suffer on the passing of Dwight David Eisenhower. It was a smile that came from the heart of a man who epitomized the great American dream. There was the knowledge from Ike's smile that he trusted people, and they returned that trust without bounds. It was, according to one writer, "the smile of sincerity in an age of contrivance."

That smile is physicially gone now, but the place it holds in the hearts of the countrymen of Dwight David Eisenhower can never be replaced.

## Hon. Chalmers P. Wylie
OF OHIO

Mr. Speaker, as we today pay honor to a great American, I welcome the opportunity to record a personal experience with Gen. Dwight David

Eisenhower. In it we find further evidence of those great qualities which made him beloved as a leader in war as in peace.

This incident took place on March 23, 1945. The 30th Infantry Division, of which I was a member, was moving into position in preparation for a night attack across the Rhine River at Wessel, Germany. We had spent many hours practicing with assault crossings of the Maas River in Holland. We knew what we were to do. But the Rhine River was wider and the attack was to be at night under cover of darkness. In practice no one was trying to keep us from landing. Still assault boats had capsized and in one instance the occupants had drowned. So, we approached our task afraid that we might never see loved ones again. Then, the paratroopers started dropping behind enemy lines in great numbers from the sky. We sensed their mission was much more dangerous than ours but would certainly increase our chances of reaching the other side. Sporadic shell fire made us ill at ease and attested to the presence of the enemy and his intention to see that our mission failed. While we were there, marching gloomily in combat column, a staff car approached and stopped beside where I was walking. General Eisenhower stepped out. For a moment, I froze with apprehension. Then, I made a poor attempt to salute, which seemed the thing to do. The general extended his hand to shake mine, flashed his warm smile, and said—I think, "Hi soldier," although in the dramatics of the moment I cannot now be certain of his exact words. The general walked up and down the column shaking hands and encouraging his troops. He came, too, I am sure, to get a better look at the tactical situation. I remember distinctly saying to a buddy, "He shouldn't be here. Doesn't he know he is liable to be killed?" General Eisenhower was up with the troops risking his life but the inspiration his presence gave cannot be imagined. Later, I was to receive the Silver Star because our battalion commander, Lt. Col. Ernest Frankland, thought I performed my small part of that battle with extraordinary heroism. As I reflect, I am not inclined to acts which would warrant any such honor. If I deserve it, General Eisenhower deserved, at least, some of the credit. Two years ago many of us as freshman Congressmen visited with President Eisenhower at Camp David. We talked briefly about the Rhine River crossing.

Our Nation is sad because of the death of our great general and President. He was loved for his courage, warmth, and understanding. Yes; we are saddened, as a nation by his passing. Yet in his death, as in his life, we are caused to reflect on the heritage of our great country, the outstanding contributions of the great Dwight David Eisenhower and the necessity just now, as perhaps never before, for an extra effort to preserve our freedoms.

## Hon. Neal Smith

OF IOWA

Mr. Speaker, for the past several decades, it seems that fame and notoriety has gone principally to those who accumulate great material wealth, commit some hideous crime, or have a reputation for abusing power or do the unusual. Many millions of Americans are honest and have a great desire to see justice but few become famous for having those attributes. General Eisenhower was one of those few. The loss of a man with worldwide fame for such characteristics is a great loss and the whole Nation and world suffers from such loss.

As Dwight David Eisenhower sleeps in the rotunda a few steps from here, the Nation mourns the loss of a truly great American, and I join those who extend their condolences to his family.

## Hon. Larry Winn, Jr.

OF KANSAS

Mr. Speaker, all the world is saddened by the death of Gen. Dwight David Eisenhower, a truly great yet humble man. The former President—who preferred to be called general after his retirement—probably will not go down in history as a politician's President, but rather as a true statesman, highly respected by the leaders of all nations of the world.

As young Kansas Congressman, I was fortunate enough to meet personally with this great man, who grew up on the western prairie of Kansas, at his peaceful Gettysburg farm. His knowledge of both national and international affairs proved to be most helpful to me as a new Congressman.

Men of all political philosophies sought his counsel and guidance on matters of importance. And all succeeding Presidents have at one time or another turned to him for help.

To the end, this uncommon man was characterized by uncommon strength.

Mr. Speaker, at the Capitol today are 50 Kansas schoolchildren who are here to pay tribute to Dwight D. Eisenhower. They have brought with them a beautiful box of long-stemmed wheat from the great State of Kansas, as a symbol of their love for our wonderful former President. They are here in person to add this wheat to the many beautiful flowers covering the rotunda of this Capitol.

One of the sponsors of this Kansas group has written a poem which I should like to read to this distinguished body today. This poem was written by Barbara Hanna Gray and endorsed by the 50 schoolchildren from Kansas.

This poem reads as follows:

WHEAT: IN MEMORY OF DWIGHT DAVID EISENHOWER

(By Barbara Hanna Gray)

A shock of wheat—Ripened in the sun of a Kansas prairie, tendered gently there from small green sprout until tall and golden—unbent by the winds that blow hard.
A shock of wheat—Filled with the grain of a Kansas youth, harvested by God to feed His flocks with the bread of his life—unbent by the winds that blow hard.
A shock of wheat—Having borne its fruit must die to live anew, returning now to the promised land of everlasting life—unbent by the winds that blow hard.

## Hon. Ed Edmondson

OF OKLAHOMA

Mr. Speaker, I brought my family to the Nation's Capital in January of 1953, at the beginning of the Eisenhower-Nixon administration.

As a freshman in the 83d Congress, I became acquainted for the first time with the warm, friendly, and genuine American who was to lead our country through most of the 1950's.

The impression I then received—of a man with a deep love for our country and a great respect for all his fellow citizens—was to continue for the 17 years which followed.

The opportunity to know the man and to appreciate his great character was one of the real treasures of my own years of public service.

Mr. Speaker, the Nation has lost one of its finest sons in the death of our beloved former President, Dwight David Eisenhower.

General Eisenhower was a soldier-patriot in the great American tradition—a worthy successor to George Washington and Andrew Jackson.

As commander of the Allied forces who liberated Europe from the tyranny of Nazi armed conquest, he was a crusader for freedom in one of history's most trying challenges to freedom.

Eisenhower leadership for freedom continued in the tumultuous years which followed World War II, as he united the NATO powers to halt the westward drive of another tyranny—that of Soviet communism lead by Stalin.

As President of the United States during the cold war years of the 1950's, Dwight Eisenhower continued to lead the free world in the quest for both freedom and peace.

As the acknowledged leader of free nations throughout the 1950's, President Eisenhower pledged the terrible power of the atom to the search for peace, in an address to the United Nations which inspired all the world.

When he completed his second term as President, he continued to serve his country, providing wise counsel and assistance to the three Presidents who have followed him—regardless of party affiliation.

A man who loved and served his country well, a man who was above partisan politics on the major questions of peace and war at all times, a man who was loved and respected by all Americans—that was Dwight David Eisenhower.

America has lost a great champion and a great leader. I join my colleagues in mourning our great loss.

## Hon. Ogden R. Reid

OF NEW YORK

Mr. Speaker, in the death of General Eisenhower America has lost our most widely loved public figure. General Eisenhower had very special qualities of humility, sincerity, spiritual conviction, and great human warmth. All of these animated his long service to his country.

I remember on more than one occasion his turning to friends and saying, "Well, the really educated member of the family is Milton." He always thought of the other person first, such as when he knew almost a year ago that his chances for the future were perhaps not the brightest. Then, he looked death in the face and he found it preferable. He said to a friend:

> I have a pretty good idea as to what my chances are. I would like to go on living for as long as I can be useful to somebody, even though I know I am not going to set the world on fire at my age. But I had just as soon the end came now as to go on living. I feel I will be a burden to my family and tie up all those doctors who could be taking care of guys with a full life ahead of them.

Mr. Speaker, I think this deep and ingrained humility was uniquely characteristic of General Eisenhower.

Few will ever forget his broad smile and his capacity to inspire confidence and accomplishment—among both men and nations—whether it was before Normandy or during Europe's troubled days while NATO was being formed or in his dramatic "open skies" proposal at the Geneva summit, which no other American could have put forward with the same effectiveness. Indeed, his smile was capable of lighting up a nation here or overseas, as the great throngs that turned out to greet him illustrated so vividly. We felt better when we saw that smile—it was unique—it was a personal one, it was a humble one, and it called forth our deepest trust.

I also remember the period during the late 1940's and early 1950's when General Eisenhower had several opportunities to consider the nomination for the Presidency. Perhaps no other American in public life turned down such clear offers for the presidential nomination as forthrightly as he did.

I think the point that finally motivated him to accept the Republican nomination was his concern over the war in Korea and his desire to work for peace. He could not have forgiven himself had he sacrificed an opportunity to save the lives of young men and to truly serve the people of the country he so deeply loved; but it was not in his nature to seek the power of the Presidency.

Mr. Speaker, General Eisenhower certainly was one of the most successful commanders of a multinational alliance. He revitalized the Republican Party and thereby strengthened the two-party system. His character and ability certainly put to rest many thoughts of isolationism of prewar America.

He was responsible for many progressive steps to strengthen our domestic policies, whether they involved the establishment of the Department of Health, Education, and Welfare or increase in social security. Neither will America forget that it was President Eisenhower who succeeded in passing the first civil rights bill since Reconstruction and warned of the dangers of the military-industrial complex.

All remember, I believe, his achievement in bringing peace to Korea. Surely history will record the unifying leadership he brought to America in the Presidency following the divisive years of war overseas.

But his overriding concern in the Presidency was to work for a world of universal peace with justice. His unqualified support of the U.N. was fundamental. His leadership in the "atoms-for-peace" program, in the Alliance for Progress, in progress toward a nonproliferation treaty, and for a détenté with the Soviet Union remains basic to the future.

I was at the White House one day when the subject of nuclear weapons was raised. He looked out the window and said very simply that he was opposed to their use, and that there would be no such thing as the use of one tactical nuclear weapon, for any such action would inevitably invite a full nuclear exchange.

Certainly, Mr. Speaker, former President Eisenhower had a real spiritual quality, character and judgment, steadiness under pressure, and a complete honesty and sincerity about him. He inspired men to work together; he had total disdain for personal public comment; he was contemptuous of narrow partisan motives, and more than once rejected temporary political gain for the greater good of our country. Such a man brought stature and trust to the White House. He represented Americans, perhaps, more faithfully than any in our time. Certainly, he was loved and trusted both overseas and here. In a unique way his life will stand as an inspiration for all those who believe in character in government.

He was a great human being, and he will be

judged kindly by future historians, not only for his positive accomplishments but indeed for those decisions which did not make the headlines, such as his refusal to be stampeded into any commitment to Vietnam.

His life is a testament to public service, and of the highest traditions of America, and General Eisenhower now clearly belongs to the ages.

Mr. Speaker, I wish to join with all of the Members of the House in expressing our grief upon the passing of General Eisenhower, and I wish to express our deepest sympathy, that of Mrs. Reid and my mother, Helen Rogers Reid, to Mrs. Eisenhower, John Eisenhower, and all members of the family.

## Hon. Roman C. Pucinski
OF ILLINOIS

Mr. Speaker, America today mourns the loss of one of her most noble sons. I deem it a great privilege to join with the Speaker and others in paying tribute to the memory of Dwight David Eisenhower.

Mr. Speaker, I like to think of Dwight D. Eisenhower in terms of three plateaus: first, as a military leader, he was without a peer. His greatest strength was his ability to bring people together. It was his genius as an organizer, as a persuader, as a mediator, and as a military tactician that helped put together the fantastic military machine that frustrated the designs of the Axis Powers upon the freedom of this country and the rest of the world.

I do not believe that even at this day we realize the enormity of his accomplishments in pulling together divergent military views, in pulling together divergent military concepts, different equipment, different ideas, and welding them into one successful effort which brought victory and freedom to the world.

I believe that Dwight Eisenhower today deserves to be called the greatest military genius of our time.

Second, as President of the United States he had abiding faith in the rugged spirit of American individualism. Many of his critics have erroneously interpreted his stubborn refusal to plunge Government controls into every facet of our American life as a record of inaction. President Eisenhower in my judgment reflected the true spirit of Thomas Jefferson. He had a social consciousness. He realized things had to be done, and he wanted to move forward, but he also realized that the dignity of an individual is supreme in a free nation, and he wanted to let the individual do as much for himself as humanly possible.

President Eisenhower gave the country a great record to build on. In the ensuing years his successors have built upon that record. There is no question but that Mr. Eisenhower has made great contributions as President of this country.

Finally, Mr. Speaker, I believe his third great achievement was as an American in his farewell address when he warned the Nation against the military-industrial complex. Here was a man who had had occasion to observe first-handedly as a military leader and as the President of the United States the inherent dangers of permitting that sort of a combination to get out of hand. The enormity of his warning is best exemplified as we look today and see that some 200 American corporations have more than $30 billion worth of Government contracts. The warning given us by President Eisenhower cannot go unheeded.

Mr. Speaker, I am not at all surprised that the political leaders of my own party exerted every effort to induce and persuade General Eisenhower to run on the Democratic ticket. Mr. Eisenhower would have been a great President on either party's ticket.

Nor am I at all surprised to learn that President Truman had designated him as his heir apparent, because we all have recognized Mr. Eisenhower's genius and his great dedication and his abiding faith in America.

Mr. Speaker, in paying tribute today to Dwight Eisenhower I would say that he gave majesty and nobility to the cause of public service. His conduct in public affairs leaves all of us in public office with a legacy we can proudly emulate.

Mr. Speaker, Mrs. Pucinski joins me in extending and expressing our deepest sympathy to Mrs. Eisenhower, the entire Eisenhower family, and, yes, to all Americans who today mourn his passing.

## Hon. Elford A. Cederberg

OF MICHIGAN

Mr. Speaker, I am honored to join my colleagues today in paying respect to the memory of General Eisenhower. Many of us in this body had the honor of serving under his command in Europe during World War II, and I recall those days as well. I was division headquaters company commander of the 83d Division.

The first time I saw the general was shortly after the invasion when he visited our division headquarters and on several occasions after that he visited our division.

As a junior officer I had the privilege of being in the division war room when he was conferring with the senior officers of the division. At no time did he ever fail to inquire about the troops of the division. He always was concerned about their welfare—were they getting enough food, were they getting the proper clothes. This was a man who was not only a great general but also a great humanitarian.

Then shortly after the war, many of us had the honor of entering into public service in the Congress at the same time he became President of the United States. We still have a number here on both sides of the aisle who came in as Members of the 83d Congress in 1953. We can recall our visits with him during those years. He understood the role of the Congress and respected it.

Mr. Speaker, I think that when history writes the record of General Eisenhower, that record is going to be one of great achievement both in war and in peace. He was a man who really cherished freedom—and a man who hated war.

He never hesitated to take such action as was necessary to preserve our Nation. The world has lost a great leader but his inspiration will live on forever.

Mrs. Cederberg and I extend our deepest sympathy to the Eisenhower family.

## Hon. Ken Hechler

OF WEST VIRGINIA

Mr. Speaker, the gentleman from Michigan (Mr. CEDERBERG), the gentleman from Ohio (Mr. WYLIE), and others have called attention to the large number of Members of Congress who served under General Eisenhower when he was commander of the European theater of operations during World War II.

The qualities of General Eisenhower's leadership as commander were manifest in the planning and launching of the great invasion of Normandy as well as in many other ways.

I would like to call attention to something that General Eisenhower wrote in "Crusade in Europe" and what he described as "one of my happy moments of the war." When he received the news of the first crossing of the Rhine at Remagen, Germany, General Eisenhower capitalized on this great event which materially shortened the war in Europe. He wrote this about the Remagen Bridge capture:

> This news was reported to Bradley. It happened that a SHAEF staff officer was in Bradley's headquarters when the news arrived, and a discussion at once took place as to the amount of force that should be pushed across the bridge. If the bridgehead force was too small it would be destroyed through a quick concentration of German strength on the east side of the river. On the other hand, Bradley realized that if he threw a large force across he might interfere with further development of my basic plan. Bradley instantly telephoned me.
>
> I was at dinner in my Reims headquarters with the corps and division commanders of the American airborne forces when Bradley's call came through. When he reported that we had a permanent bridge across the Rhine I could scarcely believe my ears. He and I had frequently discussed such a development as a remote possibility but never as a well-founded hope.
>
> I fairly shouted into the telephone: "How much have you got in that vicinity that you can throw across the river?"
>
> He said, "I have more than four divisions but I called you to make sure that pushing them over would not interfere with your plans."
>
> I replied, "Well, Brad, we expected to have that many divisions tied up around Cologne and now those are free. Go ahead and shove over at least five divisions instantly, and anything else that is necessary to make certain of our hold."
>
> His answer came over the phone with a distinct tone of glee: "That's exactly what I wanted to do but the question had been raised here about conflict with your plans, and I wanted to check with you."
>
> That was one of my happy moments of the war. Broad success in war is usually foreseen by days or weeks, with the result that when it actually arrives higher commanders and staffs have discounted it and are immersed in plans for the future. This was completely unforeseen. We were across the Rhine, on a permanent bridge; the traditional defensive barrier to the heart of Germany was pierced. The

final defeat of the enemy, which we had long calculated would be accomplished in the spring and summer campaigning of 1945, was suddenly now in our minds, just around the corner.

My guests at the dinner table were infected by my enthusiasm. Among them were veterans of successful aerial jumps against the enemy and of hard fighting in every kind of situation. They were unanimous in their happy predictions of an early end to the war. I am sure that from that moment every one of them went into battle with the élan that comes from the joyous certainty of smashing victory.

Ten years after that event, President Eisenhower assembled at the White House the heroes of that event and he told them on March 7, 1955:

Gentlemen, I have asked you to come here this morning because you know old soldiers' minds are bound to turn back once in a while to dramatic events of war—particularly of the kind that took place at the Remagen bridgehead.

Now, of course, that was not the biggest battle that ever was, but for me it always typified one thing: the dash, the ingenuity, the readiness at the first opportunity that characterizes the American soldier.

That was one of the qualities of leadership of General Eisenhower when he commanded our troops in Europe.

I would like to quote also briefly from the very last words in General Eisenhower's book "Crusade in Europe," words that mean a great deal in terms of his basic philosophy:

We believe individual liberty, rooted in human dignity, is man's greatest treasure.

If the men and women of America face this issue as squarely and bravely as their soldiers faced the terrors of battle in World War II, we would have no fear of the outcome. If they will unite themselves as firmly as they did when they provided, with their allies in Europe, the mightiest fighting force of all time, there is no temporal power that can dare challenge them. If they can retain the moral integrity, the clarity of comprehension, and the readiness to sacrifice that finally crushed the Axis, then the Free World will live and prosper, and all peoples eventually will reach a level of culture, contentment, and security that has never before been achieved.

That was Dwight D. Eisenhower.

## Hon. Robert H. Michel

OF ILLINOIS

Mr. Speaker, it was my good fortune also to serve under the leadership of General Eisenhower, both militarily and in civilian life; first as an infantryman from Omaha Beach to the Ruhr River in Germany during World War II and subsequently in Congress during his Presidency.

Among the exchanges of correspondence I have had with General Eisenhower, the first was a letter dating back nearly 20 years, which I have prized very much, for it was written at a time when there was considerable talk of his running for President while serving as president of Columbia University.

President Nixon in his eulogy made several references to Dwight Eisenhower's coming from the "heart of America" and the subject of my first exchange of letters with General Eisenhower had to do with my hope in any political ambitions he might have that he would never forget his midwest heritage.

While his first letter to me dated November 16, 1949, said in part:

So far as any personal politics may be concerned . . . I have not changed my mind in the slightest degree.

We are all so grateful and so much better off for his having reassessed the situation and changed his mind.

His 8-year administration was indeed a period of calm and tranquillity accompanied by significant progress in all levels of national life. We long and yearn for similar days in the new administration.

Of all the millions of words written about General Eisenhower I believe the true measure of the man was captured as well as anything I have seen by Mr. Hugh Sidey, writing in the August 17, 1968, edition of Life Magazine. He said:

There are even those who dare to suggest that his soothing spirit, the innate goodness of the man himself, did more to lift up the hearts of Americans and hold them together in a reasonable state of public happiness than many of the social reforms that have been propounded since.

Mr. Speaker, I ask unanimous consent that the full text of the letter from Dwight Eisenhower, referred to before, and Mr. Hugh Sidey's article be included with my remarks at this point in the Record.

I extend our profound sympathy to Mrs. Eisenhower and all the members of the family whom he loved so much as he always loved his country.

The letter and article are as follows:

COLUMBIA UNIVERSITY,
*New York, N.Y., November 16, 1949.*

Hon. ROBERT H. MICHEL,
*Representative in Congress,*
*Peoria, Ill.*

DEAR MR. MICHEL: It is always nice to hear from an old soldier, particularly one who served in the Infantry, my old arm. Additionally, of course, I must thank you for the very great compliments paid me in your letter of the 12th.

While it is obviously necessary that, so long as I am connected with Columbia University, I be officially classed as an "Easterner," it is equally true that the roots of my family and my life are buried too deep in the West for me to ever think of myself as anything but a mid-Westerner.

I assure you, though, that these facts have no implication of any kind in the political world—at least so far as any personal politics may be concerned. I have earnestly and honestly tried to make my own position clear about these matters, and I assure you I have not changed my mind in the slightest degree.

With best wishes to a former comrade of ETO.

Sincerely,

DWIGHT D. EISENHOWER.

---

THE PRESIDENCY—THE SMILE OF SINCERITY IN AN AGE OF CONTRIVANCE

(By Hugh Sidey)

Dwight Eisenhower came into the living rooms of 30 million Americans the other night, and he was old and bald and he used a TelePrompTer and still flubbed a few of his lines, but there was more power in his 10-minute appeal than in any of the presidential political oratory of the past 12 months. And it may be that the effort to make his talk brought on the heart attack that has him seriously ill.

It has been one of those mysteries of national life why all the would-be Presidents (and President) who have been frantically searching for some formula to catapult them to the heights of popularity have failed to study the example of Eisenhower. Perhaps in this age of contrivance it is too simple to be believed—decency, sincerity and honesty. It shines out of Ike like a beacon, and it should give those in the political business some pause. Because it illustrates anew that all the programs espoused and the bills passed and the billions spent are only a part of this thing of being President and maybe even the lesser part in a time of dispirited affluence.

It should be of some significance that while almost everybody else was engaged in a season of shifting views, cloaked opinions, denials of internal trouble and even espousal of the right of a government to lie to its people, the steady virtue of Eisenhower raised him to a new pedestal while all those others fell lower. He was polled the most admired man in the nation last year and probably ranks as high today. There is some kind of hunger there. Even among the unwashed and on the campus, the cry is for candor and compassion, which is the same thing.

Lyndon Johnson has used an inordinate amount of his time and energy raising monuments to his own greatness, and all the while his esteem has slipped. Ike's self-promotion runs at such a low voltage as to be undiscernible. He still acts a little embarrassed at new honors. He still wonders why people care—and that only intensifies the phenomenon. A while back in his modest office on the corner of the Gettysburg College campus he marveled at this public. He didn't have an unusually big nose or extraordinary ears or any other physical features that made him easily identifiable, he explained. Yet, there he had been in New York in the back of an unmarked limousine, almost out of sight, and as he drove down the street, "the darndest thing happened. People leaned out and yelled, 'Hello, Ike.' How did they know who I was?"

While all the candidates from Reagan to McCarthy diagnosed in detail the national ailments, Ike maintained a hearty belief that it was a fever, and the body was fundamentally sound. He could beat any of them in a runoff. While the scowl has become the symbol of this season's stump (with the exception of Hubert Humphrey), there has been that enduring smile of Eisenhower's that reached more men's hearts than social security. There is the feeling from Ike that he trusts people and they return it in spades. He has confessed that it would be nice sometime to take Mamie and go to the Metropolitan Museum and "just drift through it without having to shake hands or sign an autograph." But, says Ike, with a chuckle, whenever he brings up that complaint (one of the few anybody has heard him make about his lot in life), Mamie turns to him and says, "How would you like it if they all disliked you?"

In these days of rebellion against order, Ike has been more than ever conscious of the example he must set, which is another of those unmeasurable qualities that go into leadership and has been missing on occasion with the men now in the ring. Eisenhower confesses a liking for horses and horse racing, and yet he has scrupulously limited himself to one appearance at the track each year, simply because he believes that that is enough for a man who is held in the public gaze.

There are a lot of people who still feel that Ike never really understood his job of being President. Yet today his commonsense observations about the Presidency are more cogent than a lot of the other talk. He, for instance, does not like the disuse of the Cabinet and the National Security Council in the executive branch and the resulting deep personalization of the Presidency. "You need," he says, "bitterly debated advice and conflicting considerations." The frantic pace of today's Presidency has also disturbed him. He played golf, yet, but the business was never out of his mind. A President has got to have time to think about his main problems. There are a growing number of presidential observers who endorse that need.

He feels that the heads of the great Federal departments, should have more farreaching power in setting up their staffs. He feels that the momentum of the big bureaucracies tends to sweep the Cabinet officers right along with them, and these men are often almost powerless to combat the system which grows bigger when it is obvious that in some ways it should grow smaller. This is the theme song now of all the candidates.

So far the historians have not ranked Eisenhower very high in the presidential legend. But there is growing conviction that the measure of the man himself may be more of a factor in the national life than anyone has been willing to admit before. Ike has not been referred to as a top-drawer expediter, one who knew the machinery of government, but there are hints that the traditional assessment of those qualities may be outdated and inaccurate. The eight years of relative world calm under Ike, achieved without losing any territory or much prestige, have taken on new importance. There are even those who dare suggest that his soothing spirit, the innate goodness of the man himself, did more to lift up the hearts of Americans and hold them together in a reasonable state of public happiness than many of the social reforms that have been propounded since.

## Hon. Byron G. Rogers

OF COLORADO

Mr. Speaker, I appreciate the distinguished Speaker yielding to me so I may join with other Members in mourning the passing of our late President and general, Dwight David Eisenhower.

This is a significant day in which to pay tribute to a man who had his roots in my congressional district. In fact, he was married to Mamie in Denver, Colo., and after that Denver was his second home. Throughout the years before he became prominent as a forthright leader of the Nation, he spent many years and days in the city and county of Denver. It was during that period of time that those he came in contact with learned to know and love him. They appreciated the fact that he had the spirit and the fairness and the understanding that are not as well attributed to all men as they were to Ike.

After he became famous, so to speak, when he led our armies in Western Europe to victory and then he returned to the United States, he came back to Denver, Colo. Once again, General Eisenhower enjoyed the respect and honor and leadership that he so well deserves.

We in Denver express our thoughts this moment to the family and mourn the loss of his leadership. I express my sympathy to Mrs. Eisenhower and the family. I know his death is a great loss to the Nation, and particularly it is a great loss to the people of my district.

## Hon. Don H. Clausen

OF CALIFORNIA

Mr. Speaker, I express my gratitude to the Speaker for yielding to me, and also for taking the lead in expressing eulogies and giving us the opportunity to express our personal eulogies for our former President, Dwight David Eisenhower.

Dwight David Eisenhower, 34th President of the United States and General of the Armies, is dead, and like millions of Americans and people throughout the world, I deeply mourn his passing.

Whenever I think of President Eisenhower, the words "warm" and "human" immediately come to my mind. Will Americans ever forget that big grin—the smile, known around the world, which genuinely reflected his warm personality.

When I first met this great, dedicated, and devoted American, I was overwhelmed by his down-to-earth sincerity. Being in his presence gave me renewed confidence and faith in the goodness of unselfish public service. Having met him in person, one soon realized that he had just met greatness.

Now America has lost its most distinguished elder statesman and the world has lost one of the truly great men of the 20th century.

Dwight Eisenhower was a professional, career soldier who spoke of war as "this damnable thing." He led a great military crusade that saved Western Europe and the free world from tyranny, yet warned of the creation of a "military-industrial complex" in America.

President Eisenhower always spoke of the "greatness of America" and the "strength of the American people." He was not a flamboyant man or a great wit, but he was genuinely liked—even by his political and philosophical opponents.

Dwight Eisenhower has been called a national hero, a leader in war, a crusader for peace—and it is true; he was all of these things. But more important, he was a humble man who was called to greatness by those who recognized in him that rare quality of leadership that makes some men stand taller than others.

As a military figure, he was not a great authoritarian, or a disciplinarian. Instead, he inspired men by his example and by his logic. He had a unique ability for drawing people together in a common cause and welding them into the most awesome and proficient military armada ever assembled.

As our President, he brought to this great Nation something it desperately needed—unity, purpose, and a sense of direction. Whether they voted for him or not, most Americans were proud of Dwight Eisenhower and felt a measure of security while he was in the White House.

In the twilight of life, "Ike" displayed the same courage and tenacity that he had reflected on the battlefield and in the quiet counsels of the Presidency. I have never known a man to survive seven heart attacks and so many other medical complications and still maintain that keen insight into the future or that illuminating awareness of history that "Ike" held to the end.

In my judgment, leadership is the ability to influence human behavior, and it was for this reason, I believe, that people trusted "Ike." They trusted him with the lives of their sons in war, and with their own destinies as our President.

Though he was trained as a soldier, "Ike" was truly a man of peace.

Dwight David Eisenhower will go down in history as a humble man who responded to the call of his country in its time of greatest need—not once or twice, but whenever the need arose.

## Hon. Andrew Jacobs, Jr.

OF INDIANA

Mr. Speaker, General Eisenhower helped us win a war that could not be avoided and kept us out of several that could. In this dangerous world, no public service could be more beneficial nor earn higher marks in history. General Eisenhower has earned his greatness.

## Hon. Orval Hansen

OF IDAHO

Mr. Speaker, I thank the distinguished Speaker for yielding to me.

The people of Idaho join with the millions of Americans across this land and, indeed, the millions in other lands in mourning the death of a great leader, Dwight David Eisenhower, and in paying tribute to his memory.

I shall never forget the first time I met General Eisenhower. It was at the convention in Chicago in 1952, a short time before he was nominated to be President of the United States. I had the feeling at the time that I was meeting one of the great men of history. General Eisenhower had completed a career of distinguished service to his country as a soldier. He was about to enter upon the period of his greatest service to our country as one of its most beloved statesmen. On the occasion of this first meeting, General Eisenhower's personal warmth, his infectious smile, and the twinkle in his eye made a profound impression on me.

The pleasure of my first meeting with General Eisenhower was matched by the pleasure of meeting Mrs. Eisenhower on the same occasion. Her friendliness, her warmth, and great charm are among the qualities that have marked Mrs. Eisenhower as one of the truly great ladies of American history.

President Eisenhower honored the people of the State of Idaho by paying us a visit in 1962, when he was accorded a welcome that reflected the depth of the love and respect that the people of Idaho bear for him.

General Eisenhower was a distinguished soldier and military leader, but was also passionately devoted to the cause of peace. He dedicated all of the energy and strength he could command to the task of building an enduring world peace.

General Eisenhower's life exemplified the best in America. Because of him, all Americans stand a bit taller. All of us feel prouder of ourselves and of our country. He had a deep belief in the American dream, a faith in God and in the future of our country.

He was a leader of great strength and toughness. Yet, he was kind, gentle, compassionate, and understanding.

The high principles and purposes that motivated General Eisenhower are reflected in his speech to the men and women of the Allied Expeditionary Force at the end of his great crusade in Europe. I quote from the closing sentences of his address:

Each of the fallen died as a member of the team to which you belong, bound together by a common love of liberty and a refusal to submit to enslavement. No monument of stone, no memorial of whatever magnitude could so well express our respect and veneration for their sacrifice as would perpetuation of the spirit of comradeship in which they died. As we celebrate victory in Europe, let us remind ourselves that our common problems of the immediate and distant future can be best solved in the same conceptions of cooperation and devotion to the cause of human freedom as have made this Expeditionary Force such a mighty engine of righteous destruction. Let us have no part in the profitless quarrels in which other men will inevitably engage as to what country, what service, won the European war.

Every man, every woman of every nation here represented has served according to his or her ability, and the efforts of each have contributed to the outcome. This we shall remember—and in doing so we shall be revering each honored grave and be sending comfort to the loved ones of comrades who could not live to see this day.

Mr. Speaker, we have lost a great leader. But as we face the challenge of the future to carry on the work which was so effectively advanced by Dwight David Eisenhower during his lifetime we can, if we will, continue to draw strength, inspiration, and guidance from the life and service of this dedicated American. We can best honor his memory by learning and applying in our own public service the great lessons he has taught us.

## Hon. Tom Bevill

OF ALABAMA

Mr. Speaker, I was deeply saddened by the death of that great American, former President Dwight David Eisenhower. I join all Americans and citizens throughout the world in extending my deepest sympathy to the Eisenhower family.

The light of liberty burns brighter and the strength of our Nation is far more secure today because we were fortunate enough to have had the services of General Eisenhower.

There are no words adequate to express the love and admiration held in the hearts of all Americans for the general. Many of us were privileged to serve under General Eisenhower in the European theater during World War II.

Occasionally an individual comes along who possesses a rare quality of leadership, an insight into life, and the needs and aspirations of our people. General Eisenhower was such a man.

An individual destined to take his place as one of the great military leaders of all times, General Eisenhower was a man of peace, an individual destined to become one of his country's greatest Presidents, General Eisenhower knew when to stand strong and firm for freedom.

He brought to public life a spirit of American know-how and dedicatoin unexcelled in our generation.

A man of the people, General Eisenhower was raised in the simple, dignified tradition which molded the life of another great American, Abraham Lincoln. He lived close to the earth, and like Lincoln, received strength from it.

From the beginning, General Eisenhower was destined to carry on his shoulders the responsibilities of a growing, thriving, sometimes troubled nation. And he never shirked these responsibilities.

Throughout his illustrious career, General Eisenhower maintained the bearing of a patient, persistant worker for every American. Indeed, he leaves behind a legacy of service to his country which will enrich the lives of generations to come.

Perhaps no greater tribute can be paid to General Eisenhower than to say that "Ike" will be missed by those who love freedom and believe in the dignity of man.

## Hon. Sherman P. Lloyd

OF UTAH

Mr. Speaker, in behalf of the citizens of my Second Congressional District in Utah, I rise to pay tribute to one of the greatest of all Americans.

Dwight Eisenhower represented the American ideal. As someone has said over this weekend, he was the kind of man the American father wants his son to grow up to be.

Except for the far left or pretentiously sophisticated writers, who find something "square" about traditional virtues, the tributes to this authentic American hero have expressed the heart of America, as President Nixon said yesterday, that General Eisenhower himself represented the heart of America.

I was privileged to visit with our former President on two occasions in 1967. The first with the

90th Club of Republican freshmen. He greeted us at his home in Gettysburg from where we went to a quiet picnic grove adjacent to the canyon stream. There the general sat down with us and ate a steak and baked bean lunch from a paper plate, showing his personal consideration for our welfare by his every move and expression, and then we had the rare privilege of listening to him answering our questions for nearly an hour. I was struck by the clarity of his mind and by the clarity of his words and by his intellectual articulation of basic knowledge and basic truth.

Later with a Republican task force on Western alliances, we visited with him in his office on the campus at Gettysburg College. Around luncheon tables, he discussed with us his convictions in the field of foreign relations. Again I was struck by his modesty, the simplicity of his movements, the clarity and force of his expressions, and his constant consideration for those of us around him.

It is said that he was not a politician. However, he believed and expressed something very basic which the Members of this Congress and the American people should remember. He said that what was best for this country would prove to be the best politics. So, in a day when some use the word "statesman" in derision and glorify political cleverness, the constancy and the patriotism of Dwight David Eisenhower stands out monumentally.

It was our good fortune as Americans, that Dwight Eisenhower was granted the years to complete his work and he passes to eternal glory with the love, the gratitude, the reverence, and the eternal respect of the American people.

Sentiments of Utahans are expressed in editorials from the Salt Lake Tribune and the Deseret News, which follow:

[From the Deseret News, Salt Lake City, Utah, Mar. 28, 1969]

WHY AMERICANS WILL ALWAYS LIKE IKE

As a sorrowing nation mourns the passing of one of its greatest and most beloved leaders, there is little to be said about Dwight David Eisenhower that has not only been said before but repeated frequently.

From his early years as a Kansas farm boy to his rise from an obscure lieutenant to become supreme commander of the Allied forces that smashed Hitler's "fortress Europe," from his stint as President of Columbia University to his accomplishments as the first Republican President of the United States in 20 years, and his public services after leaving the White House, the life of Ike Eisenhower has been thoroughly chronicled as have few others.

No words can add or detract from his accomplishments, or the honors bestowed upon him all over the world. Nor can words enhance the love or ease the sadness that his countrymen feel at his demise.

As Americans reflect upon the life and works of this remarkable soldier, statesman, and leader, they would do well to ask why he won not only the admiration but also the respect of so many people in all walks of life.

Was it because Dwight D. Eisenhower was a fatherly figure to the entire country—firm but kind? Was it because he had the "common touch," being a man of simple tastes? Was it because he genuinely liked people—and they responded in kind? Was it because of his undeniable sincerity as a man of peace? Was it his clear-cut integrity?

No doubt these and many other well known aspects of Dwight Eisenhower's personality help explain his amazingly intense, widespread and enduring popularity.

But there is one facet of his character that has been generally neglected, but which speaks volumes about the man. It was a facet that was touched on in a thumbnail sketch written two years ago by Bryce N. Harlow, one of Eisenhower's closest aides during his eight years in the White House who observed:

"Take the attributes you consider the most admirable in the people you know, put them in a mixer, and you'll come up with the Eisenhower blend.

"He is vitality and power and force—yet he is profoundly sensitive to the needs and feelings of others. He dominates the people around him—yet eagerly solicits their advice and readily acknowledges error. He has great dignity and reserve, reflecting a quarter century of command and association with world leaders—yet he transforms instantly into 'Ike of Kansas' with a school-boy grin radiating amiability and warmth and the friendliness of a cocker spaniel.

"He has had the adulation of people all over the world for two decades and more—yet is humble to the point of being self-effacing. He detests the perpendicular pronoun, and has scratched out hundreds of 'I's' from speech drafts. Many of his political speeches have ended up almost sterile because of his dislike of blowing his own horn.

"During all of his White House days he forbade the use of the word 'my' before 'Cabinet,' insisting that the prestigious institution should always be called 'The Cabinet.'

"One of his favorite admonitions is, 'Always consider your job important, never yourself.' In 1942 in North Africa, General Marshall asked him what is the most important attribute of a leader. His answer was 'selflessness'."

Whatever history records of Dwight David Eisenhower's accomplishments as a soldier and statesman, the record will not be complete without his accomplishments as a man and the inspiration he provided in helping Americans live better lives of service and devotion to their country.

[From the Salt Lake (Utah) Tribune, Mar. 29, 1969]

A MAN FOR HIS TIMES

Often in this fortunate country's history the right man has come forth in times of national need. Former President Dwight D. Eisenhower was such a man.

During World War II he rose from relative obscurity to plan, then execute, the invasion of Hitler's Fortress Europe. In 1952, when Americans were frustrated and bogged down in a seemingly fruitless and unwanted war in Korea, he agreed to seek the Presidency if given a "clear call to political duty." Republican leaders saw to it that the call was forthcoming and General Eisenhower, then serving as Supreme Commander of the new North Atlantic Treaty Organization forces, answered without further hesitation.

Americans of all political persuasions turned to the former general in hope that his international prestige could restore and preserve peace and bring on the good life. To a remarkable degree these hopes were realized. The 8 Eisenhower years, though frayed at times by tense international incidents, were, in the overall, good ones.

His death Friday at the age of 78 will be mourned as one mourns the passing of a kindly relative who saw the family through troubled times in other years that now seem almost placid by comparison.

Though he was coaxed into politics and never practiced that art in the usual fashion, General Eisenhower was nevertheless reluctant to cut political ties after stepping down. He continued active in Republican affairs and spoke out frequently in criticism—and sometimes support—of the Kennedy and Johnson administrations that followed. He took a hand in reknitting the Republican Party, which strayed from his more liberal concepts and came to disaster in the Goldwater debacle of 1964. His last public utterance was addressed to the party, revitalized and then meeting in convention in Miami Beach, last August.

History has yet to pronounce its verdict on Eisenhower the general or on Eisenhower the President. Criticisms of both roles have been made by knowledgeable persons of high repute and these must be weighed. But Eisenhower of the infectious grin and fatherly aura must be audited in the abstract.

His greatness lay in his ability to instill in millions of people here and abroad the feeling that the world's mightiest power was in responsible hands and that all was well. Though hampered by illness and pressed by mounting crises that eventually eroded some confidence in his leadership, Dwight Eisenhower made good that trust. The America he handed over to John F. Kennedy was by no means perfect, but it had been calmed and rested and made ready to withstand the upheavals that have visited it since.

## Hon. George H. Mahon
OF TEXAS

Mr. Speaker, President Eisenhower's work has been finished. He has written his record. It is a brilliant and moving record. The Nation and the world are now appending the closing chapters to the biography of Dwight David Eisenhower who, in the eloquent words of President Nixon on yesterday, was one of the giants of our time. Thomas Carlyle said that the history of the world is but the biography of its great men.

It was not my good fortune to know the late President as intimately as some, but I had the privilege of many interesting associations with him, and I counted him as my personal friend. My official relations with him often came about through my chairmanship of the Subcommittee on Defense Appropriations. He was always forthright and cooperative. He had a genius for getting to the heart of the proposition and making his views clearly understood.

The late President Eisenhower was blessed with a richness of personal qualities that make great men greater—qualities that find a permanent home not only in the hearts of his countrymen but of people everywhere. Unimpeachable character and integrity, great depth of sincerity, love of liberty and country, and devotion to the service of the common good were among the shining precepts of the personal coat of arms of this unpretentious man.

A victor in so many battles even in the last days, it is hard to realize that the late President is no longer here. He was so permanent, so enduring, so indestructible throughout his long years.

All of us who have been associated with him in official matters, on the golf course, and otherwise will treasure the memory of our experiences and be glad that we had the opportunity of knowing a man of his stature. Surely his life and work will be widely noted and long remembered by this and coming generations.

May the Lord bless his memory and give strength and comfort to Mrs. Eisenhower and family and others of his loved ones.

## Hon. Thomas E. Morgan
OF PENNSYLVANIA

Mr. Speaker, in the passing of Dwight D. Eisenhower one of our greatest statesmen and national heroes has joined the ranks of the immortals. The pages of our history as a people and a nation have a special luster imparted by his life and deeds.

I shall always cherish the memories of my association and friendship with Dwight Eisenhower. He was a man to inspire respect, confidence, and admiration as well as friendship. These he won in large measure from me and from my colleagues on the Committee on Foreign Affairs in the days when he used to testify and assist us obtaining information we needed on foreign policy matters involving military aid to our allies.

These sentiments were confirmed and strengthened when he became our President. His stature as a dedicated public servant transcended politics and he retained the affection and esteem he had won during his military career.

It is sad to meditate on his passing, because it is a deep and grevious loss to his family and friends, and also in a very real way to all of us. At the same time, our grief is tempered by our gratitude and deep sense of appreciation for all that Dwight Eisenhower accomplished for his country and his fellow man.

During the war, Dwight Eisenhower led the greatest forces in mankind's history. In peace, he held the highest office in our land. His true greatness did not stem from holding these high posts. I agree with those who knew him best, that his real greatness was due to his unique personal qualities which fitted him to be the greatest hero of our time. In making these brief remarks I join my fellow Americans in saluting and paying tribute to a patriot whose devotion to our well-being has helped shape the course of war and of peace so that our Nation could survive and prosper.

## Hon. Edward P. Boland
OF MASSACHUSETTS

Mr. Speaker, I am profoundly saddened by the death of Dwight David Eisenhower, one of this Nation's greatest leaders and one of its most acclaimed public figures.

I had the honor of being elected to Congress in 1952, the year General Eisenhower was elected President. My admiration of him increased during these years as I witnessed Dwight Eisenhower's unyielding courage, high integrity, abiding faith in his fellow man, and his quest for world peace.

General Eisenhower's historic record of achievement is, in a sense, this Nation's record of achievement for the past three decades.

Chief architect of the Allied effort that rescued Europe in World War II, leader of the North Atlantic Treaty Organization, 34th President of the United States for two terms, counselor to succeeding Presidents, Dwight David Eisenhower led our Nation through one of the stormiest periods in its history.

He was not afraid to show hope instead of despair, faith instead of cynicism, honest toil instead of idle talk. He was a good and compassionate man whose words and deeds were an inspiration to all Americans and millions of people throughout the free world.

Dwight David Eisenhower embodied all that is best in American life. Through sheer hard work and determination he brought himself from humble beginnings to the pinnacle of success.

Mr. Speaker, I join my colleagues in extending my heartfelt sympathy to Mrs. Mamie Eisenhower, and son, Ambassador John Eisenhower.

## Hon. Wright Patman
OF TEXAS

Mr. Speaker, Dwight David Eisenhower occupied, even before his death, a very special position in the hearts of his countrymen, and now that his gallant soul has reached the haven of eternal peace, it is our duty and our right to claim him for posterity as the very symbol of what is means to be an American. It is necessary to use the phrase, "a self-made man," in the best possible sense of that term because he rose to great position from a home of average circumstances through the application of hard work and the intelligent use of the opportunity afforded to all young men in our democratic society—remember that his career in the public service started with a highly competitive examination for the military academies. His character was well nurtured and formed in the midst of a family that believed deeply in God Almighty, in what we have come to call the American dream, and in the power, dignity, and integrity of the individual person, in that order though dependent one upon the other. This noble character was the source from which Dwight Eisenhower derived his strength and the abilities that were later to lead his Nation through years of strife, when our future as a free people was in critical balance.

Let us not forget that Dwight Eisenhower gave superior and loyal service and invaluable advice and counsel to Presidents Franklin Delano Roosevelt and Harry S. Truman, and that under their administration he became a legend in his lifetime. As President for 8 succeeding years, he achieved a serenity and balance which enabled him to implement his basic belief and faith in our democratic institutions. Indeed his wisdom and thorough experience in every facet of the administrative process, and his tremendous gift for leadership, engendered a trust and confidence among all Americans that is unique in the history of our Presidents. Almost to the hour of his passing, his inspired guidance was significant to the course of our Government.

Possibly the most sincere indication of his concern for the continued well-being of his fellow citizens was the admonition in his farwell address that—

> We must guard against the acquisition of unwarranted influence, whether sought or unsought, by the military-industrial complex. The potential for the disastrous rise of misplaced power exists and will persist.

Coming from a man who had spent so many years with the military his warning was indeed a splendidly independent and objective guidepost—in itself it was a great and significant service to his fellow Americans; a statement worthy of the respect, admiration, and affection given to him without stint by millions of Americans and by the many millions in other countries who revere his memory as the architect of world peace and stability.

In this time of deep sadness, I join with my colleagues in expressing my heartfelt sympathy to his wonderful and gracious wife, Mamie, who shared his burdens and his triumphs, and to the other much beloved members of his family. For them the sharp pain of personal loss is greatest, but all Americans share in their grief, for this was a man much loved by all people. He, more than any man of our century, fits the often-quoted description of our first President, George Washington, for in his time, Dwight David Eisenhower was also "first in war, first in peace, and first in the hearts of his countrymen." Truly, we shall miss this great American champion whose spirit is now and forever with all people and all lands as a resplendent symbol of the United States of America.

## Hon. William H. Ayres

OF OHIO

Mr. Speaker, I stand on the floor of the House of Representatives as a spokesman for all the people of Summit County. On the subject of the qualities of Dwight David Eisenhower, we are unanimous in our homage. We well understood this great man of our own Midwest. As often as I met with him, I told him of the support our people gave his successful efforts to make us a land of peace.

The great man that he chose to succeed him in the Presidency, President Nixon, closed his eulogy of General Eisenhower by stating:

> We salute Dwight David Eisenhower standing there in our memory—first in war, first in peace and wherever freedom is cherished, first in the hearts of his fellow men.

As the Representative of the 14th Ohio District, to Mamie Eisenhower and her family, I wish to express our deepest sorrow at their great loss. We are grateful to them for having shared Dwight David Eisenhower with us.

## Hon. Robert V. Denney

OF NEBRASKA

Mr. Speaker, I join my fellow Americans and the world in mourning the death of General Eisenhower, the 34th President of the United States.

Dwight D. Eisenhower will return to his midwestern plains boyhood home after a full life, but, as described in his own words, one with "his work unfinished." Indeed, the work of the world is unfinished. His death reminds us all of the test we have before us and stresses the point that each of us must become involved if we are to count our accomplishments to this end. He was involved. He encouraged not only those around him, but all people to do the same.

Throughout his endeavors in war, peace, and politics, he was not one to lose sight of his beginnings. He had grown to appreciate the honesty and integrity of those who had surrounded his boyhood life. He was a man to be trusted and he served as an example of the virtue of our way of life. He was typically American, and yet perhaps as Rev. Billy Graham recently said, "the greatest American since Lincoln."

## Hon. Donald E. Lukens

OF OHIO

Mr. Speaker, I join with my colleagues in paying tribute to a truly great American.

On Friday, March 28, 1969, at 12:25 p.m. the world suffered a great loss—former President Dwight David Eisenhower became history.

There will be many eulogies and documentaries as well as perhaps a few books. Yet, in all this, it will be nearly impossible to express the true nature of this beloved mortal. A man of great dignity who had the respect of his fellow man, he rarely found it necessary to command it. Although greatly respected, we warmly referred to him as "Ike" as readily as if he were our closest acquaintance. Surely, "Ike" felt this way about the people who chose him as their leader, as well as the rest of the human race which was also captivated and influenced by his statesmanship.

Dwight Eisenhower was a warrior but also a peace-loving man, a political leader and a statesman, an intellectual and a firm believer in his fellow man. He was a Christian who had a keen sense of justice and who would act in a just manner; he had unlimited courage.

He will be remembered for his controversial directing of Federal forces into a city of this country to enforce what he considered to be justice. This demanded a tremendous amount of courage. As general he used every ounce of courage, physical strength, and mentality to defend this country and all people of the world from an aggressive nation. As supreme commander of Allied Expeditionary Forces, he accepted the unconditional surrender of Germany. As President he alone brought peace in Korea. History now shows that he was at this very time fully prepared to again defend this Nation and the world if necessary.

At a time when the military leadership of this Nation is coming under heavier and heavier attack, it is well to remember that one of the greatest military geniuses of our time was a proven man of peace. For eight years under his administration we experienced our longest period of peace since World War II.

Throughout his life he practiced strength and proper use of strength which was clearly illustrated when he ordered our marines into Lebanon to maintain the peace in the Middle East.

A warrior and a fighter to the end, he loved life so much that he fought for weeks grasping onto that thread of life. As with Winston Churchill and the other greats of this era, he belongs to the ages. Now, surely, he has found peace.

## Hon. Thaddeus J. Dulski

OF NEW YORK

Mr. Speaker, on this day of national mourning for President Eisenhower, I would like to convey condolences on behalf of myself and the Buffalo, N.Y., area which I represent.

As I said upon learning of the general's passing last Friday:

> I, along with millions of Americans have offered my prayers during the illness of President Eisenhower. Although aware of the gravity of his illness, I was profoundly shocked and grieved at the news of his death. During my earlier terms in Congress, I came to know him, respect, and revere him as a soldier and as President. The influence for good which he exerted, the high ideals which were voiced by him and his noble examples, all combine to stamp him as a man among men. My wife and I have conveyed our condolences to his immediate family and I shall return to Washington to pay my personal respects.

The feelings of Buffalonians are well expressed in editorials appearing in our two daily newspapers, as follows:

[From the Buffalo (N.Y.) Courier-Express, Mar. 29, 1969]

UNITED STATES MOURNS SOLDIER–STATESMAN

A grief-stricken nation mourns the death of former President Dwight D. Eisenhower, a man beloved and esteemed by the American people. His deeds as a military commander will be enshrined in history as long as Western civilization endures. It was he who directed "Operation Overlord," the invasion of the European Continent, which resulted in the defeat of the Nazis. When he became President, the energy and zeal which he had displayed in war were devoted to the objective of bringing about lasting world peace.

Probably no other President in this century was as universally popular as Gen. Eisenhower. Theodore Roosevelt, Franklin D. Roosevelt and Calvin Coolidge came close, but each profoundly displeased a minority. The two Roosevelts were disliked by conservatives and Coolidge by the progressives. President Eisenhower, who pursued a middle-of-the-road policy toward national problems, was disliked by few Americans—a fact emphatically attested to in his 1956 reelection.

Mr. Eisenhower possessed the qualities that Americans seem to admire most in their chief executive. A pleasant and photogenic man, Mr. Eisenhower possessed a personality that radiated confidence. As a soldier, he had risen to prominence through his own brilliance. As an educator, he championed academic freedom. And as a statesman, he represented the United States with dignity and honor.

The President came to the occupancy of the highest office in the land with no experience in politics and little in government. No one realized it more than he did. Hence, he did not rush into a legislative program, but permitted his first year, 1953, to pass by without major recommendations. In 1954, he submitted a comprehensive program to Congress which was designed to cover his entire term. This included tax revision and reduction, based on curbing expenditures.

Perhaps the American people felt most indebted to him for a victory scored outside the legislative realm. That was the ending of the Korean War.

The United States and the free world have lost one of the noble and justly revered soldier-statesman of history.

---

[From the Buffalo (N.Y.) Evening News, Mar. 29, 1969]

DWIGHT D. EISENHOWER

However history ranks him among Presidents or among generals, Dwight D. Eisenhower has already been ranked in the hearts of his countrymen among the best-loved Americans of all time.

Ike had that special magic of personal warmth, that glow of inner decency and dignity, that won him an all-but-universal affection—evidenced not only by the familiar "I Like Ike" buttons of his two spectacularly successful presidential campaigns, but by the millions who served under his command in World War II and the tens of millions who later greeted him wherever he traveled abroad.

As President, he could be bracketed with Washington but not with Lincoln—as an inspired unifier and team captain, but not a driving leader. His eight-year presidency was a success by the standards of those who believed deeply, with him, in a government of restraint and rigidly limited use of its vast powers—but not by those who prefer to see the Presidency played, a la FDR or LBJ, as a virtuoso performer plays a great organ.

As a general, too, Eisenhower can be ranked with history's great team captains, but not among its brilliant strategists or dashing warriors. The MacArthur style was not for him, nor the Marshall command of over-all organization. His was a kind of generalship that could keep a prima donna Montgomery, a brilliant Bradley and a swashbuckling Patton all working for the same winning team.

His greatest single contribution—indeed the very theme of his life from the "Crusade in Europe" through the organization of NATO, his eight-year presidency and on into his eight years of retirement—was his dedication to the concept of the collective self-defense of the free world.

In World War II, his triumph was the effective captaining of a multi-nation coalition of armies to defeat the most evil tyranny of modern times. In organizing NATO, he was the logical one man in all the free world to be brought back into uniform to put the free nations of the North Atlantic Community into another effective coalition against the danger of Communist aggression.

In leaving NATO to fight for the Republican presidential nomination, his main motivation once again was his devotion to the concept of collective security and his fear that America might revert to isolationism or to go-it-alonism. And throughout his presidency and on to his final illness, he never wavered in support of this nation's commitment to defend its friends and maintain a strong set of globe-girdling alliances to keep the free world free.

Looking back over his whole career, what sticks out is a passionate devotion to three words: Freedom, security, peace—and in that order.

The first he formed into this virtual credo, in a 1949 speech while president of Columbia University: "To men who have lived in freedom, there is nothing in life so valuable as freedom—not even life itself."

To the second, his nation's and the free world's security, he not only devoted his whole career as a soldier, but his deepest concern as a statesman—right up to last summer's ominous warning to the Republican national convention: "Abroad, in every major sector, we confront a formidable foe—and expansionist tyranny which respects only toughness and strength and still displays little interest in traveling the pathways to peace, with honor and justice. . . . To call for retreat by America is the best way I know to stockpile tragedy for our children."

Yet this is the same Ike who warned us in his presidential farewell speech eight years ago to be wary—in a time when our security depended on a vast military-industrial complex—of letting "the weight of this combination endanger our liberties or democratic processes." And his greatest pride in looking back on his own presidency was simply that it had kept us at peace and secure for eight years, while his bitterest disappointment, as he himself sized it up, was his inability, despite a massive peacewaging effort, to bring about a trustworthy accord with Soviet Russia.

What the world will best remember about Ike, however, is not his speeches or his sometimes fractured syntax but that marvelous Eisenhower grin and the infectiously optimistic faith in human decency that it punctuated. Rank him where you will in greatness among the unforgettable free world leaders of his momentously historic times—Churchill, Roosevelt, MacArthur, Marshall, DeGaulle, Adenauer—and Eisenhower will be remembered as long as any and probably with more sheer affection.

## Hon. William G. Bray
OF INDIANA

Mr. Speaker, following is the eulogy I wrote on the occasion of the passing of one of the greatest sons of our American Republic, Dwight David Eisenhower:

IN MEMORIAM: DWIGHT DAVID EISENHOWER, 1890–1969, GENERAL OF THE ARMY, PRESIDENT OF THE UNITED STATES, AMERICAN

"So he passed over, and all the trumpets sounded for him on the other side."

A man of unfaltering kingly bearing that was complimented by a genuine native warmth and humility, he was by nature and by character as open and as free as the western plains and prairies of his youth. Few men ever sought less; he asked for nothing more than the opportunity to serve, when called and where ordered. Few men ever received more; he is one of the scant handful of men in the history of our American Republic whose fellow citizens spontaneously and overwhelmingly elevated him to be a symbol in his own lifetime. And the symbol was not merely of an era, but of the country itself, and of its people, and of the ideals and the good in the two that were both existing and hoped for.

As soldier, as General, he directed the most awesome array of military might ever trusted to one man. It was his duty to order entire armies into some of the bloodiest combat in the history of warfare.

As statesman, as President, he gave to his country a Chief Executive with a commitment to peace that can only be known by one like himself who had carried the heaviest of the burdens and agonies of war. Six months after his First Inaugural in 1953, the guns of the Korean War fell silent. For the next seven and one-half years of his Presidency, not one American combat death occurred.

His call to serve—first as soldier, then as statesman—came from his own country, yet the scope of this service was truly worldwide. As soldier, millions in this country and abroad looked to him in time of war for the hope of victory and of liberation. As statesman, these same millions looked to him in time of peace as that symbol of the forces of good that had gained victory, and would strive to preserve the peace so dearly won.

Measure him, in part, by the nature of his critics, that small band of petty men whose stock in trade is the supercilious condemnation, the mocking jest, and arrogant condescension. Such trivia, such meanness, only made more clear the true nobility of his own character, and exposed more glaringly the shallowness of theirs.

The legacies he leaves to his fellow men are rich and many. But perhaps the greatest of them all is this: In a day when it sometimes seems that "image" is all, and that character counts for nothing, this man lived and practiced, openly and unashamedly, the old, simple precepts of "The Gods of the Copybook Headings."

The love, honor and respect that millions gave him has proven beyond any doubt that mankind is, and always will be, more receptive to, influenced by and appreciative of a basic, simple code of honor and decency such as this man practiced than all the false glitter and manufactured rhetoric that so quickly loses its luster.

The roll of the muffled drums, the rumble of the caisson wheels, and the clear, high notes of Taps will now mark the passing of one who carried and fulfilled some of the most momentous and difficult tasks ever placed upon one man. He passes into history, but he passes as one whose part in the constantly unfolding drama of human existence and civilization will be forever remembered. And the example he set by his life will be forever called to mind, wherever and whenever men lift up their eyes unto the hills, and seek from a Power beyond themselves that inner strength and support that man must have to prevail.

"Soldier from the wars returning
Spoiler of the taken town,
Here is ease that asks not earning;
Turn you in and sit you down.

"Peace is come and wars are over,
Welcome you and welcome all,
While the charger crops the clover,
And his bridle hangs in stall.

"Now no more of winters biting,
Filth in trench from fall to spring,
Summers full of sweat and fighting
For the Kesar or the King.

"Rest you, charger, rust you, bridle;
Kings and Kesars, keep your pay;
Soldier, sit you down and idle
At the inn of night for aye."

## Hon. H. Allen Smith
OF CALIFORNIA

Mr. Speaker, I wish to join my colleagues in paying tribute to Dwight David Eisenhower. Americans have lost one of their greatest leaders of all time.

Dwight David Eisenhower was a leader of soldiers; he was the leader of a distinguished university; and he was a leader of the greatest nation on earth.

A distinguished military career followed his graduation from the U.S. Military Academy in 1915, and the greatest tribute that could be paid to his services to this Nation was given by the American public in 1952 when he was elected President of the United States.

When the American public returned him to that office in 1956, there could be no higher honor, no higher tribute to the inspiration and the dedication of this great man.

History will record this man's lengthy list of outstanding contributions, taking note that he always was sought after by his fellow man. He always ascended to the highest positions of leadership, and dispatched his offices in a gentlemanly fashion with dignity and efficiency.

Mr. Speaker, Mrs. Smith joins me in extending our deepest sympathies to Mrs. Eisenhower and the members of the family.

## Hon. Garner E. Shriver

OF KANSAS

Mr. Speaker, on behalf of the citizens of the Fourth Congressional District of Kansas, Mrs. Shriver, and myself, I want to express the feeling of deep sorrow over the passing of a beloved and great American, Dwight D. Eisenhower. Our heartfelt sympathy goes out to his beloved wife, Mamie; his son, John; and the entire Eisenhower family.

Dwight Eisenhower's fight for life, his physical and mental strength in the face of suffering, was an inspiration to all of us. America has lost one of its great statesmen and soldiers. We, from Kansas, are especially proud of the heritage and accomplishments left behind by this native son of Abilene.

Every World War II GI who served under Ike will forever treasure his military leadership and organizational genius. Free men everywhere will long remember his leadership in bringing peace and stability to the world as 34th President of the United States.

We are all the beneficiaries of his lifelong devotion, dedication, and service to America and free men everywhere.

## Hon. James C. Corman

OF CALIFORNIA

Mr. Speaker, I join my colleagues in paying tribute to President Eisenhower and to underscore the deep sense of loss felt throughout the country at the death of this gallant and remarkable person.

Dwight David Eisenhower has rightly been called a great general and a great President. But, mostly, I would call him simply a great man.

The key to his greatness was the warmth and sincerity of his personality, which were reflected in his compassion and regard for his fellow men. The measure of his greatness was the strong hold he so easily retained throughout his entire career on the confidence, respect, and affection of the people of this Nation; indeed, throughout the world community.

General Eisenhower has left to America a legacy of bravery, integrity, courage, and devotion to country and to democratic principles as a way of life. He was a man of essential decency and kindness, the traits which endeared him to the Nation.

His place in history is firmly established by his many services to his country. In the dark days of World War II, he emerged as the strong commander of the Allied forces to win for the millions of Europeans their freedom from Nazi tyranny. Who of us can forget D-day and the extreme courage the general displayed in executing the invasion, which was the only hope of stemming the Nazi onslaught? The remarkable trust he instilled in the men who crossed the channel and went on to the beachheads on that May day was the hallmark of his ability to command and to lead. He sent the Allied forces on to a glorious victory that gave Western Europe its freedom, and he stayed to watch over the liberated lands and helped to rebuild them. He returned to America a "conquering hero" in the true sense of the word, and its was his just due.

His two terms as President was a grateful nation's recognition of qualities of leadership. In his person, he represented what America is—in war and in peace.

Dwight David Eisenhower will always be remembered and revered by every American now living and for all generations to come. His page in history is a shining example of a truly wonderful man and a great American.

Mrs. Corman and I extend our deep sympathy to Mrs. Eisenhower and the family. We hope they will find solace in the knowledge that the Nation mourns with them.

## Hon. John N. Erlenborn

OF ILLINOIS

Mr. Speaker, it seems to me that Dwight Eisenhower was one of those rare leaders with a genius for bringing people together. He was a maker of friends, not a maker of enemies—for himself, for his political party, for his point of view, for his country, and for the people of the world.

His administration was a time of healing, of peacemaking, and of peacekeeping. His life was devoted to goodness and mercy.

His greatness as a man overshadows his greatness as a general or as a President; and yet, his ready smile and his well-known temper marked him as being made of the same stuff as the rest of us.

Samuel Butler, the great English novelist of the 19th century wrote a line at about the time Dwight Eisenhower was born:

> A virtue, to be serviceable, must like gold, be alloyed with some commoner but more serviceable metal.

Mr. Speaker, I believe Dwight Eisenhower was a marvelous alloy. Millions of people around the world today are repeating a famous phrase: "I like Ike."

## Hon. William J. Scherle

OF IOWA

Mr. Speaker, today I am introducing legislation that would authorize the minting of all quarter-dollar pieces with a likeness of former President Dwight David Eisenhower.

This tribute to President Eisenhower is only fitting when one considers his dedicated service to his country. Our country and the world are more secure because of his efforts in times of war and peace. He was a man of courage; a man of integrity, and above all, a man of kindness. Even in death, President Eisenhower's spirit of dedication to his countrymen and his Nation will remain as an inspiration to all.

The people of Iowa have had a special feeling in their hearts for President Eisenhower throughout his career, because his beloved wife was reared in our State. I know the people of Iowa will join me in extending our prayers and sympathy to Mrs. Eisenhower and the family in this time of sorrow.

## Hon. Leonor K. Sullivan

OF MISSOURI

Mr. Speaker, with the dignity befitting his entire lifetime, and with the respect he always earned and enjoyed, the American people have been saying their personal farewells to a great and good man who served them well.

We salute his fine family for the admirable manner in which they have borne the long and trying months of General Eisenhower's final illness, and for the inspiration they have given all of us to bear our own burdens with similar courage and fortitude.

Mr. Speaker, there are unlimited tributes one could pay to our former President and great wartime leader. When I heard of his death on Friday, and the newspapers in my district asked me for my comments, I made the following statement:

STATEMENT BY CONGRESSWOMAN LEONOR K. SULLIVAN UPON THE DEATH OF FORMER PRESIDENT DWIGHT D. EISENHOWER, FRIDAY, MARCH 28, 1969

I don't think there was ever any narrow partisanship in the character of Dwight D. Eisenhower during his eight years as President of the United States, which was one of the reasons why he could serve as effectively as he did as a Republican President with a predominantly Democratic Congress during six of those eight years. I think every Member of Congress recognized in him a man of decency and of great dedication to the cause of freedom, and even when we disagreed with him—as we frequently did—on domestic issues, there was never any bitterness or attacks on his personal integrity.

Few Americans have ever left the White House with as much genuine good will and warm feeling of approval as a person. History may not regard him as one of our greatest Presidents, but it is certain to include him among the greatest Americans. And considering the fact that his entire adult life was spent in the military service until just a few years before he became President of the United States, his performance as President was indeed remarkable in many respects, particularly in recognizing the supremacy of the civilian authority over our national destiny.

Even when I was fighting him vigorously on some issues in the Congress—on food stamps, medicare, and some of the other domestic issues—I never doubted for a moment the sincerity of his views or the honesty of his approach. He was, in all respects, a man to be admired and respected. I join all of my fellow citizens in sorrow over his death following such a magnificent and dignified and courageous life of service to his country.

## Hon. Howard W. Robison

OF NEW YORK

Mr. Speaker, my family joins with the millions of others throughout the world who will mourn the loss of Dwight David Eisenhower—a great and good man.

His death, after his prolonged illness and almost miraculous recovery from prior heart attacks, comes as no great shock but it is, nevertheless, a personally difficult thing to accept the fact that his wise counsel and always-encouraging presence has been removed from us.

Dwight Eisenhower's place in history was assured long before he assumed the Presidency, but there have been some who have questioned whether or not his tenure in that most difficult of all offices added anything to his stature. I have never understood nor shared those questions. To my mind, back then and now, today, as I review the tumult and the trouble of these past 8 years, General Eisenhower was—and will forever remain—one of our great Presidents. He brought peace and a respite from both domestic and international tensions to a nation badly in need of such relief; he proved, if such needed proving, that we could have prosperity without war, a steadily rising standard of living without crippling inflation, and that true progress could be made in the field of human rights without recourse to public confrontation in city streets.

God grant that Richard Nixon, under today's worsened circumstances, can do half as well—and God grant, too, that as Dwight Eisenhower leaves us, we, the American people, will be so inspired by his precept and example as to prove worthy of the trust he always had in us.

## Hon. Edward Hutchinson

OF MICHIGAN

Mr. Speaker, I have been deeply moved by the eulogies today on the life and career of General Eisenhower. It was not my privilege to have served in Congress during the years of his Presidency. In those years I served in the legislature of my State. But on two occasions, once before his election as our Chief Magistrate, and once afterward I met him, and his personal warmth I have always remembered. When he was campaigning for the Republican nomination before the Republican Convention in 1952, he came to Detroit. It was my privilege to sit on the platform with him at that time, and to meet him on that occasion. After the close of his presidential years, during the Michigan Constitutional Convention in the spring of 1962, General Eisenhower came to that convention in Lansing. A few of us, who were delegates at that convention were privileged to have luncheon with him at the home of Dr. John Hannah, then president of Michigan State University. I sat across the table from him then, and for an hour and a half he kept us enraptured by his experiences, his philosophy, and his life as a retired President living at Gettysburg and his interest in Eisenhower College. The occasion impressed me deeply, and I shall remember him vividly as long as I live.

## Hon. Dominick V. Daniels

OF NEW JERSEY

Mr. Speaker, I rise to express the profound sorrow of the people of the 14th Congressional District of New Jersey at the passing of our 34th President, Dwight David Eisenhower.

Because in the later years of his life he was involved in the world of partisan politics, his was to some extent a controversial figure. There were those who agreed with him on particular policies and those who differed with him. Yet, while there might have been disagreement about Eisenhower the President, there was no disagreement about Eisenhower the man. I know that there has been no man who in my lifetime has enjoyed the trust and confidence of his fellow citizens to the extent that General Eisenhower did.

Mr. Speaker, General Eisenhower was a professional military man and indeed one of the great military figures of our history. He ranks with Washington, Grant, Lee, Sherman, Sheridan, Pershing, and MacArthur in our glossary of military leaders. He possessed military virtues in abundance. He was always an enlisted man's general, humble and self effacing. And it was General Eisenhower who had spent almost all his adult life as a professional soldier who warned his fellow citizens about the dangers of the military-industrial complex in a free society.

Dwight David Eisenhower brought to public life a sense of decency, a sense of propriety, and above all, a deep devotion to this Nation and its ideals. His virtues were perhaps the virtues of an earlier America, an America which was not ashamed to wear its patriotism on its sleeve, an America which believed in God and the family as the basic unit of a free and just society. At this critical time these seem to be the virtues that this Nation needs most.

His contributions to this Nation and to the free world will live after him. Of him it may be said, as Richard Henry Lee said of an earlier military man, George Washington, who served as President during trying times, he was "first in war, first in peace, and first in the hearts of his countrymen."

## Hon. Charles E. Bennett

OF FLORIDA

Mr. Speaker, every American and every freedom-loving person on this globe has lost a dear friend in the passing of General and President Eisenhower. At the end of World War II, as I was a patient in Army-Navy hospital in Arkansas, I wrote to General Eisenhower and urged him to run for the Presidency, as I felt he was just the man who was needed to lead our country in those troubled times. I was never sorry that I had made that judgment and that in the years that followed that he went to the White House and led our country so well in peace as he had in war. In the years since General Washington, no one has better earned the phrase that he was "first in war, first in peace, and first in the hearts of his countrymen." He had the uncommon quality of understanding the common man and helping him to achieve his finest potentialities. No President in our history has been better loved and it will always be one of the treasures of my life that fortune gave me the opportunity to know him personally. Our country will always be his debtor, as in fact so will we and all of humanity.

## Hon. John J. Rhodes

OF ARIZONA

Mr. Speaker, the life of Dwight Eisenhower was a very special gift of the Almighty to our contemporary world. Few men have been endowed with the personal qualities to make them, all at the same time, effective, objective, resolute, and compassionate. Few men have been able to encompass in one life the roles of warrior, statesman and peacemaker. Few men have been able to inspire, at same time, love from their friends, respect from their enemies, and confidence from their fellow men. Yet, he did all of these things.

General Eisenhower was a true moderate. In one of the first utterances he every made in my presence, he said, "No progress can be made by walking in the gutter to the far right, or the far left. It can only be made by walking resolutely down the middle of the road. This is where I plan to walk."

The world is today a poorer place than it was yesterday because President Eisenhower is no longer in it. We thank God for his life, we express our sympathy to Mrs. Eisenhower and the Eisenhower family, and we pray that Almighty God will give his great soul rest and eternal peace.

## Hon. Charlotte T. Reid

OF ILLINOIS

Mr. Speaker, I join with Americans everywhere and people the world over in mourning the passing of our 34th President—who in death as in life will be remembered among our country's greatest statesmen and patriots. He was one of those individuals who had the rare privilege of seeing himself become a living legend—hailed and admired by peoples around the world. He won the love, respect, and devotion of his fellow man. In our Nation's darkest hour of need, he came forward to lead the free world to victory.

Dwight David Eisenhower began his service to his people as a soldier of war. He ended as a crusader for peace. For both he will be long remembered by a world that knew and loved him. He believed superbly in the motto of West Point, his alma mater—"Duty, honor, country"—and he dedicated his life to these high principles. He was a man of great strength, wisdom, and compassion.

As we mourn the passing of General Eisenhower, we think first of the loss of a man who stood for America, a man whose courage, personality, and integrity lifted the Nation in times of crisis—a pillar of strength who could be relied upon for wise counsel and leadership. We think of all he exemplified, of all he did—as commanding general in World War II, as an educator, serving as president of Columbia University, as the organizer and first supreme commander of

Allied Powers in Europe within the North Atlantic Treaty Organization, as our President, twice elected by landslide majorities, and as a man still revered after he left office. But aside from all this, General Eisenhower has left our Nation a legacy to which to cling—to live by, to build on—basic principles and basic commonsense good in any circumstances.

There was his essential decency as a man, his humility as a leader, his readiness to make decisions, and his willingness to take the blame if the decisions went wrong. President Nixon, in a statement, pointed out that the one key to the character of General Eisenhower was revealed in a message the general had prepared in case the landings in France on D-Day had failed. This message—never issued because the landings were a success and led directly to the end of the war—included these sentences:

> The troops, the air and the Navy, did all that bravery and devotion could do. If any blame or fault attaches to the attempt it is mine alone.

This was typical of General Eisenhower—a man ready to take the consequences of decision.

The convictions which led to his decisions were bolstered by the thoroughness with which he made them, and one of the fundamentals in his planning was to consider the consequences if they proved wrong—what to do next—what alternatives. These were the qualities which made him a great general, and the qualities maintained through the major decisions of his years as the Nation's Chief Executive. They are qualities that too often have been lacking in Washington when great plans were pushed through with little or no thought to the possiblility of failure, or to the alternatives. But these qualities are essential to the leadership of the future—and they are General Eisenhower's most enduring legacy.

In death Dwight Eisenhower becomes no longer a man of the 20th century but a man of immortality who will live on through the ages in the hearts of his countrymen—along with Washington, Jefferson, Lincoln, and others who have made our Nation great. This generation and those to come will never forget the legend of Eisenhower the general, Eisenhower the President, and "Ike" the citizen.

At this time, I want to extend my deep sympathy to the Eisenhower family.

## Hon. Bill Nichols

### OF ALABAMA

Mr. Speaker, America has lost one of its finest citizens in the passing of former President Dwight David Eisenhower. The President leaves an outstanding record as a military tactician and former commander of all Allied forces in Europe during World War II. He was a distinguished military graduate of West Point and had the distinction of leading this country both in time of war and peace.

His 8 years as President of our country saw America prospering and under his able leadership our country was recognized worldwide for the strength of our military forces, and for our industrial growth. Also our abilities to negotiate and work with other nations of the free world were well known. During the last 8 years of his life, he sought retirement to the serenity of a small farm in Gettysburg, Pa., on lands which ironically join to the great military battlefield between the North and South during the War Between the States.

As I silently walked past the body of this great American lying in state in the rotunda of the U.S. Capitol, which traditionally is reserved exclusively for outstanding Americans, my mind went back some quarter of a century ago when the general was my own military commander just prior to the invasion of Normandy in World War II. I still treasure the individual letter which he wrote each man taking part in the invasion of France. It was a warm, personal sort of message from a leader whom we all had great confidence in and whom we would follow without question in carrying out his orders for the long-awaited and much-planned landing in Normandy.

It was a solemn hour going across on the old Navy LST's on the morning of June 6, 1944, but somehow every GI felt better about whatever he might face during the days and weeks ahead, because he carried that special letter from Gen. Dwight D. Eisenhower in his pocket or tucked away under his steel helmet.

In the after years, we may not have always agreed wholeheartedly with some of the President's decisions nor necessarily all of his political views, but make no mistake about it, he was indeed a great American. General Eisenhower will be missed, for a man of his stature does not come along every day. I am confident that both his spirit and his influence over the men he commanded in battle and over those who served with him during his 8 years as President of our country will long be remembered. His influence will be felt in this country and throughout the world for many, many years to come.

## Hon. James A. McClure

OF IDAHO

Mr. Speaker, the greatest moment to a public figure is the esteem in which he is held by his fellow man. If that is the measure, then Dwight Eisenhower was truly the man of his time.

His service to his country, to the world, and to the cause of freedom is unmatched in this century. He marshaled the greatest force for war in the history of mankind. After that, he marshaled the greatest force for peace the world has seen—the spirit of the American people. There is a certain irony in the fact that this man of war gave us the longest sustained period of peace in the last three decades.

Those of us from Idaho have always felt a special fondness for Dwight Eisenhower. We recall that the first speech he gave in his quest for the Presidency was delivered on the steps of the State capitol in Boise. From that point in 1952 to his final resting place in Abilene, Ike traveled the path of peace and freedom. It is a journey that will be remembered throughout history.

On behalf of the citizens of the First District of Idaho, I wish to extend our deepest sympathy to Mrs. Eisenhower and the other members of the Eisenhower family.

## Hon. James M. Collins

OF TEXAS

Mr. Speaker, as we assembled in the rotunda of the Capitol Sunday to pay our respects to the great President of peace, Dwight David Eisenhower, my thoughts went back to my earlier discussions with the President.

Serving him as Regional Chairman of the White House Conference on Youth, I recall how often he would urge our Nation's youth to use "commonsense." Every single individual was unique, and had something special to offer to America. Every single individual was important to "Ike," and he would often speak of the great need to provide better educational opportunities for America's youth. I remember how he outlined the "way" for our youth.

We must not look for the simple way—the easy way—but we must understand and know that the best way is so often the hardest way. Many men put forth their ideas to simplify a youngster's education and growth. "Ike" would pause a moment, then more deliberately and more thoughtfully restate his belief that America's youth could—and would—respond to the call for individual responsibility and individual development.

And because "Ike" believed in you—you believed in yourself. And you believed in the others who struggled daily beside you in the bettering of an often-troubled world. "Ike" understood Emerson's phrase:

> The only way to have a friend is to be one.

General Eisenhower was my leader during the war as this Nation forsook the easy way for the grueling, hard way that brought us the one true victory that men call peace. Dwight David Eisenhower was my leader again as he paced us as the great President for peace and prosperity. "Ike" was my friend as he befriended our Nation, and as he issued the call for individual leadership on the part of all Americans.

## Hon. Cornelius E. Gallagher

OF NEW JERSEY

Mr. Speaker, everything in the life of Dwight David Eisenhower "became him like the leaving it."

The accomplishments of Dwight Eisenhower as soldier and statesman, as general and President, richly deserve the praise and admiration they have received. But I would like to focus upon another of his great achievements: the courage of Dwight Eisenhower in the face of death.

Many times during 1968 the dark solemnity of the death watch settled over Walter Reed

31-935 O—70——5

Hospital here in Washington; just as many times the bright light of the famous grin of Ike was shed yet again upon a relieved world. The fact that we mourn him in 1969 rather than 1968 is a tribute to more than the miracles of medical science. It is a tribute to the unquenchable spirit of man—surely the greatest glory of God's earth.

Dwight Eisenhower has left us many legacies. To my mind, perhaps the greatest is the memory of his unbroken will and transcendent character when his body was at its weakest. For his refusal to slip easily into death is an enduring inspiration to all who must undergo adversity.

Mr. Speaker, no matter what they may have been in life, many men have died well. Shakespeare celebrated that fact in the famous speech in Macbeth which begins:

> Nothing in his life became him like the leaving it.

In the case of Dwight David Eisenhower, however, everything in his life became him like the leaving it.

## Hon. Louis Frey, Jr.

OF FLORIDA

Mr. Speaker, the world has lost a friend. People of all ages, all political ideologies and all nations respected and revered Dwight D. Eisenhower. He was a great military leader in times of war. But more important, he was the President who united this Nation and led it to peace. A deeply religious man, his strong spirit and will were evident even in these last days and hours. Dwight Eisenhower's mission in life was to chart a course toward permanent world peace and human benefit. The greatest tribute we can pay him is to do everything in our power to fulfill this mission.

## Hon. Robert C. McEwen

OF NEW YORK

Mr. Speaker, we are all saddened by the death of Dwight D. Eisenhower. Soldier and statesman, his life was one of distinguished and disciplined devotion to service.

As the general commanding the greatest military force ever assembled, he led American and Allied armies to victory in Europe.

Called by his countrymen to the highest office in this Republic, he brought an end to the Korean conflict and maintained the peace during his years as our President.

For his great leadership in these accomplishments, he received the deep and continuing appreciation of a grateful people. For his dignity, humility, and warmth of personality, he was held in affection by all.

To Mrs. Eisenhower and his family, I extend my deepest sympathy as we all share in their loss and bereavement.

## Hon. Albert W. Watson

OF SOUTH CAROLINA

Mr. Speaker, because of the universal esteem with which General Eisenhower was held, I deem it appropriate for Congress to take immediate action to preserve the memory of this honored American by renaming the District of Columbia Stadium, the "Dwight David Eisenhower Memorial Stadium."

Therefore, in order to pay this initial tribute to this distinguished American, I plan to introduce a resolution to attain just such a goal.

This magnificent stadium was built during the administration of President Eisenhower. As we all know, he was a sports enthusiast. His example of courage, fair play, devotion to duty, and deep humility are the attributes of a great athlete and it was this example which inspired untold millions to conquer life's adversities.

I know that all my colleagues will want to join in this worthy endeavor.

Few men of history have ever received the universal love, respect, and acclaim during their own lifetime as that accorded to General Eisenhower. His continuing strength and abiding faith were an inspiration to people everywhere, and when he finally succumbed to an illness which had plagued him for so long, we could not help but be exalted by the tenacity with which a man his age clung to life. His universal appeal as soldier, statesman, humanitarian and those other accomplishments of such a great and noble spirit will be forever enshrined in the hearts of all who aspire to make this earth of ours a better place to live. There will be countless ways in which Ike will be remembered in the years ahead.

While I am certain that each of us will recall him in a different way, I shall remember most of all his indomitable courage and boundless optimism during the dark days of World War II. Just as his contemporary, the great Sir Winston Churchill, Dwight David Eisenhower stands as one of the giants of the 20th century, because he and Churchill played such an important role in leading us through the most monumental crisis that our century has thus far been confronted with—the Second World War. The Nation, indeed the world, stands a little sadder today because of his passing. But, we can take heart. His life made it possible for us to stand taller as we face the future with renewed purpose, direction, and above all, hope.

## Hon. William E. Minshall
OF OHIO

Mr. Speaker, 1,200 miles of railroad track tie Washington to Abilene.

America's heart is on the train carrying home the body of Dwight David Eisenhower from the Capital of the Nation he served so devotedly to the vast golden wheat fields of the Kansas he loved.

Soldier, statesman, he epitomized all that we like to think is best in the American character. He was friend to the world, and the world responded to his warmth. "I like Ike" probably has been repeated in nearly every language spoken on the globe.

As President Nixon said in his beautiful eulogy yesterday in the rotunda, General Eisenhower undoubtedly was loved by more people in more parts of the world than any other American President.

Each of us who had the privilege of calling him friend has his own special memories of the 34th President of the United States.

Mine extends back to World War II when I first met him in the European Theater. He was a soldier's soldier, a commander who inspired confidence, devotion, courage, the will to win.

Yet Great Britain's Lord Moran, who knew him well, sensed even then the real Dwight Eisenhower, the man of peace. In the bleak days of 1943 Lord Moran wrote of the general that—

> Could he have had his way he would have spent a quiet life in the country stillness, near some tree-reflecting stream, but that was not to be his lot. He loathed war.

It was precisely because he knew the horrors of war and the blessings of peace, that as Commander in Chief he was able to give our Nation the only virtually untroubled 8 years this country has known since the end of World War II. The times were no less demanding, the decisions he made during his two terms in office were as critical as any during the European campaign. But while he was President not one drop of American blood was shed in battle, not one inch of free world soil lost.

First and foremost his objective was a world in which free men could live in harmony together. This was his crusade. It was his fervent prayer during the years after he left the White House.

The last time I visited General Eisenhower, a little more than a year ago, at Gettysburg, the famous grin was as infectious as ever, the twinkle in his blue eyes seemed to mock at time. It came with a stab of pain to realize that he was, indeed, growing old.

We who fought under him in Europe and shared his victories, we who worked with him to carry out his programs in Congress, we who were privileged to counsel with him at Gettysburg in later years—we had grown accustomed to Eisenhower victories over impossible odds, even those posed by his failing health.

After so many victories, it was hard to accept the inevitable, that one day he would fight his last great battle and would lose, as all men must. We are grateful that death came to him quietly and gently.

His long life was filled with mighty and heroic struggles. His valiant spirit endures to inspire all men who love freedom.

Dwight David Eisenhower combined the best qualities of ordinary Americans and thereby became the most extraordinary American our country has produced. He was a man who loved the outdoors, who once wistfully remarked, of the squirrels on the White House lawn:

> They have a freedom I would personally dearly love.

And now, after so many years of striving to bring new understanding of the word freedom and brotherhood to the world, his work is finished.

Abilene was little more than a frontier town

when young Dwight Eisenhower moved there as a boy. The names of Bat Masterson, Wyatt Earp, and other Kansas heroes were not mere legends to him, they were vivid memories on the lips of his elders. He grew up on stories of pioneers, hardships, of the right and wrong of the western frontier. He was taught, and believed, and proved, that a man can be anything he aspires to be, if he is honest, willing to work hard, has courage and faith in his Creator.

Speaking of his childhood, General Eisenhower once said:

> I found out in later years that we were very poor, but the glory of America is that we didn't know it then.

The boy from Abilene now is part of the glory of America. He has left a heritage neither time nor death can extinguish.

After a life of devotion to his country, to the cause of freedom throughout the world, he is going home to what he always called "the heart of America." Not far from his resting place flows the "tree-reflecting stream," the Smoky Hill River. Spring is a burst of loveliness on the Kansas plains, summer a blaze of heat and ripening grain, fall a triumph of harvest time, winter harsh and cold and a time for fireside stories of the days when Kansas was young, stories Dwight Eisenhower loved all his life.

And he can say, with Benet's "William Sycamore":

> My youth returns, like the rains of Spring
> And my sons, like the wild geese flying,
> And I lie and hear the meadow-lark sing,
> And have much content in my dying.
>
> Go play with the towns you have built of blocks,
> The towns where you would have bound me.
> I sleep in my earth like a tired fox,
> And my buffalo have found me.

God speed the train to Abilene.

## Hon. Roger H. Zion

OF INDIANA

Mr. Speaker, Ike is gone. The courageous heart is finally stilled.The grand old soldier whose life and career were so closely entwined with the destiny of his country has been permitted to rest at last.

Dwight David Eisenhower was never a quitter. He fought his way from the poverty of a prairie farm boyhood to the ranks of West Point. His career sent him to the summit of military achievement as commander of allied forces in World War II. A grateful nation refused, as they had refused General Washington, the opportunity of a quiet retirement following the conclusion of his military career and bestowed upon General Eisenhower the Presidency of the United States. His tenure as President marked one of the great eras of prosperity and peace in the national history.

Ike was no speechmaker. He had little familiarity with the clever turn of phrase that characterizes the experienced politician. His own formal politics were, at best, uncertain. But his philosophy of living, of duty, of loyalty to country, of honor—these were firmly rooted in the great traditions of America. From these he never swerved. Successful politics involves the art of compromise. And history will thus not record Dwight Eisenhower as a master politician. For the principles of decency and honor learned in midwest farm upbringing simply would not be comprised by this man.

Americans sensed the character of which Ike was made. He was elected and reelected to the Presidency by overwhelming majorities. The Nation that he had served so well for so long was strangely moved by this kind, good President who cared little for the entrapments of power. He left the Presidency in 1961 enjoying a pinnacle of esteem that few men in the history of this world have enjoyed.

His greatest battle was yet before him. The ravages of world wars and 8 years in the Presidency had taken their toll. His weary heart began to fail. A nation waited and prayed with the family of Dwight Eisenhower through each new crisis—each terrible onslaught on the gallant heart.

Now, kind providence has stilled his suffering and a nation remains to mourn the passing of her faithful son. I may only hope that the collective memory of what he was will remind all of our people of what we, as a nation, have been and what we still can be.

## Hon. Clement J. Zablocki

OF WISCONSIN

Mr. Speaker, in General Eisenhower's death our entire Nation, regardless of our individual views and perspectives, mourns the passing of one of our great leaders.

I join all Americans in mourning the passing of Gen. Dwight D. Eisenhower. His page in history will indeed be an illustrious one and his contributions to the free world and his search for lasting peace have endeared him to all people.

General Eisenhower was in many ways the embodiment of the virtues which have sustained our Nation through the nearly 200 years of our existence.

Some people said that he projected a "father image." This to me is a high compliment. For in times of stress and uncertainty he was the man in whom the Nation placed its highest trust, and he lived up to that trust to the best of his ability.

He was a good soldier, an outstanding general, and above all, in a time of tension and division, a unifying force for a nation surrounded by a world of peril and trouble.

General Eisenhower's influence went beyond the years of his Presidency. Nearly to his dying day, he was a leader who provided counsel and guidance to the men who have been and are responsible for carrying on the highest responsibilities of this Nation.

Although he was elected as a Republican, he was not at heart a partisan man. He championed causes which he believed were good for this Nation and the cause of freedom. And he did it at times by rallying some fragments of his political party to the support of the undertakings of Democratic administrations.

General Eisenhower came from the Midwest, the heartland of our Nation. All of us mourn him. My wife joins me in extending heartfelt sympathy to his beloved wife and family. May they be comforted in the knowledge of the love and hope he inspired throughout the world.

## Hon. H. R. Gross

OF IOWA

Mr. Speaker, President Eisenhower was a strong man, physically and morally.

I admired, as did all Americans, his courageous fight for life through a long series of operations and heart attacks.

History will probably record as the two greatest accomplishments of his life the fact that during the 8 years in which he served as President he kept the United States at peace, and his administration was untouched by the scandals that tarnished preceding and subsequent administrations.

In the most respected sense of the word, President Eisenhower was a simple man, uncomplicated and unpretentious in his great affection for his country.

I extend my sympathy to Mrs. Eisenhower and members of the family.

## Hon. Mario Biaggi

OF NEW YORK

Mr. Speaker, tributes can hardly do justice to the service that Dwight D. Eisenhower gave to his country and the entire free world. His kind does not often pass among us.

He was surely one of our greatest generals and one of our truly peace-loving Presidents. His successful leadership of the United States in war and peace made every home in our Nation safer and many times contributed to the protection of our free Western civilization.

He was both a great man and a good man who was possessed of moral courage and genuine kindness; a man you would be proud to call your friend.

Though he has fallen, his greatness and his deeds will never die.

## Hon. Charles E. Chamberlain

OF MICHIGAN

Mr. Speaker, the people of America—indeed the people of the world—mourn the death of a great man, Gen. Dwight D. Eisenhower. He gained the affection and respect of all men as a hero of peace as well as a hero of war.

As president he brought us a peaceful end to the Korean conflict. Just as he ended the war with Germany by military action. Rarely has a military leader so completely earned the world's attention and trust as a statesman. The sympathy of our Nation and the world goes out to Mrs.

Eisenhower and her family in their hour of grief. Their loss is truly our loss.

Great men need no eulogies. Their character and deeds require no external illumination and in fact none is possible.

They shine out of the past unaided or not at all.

Through them the world is permanently changed and goes on changing.

Their truth, we may imperfectly understand and express, neglect and forget, but it remains unalterably part of our history.

It falls upon us, the living, however, to preserve that past in the living memory of each new generation. It is this duty particularly that prompts us to offer our thoughts at a time when a reverent and grateful silence would speak best our deepest feelings.

Many have noted the presence of many young people amidst the thousands that have come to pay their final respects to General Eisenhower. Many of these were born since the end of his final term as President and a great many more did not live through the trials and triumphs of World War II. It is for these new citizens of our country that we should direct our praise for the man we honor today.

Yesterday President Nixon eloquently stated the essential quality of General Eisenhower, saying:

> It was the character of the man, not what he did but what he was.

It is the example of this simple, honest man that commends itself to us today as our Nation strives to heal the wounds of discord that have come to trouble its spirit. The challenges that Dwight D. Eisenhower faced in his day, while perhaps different, were no less difficult than those we face today or will face tomorrow. He met and conquered them without fear or malice in the finest tradition of "duty, honor, country."

In his death by reminding us all of the immortality of these truths General Eisenhower has served his country as he served it in his lifetime.

## Hon. Peter W. Rodino, Jr.

OF NEW JERSEY

Mr. Speaker, I join with my colleagues, my country, and the world in mourning the death of Dwight David Eisenhower, the 34th President of the United States. The world has lost a leader; the country has lost a devoted servant; and all Americans have lost a man that was a source of courage and inspiration to them.

President Eisenhower will long be remembered for his leadership during the Second World War and later during the Korean conflict. He will long be remembered for his courage and determination in his long battle with death.

The Newark Evening News and Star Ledger has both captured the spirit and the bond between General Eisenhower and the people. They are words well and justly spoken, and I include them herewith:

[From the Newark (N.J.) Evening News, Mar. 31, 1969]

### Nation in Mourning

A great American has died and no presidential proclamation was required to impel the nation to mourn his passing. His countrymen gave Dwight David Eisenhower honors and gratitude. And they gave him the greatest office within their power to give. But more than acclaim and reward, they gave him their affection.

To the people he was no remote hero, no aloof statesman. To the people he was Ike.

What special quality did he possess that evoked this bond? It was, it seems, a national response to a man of warmth and simplicity to whom it gave its confidence and votes in unprecedented degree. And with the presidency went a personal affection that few Americans have attained.

Dwight Eisenhower had gained world fame. He was the man who, having led an army to victory in the greatest of all wars, hated war as a "damnable thing." He hated it for what it meant in hardship and sacrifice to the countless young men he had to commit to the hazards of battle. A compassionate man, it was this bitter experience which had its origin in the fires of war that inspired his deep devotion to peace so manifest during his eight years in the presidency.

He was a man who wore his honors with easy dignity, born of a strain of religious humility so alien to the cynicism of today's world. He spoke often and proudly of his mother's training in his formative years and he did so without affectation or hesitation. He grew up in simpler, if harder, times and for today's young there is a lesson in the disciplines that he accepted without question in his youth.

Now the general of the army, the two-time president, the man from Abilene is dead, and his mourning country is diminished by the loss.

---

[From the Newark (N.J.) Star-Ledger, Mar. 29, 1969]

### Ike: Soldier, Politician

For Dwight David Eisenhower, it was a full, productive and eventful life; it was a life divided into two diverse, distinct worlds, the military and politics, and profoundly influenced the life and times of hundreds of millions, in war and in peace.

Ironically, it seemed Eisenhower was ever completely at ease in either pursuit that occupied his adult life . . . one for which he was trained, the other for which he was drafted to resuscitate a long mordant Republican Party.

Millions of Americans had a deep and abiding affection for the Kansas farm boy; they cast him in a heroic mold as a military leader and as a reassuring father image in political life.

Like other world leaders before him, Gen. Eisenhower was a product of his times. His early military life could hardly be described as distinguished; as a professional soldier he was resigned to rounding out his career as a colonel, but cataclysmic events dramatically decreed otherwise.

And later in private life, when he was content to live out the years in the tranquillity of the academe, he was thrust into the political arena, a reluctant candidate who only four years earlier had observed that a military man should not run for President unless there were exceptional circumstances to make it necessary.

In both spheres of his life there were personal conflicts, close to the surface of this leader, that occasionally broke through the characteristic Eisenhower grin, a lifelong trait that established a warm relationship with Americans and foreigners alike.

Born of pacifist origins, he chose the Army as a profession and was later to lead three million men into battle in history's greatest military operation. But he was intrinsically a man of peace who never really strayed far afield from the pacifist teachings of a mother who frowned on his choice of a career.

As a militarist who knew on an intimate level the essential evil of war, Gen. Eisenhower was avowedly dedicated to peace in his private and political lives after he left the Army. He was a world leader who made a number of fateful decisions, including one that assured his election as President when he declared that he would go to Korea to seek an armistice.

But while there was unrestrained praise for Gen. Eisenhower, there were detractors for President Eisenhower who never seemed to get over an elemental distaste for the rough-and-tumble milieu of politics. His reluctance to exert his immense popularity as a potent lever in the civil rights area, after this volatile social issue drew an unprecedented constitutional vitality from Supreme Court landmark decision on school desegregation in 1954, was deplored in a number of quarters.

He was a caretaker President at a time when the nation was at the height of its power and vigor, determined to keep the ship of state on an even keel in foreign and domestic waters. It was a sense of caution that marked his early military life and carried over into his tenure as President.

In World War II, as commander of the European theater, the general established his niche in military history; he did not come up quite as well as the nation's peacetime commander-in-chief. He was not a social innovator like President Roosevelt before him and President Johnson after him; nor did he display the combative personal stamp that marked the Administration of President Truman.

As President, Mr. Eisenhower was a chief executive who chose to remain aloof from the fires of partisan conflict, nor was he a strong influence on Congress. It is likely that when his Administration is reviewed in historical terms, Ike will likely be categorized as a good president, not a great one.

It was an Administration largely influenced by the so-called Assistant President, Sherman Adams, a stern, implacable New Englander who became embroiled in an unsavory episode involving a Boston industrialist, and John Foster Dulles, the architect of a foreign policy that was blamed for much of America's present difficulties overseas.

Eisenhower had misgivings about running for the presidency, and there were periods when he was neither comfortable nor happy in this most demanding and lonely citadel of power. It was in one of these moments of self doubts that the President once told the late House Speaker Sam Rayburn that historians would probably rank him with George Washington and Robert E. Lee as one of the great military leaders of the nation. As President, he wasn't sure how he would be graded in history.

It was a perceptive self-appraisal that could stand as an objectve accounting of this leader's life in war and peace, a dominant, influential figure whose stature never diminished in the eyes and hearts of his grateful countrymen.

## Hon. Philip J. Philbin

OF MASSACHUSETTS

Mr. Speaker, I am profoundly touched and deeply grieved by the passing of President Eisenhower. He was one of our greatest Presidents and one of our greatest Americans.

His entire life was unselfishly and brilliantly devoted to our country. He was a superb military leader, who won the hearts of his men and the gratitude of our country and allies, by his inspiring, victorious leadership of our united military forces in a most crucial war.

This great American stood out for his truly illustrious service to our country and the American people as President for 8 long critical years in our history.

His motivations were always lofty; his principles were based on solid American values; and his concerns and contributions encompassed the Nation, the world, and all mankind.

He was a personal friend, and I looked upon him with highest regard, admiration, and affection.

He was kindly, generous, and humane, instinctively dedicated to the higher concepts of duty, not only in his career as a soldier but in the Presidency and throughout his entire life.

He will be greatly missed by all of us, the American people he served so well, and peoples everywhere whom he was so eager to help toward prosperity, freedom, and peace. He has left a great legacy of honest, distinguished, loyal service to our country, which will always be gratefully remembered.

I extend my prayers and most heartfelt sympathy to his wonderful, devoted wife and all his dear ones, and join them in mourning him.

## Hon. Henry B. Gonzalez
OF TEXAS

Mr. Speaker, all Americans, regardless of political persuasion, mourn the passing of former President and General of the Army Dwight David Eisenhower. He was a singularly beloved President and a great military leader. Born in Texas and raised in Kansas, his achievements have made a profound mark on the history of this Nation.

Not only was "Ike" one of our most loved Presidents and a great leader of the Allied military effort in World War II, but he was prophetic in his farewell address as President in his assessment of the risks inherent in a growing military-industrial complex in a democratic society. As one who has drawn inspiration from his valedictory address before it became currently popular to do so, I have long been impressed with his perception. Nothing indicates the greatness of this fine old soldier more than his respect for rule by the people and for the due process of democracy.

San Antonio is proud of its connection with the career of this great American during his years of service at Fort Sam Houston. It was on our historic Army base in 1915 that First Lieutenant Eisenhower first met Miss Mamie Doud, and where they started their married life. "Ike" was reassigned from Fort Sam in 1917, preparatory to fighting in World War I, and it was not until 1941 that the Eisenhowers were again in residence at Fort Sam. But certainly this assignment was again a most memorable one for them, because it was at Fort Sam that "Ike" was promoted to brigadier general, receiving his first star. A recent article from the San Antonio Light which I am inserting at the end of my remarks contains interesting details of General Eisenhower's tours of duty at Fort Sam Houston.

The sympathy of the Nation goes out to Mrs. Mamie Eisenhower and the Eisenhower family. Their personal loss is shared in a very real sense by the entire country.

The article referred to follows:

EISENHOWER, MAMIE, AND FORT SAM HOUSTON

(Gen. Dwight D. Eisenhower, who died Friday, felt a special attachment to Fort Sam Houston and San Antonio. So did his widow, the former Mamie Doud. Here is the story about the couple's close affiliation to historic Fort Sam Houston.)

The most distinguished military leaders of this nation have served tours of duty at historic Fort Sam Houston.

Gen. Douglas MacArthur, Gen. John J. "Black Jack" Pershing, Gen. Jonathan M. Wainwright, Gen. Walter Krueger, were all men in whom the U.S. Army and Fort Sam Houston personnel take great pride. But for Dwight David Eisenhower, President of the United States, General of the Army, this feeling of pride and admiration has always been a little special.

Perhaps this feeling of kinship and affection for Gen. Eisenhower stems from the fact that he began his career at Fort Sam Houston as a young second lieutenant fresh from West Point, in September 1915, while assigned to the 19th Infantry, that he brought his 20-year-old bride to Fort Sam Houston on July 11, 1916, 10 days after their marriage.

He received his first star in ceremonies held at Fort Sam Houston in 1941 and from here he departed at the onset of World War II, to make military history as one of our greatest soldiers.

In his book "At Ease—Stories I Tell My Friends," the general said: "One Sunday afternoon after I'd been in Texas for some months, I walked out of the bachelor officer quarters to make a guard post inspection as Officer of the Day.

MAJOR'S WIFE

"On the sidewalk across the street was a small group of people, one of whom was Lulu Harris, wife of a major.

" 'Ike,' she called, 'won't you come over here? I have some people I'd like you to meet.'

" 'Sorry, Mrs. Harris,' I called back, 'I'm on guard duty and have to start an inspection trip.'

"She then turned to one young girl, as I discovered later, and said, 'Humph! The woman hater of the post.'

"The girl said something to Mrs. Harris that caused her to call once more. 'We didn't ask you to come over to stay. Just come over and meet these friends of mine.' "

CROSSED STREET

Lt. Eisenhower did cross the street in front of Bldg. 688, on Infantry Post Road and was introduced to the

Doud family of Denver, Colo., who were spending the winter in San Antonio.

This was the first meeting of Ike and his beloved Mamie. And it did not end with a simple introduction. The young officer promptly asked the attractive and captivating 18-year-old Miss Doud if she would care to walk along with him on his rounds of the guard posts. She just as promptly accepted the invitation, although she admitted in later years that walking was not one of her favorite forms of exercise.

On Valentine's Day, 1916, Ike gave Mamie his West Point class ring and formally asked her father for her hand in marriage. He almost didn't get it.

Only his deep love for little Mamie kept Dwight D. Eisenhower from becoming one of this nation's first pioneer pilots. He desperately wanted to join the aviation section of the Signal Corps, as the Air Force was called in those days. However, Mr. Doud considered flying the sign of an irresponsible character and threatened to withdraw his consent to the marriage, Ike stayed on the ground.

On July 1, 1916, the Eisenhowers were married in Denver, Colo., at the Central Presbyterian Church. The bride received a wedding ring purchased from Hertzberg's Jewelry Store in San Antonio and the groom received a promotion to first lieutenant.

Following a 10-day honeymoon, the couple returned to Ft. Sam Houston to take up life in Ike's old quarters at 688 Infantry Post.

BRIEF VISIT

In February 1959, Mrs. Eisenhower paid a brief visit to San Antonio. Asked about her first home at Ft. Sam Houston she was most explicit in describing the quarters. She said that she and the general had started their married life in "the building to the left hand entrance of Infantry Post, the second stairway, the first floor, the apartment on the left."

With this information officials of the Army post were able to place a historical marker over the entrance to the quarters.

Shortly after their marriage, Lt. Eisenhower was made Ft. Sam Houston provost marshal, a job he held until the spring of 1917 when his unit, the 19th Infantry, was detailed to Camp Wilson adjacent to the main post. Ike went to Camp Wilson as regimental supply officer and assistant mustering officer for the Southern Department.

LEON SPRINGS

When the 19th Infantry formed the 57th Infantry and moved to Leon Springs for training, Ike went along with the unit. It was at Leon Springs that one of the most unusual experiences of his life occurred. He was struck by lightning while standing under a tree in front of his tent.

Not only was Eisenhower knocked unconscious by the bolt, but the 57th's adjutant, Capt. Walton Walker, was also hit. Neither man suffered any permanent damage and, in fact, received a certain amount of local acclaim after their commanding officer Col. David J. Baker, made it known that he was the only regimental commander in the Army whose entire staff had been struck by lightning and lived to tell the tale.

On Sept. 18, 1917, promoted to captain, Ike left Ft. Sam Houston for Ft. Ogelthorpe, Ga., here he served as an instructor in the officer training camp. The Eisenhower family did not return to Ft. Sam Houston for almost 25 years.

YEARS BETWEEN

The years between World War I and the fall of 1941 were years of peace and years in which a career Army officer moved slowly up through the ranks while serving in various positions within the military establishment. Eisenhower was a tank corps commander, an executive officer and a recreation officer, at different times and places during this period of time.

He was promoted to major on June 17, 1918 and to lieutenant colonel on Oct. 4, 1918. These were temporary ranks however, and it was not until July 2, 1920 that he was given the permanent rank of major and not until 16 years later, on July 1, 1936, that he became a permanent lieutenant colonel.

On July 1, 1941, their 25th wedding anniversay, with Eisenhower newly promoted to the rank of full colonel, Mamie and Ike returned to Ft. Sam Houston, where their life together had begun. They moved into Bldg. 177 on Artillery Post Road and two months later to Bldg. 179, quarters the couple were to occupy until the outbreak of World War II, a few short months later.

CHIEF OF STAFF

On Aug. 1, 1941, Col. Eisenhower was assigned to duty as chief of staff of the 3rd Army under Gen. Walter Krueger.

In the months of August and September 1941, Eisenhower, Gen. Krueger and the 3rd Army met the forces of Gen. Ben Lear's Second Army in the famous Louisiana maneuvers.

At the close of the Louisiana maneuvers, Col. Eisenhower received his first star and promotion to brigadier general in ceremonies held on Ft. Sam Houston's Treat Field, directly across the street from his quarters at 179 Artillery Post.

On Dec. 7, 1941, Brig. Gen. Eisenhower ate lunch and took a nap. The nap was very brief. Shortly after he had retired his aide woke him to bring the news of the bombing of Pearl Harbor.

WEEK LATER

One week later on Dec. 14, Eisenhower, on verbal orders from Gen. George C. Marshall, chief of staff, reported to Washington, D.C. and the War Department.

He did not return to Ft. Sam Houston again. However, he and Mrs. Eisenhower remembered the old Army post where they had met and established their first home.

In September, 1967, a large package arrived at the Ft. Sam Houston Military Museum. It contained a pair of polished riding boots, one tropical worsted shirt and a pair of wool riding pants. The uniform was from Gen. Eisenhower and was one he had worn during the North African campaigns of World War II.

COLOR PHOTO

In 1968, he and Mrs. Eisenhower autographed a color photo of their quarters at 179 Artillery Post for historical purposes and Mrs. Eisenhower wrote a personal letter to the post's Historical Society, describing their experiences while serving in the house at the outbreak of World War II.

Ike did not forget Ft. Sam Houston—and Ft. Sam Houston will never forget him.

## Hon. John O. Marsh, Jr.

OF VIRGINIA

Mr. Speaker, the late President Eisenhower had a close association with the Seventh Congressional District of Virginia. His mother was born in Augusta County, a short distance from Fort Defiance, a small community near Staunton, in the historic Shenandoah Valley. In fact, a number of the late President's distant kinsmen are residents of that area today.

This association was a source of great pride to the citizens not only of this area but, indeed, of the entire Commonwealth of Virginia. The general received an enthusiastic welcome when, in the fall of 1960, he paid a visit to his mother's birthplace and to Staunton, Va.

His death marks the passing of one of the remaining few world figures who were the architects of allied victory in World War II. In this regard, we see the passing not only of a man, but of an era. Countless thousands have honored by word and respectful presence the virtues of this great American leader whose public service covered such a broad horizon of human endeavors ranging from military leader to college president to Chief Executive. Many can extol better than I his innumerable achievements and contributions to his country and to humanity.

In a world that is a violent one, where many governments are likely to be dictatorial and tyrannical as opposed to democratic, we see in this national loss the passing of a leader elected by the people because they respected and admired him.

When you look at the life of Eisenhower, his dedication to democracy, to the dignity of the individual, and basic decent morality, he stands as an outstanding example of leadership in a world that needs such examples.

His life is in contrast to a number of contemporary heads of government. How unlike Hitler, Mussolini, and Stalin does he stand forth as a head of state.

How unlike Castro, Kosygin, Khrushchev, and Ho Chi Minh is this man who dedicated his life to the service of his country and recognized the innate worth of the individual.

To him, power came from the people and should be used on their behalf, rather than for the ambitions and whims of any individual or privileged few.

Like so many others, I had hoped for him a recovery in order that he might return to Gettysburg and continue to enjoy what was a well-earned and looked-forward-to retirement, while ready to serve his country, as he always was, with wise and straightforward counsel to younger men who acceded to the responsibilities of national leadership.

He was a fine example of what this country can produce, and the most fitting monument America can erect to him is one honoring him for this example of the greatness this country can produce for the service of humanity.

It is an example the world will miss.

## Hon. Jack Brinkley

OF GEORGIA

Mr. Speaker, as an Air Force pilot during the Korean war, the words "I like Ike" summed up for me a genuine, honest-to-goodness affection for my Commander in Chief. Although I never met him, he was a friend—one could accept this with complete assurance because of the quality of Dwight David Eisenhower, the man.

And this afternoon the bells will toll.

Can we hear them?

For whom do the bells toll, Mr. Speaker? They toll for me; they toll for you; they toll for the American people; they toll for all men. We are all diminished by his passing.

My thoughts and prayers are with his family and loved ones.

## Hon. Clarence E. Miller

OF OHIO

Mr. Speaker, General Eisenhower was a great man in every sense of the word. He was an all-

American man, universally accepted as the epitome of all that is good. Honest, able, courageous, his every act was in keeping with the highest standards of human behavior.

As I stood in the rotunda of the U.S. Capitol yesterday afternoon and witnessed the placing of General Eisenhower's casket on the catafalque, I was overwhelmed by the memory of the man.

As the leader of our combat forces in the European theater in World War II, I can well remember the manner of the man, the positive nature of his remarks, the assurance he exuded to the free world on the evening of the Normandy invasion on June 6, 1944. I clearly recall the series of military successes that followed which brought about the ultimate surrender of the Axis Powers the following May.

As the elected leader of our Government, he again exhibited his ability to lead and to bring about peace to a fractured international scene. Shortly after his assumption of the Presidency in 1952, he announced the signing of an armistice in Korea, which brought to an end another era of costly conflict.

General Eisenhower's long and successful career can best be summarized by the expressions of those that come to pay their last respects to him as he lies in state this very moment in the rotunda of the U.S. Capitol. The people come out of admiration for a man who was loved and revered by all who knew him, who imbued in the world in which he lived a spirit of good will and cooperation. They come because "they liked Ike." We all did, and we will sadly miss him.

## Hon. Frank Horton

OF NEW YORK

Mr. Speaker, "Ike" Eisenhower was a unique American hero.

He was a military leader whose biggest battle was for peace. He was a President who gave outstanding moral leadership to his people. He was an exemplary family man.

Affection for this late President transcends national boundaries. He was a world leader loved by men everywhere. His passing creates a void in our Nation that may never be filled.

The greatness of America and the promise it holds for all its citizens is exemplified in the life of President Eisenhower. He was born of parents poor in material wealth but rich in moral strength. He drove himself to fulfill every obligation he undertook.

President Eisenhower rose to world stature. His death takes from us an inspiration of a past era.

The Nation stands still at this moment. We bow our heads in a silent prayer that we may gain strength and wisdom in following the path laid down by this great man.

Mrs. Horton and I, who both served under his command in North Africa and Europe, joined the tens of thousands of people who came to the Capitol Sunday to pay last respects to the late President. I watched as the historic, black-draped caisson moved with slow and stately majesty on its sad journey to the Capitol.

Throngs of people lined the hushed streets of Washington to watch the progress of the flag-covered casket.

Despite the damp, bone-chilling cold of the afternoon, and even through snow and rain that fell briefly, the people stood patiently and respectfully. Many brought young children.

I heard one woman explain to a preschool youngster: "The old President was a great and good man. All these people have come to say goodby to him, to show that they loved him."

The love and respect in which President Eisenhower was held was reflected in many ways Palm Sunday as the Nation paid its final tribute to him.

There were the traditional rites of the funeral march, the 21-gun salute, the honor guard from all the services.

But perhaps the greatest tribute was the heartfelt one paid by great and small, old and young, rich and poor as they gathered together at the Capitol to say a sad goodby to the man they had called Ike, a man they all felt had served his country with noble self-sacrifice, far beyond what a nation could expect.

Dwight D. Eisenhower, five-star general, President, and elder statesman, was a man truly of the people. He rose from humble beginnings in a Kansas farming town to lead the Allied Armies to victory in Europe during World War II. General Eisenhower, the war hero, then became President Eisenhower, a man who searched as hard for peace in the postwar world as he had for victory during the massive conflict before.

Although he first came to fame as a war leader, I will remember him as a seeker for peace.

President Eisenhower led us through those first frightening years of history when men possessed the power to destroy civilization.

The great affection of the people for him certainly sustained him through those difficult years. I could see, in the solemn faces of those who lined Washington's streets as the funeral cortege passed by, the affection held for President Eisenhower.

To honor the late President, the heads of state from scores of countries came to Washington for the funeral services. Tens of thousands of mourners filed past the closed casket in the rotunda of the Capitol.

As if in tribute to the late President, pink buds on the magnolia trees which line many of Washington's streets started to bloom early this morning.

In a stirring eulogy, President Nixon told of the general's last words to Mrs. Eisenhower. President Eisenhower had said:

> I have always loved my wife. I have always loved my children. I have always loved my grandchildren. And I have always loved my country.

The people he loved and the people who loved him came in those few days to say, "Thank you, 'Ike'—and goodbye."

His life and his accomplishments should be a constant reminder that in these times of turmoil, unrest and tension, human qualities of sincerity, integrity, duty, love and goodness are our ultimate solution.

## Hon. Edward J. Patten
OF NEW JERSEY

Mr. Speaker, Dwight D. Eisenhower was not only one of the most popular Presidents in American history, he was also a great patriot, whose deep love for freedom helped him achieve distinction in both military and political fields.

People of all political faiths found him a warm and sincere man, whose integrity was never questioned. Let us remember that the freedoms Americans enjoy today were preserved by his military brilliance and leadership.

Dwight D. Eisenhower's leadership qualities were so unique and strong, he was selected Supreme Commander of Allied Forces over hundreds of officers of higher rank in World War II. That decision helped America and her allies triumph over an enemy that was determined to not only rule Europe, but to subjugate the entire world.

Mr. Speaker, because of his magnificent service, he earned the permanent gratitude of not only our Nation, but the other free nations of the world. Dwight D. Eisenhower was respected for his abilities, admired for his courage, and loved for his great compassion for mankind.

## Hon. William A. Steiger
OF WISCONSIN

Mr. Speaker, Dwight David Eisenhower was very much an American.

As the Christian Science Monitor put it in its March 29, editorial:

> Perhaps no President in history was more deeply and recognizably American than was Dwight D. Eisenhower. It was this quality—

The Monitor continues—

> which so many millions abroad instantly felt upon meeting or seeing him. It was a quality of strength which served him admirably, not only during the Presidency but during his equally distinguished career as an Army officer.

The words so eloquently spoken by those in this chamber today are testimony to General Eisenhower's character, ability, leadership, and humility.

I am deeply saddened by the death of General Eisenhower. Saddened in a personal sense and also because this man represents one of that group of men who brought us through some of our darkest days. The stature of an Eisenhower is not achieved without sacrifice or tribulation.

General Eisenhower was truly a hero, and this Nation can never repay its debt to his leadership of nations and people during the war, and as President of the United States.

Because I began my involvement in politics in that first Eisenhower-Nixon campaign by placing an "I Like Ike" bumper strip on my bicycle, I pause today to join the millions of people who are sad at his death. I want to express my respect for the man who today lies in state in this building.

## Hon. Hastings Keith
OF MASSACHUSETTS

Mr. Speaker, when I searched my thoughts and feelings to find the words of praise and commemoration appropriate for our late and beloved Dwight David Eisenhower—the one which seems to best fit is "supreme" in every sense of its meaning.

Dwight Eisenhower's service to America as a nation; to its people as citizens and, indeed, to all mankind is uniquely unparalleled in modern times. Perhaps the foundation for this supremacy was inborn at his birth; only God knows that for a certainty. However, during the course of his lifetime, from 1890 to 1969, he developed his inborn characteristics through his love of God and for his country, so as to become known and cherished by his fellow countrymen, civilian and military in every walk and rank of file. The citizens of the world—no matter whether friend or foe—came to know this man as a soldier of war who fought valiantly in the name of peace, and did just exactly that—brought peace to our world during his lifetime on it. Never before has so small a word in measure, so colloquial in sound, meant the supreme recognition of everything good in a man as "Ike."

"Ike" fought for peace, for justice, and for tranquillity.

As Supreme Allied Commander in Europe, he united the free world advocates into a victorious battle, but first he called upon Almighty God and beseeched Him to bless this crusade.

During his term as president of Columbia University, his countrymen called upon his qualities and characteristics of leadership to serve them as their President.

As the 34th President of the United States, he led America toward the goals of peace, justice, and tranquillity. He once again brought peace to the forefront—this time in Korea. He applied his tact as a general to his performance as President, and he called upon the American people to unite into a great freedom loving force and moved them along the paths of peace, progress, and a better world relationship.

Then, as "Ike" began to fight the most difficult battle of his own personal life, the world prayed and fought in heartfelt sincerity of spirit, this battle which only he could really wage alone. He now lies within the peace and tranquillity of the almighty defender of us all.

Personally, as a major in the U.S. Army, I served as one of General Eisenhower's staff during World War II.

Later, as a Member of Congress, I again had the good fortune to serve while he was our Nation's Chief Executive. He was a perceptive planner; he was a man who could reach into the hearts of people, and a man who could get people to work together. As our President, he moved our country forward in the true tradition of its Founding Fathers.

We can best honor him by striving, whether as a private citizen or a public servant, to heed our Nation's calls or causes by continuing to work for the goals which he sought during his lifetime—goals which, if realized, will make this Nation and this world a much better place in which to live.

Such peace as we have now, even in these troubled times, is to a large degree, because of the leadership of this soldier-statesman. He achieved it through his qualities of warmth and candor and because of his confidence in the essential goodness of man. His selflessness was a unique quality in this age where most men and most countries are seeking to satisfy their physical want.

Mr. Speaker, often I have seen these past few days, the American flag flying at half mast in full dignity and honor of the man we all knew as "Ike"—I can only pray that, as the flag of this country rises once again to its full height, so also will the principles for which "Ike" stood, will rise anew in the hearts and minds of the citizens of our great country and spill over into the hearts and minds of the world, in order that peace and tranquillity may reign supreme.

## Hon. Robert L. F. Sikes
OF FLORIDA

Mr. Speaker, I think every American feels a sense of personal loss at the death of General Eisenhower. He has been prominently identified with American history and progress since the early days of World War I, and this spans more than a generation.

During wartime he was entrusted with the

highest allied command in the European theater, and subsequently a grateful country called him to the Presidency. His leadership both in peace and war was of the highest caliber and the heritage which he leaves is one of dedication to our country, to duty, and of calm acceptance of responsibility.

He knew the cost of defense, but he also knew a strong defense was essential to our Nation's security. He strove with dedication to chart a safe course for a lasting peace. No man could do more and at the time of his death a sorrowing America pays homage to a great leader and remembers him with great appreciation.

## Hon. Edith Green
OF OREGON

Mr. Speaker, Dwight David Eisenhower served the American Nation for more than half a century: as a great soldier who led us and the European democracies against brutal totalitarian regimes; as president of a great American university; as President of the United States through difficult and demanding years; and as an inspiring source of courage and resolve in his later years when illness never conquered the greatness of his spirit. He symbolizes the strength of our Nation which drew him to the highest seats of power and responsibility from humble origins in the prairie. In his life he enacted the ideal of America, to work with each other and with other nations with reason and compassion. Above all else, he advised against despair, against giving up on ourselves. He counseled all Americans to face the perils of our future with the courage of our fathers.

General Eisenhower lived a full and rewarding life, and his courageous struggle to live is in itself a memorial to his immense personal integrity, his joy in living and serving. His struggle was long and painful. Yet his will to live, along with his ability to live fully, provide example for all.

His own admonition to the cadets at the Air Force Academy in 1959 is an excellent comment on his own life. He said then:

> The one admonition I would give you is this; make sure you get enjoyment out of every day. Life should be a thing to enjoy. Make certain your face doesn't grow long as the day grows older. Go to bed with a smile and remember a fine day. And with that custom, I am quite sure you will find a long, happy, and fruitful life, fruitful to yourself, to your country, and to humanity.

## Hon. Barber B. Conable, Jr.
OF NEW YORK

Mr. Speaker, like many of my colleagues, I never had the privilege of serving in a National Government headed by Dwight David Eisenhower. Time flows quickly, and people come and go in our National Legislature. Nevertheless, I do not speak only as a citizen when I express my admiration for his contribution to the life of America. No one who has at any time served in Washington and understood the burdens of the Presidency can fail to have some special feeling about the grace with which General Eisenhower exercised the power of the greatest office in the world. He sensed the mood of the people, he understood their heartfelt thoughts, he identified with their fondest hopes in ways which permitted him to be much more than a leader in the classical sense; he was instead a friend, a kinsman, a partner in a common endeavor. Confidence is born of this feeling of identity, and confidence is the ingredient which makes democracy possible.

When such a man passes into history we feel a sense of personal loss even though we know that Government leaders must come and go, each leaving his own legacy. Who of us can judge the historic legacy of Dwight Eisenhower? Let us say, however, that we have lost a friend in whom we had confidence, a counsellor whose judgment we trusted, a warm and honest and unfettered spirit.

Mr. Speaker, may I add a special word of tribute to Mrs. Eisenhower, a lady I have never met, but of whose sympathetic contributions to her husband's career I am as sure as I am of today's sense of loss in his passing. We offer her our heartfelt best wishes at a time which must be very difficult for her.

## Hon. Joel T. Broyhill
OF VIRGINIA

Mr. Speaker, death came Friday to a great American. While it may have stilled one great and noble heart, it stirred anew in other hearts, including millions who fought beside him for freedom, solemn thoughts of the massive debt mankind owes to his memory.

Not since our Founding Fathers has an American soldier-statesman received the respect, reverence, and love accorded Dwight Eisenhower by the people of the world. He was a man worthy of any age. He belonged to our generation. He needs no monument, no cause, no cult. He was indeed a great American. I can think of no greater accolade—the true greatness of a humble man who responded to the call of duty from his countrymen. We shall all miss him.

## Hon. Delbert L. Latta
OF OHIO

Mr. Speaker, General Eisenhower was not only a great military and political leader but he was a great moral leader, as well. History may well record him in this capacity ahead of the other two. He possessed a unique moral quality that few men possess and never failed to show it wherever and whenever he appeared. His deeds and his actions made people so aware of this quality that no one ever doubted that actions taken by him were morally right. Such a quality is indeed a rarity and it was good for America and it was good for all humanity. The world will miss his goodness.

Mrs. Latta joins with me in extending deepest sympathy to Mrs. Eisenhower and members of her family.

## Hon. Louis C. Wyman
OF NEW HAMPSHIRE

Mr. Speaker, there are many Members of this Congress assembled here today who have lost, with the death of Dwight David Eisenhower, more than a general and a President, more than a great man to be admired from a distance, and more than an image to which we pay respect because of his noticeable accomplishments. To us, as is the case with thousands of Americans and other citizens of the world, his death marks the passing of that rare kind of leader whose humility, energy, and understanding drew toward him our deepest confidence and highest respect. We looked to him as a man who enjoyed virtually every honor which the world could bestow on a single individual, but who remained unspoiled by the tributes. As a great soldier and hero, he was yet a man who longed only for a just and lasting peace. As a distinguished President, he was a man who used political power only to build and strengthen his country, and abhorred the weaknesses that the abuse of political power brought forth in lesser men.

His accomplishments as a military leader need not be glorified for the fact that we are here today as free men to express ourselves in this manner is in no small part a result of his efforts. As a commander of the armies of many nations in an allied cause, his qualities of leadership earned the praise of the leaders of the free world and the confidence of its fighting men.

His accomplishments as a President can now, in retrospect, be looked upon with longing. He successfully guided us through two terms of peace and prosperity. He served us in a time when anything short of his great knowledge of the realities of power, how it should be regarded and used, could have brought grave consequences. He brought to the presidency a calm, quiet resolve to be guided by God and commonsense, to accomplish what he could with a humility and a trust in what is good and in what is right. And accomplish he did, for the trust was returned to him a thousandfold, and the love which he felt for his country is now and has been reflected by the love which his country feels for him, as well as the grateful thanks given to him for his role in making America mean what it does to all the people of the free world.

## Hon. James C. Cleveland
OF NEW HAMPSHIRE

Mr. Speaker, Dwight Eisenhower leaves us in the fullness of years, weighted with all the honors a grateful, admiring people can bestow.

Even though within the divine order of things, his loss is a grievous one. We will miss his breadth of experience, the sense of proportion and judgment which he aways applied to great problems, and the smile that warmed our hearts.

We have lost one of the truly great men of American history. In war and in peace, the

Eisenhower record will stand always as a testament to his enduring qualities of greatness. His courage, integrity and wisdom, his abiding faith in God and country, his humility, his uncomplicated, forthright character are qualities in the American tradition. They are the qualities which have made our Nation great and which have sustained us in hours of darkness.

They are qualities without which our Nation would be destroyed, as with other nations who have lost the faiths and strayed from the simple truths which inspired their foundings.

To have been acquainted with Dwight Eisenhower I shall always count as among the highest privileges of my life. He radiated integrity and unselfishness. He buoyed you up and lifted your spirits. One of the happiest benefits of our electronic age is that men like Eisenhower can be seen and studied by each new generation. What a tremendous advantage they have if they will but use it.

Through this wonderful medium coupled with his written word they, too, can come to know and understand the qualities of this great man. They, too, can someday sense something of the magic of his personality which no mere words in history books can quite convey.

So the sadness and loss we bear today is leavened by our sense of good fortune in having shared some portion of our life and times with Dwight Eisenhower. It is leavened, too, by our sense of triumphant pride in his human greatness. I think it is fair to say that no President except, perhaps, Washington has ever left office enjoying greater public affection. As President Nixon told us yesterday in the rotunda, that affection is worldwide, wherever freedom is cherished, deep rooted in the hearts of his fellow man.

I cannot close these heartfelt remarks without paying homage, too, to Mrs. Eisenhower. Her faith and graciousness and love for her husband have endured through these grievous days and set for us all yet another example of extreme grace under great stress.

## Hon. Charles H. Griffin

OF MISSISSIPPI

Mr. Speaker, I join in paying tribute to the life and character of Dwight David Eisenhower—one of America's foremost leaders. On March 28—last Friday—the inevitable took from our midst a patriot, a soldier, a statesman, a gentleman. Throughout his entire life, Dwight David Eisenhower exhibited those traits of virtue and decency which are required of men who must lead men in time of war and in time of peace.

Mr. Speaker, Ike is gone; but his good deeds will linger in the memory of Americans as long as there is an America.

In an eloquent, front-page editorial, the Vicksburg, Miss., Evening Post noted the Nation's loss and recalled the occasion on July 4, 1947, when, as Army Chief of Staff, General Eisenhower was in Vicksburg to accept the city's "surrender" to the United States. As a part of my remarks, I include the editorial, which follows:

### Ike Is Gone

The word-flashed around the world. One of the great figures of modern history has gone to his reward. The old soldier just "faded away." The rugged constitution which had withstood numerous heart attacks, three major surgeries, pneumonia and other ailments, finally won the victory over the stout-hearted soldier who not only won his victories in the greatest war of history, but also conquered the hearts of his countrymen and of the world. He was "Ike" to America—a military genius, a great president, but more than that, he was possessed of a wonderful personality which endeared him to his countrymen and to those who served under his various commands.

He is remembered with great affection in Vicksburg, where twenty-two years ago he came as the featured speaker at a great July Fourth celebration here. We well remember his words—"Instead of accepting the 'surrender' of Vicksburg, I confess that I have surrendered to the warmth of your welcome and to the graciousness of your hospitality." He took Vicksburg by the force of his great personality, and this was genuinely reflected in the splendid vote he received each time he ran for the Presidency. Vicksburg voted for "Ike".

He was the greatest military figure of the century, and the manner in which he forged into a great command the armies of many nations, remains as one of his most brilliant feats. It was this ability to bring forth a united force that resulted in the fall of the German empire.

A great man, a splendid citizen, a truly great American has answered the last roll call. As the nation pays homage to his memory, the spirit of this outstanding American should rekindle in the breasts of the people of our nation, a dedication to our country, which was the foremost quality of our former President.

The drums are muffled. Taps is sounding. Ike has gone. May he gain the reward promised to all who serve, and serve well.

## Hon. Wm. Jennings Bryan Dorn
OF SOUTH CAROLINA

Mr. Speaker, while we knew of General Eisenhower's declining health we were still unprepared for his passing. We are deeply saddened that his intense personality and famous smile that radiated confidence throughout the world will no longer be with us.

General Eisenhower symbolized and typified an entire era. He played a major role in the struggle of free peoples to remain free as an officer in World War I, as Supreme Allied Commander in Europe, as commander of NATO, as President in ending the Korean war, and in his decision to support South Vietnam. He encouraged the cause of freedom to stand fast when the world was threatened with total war and anarchy.

As Supreme Commander of the Allied Forces during World War II in Europe, I knew first hand of his superb accomplishments. He was unsurpassed in welding together an invincible fighting machine from so many diverse elements. As a soldier, near General Bradley's headquarters in Normandy, I learned of his diplomacy, his tact, and his ability to inspire confidence and cooperation from all branches of the service and from the armed forces of our allies. His selection by the President, and by General Marshal, as Supreme Commander in Europe proved to be a wise choice. His name became the symbol of a great crusade. He was admired and respected and loved by the free world. He even became the hope of many of the German people who had been enslaved by the raving Hitler and who saw in Eisenhower relief from slavery and oppression. His name became synonymous with justice as opposed to infamy and oppression.

When General Eisenhower became commander of NATO, it was my privilege to visit with him there at headquarters near Paris as a young Member of the Congress. I remember General Eisenhower telling us that 95 percent of his work as Allied commander and as NATO commander was diplomatic and political. He simply had, in a magnificent way, the ability to reject jealousy and envy and get people together. He was NATO commander during a critical time. When the forces of oppression and slavery threatened to engulf Europe, he inspired the peoples of Western Europe and caused them to stand firm during those critical years.

Dwight David Eisenhower, as President of the United States, provided for the American people, and those of the free world, a fatherly image of kindness and fairness. His smile, his winning personality, his character, and his modesty led America to the heights in the postwar era. We have not had a more popular President or general. The people loved "Ike." He was the one they wanted their sons and daughters to serve under in war. He was the one they wanted to lead them in peacetime. He respected the Office of the Presidency and advised and consulted with succeeding Presidents.

As an elder statesman, he was truly great. As a general, he will rank with Douglas MacArthur, George Washington, the Duke of Marlborough, the Duke of Wellington, and Robert E. Lee. Like them, he will be noted for his integrity, compassion, and devotion to, and respect for, the individual and those less fortunate. As President of the United States he will be associated with those virtues and attributes of character associated with the greatest.

I extend on the part of my fellow South Carolinians our deepest sympathy to Mrs. Eisenhower, his distinguished and devoted son, and all of their great and wonderful family.

## Hon. Charles A. Vanik
OF OHIO

Mr. Speaker, our former Commander in Chief, leader of the crusade in Europe, and two-term President has left us. We are all better men in a greater Nation because of our work with him.

Dwight David Eisenhower, general and President, gave his whole life to the service of his country. He led America's armies and then the whole Nation with rare strength and ability.

General Eisenhower believed strongly in the right and in the necessity of America pursuing the moral and right course. He had great spiritual faith and he tried to give that faith to America. He said that "faith is our surest strength, our greatest resource." Much of the courage and strength of America, through World War II and the darkest days of the cold war, was strength gained from the example of this leader of men.

It was my privilege to serve in the Congress

for 6 of the years of President Eisenhower's two terms. He was never partisan; never a leader of part of the people. He was truly a national leader; a leader of all Americans—loved by all Americans.

No one can question that his greatest accomplishment was to lead us to peace and keep us in peace.

Yet he may be remembered even more for his spiritual accomplishment, for his integrity, for his honesty, for the moral example he gave us all. General Eisenhower's great contemporary, Sir Winston Churchill, wrote most beautifully of the place of men in history:

> History with its flickering lamp stumbles along the trail of the past, trying to reconstruct its scenes, to revive its echoes, and kindle with pale gleams the passion of former days. What is the worth of all this? The only guide to a man is his conscience; the only shield to his memory is the rectitude and sincerity of his actions. With this shield, however the fates may play, we march always in the ranks of honor.

General Eisenhower always marched in the ranks of honor; he will always live in the minds of honorable men.

Dwight David Eisenhower said that "men grow in stature only as they daily rededicate themselves to a noble faith." With the example of this leader before us let us all rededicate ourselves to the faith which he had—to his faith in man, to his faith in America, to his faith in the right.

Again, my sympathy to his courageous family. May God bless them in this hour of grief.

## Hon. Carl Albert

OF OKLAHOMA

Mr. Speaker, I offer a resolution.

The Clerk read the resolution as follows:

H. Res. 351

*Resolved,* That the House of Representatives has learned with profound regret and sorrow of the death of General of the Army Dwight David Eisenhower, beloved former President of the United States of America.

*Resolved,* That in recognition of the many virtues, public and private, of the illustrious soldier and statesman, and as a mark of respect to one who has held such eminent public stations, the Speaker shall appoint a committee of the House to join with such Members of the Senate as may be designated, to attend the funeral services of the former President.

*Resolved,* That the House tenders its deep sympathy to the members of the family of the former President in their sad bereavement.

*Resolved,* That the Sergeant at Arms of the House be authorized and directed to take such steps as may be necessary for carrying out the provisions of these resolutions, and that the necessary expenses in connection therewith be paid out of the contingent fund of the House.

*Resolved,* That the Clerk communicate these resolutions to the Senate and transmit a copy of the same to the family of the deceased.

The resolutions were agreed to.

*The Speaker.* The Chair appoints the Speaker and the entire membership of the House to attend the funeral services for former President Dwight D. Eisenhower this afternoon at the Washington National Cathedral.

Members' wives have also been invited to attend these services.

The Chair appoints as members of the committee on the part of the House to attend the funeral services in Abilene, Kans., the gentleman from Texas, Mr. Fisher, and the gentleman from Kansas, Mr. Mize.

Transportation will be furnished to the cathedral this afternoon for Members and their wives and will also be available for the return to the Capitol at the completion of the services.

Buses will leave from New Jersey Avenue, between Independence Avenue and C Streets, promptly at 3:15 p.m. for the trip to the cathedral.

The Clerk will report the remaining resolution.

The Clerk read as follows:

*Resolved,* That as a further mark of respect to the memory of the former President, this House do now adjourn.

The resolution was agreed to.

A message from the Senate by Mr. Arrington, one of its clerks, announced that the Senate had passed a resolution of the following title:

S. Res. 175

*Resolved,* That the Senate has heard with profound sorrow and deep regret the announcement of the death of Dwight David Eisenhower, the former President of the United States and General of the Army of the United States.

*Resolved,* That as a token of honor to his illustrious statesmanship, his leadership in national and world affairs, his distinguished public service to his Nation, and as a mark of respect to one who has held such eminent public station in life, the Senate hereby expresses its deep sensibility of the loss the Nation has sustained by his death, and its sympathy with the family in their bereavement.

*Resolved,* That the two Senators from Kansas be appointed by the President of the Senate to attend the funeral of the deceased, to be held at Abilene, Kansas.

*Resolved,* That the Secretary of the Senate transmit these resolutions to the House of Representatives and transmit a copy thereof to the family of the deceased.

*Resolved,* That as a further mark of respect to the memory of the deceased the Senate do now adjourn.

## Hon. W. C. Daniel

OF VIRGINIA

Mr. Speaker, permit me to associate myself with the good and kind things which have been said here on the floor of the House about Dwight David Eisenhower.

Saturday night, March 29, I spoke to a junior chamber of commerce chapter at Clarksville, Va. A memorial service was held for General Eisenhower during the course of the meeting at which time I spoke briefly, and I should like to submit my remarks for the Record.

Of all the noble characteristics of General Eisenhower, perhaps his greatest was humility. Let me relate to you a personal experience that occurred during my term as national commander of the American Legion.

General Eisenhower gave me the opportunity to meet and discuss with him some of the problems with which we were faced at that time. During our discussion he evinced this humility in a remark about Gen. Omar Bradley. The general said:

> When Stonewall Jackson was killed at Chancelorsville, General Lee is reported to have said, "With the death of General Jackson, I have indeed lost my right arm."

General Eisenhower continued—

> Had I lost Bradley in Europe, I would have lost both arms.

General Eisenhower was a man of God who manifested deep feeling for his fellow beings. He served his Nation and the cause of freedom well. It is my prayer that God will grant him the peace and the rest that He has reserved for those who served Him well.

## Hon. William H. Ayres

OF OHIO

Mr. Speaker, the physical presence of Dwight David Eisenhower has departed from this earth but if we would only follow the principles and beliefs he exemplified, this world would at long last know once again that peace which marked his 8 years as President of the United States.

While we mourn his passing with a sorrow that is usually reserved for members of one's immediate family, we must be grateful for the long life granted to him so that not only this Nation, but also the free world might benefit from his wisdom and guidance.

We who served under him in World War II developed not only great confidence in his military leadership but also a great sense of affection for the man himself. As I donned my issue Eisenhower jacket, I can well remember my great sense of pride in becoming a part of the Eisenhower team. Even as an enlisted man, I could sense that his leadership would bring us victory over the mighty Hitler hordes.

Although we were a heterogeneous force when he took command, he soon knit us into a united team whose sole purpose was to bring freedom to all. It was only through this unification that Hitler's nefarious effort to enchain the entire world in slavery went down to permanent defeat.

No man has led armies into a more purposeful victory. All freedom-loving people called him "savior."

Upon my discharge, I, as well as all ex-servicemen, followed his career with great interest. We were pleased when he turned to the field of education, since we felt that he could instill in our sons that great sense of humanity and responsibility that characterized his own life.

When the Nation called on him to resume a military role as the leader of an international army to maintain the peace, we gained the feeling that free Europe would be secure. Time has justified our feelings.

We who knew him well, realized that this man, trained for war, was truly a man of peace.

Once more, I had this same sense of security when he became President of these United States.

Though many, during his campaign for that office, had expressed fears that he would lead us into wars abroad, we who had followed his every word knew differently. Again, our faith was justified. His two terms were periods of peace.

As he took over the Presidency, those of us who had served under him were immensely pleased that we were once more to become members of "Ike's" team. Although I was only a one-term Congressman when he assumed office, he accorded me the privilege of a lengthy, private discussion in order that I might make known to him my legislative views.

Here I learned of the similarity in our upbringing. We both came from families that not only lived by the Bible but raised their children to govern their actions by its teachings.

If only the parents of today would read the story of the early life of Dwight D. Eisenhower, as he himself told it, I believe that they would learn a method of child raising that would lead a fuller and more meaningful life for their children. His parents impressed upon him that service to his fellow man was a law of God. They also told him that such a service was futile unless it was accompanied by love.

It will be noted that even on the last day of his life, he spoke of his love for others. President Nixon has told us of the words that he spoke to his lovely wife from his deathbed.

He said:

I've always loved my wife. I've always loved my children. I've always loved my grandchildren and I've always loved my country.

I realize that I cannot speak for our Nation, but I can and do speak for the people of the 14th Ohio District when I say that we return the love of General Eisenhower from the depths of our being.

God was not dead to this man, and we know that he is now under His mantle.

To his beloved wife of 52 years, we can only say that the love that we felt for him encompassed the rest of those so dear to him. No tribute to Dwight David Eisenhower would be complete without the inclusion of Mrs. Mamie Eisenhower. She still remains in our hearts. Our hearts go out to her and the family in this hour of her greatest sorrow. All of our tears are intermingled with hers.

We are indeed fortunate that a man of Ike's own choosing and training occupies the White House. I am certain that he shares the dedication of Dwight Eisenhower for the welfare of all the people. Again we have a leader in whom we can have total confidence. We know that we will strive for that peace with justice that characterized the Eisenhower administration.

The Akron Beacon Journal recently ran an editorial about General Eisenhower's passing. That newspaper's president and editor, who is the chairman of the board of all Knight newspapers, was a personal friend and adviser of our late President. Excerpts from that editorial follow:

[From the Akron (Ohio) Beacon Journal, Mar. 29, 1969]

DWIGHT D. EISENHOWER

"Stand firmly for America."

This is Ike's legacy to the American people.

These are his final words, his final exhortation to those he loved and served and to those who loved him.

"Stand firmly for America" on the battlefields, in the halls of Congress, in our courts, in our schools, at the polling places and, most of all, in our homes.

Teach our children to love, respect and honor the principles of true American patriotism that Ike made the guideposts of his entire life. Teach our people that the only route to dignity, to prosperity, to individual greatness is the American way.

In the image of Washington, Lincoln and all the others who have built this nation to greatness, President-General Ike Eisenhower dedicated his life to standing firm for America in war and in peace.

He led us safely and well along the dangerous routes during war and peace. The inspiration and leadership he has given do not die with him.

While history must hand down the final verdict on the stature of this soldier, this statesman and this patriot, all of us must recognize the fact that General Eisenhower, as President during a critical period, inspired the American people to greater unity and confidence and courage.

As a leader in peace and war, we liked Ike. We shall treasure his memory.

Another good friend and confidant of General Eisenhower was Harvey S. Firestone, Jr., national chairman of the United Service Organization—USO—and retired chairman of the board of Firestone, I include, Mr. Speaker, his message to Mrs. Eisenhower:

The world has lost a leader and the nation mourns a friend. The valor, leadership, love of country and humanity of your gallant husband will keep his memory alive in the hearts of men for the ages and will be a continuing inspiration to those of us who counted ourselves among his friends.

As a statesman and as a soldier, he heard the drums of history and marched to them as the liberator of the free world.

## Hon. Clarence D. Long
OF MARYLAND

Mr. Speaker, I join my colleagues today in paying last respects to a great American, general of the Army and former President, Dwight David Eisenhower.

Dwight D. Eisenhower was a gallant and courageous man who gained the affection and respect of his countrymen and of all humanity.

His contributions, in war and in peace, are without measure. As the Supreme Commander of Allied Forces in Europe during World War II, as Supreme Commander of NATO, and as our 34th President, Dwight D. Eisenhower served his Nation well. As a former member of the staff of the Council of Economic Advisers to President Eisenhower, I had opportunity to observe the dignity and strength that he brought to that Office.

In a letter written in 1966, Dwight Eisenhower listed what he felt were 23 of the chief accomplishments of his administration. First among these in all our hearts was the peace that the Nation enjoyed under his leadership. And, as much as any other President of the United States, he unified the Nation.

With what a deep sense of loss we mourn his passing.

## Hon. Dan H. Kuykendall
OF TENNESSEE

Mr. Speaker, like millions of other Americans, I served under General Eisenhower in World War II, and I became a member of the Republican Party because of him. So it is no exaggeration to say that I owe him my present position in life.

But that is only a small part of the debt.

I owe him the same thing we all do—his immeasurable contribution to our Nation, and to the world.

His atoms-for-peace program; the Nation's system of superhighways begun under his guidance; the dramatic trip to Korea that laid the groundwork for the negotiations at Panmunjom—these are only a few of the items in his legacy.

There are the other things, the human things. The jokes about his golf game, at which he laughed as heartily as anyone. The charm of the photographs in the Nation's press of a proud grandfather romping with his grandchildren. And above all, that fantastic charming grin that lit up his face like sunrise over the White House.

Rather than mourning his loss, Mr. Speaker, we should be profoundly grateful for having had him among us, at a time when we needed him so desperately. We will be remarkably lucky if we see another world leader in our lifetimes who can begin to measure up to him.

## Hon. Thomas P. O'Neill, Jr.
OF MASSACHUSETTS

Mr. Speaker, the long lines of people waiting outside the Capitol to pay tribute to Dwight David Eisenhower express more eloquently than words the esteem in which he was held by the people of this Nation.

General Eisenhower once said "I came from the heart of America" and so he did. He came from the vast heartland of our Nation and grew up in the open country of Kansas. In another generation there will be few men left who remember America as it was when Dwight David Eisenhower was a boy.

Since its inception our Nation has grown and changed and the urban America of tomorrow will bear little resemblance to the land that Washington and Jefferson knew. It will bear little resemblance that is in physical characteristics. But the heart of America is not the geographical center of the Nation, but rather that enduring quality composed of a history of democratic institutions and a belief in equal opportunity for all. This is the heart of America from whence came Dwight David Eisenhower.

He will be remembered best as the 34th President of the United States not for programs or policies, but rather for an attitude and a way of looking at life. He was honest and fair. He loathed to question the motives of others. He liked people and saw the best in each man. In those dark days of the early fifties when suspicion and accusation were rampant in the land, a man like General Eisenhower was needed. He feared no one and trusted both friend and foe alike. He believed in the basic goodness of mankind and understood that good intentions could produce varying viewpoints.

In 1953 when he assumed the Presidency, the world was beset by division and mistrust. General Eisenhower brought with him the experience as the Supreme Commander of the Allied Expeditionary Forces. As such, he had brought together the military leaders of all the Allied Nations who worked with him to assure the victory of the free world. He saw no reason why that spirit of cooperation and dedication to principle could not be continued and indeed expanded during peacetime. His foreign policy reflected this attitude. He was a man of principle, a man above party. When I came to the Congress in 1953, he assumed the office of the President. I remember the spirit of cooperation that existed between both sides of the aisle and between the legislative and executive branches.

His obvious and enormous dedication to the Nation was the motive force in his life of public service. We shall miss his honesty, his integrity, his devotion to duty. We shall also miss his smile and the warmth that reflected the heart of America—the love of mankind. It was to this heart that he appealed. It was this heart from whence he came.

## Hon. Glenard P. Lipscomb

OF CALIFORNIA

Mr. Speaker, the late great President Dwight D. Eisenhower on January 17, 1961, just prior to leaving office after 50 years of service to our Nation delivered his farewell address to the American people.

President Eisenhower delivered the message, he said, "to share a few final thoughts" with his countrymen. As he discussed the need to work for peace and human betterment, he discussed the challenge we face from communistic ideology and the need to be fully prepared. He discussed problems for our Nation as he saw them and called for caution, balance, and reason as we meet the challenges ahead.

In the intervening years, there have been many references to Mr. Eisenhower's farewell address. Unfortunately, however, it seems most commentators and speakers have concentrated on only one term used by the President in that talk, and that term is "military-industrial complex."

It is not that the term "military-industrial complex" as used by the President does not deserve attention, for it clearly does. But what is unfortunate is that at the same time so many other of the President's thoughts contained in that farewell address are glossed over or neglected.

I believe it would be well for Americans of all ages to refresh their memories as to what President Eisenhower said just a little over 8 years ago because so many of his thoughts are as valid today as when delivered.

In that address, he prayed "that the coming years will be blessed with peace."

But tragically in the 8 years which followed, we have not been blessed with peace.

President Eisenhower on January 17, 1961, also reminded us how essential is our Military Establishment in keeping the peace:

> A vital element in keeping the peace is our Military Establishment. Our arms must be mighty, ready for instant action, so that no potential aggressor may be tempted to risk his own destruction.

The President stated why an American armaments industry is required:

> We can no longer risk emergency improvisation of national defense; we have been compelled to create a permanent armaments industry of vast proportions.

President Eisenhower recognized that the total influence of an immense Military Establishment together with a large arms industry was felt in governmental offices throughout the land and he stated:

> We recognize the imperative need for this development.

It was at this point, having recognized the need for this development, that the President quite properly expressed the need for caution. He said:

> In the councils of government, we must guard against the acquisition of unwarranted influence, whether sought or unsought, by the military-industrial complex.

These words are, of course, still valid and pertinent today.

But at the same time we should not overlook the important warning contained in President Eisenhower's farewell message concerning the danger communism poses to achieving freedom and progress in the world. He said:

> We face a hostile ideology—global in scope, atheistic in character, ruthless in purpose, and insidious in meth-

od. Unhappily the danger it poses promises to be of indefinite duration. To meet it successfully, there is called for, not so much the emotional and transitory sacrifices of crisis, but rather those which enable us to carry forward steadily, surely, and without complaint the burdens of a prolonged and complex struggle—with liberty the stake.

With our Nation now actively engaged in war against forces nurtured and sustained by the Soviet Union and others, those words of warning were all the more prophetic and timely.

Mr. Speaker, in view of the frequent references we have been hearing about the phrase "military-industrial complex" as contained in Mr. Eisenhower's final message, I believe it is important that the entire message be available for study and consideration. I am, therefore, including at this point the full text of President Eisenhower's farewell address of January 17, 1961:

FAREWELL RADIO AND TELEVISION ADDRESS TO THE AMERICAN PEOPLE, JANUARY 17, 1961

(Delivered from the President's Office at 8:30 p.m.)

*My fellow Americans:*

Three days from now, after half a century in the service of our country, I shall lay down the responsibilities of office as, in traditional and solemn ceremony, the authority of the Presidency is vested in my successor.

This evening I come to you with a message of leave-taking and farewell, and to share a few final thoughts with you, my countrymen.

Like every other citizen, I wish the new President, and all who will labor with him, Godspeed. I pray that the coming years will be blessed with peace and prosperity for all.

Our people expect their President and the Congress to find essential agreement on issues of great moment, the wise resolution of which will better shape the future of the Nation.

My own relations with the Congress, which began on a remote and tenuous basis when, long ago, a member of the Senate appointed me to West Point, have since ranged to the intimate during the war and immediate post-war period, and, finally, to the mutually interdependent during these past eight years.

In this final relationship, the Congress and the Administration have, on most vital issues, cooperated well, to serve the national good rather than mere partisanship, and so have assured that the business of the Nation should go forward. So, my official relationship with the Congress ends in a feeling, on my part, of gratitude that we have been able to do so much together.

II

We now stand ten years past the midpoint of a century that has witnessed four major wars among great nations. Three of these involved our own country. Despite these holocausts America is today the strongest, the most influential and most productive nation in the world. Understandably proud of this pre-eminence, we yet realize that America's leadership and prestige depend, not merely upon our unmatched material progress, riches and military strength, but on how we use our power in the interests of world peace and human betterment.

III

Throughout America's adventure in free government, our basic purposes have been to keep the peace; to foster progress in human achievement; and to enhance liberty, dignity and integrity among people and among nations. To strive for less would be unworthy of a free and religious people. Any failure traceable to arrogance, or our lack of comprehension or readiness to sacrifice would inflict upon us grievous hurt both at home and abroad.

Progress toward these noble goals is persistently threatened by the conflict now engulfing the world. It commands our whole attention, absorbs our very beings. We face a hostile ideology—global in scope, atheistic in character, ruthless in purpose, and insidious in method. Unhappily the danger it poses promises to be of indefinite duration. To meet it successfully, there is called for, not so much the emotional and transitory sacrifices of crisis, but rather those which enable us to carry forward steadily, surely, and without complaint the burdens of a prolonged and complex struggle—with liberty the stake. Only thus shall we remain, despite every provocation, on our chartered course toward permanent peace and human betterment.

Crises there will continue to be. In meeting them, whether foreign or domestic, great or small, there is a recurring temptation to feel that some spectacular and costly action could become the miraculous solution to all current difficulties. A huge increase in newer elements of our defense; development of unrealistic programs to cure every ill in agriculture; a dramatic expansion in basic and applied research—these and many other possibilities, each possibly promising in itself, may be suggested as the only way to the road we wish to travel.

But each proposal must be weighed in the light of a broader consideration: the need to maintain balance in and among national programs—balance between the private and the public economy, balance between cost and hoped for advantage—balance between the clearly necessary and the comfortably desirable; balance between our essential requirements as a nation and the duties imposed by the nation upon the individual; balance between actions of the moment and the national welfare of the future. Good judgment seeks balance and progress; lack of it eventually finds imbalance and frustration.

The record of many decades stands as proof that our people and their government have, in the main, understood these truths and have responded to them well, in the face of stress and threat. But threats, new in kind or degrees, constantly arise. I mention two only.

IV

A vital element in keeping the peace is our military establishment. Our arms must be mighty, ready for instant action, so that no potential aggressor may be tempted to risk his own destruction.

Our military organization today bears little relation to that known by any of my predecessors in peacetime, or indeed by the fighting men of World War II or Korea.

Until the latest of our world conflicts, the United States had no armaments industry. American makers of plowshares could, with time and as required, make swords as well. But now we can no longer risk emergency improvisation of national defense; we have been compelled to create a permanent armaments industry of vast proportions. Added to this, three and a half million men and women are directly engaged in the defense establishment. We annually spend on military security more than the net income of all United States corporations.

This conjunction of an immense military establishment and a large arms industry is new in the American experience. The total influence—economic, political, even spiritual—is felt in every city, every State house, every office of the Federal government. We recognize the imperative need for this development. Yet we must not fail to comprehend its grave implications. Our toil, resources and livelihood are all involved; so is the very structure of our society.

In the councils of government, we must guard against the acquisition of unwarranted influence, whether sought or unsought, by the military-industrial complex. The potential for the disastrous rise of misplaced power exists and will persist.

We must never let the weight of this combination endanger our liberties or democratic processes. We should take nothing for granted. Only an alert and knowledgeable citizenry can compel the proper meshing of the huge industrial and military machinery of defense with our peaceful methods and goals, so that security and liberty may prosper together.

Akin to, and largely responsible for the sweeping changes in our industrial-military posture, has been the technological revolution during recent decades.

In this revolution, research has become central; it also becomes more formalized, complex, and costly. A steadily increasing share is conducted for, by, or at the direction of, the Federal government.

Today, the solitary inventor, tinkering in his shop, has been overshadowed by task forces of scientists in laboratories and testing fields. In the same fashion, the free university, historically the fountainhead of free ideas and scientific discovery, has experienced a revolution in the conduct of research. Partly because of the huge costs involved, a government contract becomes virtually a substitute for intellectual curiosity. For every old blackboard there are now hundreds of new electronic computers.

The prospect of domination of the nation's scholars by Federal employment, project allocations, and the power of money is ever present—and is gravely to be regarded.

Yet, in holding scientific research and discovery in respect, as we should, we must also be alert to the equal and opposite danger that public policy could itself become the captive of a scientific-technological elite.

It is the task of statesmanship to mold, to balance, and to integrate these and other forces, new and old, within the principles of our democratic system—ever aiming toward the supreme goals of our free society.

V

Another factor in maintaining balance involves the element of time. As we peer into society's future, we—you and I, and our government—must avoid the impulse to live only for today, plundering, for our own ease and convenience, the precious resources of tomorrow. We cannot mortgage the material assets of our grandchildren without risking the loss also of their political and spiritual heritage. We want democracy to survive for all generations to come, not to become the insolvent phantom of tomorrow.

VI

Down the long lane of the history yet to be written America knows that this world of ours, ever growing smaller, must avoid becoming a community of dreadful fear and hate, and be, instead, a proud confederation of mutual trust and respect.

Such a confederation must be one of equals. The weakest must come to the conference table wth the same confidence as do we, protected as we are by our moral, economic, and military strength. That table, though scarred by many past frustrations, cannot be abandoned for the certain agony of the battlefield.

Disarmament, with mutual honor and confidence, is a continuing imperative. Together we must learn how to compose differences, not with arms, but with intellect and decent purpose. Because this need is so sharp and apparent I confess that I lay down my official responsibilities in this field with a definite sense of disappointment. As one who has witnessed the horror and the lingering sadness of war—as one who knows that another war could utterly destroy this civilization which has been so slowly and painfully built over thousands of years—I wish I could say tonight that a lasting peace is in sight.

Happily, I can say that war has been avoided. Steady progress toward our ultimate goal has been made. But, so much remains to be done. As a private citizen, I shall never cease to do what little I can to help the world advance along that road.

VII

So—in this my last good night to you as your President—I thank you for the many opportunities you have given me for public service in war and peace. I trust that in that service you find some things worthy; as for the rest of it, I know you will find ways to improve performance in the future.

You and I—my fellow citizens—need to be strong in our faith that all nations, under God, will reach the goal of peace with justice. May we be ever unswerving in devotion to principle, confident but humble with power, diligent in pursuit of the Nation's great goals.

To all the peoples of the world, I once more give expression to America's prayerful and continuing aspiration:

We pray that peoples of all faiths, all races, all nations, may have their great human needs satisfied; that those now denied opportunity shall come to enjoy it to the full; that all who yearn for freedom may experience its spiritual blessings; that those who have freedom will understand, also, its heavy responsibilities; that all who are insensitive to the needs of others will learn charity; that the scourages of poverty, disease and ignorance will be made to disappear from the earth, and that, in the goodness of time, all peoples will come to live together in a peace guaranteed by the binding force of mutual respect and love.

## Hon. Henry Helstoski

OF NEW JERSEY

Mr. Speaker, Dwight David Eisenhower, the wartime leader of the Allied Forces in Europe during World War II, the 34th President of the United States, passed on to his Heavenly reward after a long battle against an overwhelming illness.

He was a great patriot and as a soldier and statesman has earned our thanks and our respect. America's heart is heavy with sorrow because of its deep affection for this man, and mankind owes a massive debt to his memory for he has left a legacy of devotion to duty and to his fellow man.

The historian of the future will have to assess the many accomplishments of Dwight Eisenhower; however, we do not have to wait for some future date to determine his strong character and his determination to complete the tasks to which he was assigned.

When "Ike," as he was known throughout the world, left the United States for Europe on an assignment that led to his choice as the Supreme Commander of the Allied Forces, he was unknown to the American people. When he came home several years later he was known to everybody. He was then a world figure, winning fame during the war which carried over into the peacetime years and into the political arena as our President.

What would have been the future of Dwight Eisenhower if he had entered the Naval Academy instead of West Point cannot be assessed by any living mortal. It was only by a quirk of fate that "Ike" entered West Point. He had taken competitive examinations for both academies; finishing first in the Annapolis test and second in those taken for West Point. He was appointed to the Naval Academy, only to find out that he would be over the age of 20 years before the term started and which age was the limit for the new naval cadets. As fate would have it, the first man on the West Point list was unable to accept the nomination and it went to Dwight Eisenhower.

His military achievements alone would have given him the greatness he gained throughout the world, but a brief portion of his civilian life added much to it, the office of the President of the United States.

Elected in 1952, and reelected in 1956, he served his Nation during a predominantly relaxed state of mind of the American citizens, which became known as the "Eisenhower years."

President Eisenhower was consulted many times by the two men who followed him into the White House—President John F. Kennedy and President Lyndon B. Johnson. In this way he showed the American people his continued interest in politics and in the affairs of our Nation.

A grateful Congress restored to General Eisenhower the title he once held—before assuming the office of the Presidency—General of the Army, again, a grateful Nation paying its respects to a great man.

Dwight David "Ike" Eisenhower always marched in the ranks of honor; he will always live in the minds of men as one of character and honor.

A great man, an American-minded citizen, a truly honorable man has answered the final rollcall. The Nation has paid homage to his memory and the spirit of this outstanding American should rekindle in the hearts of the people of this Nation, a dedication to our country, which was the foremost quality of our former President, and soldier.

"Ike" is gone. May he gain his reward promised to us all who serve, and serve well.

Today, Mr. Speaker, my sorrow and prayers are with his family and loved ones. My deepest sympathy goes out to the Eisenhower family for their loss is shared by the entire country—yes, even the entire world.

## Hon. Samuel S. Stratton

OF NEW YORK

Mr. Speaker, with the passing of General Eisenhower we all feel that we have lost a personal friend, whether we really knew him closely or had just read about him and seen his pictures. His passing comes as something of a surprise because in these past few months Dwight Eisenhower had made such a valiant and vigorous fight against recurring illness that all of us had come, I am sure, to regard him as virtually indestructible. His passing makes us sad, and yet there is also a feeling of quiet pride in the very full and very rich life which he lived, and the great inspiration and leadership that we were able to benefit from during the years that he occupied positions of great responsibility in our Nation. The sadness that we feel today is not so much the sadness of what has been left undone, what might have been accomplished, that we felt in the sudden passing of John F. Kennedy, Martin Luther King, and Robert F. Kennedy; but instead a certain sadness for ourselves that we should henceforth be left without his wise counsel and encouragement, and sadness for our country and the world in realizing that with the departure of Dwight Eisenhower a unique and brilliant era in our history has finally come to an end.

Though I first saw General Eisenhower in the summer of 1952 when he returned from Europe to run for the Presidency; stood on the fringes of the crowd in January 1953 at his inauguration; and served in the Congress during the last 2 years of his administration, it was not until September 1965 that I actually met the general personally. He came to Seneca Falls, N.Y., in my district, to turn the first shovel-full of earth in the construction of the new Eisenhower College, named in his honor. The general's close friend, Bob Hope, was on hand for that historic occasion and Mr. Eisenhower joined in the laughter and applause when Bob Hope quipped:

> Where but in America could a poor Kansas farm boy grow up to be a 5-star General and President of the United States, and then end up as a ditch-digger in Seneca Falls!

I had another opportunity to chat with the general at his office in Gettysburg in 1967. At that time he was considering an invitation to fly to Vietnam to see the situation there at first hand, and I encouraged him to go, because I knew he would be a tonic to the troops out there, and his personal appraisal of the war when he returned would be valuable to all of us. The general told me he was eager to go if his doctors would permit it, and I believe he would have gone, but unfortunately, only a couple of weeks later, he was rushed from Gettysburg to Walter Reed with the first of several acute stomach upsets.

Mr. Speaker, I am especially proud of the fact that I was the original author of the legislation, enacted last year in the 90th Congress, to establish Eisenhower College, now in full operation, as the living national memorial to President Eisenhower, and to extend to that new college some $5 million in matching Federal funds in tribute to the former President. I was pleased to notice that Eisenhower College was one of the five charitable causes which members of the general's family had specifically urged friends who so desired to send their contributions to in lieu of flowers.

Eisenhower College will, I am confident, keep alive the magnificent buoyant spirit of Dwight Eisenhower that we honor today, so that in years to come he may continue to be for succeeding generations of young Americans as great a source of inspiration and encouragement as he has been to ours, to those of us who served in uniform with him, if not directly under him, during the historic days of World War II.

## Hon. William C. Cramer

OF FLORIDA

Mr. Speaker, America has lost one of her greatest sons. His legacy of personal warmth, exemplary leadership, and religious and family devotion will live forever as an inspiration not only to Americans but to people throughout the world.

Having served under him in the military and with him as our President, I am saddened by his passing, but inspired by his life.

No greater honor, privilege, or inspirational experience could befall any American citizen anytime in the history of our country, than to have served in Washington under the Eisenhower administration, and in the military during World War II under Dwight Eisenhower's watchful and guiding hand.

Having attended numerous conferences at the White House during his administration, I recall many discussions about the future of our country, the necessity of a balanced budget, and the tough decisions on preserving peace. The ever-present compassion for the people of this country stood out as the touchstone of his convictions and of his administration. He was a man who practiced what he preached and during his 8 years in office set the highest moral tone of this century for the National Government.

His philosophy, which supported the federal system through a strengthened local-State-Federal relationship, was clearly enunciated when he proposed in his famous Williamsburg address that certain taxing powers be turned back to the States in an overall attempt to strengthen State and local government and to preserve and strengthen the true federal system.

The depths of his convictions were clearly evidenced by his vetoes of bills which could have had a budget-busting effect. In particular he vetoed numerous public works bills. He vetoed them because he believed they were too costly, yet knowing full well that sustaining vetoes in the area of public works is extremely difficult. He succeeded in removing the unnecessary fat from public works appropriations until the last year of his administration, when the only Eisenhower veto ever overridden was one relating to public works. Even though the votes sustaining his veto became closer and closer, he never wavered from his deep conviction on this subject and was willing to run the risk of being overridden in order to try to control inflation through responsible Government spending. This is just one example of the dedication and firm convictions which President Eisenhower displayed as our Nation's leader.

Despite what some historians have already suggested as their judgment of the Eisenhower administration, President Eisenhower proved to be a man of action, compassion, and a man who was loath to make unattainable promises or to propose programs he knew could not succeed. I believe history will record the Eisenhower administration as the administration which not only kept the peace but brought a period of stability and reasoning to America.

During his first 2 years in office he brought the Korean war to an end, reduced taxes substantially, increased social security payments and coverage significantly, and provided needed leadership to bring our country together. His administration also created the Department of Health, Education, and Welfare; provided statehood for Alaska and Hawaii; started the most significant highway program in the history of the country, the Interstate Highway and Defense System; began the water pollution control fight; and even though a military man himself, constantly strived to keep military programs and budgets within reason. He commenced the Nation's efforts in outer space, successfully met the challenges of the uprising in the Middle East, and refused to permit the United States to get dragged into the confrontation in South Vietnam. These monumental accomplishments undoubtedly came about largely because of the nature of the man himself, resulting from his basic honesty, unquestionable sincerity, and gentle friendliness, tempered with a firm decisionmaking capability and backed by the love and affection of the people of this country and throughout the freedom-loving world.

No one could be on the scene during his life of service without being impressed by him as a leader.

No one could attend the services in the rotunda of the Capitol where his body lay in state, or the funeral services at the National Cathedral and see the outpouring of love, affection, and respect by the leaders of the countries of the world, as well as by his fellow citizens at home, without realizing that one of the great men of history had passed away.

## Hon. Glenard P. Lipscomb
OF CALIFORNIA

Mr. Speaker, this is a time of sadness for America. With the passing of our beloved former President Dwight David Eisenhower, our Nation has lost an outstanding leader and a great man.

General Eisenhower will be remembered for many things. He was highly successful both as a soldier and as a statesman, achieving the ultimate of success in our Nation by being elected our 34th President.

He was a devoted family man, a man of religion, and a stanch patriot. He was passionately dedicated to achieving and maintaining peace. Above all, he will be remembered as a very warm and compassionate human being.

I feel greatly honored to have had the privilege of serving in the Congress during the Presidency of Dwight Eisenhower. His terms in office were marked with many accomplishments.

Ike's life and achievements and the high principles he stood for will continue to serve over the years as an inspiration to us all.

To Mrs. Eisenhower and their son John and family we express our deepest sympathies.

## Hon. E. Ross Adair
OF INDIANA

Mr. Speaker, I would like to add my voice to those who have already publicly expressed their sorrow at the passing of Gen. Dwight David Eisenhower. His death is a time for national mourning and also for renewed idealism.

We who knew him both in time of war by serving under his command in Europe and in time of peace as a Member of Congress during his administration know well how he fully committed himself to the United States of America. He constantly endeavored to make the words "individual freedom and liberty" in the Declaration of Independence meaningful both to Americans and to nations of the world which were threatened with outside aggression or internal subversion.

Although we are saddened by the passing of this friend and great leader, we can be heartened by the inspiration which his life will be for today's and tomorrow's leaders. His unselfish devotion to the service of his country will serve as a constant reminder of the quality of leadership required to preserve freedom. The decisions which he had to make both in war and in peace were oftentimes "hard" decisions requiring thoughtful answers. General Eisenhower's courage and ability to make such decisions, rather than take the easier or more politically expedient way out, marks him as a true patriot.

## Hon. Rogers C. B. Morton
OF MARYLAND

Mr. Speaker, the country has lost one of its great leaders. Much will be written about his accomplishments, his life and service to the Nation. Anything I add here would be redundant.

However, I am deeply conscious that he was a man of his time. No man on the political scene of America could have filled so well the role of leadership which this country needed after the trials of World War II. His great sense of purpose, his overpowering devotion to duty, his perfect sense of integrity brought our country through some difficult times. The struggle for life during his last weeks typifies the character of this great man.

With every American I share deep sympathy for his family in this their tragic hour. Also with every American I share a great sense of gratitude for the life which this native Kansan gave to his fellow man in public service.

## Hon. Jackson E. Betts
OF OHIO

Mr. Speaker, so many tributes have been paid General Eisenhower that it is difficult to add anything new. But I do want to be among those who have expressed their deep appreciation of the life and character of this great man.

To me, the lasting impression I have is that in a world that questions some basic beliefs such as religion and clamors for the leisure life and a permissive society he was a steadfast Christian gentleman who rigidly believed in discipline—including self-discipline. To him the rules of the game were made for some good purpose and should be followed without complaint or equivocation.

Loyalty was bedrock in his character. Whether it was West Point, his country, his church, or his party, he felt that his association with these institutions demanded allegiance and loyalty.

These virtues of loyalty and discipline are part and parcel of America's greatness, and for that reason make Eisenhower one of the great men of our day and give him a place of prominence in the history of our country.

Possibly above this, or at least part of it, was his personal and family life. Here he was an example of the kind of man Americans want to see in their leaders.

All of these qualities made him a great soldier and a great President. His passing has emphasized them in the tributes that have been paid him during these recent days. But they are enduring virtues which will fill a place in the hearts of Americans for all time.

## Hon. Patsy T. Mink
OF HAWAII

Mr. Speaker, today we mourn the loss of another great American leader, President Dwight D. Eisenhower. But our sorrow is tempered by the knowledge of the fullness and richness of his life; a life that was devoted entirely to the service of this country.

Involvement and service were the hallmarks of his life which encompassed all of the great trials and the great victories of this Nation in the 20th century.

From his early manhood at the time of World War I, Dwight Eisenhower moved inexorably to the leadership of the most powerful military forces ever assembled in the history of the world. He led those forces with valor and devotion and presided at their victory in World War II.

One might have expected that to be the end and the zenith of a great general's career, but for Dwight Eisenhower, it was only the beginning. The unprecedented faith and affection which he inspired in his fellow Americans moved the Nation to call him to still further service in the highest office in the land where he served as long as the law allows.

He was a great leader in war and a great leader in peace.

Today we grieve at his passing, but we rejoice in his life which is an inspiration and an example for all of us.

His words as he ended his second term as President of the United States shall continue to be of particular significance to me. Let us never forget that being a great military leader, and as a President leaving office, he still warned us against the dangers he saw ahead:

> In the councils of Government, we must guard against the acquisition of unwarranted influence, whether sought or unsought, by the military-industrial complex. The potential for the disastrous rise of misplaced power exists and will persist.
>
> We must never let the weight of this combination endanger our liberties or democratic processes. We should take nothing for granted. Only an alert and knowledgeable citizenry can compel the proper meshing of the huge industrial and military machinery of defense with our peaceful methods and goals so that security and liberty may prosper together.

I join the multitudes to pay him homage and tribute that he so justly deserves.

## Hon. Bertram L. Podell
OF NEW YORK

Mr. Speaker, Dwight David Eisenhower has passed away and America is much the poorer because of it. Reared in its heartland, he personified traditional virtues. Born to service, he lived his entire life on behalf of his country. Inured to sacrifice, he gave unstintingly of himself whenever his country asked anything of him. Altruistic to the core, he set an example for the entire Nation.

Leading America's military forces to victory in World War II against Germany, he was an exemplary soldier in a democracy. Standing firmly against the Soviet menace in the cold war, he lent his strength to our international role. Stepping out of the service, he answered the call of his country as its President.

In all of these endeavors, he showed what the American spirit and fiber were really made of. Through every challenge and crisis, he maintained his courage, bringing honor to our country. Never was that courage better displayed than during his last illness.

History will treat him kindly. America will always be in his debt. He left us many legacies. That of courage in combat, honesty in office, and devotion to country.

He also left us a warning—one that it would do us well to heed. It stays in my mind always. He warned us of the military-industrial complex, and what dangers it poses to our society. Never was he more correct than when he delivered that warning.

His message has been taken to heart along with his other legacies. May God give him peace and receive his soul.

## Hon. John W. Byrnes
OF WISCONSIN

Mr. Speaker, few men have ever enjoyed such universal respect from their countrymen as Dwight David Eisenhower.

He was beloved because of his great accomplishments, of course—accomplishments which, with the perspective of time, we are beginning to appreciate even more.

But he was also beloved because of his noble character which inspired trust and belief. No man had a deeper love for his country or a stronger desire to do what was "right" for all of us. And I think most of us instinctively recognized this.

Even those who did not always agree with his views or actions did not question his integrity or sincerity. Because of his character he had the unique ability to inspire the best in all of us. As Field Marshall Lord Montgomery said last week, "He had only to smile at you and there was nothing you would not do for him."

As others have pointed out, as a general and as President he fought to defeat tyranny and to achieve lasting peace in the world. These efforts arose from the depth of his character. I can personally testify that his intense dedication to freedom and peace was apparent in his private discussions as well as in public.

I am grateful, therefore, not only for his accomplishments but also for the spiritual inspiration and example he has given us.

I feel a great personal loss and I join the Nation in mourning the death of a great hero and patriot.

## Hon. Thomas M. Pelly
OF WASHINGTON

Mr. Speaker, my service in the Congress during the 8 years of the Eisenhower administration carry with it many cherished memories of Dwight David Eisenhower. These memories of my President and my leader are personally very dear and are historically significant chiefly because in essence they bear out the character and integrity of this great American.

From the time General Eisenhower visited Seattle and I had the privilege of presenting him to a huge audience during his first presidential campaign, until now, when his service to the Nation is completed, I have associated his life and achievements with the line of Alfred Lord Tennison describing Sir Galahad, "His strength is as the strength of 10 because his heart is pure."

No man I ever met, save only my own father, represented so much in the way of personal integrity.

Today I cannot add to what has been said during the past few days when a grateful and grieving nation, and indeed the world, paid tribute to the general's life and service. But, in all humbleness as an American, I do honor and pay my respects to him and to his family.

In addition, my greatest sympathy goes to his devoted wife, Mamie, who have given us strength during these past few trying days.

Meanwhile, in our hearts Dwight D. Eisenhower will live while we live, and after we are gone, his monumental achievements will live throughout history.

## Hon. Joseph M. Gaydos
OF PENNSYLVANIA

Mr. Speaker, Americans throughout the Nation and free people the world over join together in mourning the passing of a great American, Dwight D. Eisenhower.

His was a full and fruitful life dedicated to the services of his country as Supreme Commander of the Allied Forces when the drums of war sounded in World War II, and later as a leader for peace as Chief Executive of our Nation. He was blessed with an inherent ability to unite people and infuse in them the spirit of mutual assistance and collective action under the most trying circumstances.

He had about him a very sincere and genuine love for his fellow man and though he walked with kings, he never lost the common touch. It was this common touch that endeared him to his fellow Americans. This faith, trust, respect, and admiration accorded him by the American people was a reflection of the deep love and respect he had for his country.

His brilliant and illustrious career has come to a close. A Nation grieves, the world mourns, and people of all nations join together in final tribute to Dwight David Eisenhower; general, President, statesman, patriot, and above all, a most remarkable human being.

## Hon. Samuel L. Devine
OF OHIO

Mr. Speaker, many words have been spoken in honor of Dwight David Eisenhower, but few of us will ever realize how much we asked of him as a man. We should indeed mourn his passing but also be grateful for his life as an American. He rose through the ranks of the service and led us through a world crisis as Supreme Commander of Allied Forces in Europe in World War II. We turned to him again and asked for his leadership as President of the United States. His great deeds and efforts toward the fight for peace in his capacity as both Commander and President will long be remembered.

"Ike" will not merely be a figure for future generations to recall as just the 34th President of the United States; he was a part of the history of our Nation. Throughout the world he gained lasting friendships for America as was demonstrated by worldwide leaders attending his funeral services.

In his retired life "Ike" was referred to as the "father image." Many leaders and politicians turned to him for his advice and wisdom. His unique leadership qualities assisted in uniting clashing political views, and he was loved and respected by all. His warmth and sincerity can only be measured by those who knew him personally; but Americans at home will always be indebted to him for his contributions as a great leader.

## Hon. G. Elliott Hagan
OF GEORGIA

Mr. Speaker, I join my colleagues and all Americans in the expression of my sorrow and heartfelt sympathy on the death of a truly great American—Gen. Dwight David Eisenhower.

General Eisenhower will be remembered by all as a man of high integrity, a man of great determination and, most of all, a man of such loyalty and patriotism that he will stand out for centuries to come as one of the greatest of American patriots.

We who have been fortunate enough to have lived in his lifetime will not forget this great general, who epitomized the American ideal of a devoted public servant. We will also remember him as our Chief Executive—and we will look back in years to come on his earnest devotion and loyalty during his tenure of office which will in no way diminish as time goes by.

We have indeed lost a great American, but we can proudly recall his name and the principles he represented with deep and everlasting pride.

America is sadder today—but we should also give thanks that we were fortunate to have had Dwight David Eisenhower in our midst—for he now "belongs to the ages."

Although mere words at such a time are grossly inadequate, I believe the following sensitive and expressive editorial and accompanying articles from the Savannah Morning News come close to perfection in describing the man we affectionately thought of as "Ike":

[From the Savannah (Ga.) Morning News, Mar. 29, 1969]

DWIGHT DAVID EISENHOWER

Death came finally for the General. He had suffered too long, bedridden for months at Walter Reed Hospital, victim of at least seven heart attacks in less than 15 years. One marveled at his endurance.

Dwight David Eisenhower, much loved, reflected an image which was comprehended by every American, and yet the whole man seems to be beyond our understanding.

We liked Ike. So did millions of his countrymen who twice elected him to the nation's highest office by an overwhelming number of votes. As Washington, Jackson, Grant—he, too, had won his honors on the battlefield and did not need the presidency for his page in history. He smiled, and that was all that was needed, and in a certain era it was all that most of us wanted. We trusted him. There were ignominious embarrassments during his second term and the country despaired, but if the postwar Republicans had not fought so hard for the 22nd amendment, his tenure of office might have equalled Franklin D. Roosevelt's.

He had his critics. Douglas MacArthur, his former chief, disparaged his abilities and saw him first as an equal in Europe and later as a rival for the Republican nomination. He was a man of the people, and this, of course, earned him the enmity of intellectuals.

But the people liked Ike. If the public came closer to having a common love for a President, without the opposing hatred which also was directed toward FDR, it was with this man they entrusted it. Lyndon Johnson was also a man of the people, but his mistakes were never forgiven. For the most part, Mr. Eisenhower's were. If he, unlike Washington, was not first in the hearts of his countrymen, he was close by, particularly to a generation which yearned for a proud America.

His success which led him to the highest office has been waved aside by some as political charm first recognized while he was an Army officer. There were intricate maneuverings by politicans on all sides of the Allied cause during World War II. Charles de Gaulle wanted immediate action to recover France from the Nazis. Winston Churchill, wary of a second front which would aid the Russians, and mindful that a premature invasion might be defeated and thus injure British morale, differed with Gen. George C. Marshall who also preferred a cross-Channel invasion early in the war. Mr. Churchill wanted instead to move through the "soft underbelly of Europe." A compromise resulted, but it also led to Gen. Eisenhower being named commander in chief of Allied forces. The General, whom many were to call apolitical later on, led this often haggling Allied army to victory.

If he served also as a mediator during the war, bringing opponents around and making true allies of the Allies, he is still best remembered as the President. And it is this which poses the problem of what the man was really like.

It was something basically American in his makeup, a certain honor which most of us yearn to see in the leaders of our country. It was a quality rare enough to cause us to forgive his errors, his stumblings in foreign affairs because many of us still think we have no business being in such things and that the rest of the world is out to despoil us. He was a native American who made good. He was, to Americans, "There but for the grace of God go I—but I'm rather pleased that it's he."

We admired his honesty. Though his administration, Mr. Eisenhower seemed above politics rather than incapable of understanding. He was a man grasping at the straws of peace, at a time when the Communists wanted anything else but. If he had any political coloration, it was that of a moderate, unwilling to turn the clock back and yet steady enough to sound warnings about government plunging into areas previously unknown.

This was how many saw him. Whether he was always thus, or whether he became this, matters little. Perhaps for the first and only time a contemporary politician and his image were true to each other.

Mr. Eisenhower, in truth, represented America as much as the Stars and Stripes in his time. It is a decency, a reverence in fact, that finds constant belittlement today. It is feared that he may one day represent in the minds of many something of a vital cog in the machinery of war, just as some today take the flag to represent all that is deplorable about this country rather than all that is represented as the hope of free men. It is a vile twisting of history to meet ideologies that are currently in fashion, and the damage is never completely repaired.

But today, in our own hearts, the man stands tall. The critics are stilled. The country has halted momentarily, to go forward again within a few days. What Dwight Eisenhower bequeathed us was his unblemished honor, and we must protect it. It is the key to what we continuously reach for, and to lose it, to lose him entirely, is to open the door to an existence which we have long fought against, which is the obituary of the American nation.

[From the Savannah (Ga.) Morning News-Evening Press, Mar. 30, 1969]

IKE'S EXAMPLE WILLINGNESS TO LISTEN: A STERLING QUALITY

(By Tom Coffey)

A few months back when General Eisenhower was fighting (and for the moment winning) one of his battles to stay alive, I wrote a column about Ike's smile, his strong point.

We alluded to that smile in yesterday's beautiful editorial tribute, written by Dave Hardin—"He smiled, and that was all that was needed, and in a certain era it was all that most of us wanted."

But the General was not one who made his way just by smiling. There was more to the man than his countenance.

So many have attempted to fathom Dwight Eisenhower. We have read reams about his organizational ability, his perception of the big picture, how he could rise above politics, etc., etc.

But I think one who was close to the General summed it up best of all. "His willingness to listen" was the Eisenhower quality cited by Maj. Gen. Henry B. Sayler, who lives here in retirement, during an interview he granted me Friday afternoon, about an hour after General Eisenhower had died.

General Sayler was in the famous West Point Class of 1915, eighty per cent of whom became generals. Eisenhower, Bradley, names like that. General Sayler became Eisenhower's ordnance chief in Europe. He passed the ammunition in the biggest single fight the nation ever waged.

There's something almost of a virtue in a willingness to listen. General Sayler said this was why Eisenhower was a great organizer, why he could bring differing factions together. He listened to what they had to say, then made his decisions based upon what he had heard.

Don't all of us wish that we could? Aren't so many of us so headstrong, so pre-conceived in our notions that we fail to listen?

I couldn't help noting a similarity between what General Sayler said about his former chief and what President Nixon said in his inaugural speech.

The President said that for too long we have been shouting. He exhorted us to listen—to one another, and to learn, each from the other.

I am certain now that President Nixon listened to his former boss—and learned.

It might well be that if Nixon sensed Eisenhower's willingness to listen, and identified it as a sterling quality, it was the most important single piece of the basic training that our present President received during his eight years as Vice President under Eisenhower.

Surely it was the most important piece of advice that he could give to the nation when he took office.

I pass this along, and note the similarity aforementioned, merely through circumstance of General Eisenhower's death and my acquaintance with a Savannahian who knew him better than a great many people did.

But I consider it highly significant, not only in offering a keener insight into Dwight Eisenhower but its sobering impact as an example by which we can profit.

Coincidentally, this column makes print at the beginning of Holy Week, a period which solemnity dictates, and four days before Passover, which involves the historical ideal of freedom.

We can solemnly contemplate the idea of listening.

It might enhance our freedom.

---

[From the Savannah Morning News, Mar. 29, 1969]

B-17 CREW RECALLS IKE

(By William H. Whitten)

For two Savannahians the news of former President Eisenhower's death Friday came home much more personally than perhaps for the millions to whom "Ike" was mostly a public figure.

To V. J. Romagosa and William G. Nelson the news brought memories of many hours of close association with Eisenhower as members of the crew of his World War II Flying Fortress plane.

Both men described their former commander as one of the finest officers and nicest men with whom they had ever served.

MYSTERY ASSIGNMENT

Nelson, a flight engineer who served with Eisenhower for 14 months, recalled Friday the day in 1942 when he learned he was assigned to the Allied commander's crew.

"I thought I was coming home," he said. "We had taken off from England with sealed orders not be opened until we were airborne. Heading into Gibraltar I learned instead I was assigned to Ike's crew with headquarters in Algiers.

"I was with him during the North Africa campaign and the landings in Italy. At the Italian surrender some newsreel cameramen photographed all of us together but I didn't know it until my wife saw the newsreel at the Lucas Theatre and recognized me," he said.

ROMAGOSA CALLED IN

It was through the action of Nelson that Romagosa was assigned to the crew.

"We needed an expert mechanic because of all the flying he had to do so we got Romagosa on the team. I had never met him before the war," Nelson said.

"I sort of fell into the job," Romagosa recalls. "I flew about 500 hours with Gen. Eisenhower over 18 months. When the general went back to England he chose a B-25 to fly in, that became the plane that took him first to the battle in Normandy.

"The general spent most of his time at the rear of the plane. There he would work on plans and maps. To relax, he'd read wild west stories, which I understand he enjoyed a lot."

WELL-PROTECTED GENERAL

Asked about protection for Ike and the crew, Romagosa said, "our plane was always well escorted. We had gunners in the crew while in Africa but not after that. We were never bothered by Jerry (German) fighters. They wouldn't have had a chance anyway," he said.

Nelson, however, remembers at least one incident where there was immediate danger.

"It was in Africa," he said. "The officers had left the plane and gone off in three staff cars. We saw two cars returning and Eisenhower came aboard and told me to get that plane up in a hurry—the Germans were coming.

"Sure enough, just after we took off the field was bombed."

There was more to the crew's responsibilities than maintaining the plane, Nelson recalled Friday.

EMERGENCY RECALLED

"We were on our way to the Casablanca Conference," he said, "to meet President Roosevelt when a propeller shaft broke. We were afraid the engine would catch fire (it didn't) so I put a safety harness on the general. I remember him saying, "I hope I don't have to use this thing.' I told him I hoped he didn't have to either."

Being that close to the Supreme Allied Commander meant that most of the topranking generals of the war were seen close up by these men. One of the most remarkable was "Blood and Guts"—Gen. George Patton, tank commander, innovator, egotist and always controversial.

"When the Germans started getting too close Eisenhower would say 'Sergeant, bring me my steel helmet.' Patton fined men $25 if he caught them without their protective helmet.

"When I didn't have mine on Eisenhower would remind me that Patton wasn't above fining a member of the commander's crew."

IKE GOT MEDAL

This was during the dark days of the war when the outcome was still in doubt. As victories came and D-Day moved closer to a reality Sgt. Romagosa's mother in Savannah attended a nine-day Solemn Novena for Peace and about a week before the invasion of France sent a letter and Miraculous Medal to Eisenhower. His personal reply came on the 29th of May, seven days before the Allies swarmed into France.

After the war, when Eisenhower began visiting Augusta to play golf and later as President, Nelson and Romagosa had an open invitation to see Ike.

"We did see him one time," Nelson said "and spent about three hours with him but he was so busy as President that we did not want to bother him."

## Hon. John M. Zwach

OF MINNESOTA

Mr. Speaker, America and the world lost a great leader, a great man, in the death of Gen. Dwight D. Eisenhower. His name will live in history as the architect of a great crusade for freedom, an apostle of peace. He was universally loved. He was respected alike by friend and foe.

The life of General Eisenhower is an inspiration to all. Born of poor, humble parents, he proved again to what heights a man can rise on his own strength of character, hard work, ambition, and perseverance.

For his efforts as a world military leader, educator, an outstanding President, and elder statesman, he added beyond words to the strength of America and the free world.

It was my very great fortune to meet and visit with this extraordinary citizen. It was a privilege I will never forget.

His valiant fight against the ravages of ill health typified his courage and tenacity. His death brings an end to the "Eisenhower era."

The entire world is saddened by his passing.

My prayers and sympathy go to his bereaved family.

## Hon. Chester L. Mize

OF KANSAS

Mr. Speaker, many have been the words of tribute written and spoken these last few days to honor the memory of Dwight David Eisenhower. Standing out among them is a statement by Dr. John Wickman, director of the Eisenhower Center in Abilene, Kans. In carrying out his duties at the center, Dr. Wickman has probably been exposed to more of the many-faceted greatness of General Eisenhower than anyone outside the Eisenhower family. I find his words particularly appropriate at this time and consider it my obligation to bring them to the attention of my colleagues, as follows:

### The Eisenhower Legacy

We can do no better, I believe, than ponder the words with which former-President Eisenhower began his address upon his homecoming to Abilene, Kansas, on June 22, 1945. Looking back over the ordeal and triumph in his role as Supreme Allied Commander in Europe, he said, "Every boy dreams of the day when he comes back home after making good. I, too, so dreamed, but my dream of forty-five or more years ago has been exceeded beyond the wildest stretch of imagination."

Today we look back over a career which spans 24 additional years after that warm, soggy June day in Kansas, and nod our concurrence. Few men came from such humble beginnings to rise to such heights. Few men have been able to make the journey as did Dwight D. Eisenhower, and still preserve, as he did, the affection and respect of his fellow citizens.

In General Eisenhower's life there was a concept which is still appealing to young and old in this country. It was the concept of service. Not a self-negating service, which so easily slips into the servile; but rather service performed for country and family, and accomplished out of the genius and strength of the individual.

Where did that concept come from? Was it born out of necessity dictated by a large family living on modest means in an Abilene, Kansas, at the turn of the century? Was it the result of loving and devoted parents who understood that character development in the young is neither easy, nor necessarily enjoyable, for both teacher and pupil?

Whatever its source, there is no question that President Eisenhower had it throughout his adult life. In choosing pathways, whether through the maze of organization which is the Army, or the complications and intrigues of the Supreme Allied Command in Europe, or through the politics of his party and country, he always chose those roads which lead to duty and honor.

Such choices were not easy for him, any more than they are easy for any of us. That they were not more difficult may be attributed to strengths of practicality, perseverance, intelligence, and self-knowledge which came from his inheritance, and his early development in America's heartland. It is too easy to wish away the influence that his early environment had on this man. He was not the product of what the America of his day deemed the best education, nor favored with the best of economic circumstances, nor thrust forward by reason of his parents' social standing. Yet the shaping forces, so necessary and so mysterious in their combinations, were there. The positive strengths were there for life's greatest challenges.

At the Dwight D. Eisenhower Presidential Library in Abilene there is a slide-sound show which all visitors to the Center may see. For a portion of it General Eisenhower recorded these words which seem especially fitting today:

". . . As you enter these buildings do not think of them as a monument to one man, or to one family. Rather, regard them as a tribute to our nation and to those who have defended it throughout its history. These structures are above all a tribute to what America gives to its children, no matter what the circumstances of their upbringing—the opportunity to aspire and achieve."

Dwight D. Eisenhower took hold of his opportunity, and his aspirations and achievements have become his monument. That monument is a full measure, and measuring up to it is the legacy he has left to each of us.

## Hon. Walter S. Baring
OF NEVADA

Mr. Speaker, I join in deep sympathy with my colleagues and my fellow citizens as we mourn the death of one of our greatest American leaders, President and General Dwight David Eisenhower. In my eulogy to the general, I want to state that his heroic and lengthy struggle to live these past days exemplifies the life the great general lived during his years as a soldier, military commander, and President of the United States. He dedicated himself to every job he took on.

On behalf of my State of Nevada, Mrs. Baring, myself, and fellow Members of the House of Representatives, I am honoring the life of Dwight David Eisenhower.

It was always President Eisenhower's integrity and dedication to duty and mankind that guided him then and for which he will be remembered forever.

Another note about the general is the statement I recall him making regarding how much he detested war and the killing that regretfully always comes with war. Mr. Eisenhower said, as he spoke referring to his rank in the military, that he hoped someday soon people in his own type of employment would be permanently out of work. He hoped then as we all do now, that there will nevermore be a need for our country or other nations to maintain great armies.

So, as the general now is history, it will be remembered that, despite his distaste for war, his leadership as a military commander will be well marked when he directed allied armies to put an end to the terrorism and devastation of countries and mankind during World War II.

Then too, his role as peacemaker in the Korean war shall not be forgotten when he served as President of the United States.

And, at all times, President Eisenhower felt deep compassion for his fellow man and wanted the best for everyone.

Truly he was a leader and truly will he be missed.

## Hon. Burt L. Talcott
OF CALIFORNIA

Mr. Speaker, Mrs. Talcott and I feel inadequate to eulogize General Eisenhower. We can merely express our gratitude to have lived in his era and to have known him.

His appeal was almost universal—which is quite extraordinary for a military or political figure.

When we contemplate what contemporary times or our future might be without his influence, we could shudder with forboding or tremble with trepidation.

The most his small, miniscule detractors could say was that "the Nation took no bold new courses during his Presidency." Perhaps, but he held us on course during perilous, troublesome times. He rescued us from the ravages of war in Korea and returned us to peace—a most welcome new course for us—and he avoided new wars for the world—no mean accomplishment. We enjoyed domestic tranquillity. We had pride in ourselves. We believed in the worth of the individual human being more than in the power of government. We can ask little more of leadership.

A few writers who excel in turning a phrase more than reporting the facts or drawing logical conclusions from correct premises, suggested that "as a general, he was a good politician and as a politician, he was a good general." We believe he had the unique, superior qualities of both and used them appropriately in each role. He also had the attributes of an ordinary man which affected and moderated his every decision, including those at the summit.

We like a general who can lead a coalition of nations yet who is compassionate and cares about each individual in his command. We like a politician who is straightforward, honest, and humble. We liked Ike.

We liked and admired his basic honesty. This may be his greatest, most impressive contribution to politics, diplomacy, and societal living. We believe it will endure.

We remember the U–2 incident. All nations spy; they must. The diplomatic code among spies was simple and well known. If a spy was caught, everything was denied. Our State Department initially followed the conventional universal rules of spying and denied the incident. When President Eisenhower learned the facts he admitted them straightforwardly—a diplomatic first and a strong leap forward in returning integrity and mutual confidence to diplomacy and international relations.

General Eisenhower was a humble man. This

characteristic made him beloved. His life and service demonstrated that humility contributes to greatness.

As Supreme Commander of the Allied Forces in Europe and as President of the United States, he possessed more power than any individual in history. He used that enormous power prudently. He carefully matched responsibility with power. He made many momentous and delicate decisions, but he always assumed full responsibility for his decisions. He was so universally respected and his decisions so nearly always correct, simply because he was basically such a good man.

Because of his basic honesty he evoked trust; because of his genuine humility, he was beloved by all regardless of nationality, age, or station in life; he understood the meaning and demands of duty and was therefore one of our greatest patriots; he applied the full dimension of responsibility to himself, his family, his countrymen, his fellow man.

From an obscure background and an ordinary childhood, he developed into one of the world's most uncommon leaders. I trust his simple virtues of decency, honesty, humility and responsibility will be his legacy to future generations. No greater legacy could one man leave to posterity—in his day or ours—to us as individuals or to nations.

We extend our condolences to his Mamie and his family.

## Hon. Dante B. Fascell

OF FLORIDA

Mr. Speaker, Dwight D. Eisenhower served his country nobly both in times of war and peace.

As one of our Nation's few five-star generals, he was instrumental in leading us to victory on the battlefield in World War II, a crucial time in our history.

As one of our most popular Presidents, he devoted his best efforts to achieving peace, progress, and prosperity at home.

For his magnificent contributions, a deeply sorrowful nation can only express its humble appreciation of a man who became a legend in his own time. He stood with the giants of our history.

I join with all Americans who now are personally saddened by the loss of so great an American, and call to the attention of our colleagues the editorial tributes paid to General Eisenhower by the Miami Herald, the Miami News, the Key West Citizen, and the Miami Beach Sun:

[From the Miami Herald, Mar. 29, 1969]

GREAT HEART AND GRIN AND IKE HAVE LEFT US

Ike and his grin are gone. And a great nation mourns.

If the American people had one authentic, consistent hero in the 20th century he was Dwight David Eisenhower. A superb soldier, he was no politician. A man of instinctive common sense, he had little finesse as a statesman. A very human person, he could not bear the minutiae and red tape which every successful administrator must master.

He was simply Ike, an antidote to the political boredom of the postwar years and pacifier of a people weary of government bureaucracy.

President Eisenhower's first term was distinguished by budget reductions, economy and an income tax cut. His second appeared inconsistent with his first, for there then emerged "Modern Republicanism." An element in the party had succeeded in beating its way back to the 19th century, and it was critical of Ike. Many forgot his credo:

"We will be liberal in programs that affect the lives and welfare of people, and conservative in the handling of their money."

Both are possible. The Eisenhower administrations proved it. A budget can be balanced. The needs of people who cannot help themselves can be met.

If there was any slippage it was in foreign policy under the unfortunate aegis of the late John Foster Dulles. As generals must do, Gen. Eisenhower delegated authority—too much of it. Surely he must have been privately appalled by the course of history which has led to a hapless land war in Asia.

The people, however, will remember the man—big, genial, straightforward, amusingly wrathful, tender, word-boggler, loyal and courageous.

Countless times men sat down as we do now to write his obituary in momentary expectation of his death. Then that great heart rallied to the amazement of medical science. At last it has worn itself out. The 34th President, the Ike everyone loved and none could hate, the President whose popularity exceeded Washington's (a man often reviled, as an examination of history will show)—Ike is gone.

The lines written on Gladstone's retirement seem appropriate:

"Behold him in the evening time of life . . . By imperceived degrees he wears away, yet like the sun, seems larger at his setting."

---

[From the Miami News, Friday, Mar. 28, 1969]

ABLE PRESIDENT: EISENHOWER SERVED HIS COUNTRY WELL

Dwight D. Eisenhower didn't want to be President of the United States. He was talked into it. As with every

President, General Eisenhower had his pluses and his minuses, but the former far outweighed the latter.

When the historians finally get around to writing about the years of 1952 to 1960 in the United States, they will surely record that the most important event of the Eisenhower Administration was the beginning of the end of racial segregation.

The General had a special talent in the complex business of matters military, and one of his greatest achievements was in commanding, with success, the likes of Field Marshal Montgomery, Charles de Gaulle and George S. Patton, among others. He was able to create an order which successfully concluded World War II, and in turn this led to the general being talked into a campaign for the Presidency.

As President, Mr. Eisenhower was very much aware of George Washington's Farewell Address in which the first President warned the nation against unnecessary foreign entanglements. Mr. Eisenhower accented his understanding clearly when he refused, despite pressure from his friends and his own Secretary of State, to send American combat soldiers to Vietnam.

This was a difficult decision for the President because his old friends were Generals and members of the Chiefs of Staff with whom the President had served in the European conflict.

Mr. Eisenhower was a popular General and a popular President who suited the happier mood of the American people in the '50s.

---

[From the Key West Citizen, Mar. 30, 1969]

### Ike Was There

If the essence of Dwight David Eisenhower could be summed up in a one-word epitaph, it would be simply: "Ike."

Here was the professional soldier who rose from relative obscurity at the beginning of the greatest war in history to supreme command of the greatest assemblage of armies in history, who later served his country for eight years in the highest position of responsibility any man can attain.

Yet he was always "Ike."

Looking back from the turbulent present, the years of the Eisenhower administration seem calm and stable. They were not, but if they seemed so then as well as now, it was only because of the presence of this immensely popular president in the White House. There was something about this most uncommon common man that inspired confidence and faith that no matter how beset the nation was by crises and challenges, nothing dire would happen as long as Ike was there.

Beset the nation was:

Those were the years when the cold war was really frigid—when a man named Khrushchev came to power in Russia to strut the world's stage for a time with his rhetoric of nuclear diplomacy and ballistic blackmail; when a man named Ho Chi Minh was mauling the French in Indochina; when a man named Joe McCarthy was finding Communists in every State Department closet and setting neighbor suspiciously against neighbor; when a man named Faubus in Little Rock, Ark., was fomenting the gravest federal-state crisis since the Civil War; when a U.S. vice president was being spat upon in South America; when the world hovered on the edge of Armageddon as war broke out in the Middle East; when freedom-loving men everywhere agonized as Hungary was ground under the heel; when the nation plunged briefly into its worst recession since the 1930's; when Americans indulged in an orgy of self-doubt because Russia had launched something called a Sputnik into space; when words like "agonizing reappraisal," "brinkmanship," "U–2," "summit" and "missile gap" were part of the vocabulary of reproach against the administration.

Yet they seemed like calm years, because Ike was there.

Now the general has lost his last battle, after beating the scythe-bearer in encounter after encounter. He went down fighting, he surrendered reluctantly. More than that can be asked of no soldier.

Dwight D. Eisenhower is not rated as one of America's great or even strong presidents, and it is not likely that another generation of historians will differ with this estimate. Of one thing we can be certain, however:

If, in their study of this man, his life and his accomplishments, Americans of the future can come at all close to knowing him as his contemporaries did, they will call him "Ike."

---

[From the Miami Beach Sun, Mar. 30, 1969]

### An Editorial

Dwight D. Eisenhower will be remembered by his fellow Americans and a multitude around the world for whatever endeared him to them personally.

In history, however, there will stand out the fact that he devoted a full lifetime—from youth to old age—to this land of ours.

The fact that he rose, on moment's notice, from a desk-bound lieutenant colonel in Washington to the general in London who welded together the manpower of some 24 free nations and forged that striking force which sailed across the British Channel to storm the fortress of tyranny and man's bestiality to man.

The fact that there came, in the history of this nation, the day when the need to fill the White House with a man of stature became so dire that both Republicans and Democrats tried to claim him.

And, beyond all that, this other one: That in the final days of his Presidency he had the courage and the vision to warn America and Americans of the ever growing, overpowering influence of the "military-industrial establishment" on its domestic and foreign policy. Of the threat that has since become reality!

It is for these marks left behind—marks that will stand as tall tomorrow as they stood yesterday and thus remain indelible in the annals of American and world history—that this newspaper salutes him and bids him farewell.

## Hon. Hugh L. Carey

OF NEW YORK

Mr. Speaker, as the family of General Eisenhower travel with their memories and our beloved

31-935 O—70——6

Gen. Dwight David Eisenhower to Abilene, our hearts and our deepest sympathy are with them.

I feel a special sense of loss at the passing of this old soldier who indeed will never fade away.

It was my privilege and honor to serve under General Eisenhower when he commanded the Supreme Headquarters Allied Expeditionary Forces—SHAEF—and I was an officer in the 104th—Timberwolf—Infantry Division.

As we attended the services in National Cathedral I looked around me at the General's officers and others who were his pallbearers and I heard again the sounds of armor and small arms fire and the thunder of artillery as they once sounded in Normandy and along the Maas River in Holland, along the Rhine, over the bridge at Remagen, and the dash to the encirclement at the Ruhr, and the sudden silence of VE Day. Through all of this I was with General Eisenhower and down to the last man in every squad we felt his presence, his guidance, and his comradeship. Not only did we all wear the Eisenhower jacket but as trained, determined soldiers we wore the Eisenhower breastplate which meant cool courage under fire and the eye constantly on the objective of driving tyranny from the field of Europe.

Under his command I was privileged to be advanced in a battlefield promotion and when I received his orders advancing me to the rank of major I suddenly aged from a man in his 20's to one with a sense of the full responsibility for the lives and leadership of men which he managed to instill in all his officers by his own example.

Once again from his life I take this example that a great general is as much known for finding ways to peace as he is for the winning of wars. During his time as President he found that uneasy and unsettled peace but it was peace of a sort. In his memory I hope our generals of this day and all others who lead us will have his courage to seek the ways of peace for I know this would be his wish for all of us as he leaves this world for his eternal reward.

## Hon. David W. Dennis
OF INDIANA

Mr. Speaker, an American hero has passed from this world to his reward after a last fight as gallant as any of those he waged before. His death reduces further the dwindling band of those who led the forces of the free world in World War II. All of us owe an immeasurable debt to those men who led us to victory in those dangerous times, and to no one do we owe more than to General Eisenhower, the supreme commander of our military forces. His is an American success story—from a poor boy at Abilene to our President and Commander in Chief—and General Eisenhower carried all his honors with a modesty possible only to a great gentleman. The Nation and the people he served, and the world he did so much to save, join in mourning his passing.

## Hon. Durward G. Hall
OF MISSOURI

Mr. Speaker, once again Washington prepared and the Nation participated in another large "state" funeral. This time it occurred because of the death of former President Eisenhower. These proceedings were not made with shock, but with sober reverence and appreciation for a giant of a man that had played a dominant role in world affairs for the last generation.

During this period of time "Ike"—as he was affectionately known—represented the best qualities of America. His compassion, humility, and friendliness made him beloved by millions throughout the world. His ability to disagree without being disagreeable, contributed to his success in dealing with both quarreling allies and the conflicting interests in American society. That big Eisenhower smile served for nearly 30 years, as one of the best prescriptions for a troubled and sick world.

Beyond this, Dwight Eisenhower represented men's aspirations for individual freedom, justice, and peace with honor. He certainly believed in the worth and merit of the individual. He knew the enormous qualities and capabilities that the individual possesses, and he knew the accomplishments they can produce. In this regard, he spoke frequently of the "uncommon man." He perceptively observed that it is the "uncommon man" that produces a better life and world, and he quite correctly discovered this quality in every man. He further knew that these qualities could only be developed in an atmosphere of freedom.

Coupled with this individual freedom, President Eisenhower believed that justice was an essential ingredient to development of man's aspirations. His "crusade in Europe" was just such a quest for restoring justice and freedom—from the Nazi tyranny.

He realized that peace could not exist without justice. His entire term as President was dedicated to this quest. As a successful warrior he knew too well the horrors of war. This prepared him as a "warrior for peace." Not peace at any price, but a peace where the weaker nations would be protected from the stronger; a peace where men would not be subjected and forced to live under a government that was not of their own choosing.

As in war, Dwight Eisenhower waged a successful fight for peace. His years in the Presidency were marked with a period of stability unseen since the days following the First World War. Communist aggression was curtailed, the Korean war was ended, and the letting of American blood on foreign soil all but stopped.

The lack of strife and conflict on the domestic scene was also quite apparent during the Eisenhower years. There was no exploding racial antagonism nor were our cities in flames. General "Ike" showed that economic and social progress could be made without violence and demonstrations.

Much more could be said concerning this man who had a humble beginning on the Kansas plains. His life was lived as a classic example to all. I doubt that there is a mother and father who would not want their son to emulate Dwight Eisenhower's personal qualities and life. He is no doubt our greatest soldier-statesman since George Washington. There is no doubt that like George Washington, "he is first in war, first in peace, and first in the hearts of his countrymen."

## Hon. George A. Goodling

OF PENNSYLVANIA

Mr. Speaker, Friday, March 28, 1969, was a bright and sunny day in the Nation's Capital. The brightness suddenly turned to gloom at 12:25 a.m., with the announcement that General of the Army and former President Dwight David Eisenhower had passed away.

Probably no President in history received greater recognition as an "all-America American." The phrase "I like Ike" was a three-word testimonial to the great affection which people had for him, not only in his native land but throughout the world. He remains both at home and abroad one of the most beloved American figures of all times.

His was a remarkable life in that he served in so many capacities, all of them marked with distinction—as a military man, as an educator, as President of the United States and, finally, after a full life of public service, as a private citizen. Few men in history could match his profound dignity or his deep sense of humility.

Some men seem to have been born for a distinct purpose. Dwight D. Eisenhower was such a man. He will forever be associated with the great Allied effort to free the European Continent from tyranny brought about by a madman. He was chosen because he possessed the qualities of humanity, tolerance, and an outstanding ability to work with others and win their trust and cooperation. History shows this selection was a wise choice.

While he was supreme commander of the largest body of fighting men and the greatest army of armament ever assembled, Dwight D. Eisenhower will always be remembered by those who knew him best as a man of peace.

I was privileged to know Dwight David Eisenhower. He was my best known constituent. "Ike" had that unique blend of friendliness and competence that is too rarely found in men today. Against the background of these rare traits he had the distinction of living to see himself become a legend, certainly a fitting reward for his outstanding service.

This is an hour of great sadness because Adams County has lost a true friend and neighbor, Pennsylvania has lost a grand citizen, America has lost a great leader, and the world has lost a man it loved, respected, and revered.

We can take consolation, however, from the realization that as Dwight D. Eisenhower gave so generously and unselfishly of himself, so, too, did he succeed in weaving himself into the fabric of America and into the hearts of all men. As we mourn his passing, we should recall his strong spirit which can guide and sustain us in whatever troubled days might lie ahead. This man was an inspiration to untold millions, and ours is a better world because he walked among us.

To paraphrase the poet's words, "Dwight

David Eisenhower has joined the innumerable caravan that moves to that mysterious realm. He went sustained and soothed by an unfaltering trust. He approached his grave like one who wraps the drapery of his couch about him, and lies down to pleasant dreams."

## Hon. Silvio O. Conte
OF MASSACHUSETTS

Mr. Speaker, the death of General Eisenhower removes from this Nation, the world, and all of us a towering and noble figure.

General Eisenhower led the most powerful military machine that has ever existed in the history of this world. From north Africa, through the "great crusade" at Normandy on June 6, 1944, and on to the unconditional surrender of Germany at Rheims, France, on May 7, 1945, he gallantly led and inspired his forces.

But above all, he was a "soldier of peace." His foremost desire and hope was to witness the establishment of peace upon this earth. His Presidency was characterized by a fervent belief in the goodness of man, and therefore in the possibility of man achieving this peace.

He stood out magnificently above the frictions that existed during his administration. His humility and honesty defied the efforts of his most ardent critics. His character earned the respect and admiration of all humanity.

As a previous generation looked back upon the pre-World War I era, so we look back nostalgically to "the Eisenhower years." They were the last great period of peace this country has enjoyed.

Peace did not just come. President Eisenhower worked to achieve and maintain it. He worked with all that was at his disposal. Foremost among these "weapons" for peace was he, the human being, deeply concerned about our Nation and about all of us.

It was during the last 2 years of his Presidency that I came to Congress. I then had the privilege and honor of getting to know him personally. This was one of the truly great experiences of my life. I shall treasure the memory not only in these days of national mourning but also in the years to come. And in those years, I hope that we will all work to achieve the goals he set for himself and our country.

The general told President Nixon just the other day that "understanding" is the most needed thing in the world today. He knew that understanding, and not the "acquisition of unwarranted influence by the military-industrial complex," was the key to the survival of this Nation and of the human race.

Let us all strive toward this understanding. The future may well depend upon our achieving it.

I speak for all the people of the First Congressional District of Massachusetts in extending my deepest sympathies to his beloved widow, Mamie Eisenhower, to the entire Eisenhower family, and to all his close associates. May they be comforted by the knowledge of our great love and affection for Dwight D. Eisenhower.

## Hon. John E. Hunt
OF NEW JERSEY

Mr. Speaker, I join my colleagues and Americans everywhere in mourning the loss of a great man, a great leader, and a great American, Dwight David Eisenhower.

I was temporarily assigned to General Eisenhower's command during World War II, and it was my personal pleasure over the years to meet him on several occasions. I knew him to be a man of high moral character, impeccable integrity, and possessed of a rare quality; namely, wisdom, born of inherent compassion for his fellow man, an understanding of the times in which he lived, a depth of insight known from experience, and a capacity to apply the lessons of history to contemporary realities.

As the 34th President of the United States, General Eisenhower was to deal with yet another war whose conclusion was a prelude to an era of peace, prosperity, and stability He brought to this Nation the highest respect among the free nations of the world, the confidence of its people, and a renewed faith in our American heritage as set by his own example. His courage and leadership were dedicated to the moral right that men everywhere might live in peace and freedom, and his memory will live on in our hearts as an inspiration to give us the spiritual strength to meet the challenges both present and future. He once said:

> Faith is our surest strength, our greatest resource.

Mrs. Hunt and I extend our deepest and heartfelt sympathy to Mrs. Eisenhower and her devoted family.

## Hon. John L. McMillan

OF SOUTH CAROLINA

Mr. Speaker, we are all deeply touched over the passing of one of our country's greatest leaders. The entire world is paying tribute to the late Dwight Eisenhower for the great leadership he gave, not only the United States, but the entire world during the time we were giving our lives to preserve peace in the world. I think General Eisenhower was unanimously liked by the generals of all the armies in the world when he was the commander in chief during World War II when armies from many countries served under his command. We all know that he did the best he could to solve some of the numerous problems confronting this country during the time he was President of the United States and his service shall be long remembered. As a Member of Congress during the time he was President, I did not always agree with everything suggested by the Eisenhower administration. However, I never at one time doubted the President's sincerity and his extreme desire to keep this country solvent and at peace with the world.

We must all admire the great fight he has made over the years in conquering numerous heart attacks and other types of illness which would have taken the life of an ordinary citizen. His fight to live was equal to his fight to keep peace throughout the world during the time he was serving as commander in chief of all the armies and as President of the United States. I am certain that everyone will agree that this country is a better place to live by having General Eisenhower serve as one of our military leaders and statesman. My heart goes out to his wife and son and his brothers.

## Hon. Joe D. Waggonner, Jr.

OF LOUISIANA

Mr. Speaker, with the passing of Dwight David Eisenhower we are witnessing also the passing of an era, and we are all the less for it.

This great general, this beloved man represented a time in our history in which men spoke with unabashed pride of their love for our country, in which men professed Christian moral codes because they were proud to be called Christians, in which men had no hesitancy to stand up for right because they were taught that honorable men did not deal in expediency.

He was the epitome of that era, as much the exemplification of all that makes a man great as was George Washington in his time. He ennobled mankind with his simple honesty and his strength of character.

The Nation was fortunate to have had this man as its son. He discharged with full honors every obligation imposed upon him by God, family, and country. We have stood in the shadow of a noble man and I am grateful for the opportunity.

God rest you now, Mr. President.

## Hon. Fernand J. St Germain

OF RHODE ISLAND

Mr. Speaker, Dwight David Eisenhower lived a full human life; he used his great abilities in long and successful service for his fellow Americans. We have mourned other heroes in recent years: President John Kennedy, Martin Luther King, Senator Robert Kennedy. How different it is when death cuts off men whose work is not yet done, whose potential is not fulfilled. While we are saddened at the death of Dwight Eisenhower, we are grateful for his long and full life among us.

He rose from obscurity in a time of crisis when leadership was needed to direct the military forces of threatened nations against a common foe. The peoples of Europe remember with gratitude how he united and organized American, British, French, Canadian, and the other allied forces in that mighty and victorious campaign against Nazi oppression. After the war, Eisenhower continued to serve this Nation at Columbia University, at NATO, as President of the United States; a world-famous leader and a remarkable man.

He was a man of inner strength. Resolute and determined in the cause of peace and justice, he held unequaled power as Supreme Allied Commander of the greatest military force ever put in the field, and again as President of the greatest Nation in mankind's long history. Yet his strength of character was such that military and political power did not corrupt or distort his moral power—his integrity, his humility, and his respect for his fellow man.

He was a man men trusted. There was no question about his motives. He was not self-serving. His fellow Americans knew that he was totally dedicated to the service of his country and its people. His straightforwardness earned respect and admiration both at home and abroad.

He was a man of compassion; a man of heart and of conscience determined to bring peace and freedom to mankind. He believed firmly in the dignity of man; and because of this, in spite of the awesome power at his command, he kept a gentle spirit and displayed that extraordinary comradeship with his subordinates that made him so beloved.

It has been said that Eisenhower embodied the American ideals, that the American people felt that his virtues were somehow the virtues of the Nation as a whole. His death may remind Americans to ask if the strength of character which was so strong in him to the end, and which he symbolized for the Nation, has somehow weakened in our land. How we need his strong and compassionate spirit in today's world. Our greatest tribute will be to maintain and, where necessary, to restore in full measure for our Nation the strength and spirit of Dwight Eisenhower.

## Hon. Richard Fulton
OF TENNESSEE

Mr. Speaker, our Nation and our people mourn the passing of General of the Army Dwight David Eisenhower, the 34th President of the United States.

If one word were used to describe General Eisenhower, I believe that word would be "dedication." Dedication to his country, dedication to his duty, and dedication to his family.

His military career spanned the victorious conclusion of the greatest world conflict in history.

His political career was climaxed with the ending of hostilities in Korea, the first direct armed conflict our Nation faced with Communist aggression.

He was truly a man of peace.

Personal integrity and honor marked his years as our Commander in Chief, and its impact was so profound that those years have been designated the "Eisenhower Era."

General Eisenhower, through his example as a leader, as a father, and as a man, exemplified those values we cherish most highly. He was a symbol of the best our country can produce.

From the heartland of our Nation, at his birthplace in Kansas, he acquired his basic sense of values of honesty, integrity, love of family, respect for authority, reverence for God, and dedication to country. These were his contributions to the highest office of the land, the Presidency of the United States.

As a patriot, a leader, as a father, and as a man, General Eisenhower exemplified our most cherished values. He was a symbol of the best our country can produce.

He will be missed, and he will be long remembered.

## Hon. Charles R. Jonas
OF NORTH CAROLINA

Mr. Speaker, everything that can possibly be said about the life and accomplishments of the late President Dwight David Eisenhower has already been said so I cannot hope to add anything new. But I could not allow the occasion to pass without joining my colleagues in the House of Representatives in paying a final tribute of respect to his memory.

General Eisenhower has now passed from among us and the entire world mourns his passing. And I predict that he will live throughout all time in the hearts of his countrymen and in the hearts of millions around the world who love liberty and pray for peace.

While in my book President Eisenhower was a great statesman, I shall prefer to remember him as a man of understanding and good will. He was entirely without guile. Although he occupied the exalted position of the Presidency, millions of people in this country always referred to him by his nickname.

While I had the privilege and pleasure of meeting General Eisenhower on numerous occasions before his inauguration as President in 1953, it was not until he came to Charlotte, N.C., to help the people of Mecklenburg County celebrate Mecklenburg Declaration of Independence Day that I came to realize the impact his personality had on people in every walk of life. Riding with him from the airport to Freedom Park on that occasion, I was struck by the attitudes of the thousands who lined the streets.

In the crowds were business and professional people, workers in overalls, and many mothers holding small children in their arms. All were smiling, waving and uttering such expressions as: "Hello, Ike" and "I Like Ike." In the course of that ride I did not hear a single formal salute. The people who lined the streets were uniformly informal, which I considered to be a personal tribute to the warm personality of this man who walked with kings yet never lost the common touch. "Ike" loved it and responded to the informal salutations with a wide grin and a cordial wave of the hand.

Since that day I have had numerous opportunities to spend time in his presence, to hear him speak on many formal occasions, and to observe his superb conduct of the affairs of state during his 8 years in the Presidency; but I think I shall always remember him as he was that day in Charlotte—so warm, friendly, and responsive to the multitudes who stood on the streets and who assembled in the park to give him an official greeting and hear him speak.

In my judgment General Eisenhower will be remembered as one of our most beloved Presidents. To the cynics who sneer at the accomplishments of the Eisenhower administration, I would respond that our country has not in modern times enjoyed 8 more peaceful and prosperous years than during his Presidency. His was a decade of good will among men and I dare say that millions of Americans will always praise him for giving us that kind of an administration.

We have been told that, as the end neared, after expressing his love for the members of his family, General Eisenhower said:

And I have always loved my country.

As we remember Dwight David Eisenhower and mourn his passing, we all realize that—just as he always loved his country—his country loved and will always love him.

## Hon. William D. Hathaway

OF MAINE

Mr. Speaker, the Nation mourns the passing of Dwight David Eisenhower, soldier, statesman, and humanitarian; a great American, a great and gentle man whose life and works will stand as a monument to all that is good in 20th century America.

By any measure, he must be counted among the giants of his age. History will recall him as a great leader; as the brilliant Commander of the Allied Forces in Europe during World War II and as a President who gave our Nation a pause from strife, a period of tranquillity and dignity.

Our grief that he is dead is profound, but we are consoled by a rising sense of gratitude that he lived among us and in the service of our Nation.

## Hon. Joseph P. Addabbo

OF NEW YORK

Mr. Speaker, I join in the national mourning for a great leader, a man who placed his country above all else in times of war as well as of peace. President Eisenhower's life and devotion to his nation will be a permanent guide for the leaders of future generations.

The Long Island Press editorial sums up the Nation's loss in the passing of Dwight David Eisenhower. The text of the editorial follows:

DWIGHT EISENHOWER: 1890–1969

In mourning Dwight David Eisenhower, the sorrow is eased by the fact that his 78 years of life mirrored a glowing picture of all that is best in American life.

His initial impact upon his countrymen was as a military leader, but his first achievement as President was as a man of peace, fulfilling his campaign promise to go to Korea to end the slaughter.

Born in Denison, Tex., he grew up in near-poverty in Abilene, his mother a pacifist who wept when her boy was appointed to West Point. Perhaps that is why he was a warrior who hated what he called "this damnable thing of war," and as a President, he wielded power sparingly.

He was also a politician who told a news conference: "I think in the general derogatory sense you can say . . . that I do not like politics."

As a soldier he commanded the greatest military machine in the history of mankind and led it to victory over the most infamous enemy in memory.

A measure of this man was his popularity with the troops. Traditionally generals are fair game for the men in the ranks, but not General Ike. One of the reasons may have been his "enlisted man response" to the ingrained "chicken" of Army life.

For example, at the end of the war soldiers on leave flocked to Berchtesgaden, Hitler's Bavarian retreat. Only one elevator was available to take visitors to the top of the mountain fortress. The alternative was a long, winding climb up a path. The elevator bore a sign: "For Field Grade Officers Only." When Gen. Eisenhower saw it, he yanked the sign off and scaled it down the hillside. After that, field officers stood in line with privates to ride the elevator.

As President, he gave America no ringing slogans and made no glowing promises, but he was elected by majorities matched previously only by Franklin D. Roosevelt.

The same warmth that existed between Gen. Eisenhower and his troops carried over to civilian life. "I like Ike" was more fact than slogan, and his appeal was so magnetic that the Democrats sought him as a candidate before he identified himself as a Republican.

As he rode in an open car through Long Island—as in other parts of the nation—tens of thousands turned out to see the tanned, fit, hero, and to smile back at his famous grin.

Under the Eisenhower Administration the Korean War was brought to an end, the hydrogen bomb was developed and America entered the space age.

It was President Eisenhower who appointed Earl Warren Chief Justice of the Supreme Court, and later sent federal troops to enforce the court's order to integrate the schools in Little Rock, Ark. He sent Marines into Lebanon at that country's request, but he avoided massive involvement in French Indo-China when Dien Bien Phu fell.

The cocktail party psychologists talked glibly of the "father image" when he was in the White House. And there may have been some truth in the trite phases because he came at a time when America yearned for the comfort of a fatherly leader.

Although he was of the military, his outlook was never narrowly militaristic. The generals and admirals enjoyed no special influence over policy or budget decisions while he was President.

His military leadership made him aware of the parallel interests of the makers of arms, and military careerists. When he left the Presidency, he warned the nation to beware of an alliance between these parallel forces, and to guard against the danger of inertia in the defense establishment.

History may not rank him as our most brilliant general or our most extraordinary President, but history occasionally does not measure the quality of integrity or nobility in a man.

He was as popular when he left office as when he entered it, and there is little doubt he could have won a third term had he not been barred by the Constitution from running again.

The affection the nation felt for Ike did not diminish in the years afterward. He was always the elder statesman of the nation more than of his party.

His typically American optimism was deeply rooted in his firm faith in the strength of America. In his last public address—via television to the 1968 Republican convention in Miami—he said: "Let us first remind ourselves of the greatness of this nation and of its people. Let's not waste time this year searching out someone to blame, even though some seem more disposed to concede rather than to stand firmly for America."

A gentle man and a patriot has left us.

## Hon. James A. Haley

### OF FLORIDA

Mr. Speaker, I think little more need be said about the nature and character of Dwight David Eisenhower than that when death came to him, it found his stature undiminished in the eyes of the American people—his countrymen who had lived intimately with him for more than a quarter of a century.

In those years, the people of this Nation had known General Eisenhower in many roles, as a man of war and a man of peace, as an educator, an author, as a President, and as an elder statesman. And it is nothing less than a tremendous monument to him that the man Eisenhower, known to millions as "Ike," commanded from his fellow Americans the same respect, the same confidence, the same affection he had known at the peak of his public years.

Americans began recognizing the name Eisenhower in 1942 after he was named to direct the free world's first major offensive action of World War II—the invasion and ultimate liberation of North Africa. It was a task demanding more than the talents of a soldier, for the human problems posed by the occupation of North Africa were very nearly as difficult as the military problems. The task required tact, patience, the ability to induce men of divergent backgrounds, views, and personalities to work together for a common end.

It was General Eisenhower's exercise of that tact and patience that marked him as unlike any other military figure in World War II—and these were the qualities that put him in command of the invasion of Western Europe, the most ambitious and elaborate operation in human history. These also were the qualities that accounted for his recall to active duty to command the military arm of the North American Treaty Organization—and, ultimately, these were the qualities that made him President of the United States.

Dwight Eisenhower went into that office with the same purpose with which he approached his military assignments in North Africa and Western Europe. He aspired to unite. He sensed, accurately, I think, that the American people had been wearied by the exertions of two wars abroad and by a long series of conflicts at home, that they wanted more than anything else to pause, to catch their breath, to see how far they had come and how far they had yet to go.

Some will say that the 8 Eisenhower years were years of inaction, and in a sense they were. But they were the kind of years the American people had earned. And this is not to say that the Eisenhower years were empty, for they were not. They were years of repeated American testing on the world scene—years that found the United States reacting, in Lebanon, in the Formosa Straits, in Berlin, in Southeast Asia, with charity, courage and force.

They were the years that produced the concept of massive retaliation, the most effective instrument yet devised for arresting the forward thrust of international communism. They were years that formulated, more clearly than ever before or since, the great moral issues at stake in the confrontation between communism and freedom.

At home, they were the years that saw the launching of the Interstate Highway System—the most elaborate highway-building program in world history. A program without which much of the Nation would be close to transportation paralysis today.

Dwight Eisenhower was moved by the passionate dedication to peace that only one who has known war can have. To build understanding, to avert conflict, to relieve tensions, he was invariably willing to go the second mile—in the spirit that took him to Geneva and Paris, that brought Nikita Khrushchev to America.

The legacy that Dwight David Eisenhower leaves to the people to whose service he devoted his entire adult career is a legacy of devotion to duty, a legacy of leaving America a happier and sounder and spiritually stronger land. As his deeds are weighed in the scales of patriotism and integrity and humanity and duty, Americans know that he was a giant.

And because he was the personification of that which is good in America and in Americans, there is in the Nation this week a universal mourning, universal sharing, in which I humbly join, in the grief of Dwight Eisenhower's wife and of the entire Eisenhower family.

## Hon. Edward P. Boland

OF MASSACHUSETTS

Mr. Speaker, Dwight David Eisenhower established a truly remarkable record of accomplishments in his career as soldier and statesman. Editorials published last weekend in the Springfield, Mass., Union, the Springfield Daily News, and the Springfield Republican outline the former President's historic contributions to his Nation and to the world. With permission, Mr. Speaker, I include these editorials in the Record at this point:

[From the Springfield (Mass.) Republican]

### A Great American

Dwight D. Eisenhower was a great American; he was also a typical American, in the best sense of the term, perhaps to a larger degree than any other President of modern times.

In family background, boyhood and youth, in his West Point days and the first part of his Army career, Eisenhower generally resembled thousands of other Americans following the same sort of pathway in life.

Although he had the exceptional qualities of leadership which enabled him to take effective command of the most successful military operation in history, Eisenhower was typically the average American.

In his favorite pastimes, in his buoyant spirit, his progressive outlook, his forthright warmth and unfailing optimism, Ike personally summarized all the qualities that Americans most admire and appreciate.

And while Eisenhower was a professional soldier, he was also a man of peace. Like countless millions of Americans who have served in the armed forces, he fully knew the terrible horrors, agonies and human wastes of war; like millions of servicemen, he was dedicated to the proposition that the nation should never be an aggressor, should fight only for the defense of freedom, and should do all it could to advance the cause of worldwide peace.

Historians may well catalogue Ike for his genuine contributions toward peace as well as for his military achievements.

He typified the best of the American spirit.
He aimed for the general improvement of all people.
He sought an elusive peace for the brotherhood of man . . . and he warmed the world with a grin.

---

[From the Springfield (Mass.) Union, Mar. 29, 1969]

DWIGHT DAVID EISENHOWER

Dwight D. Eisenhower, as soldier and statesman and public figure revered in the hearts of his countrymen, came closer to the hallowed tradition of George Washington than any man in American history.

Certainly no other personality made famous by the glory of military victory went so deeply into the civil-political life of the nation and emerged with his popularity still so wide, his record of service still so clean that his critics could do no more than scratch the surface and admit in the process that they "liked Ike," too.

The images of Gen. Eisenhower, President Eisenhower, and Citizen Eisenhower (author of books, once president of Columbia, raiser of cattle) blend into a composite whole, even considering that without the first, the others might well never have evolved. It is, then, all the more remarkable that the career was marked with distinction in one or another degree in each of its undertakings.

Of the military phase, there are no doubts. Gen. Eisenhower was at the top of the small pyramid of Allied strategists in World War II to whom the free world owes its salvation. His genius for military organization was the touchstone of the successful drive for the Continent and the eventual engulfment of the German war machine. Later, as NATO commander, he headed the Allied force designed not to win wars but to keep peace in Western Europe when one old ally, Russia, threatened to disturb it. The Western world's debt to him thus was increased.

Of the political phase, criticism is easier to find. Gen. Eisenhower brought his Crusade in Europe home to a virtually assured presidential victory when he agreed to run in 1952. His innate distaste for politics seemed to grow in the next eight years. His popularity grew, too, enhanced if anything by his conquest of illnesses, but so did political opposition charging in vague and loose terms a standstill at home and ineffectiveness of policy abroad. It is a modern paradox that the Democrats gained against his party in Congress while Mr. Eisenhower himself could have won an easy third term had he chosen to seek it and had the Constitution permitted.

Part of the explanation lies in the sense of national security engendered by the man Eisenhower in the White House. But the fact also is that under the Eisenhower policies the free world was holding its own securely against Communist designs. A common complaint was that it was not doing more than that. But the cycle of events was not then conducive to breakthroughs. Whether the Eisenhower years might have been crowned by significant progress toward world peace had the summit conference of 1960 not been aborted by the U2 incident is still a matter of conjecture.

History will assess the Eisenhower presidential years in better perspective than is possible now. But one great domestic failure the general admitted himself occurred in his efforts to stem the trend toward federal centralization and to return more power and responsibility to the states. The political system, and the political figures who ran it, were the insurmountable obstacle.

Gen. Eisenhower's unswerving personal integrity was the hallmark of his presidency and doubtless what sustained his immense personal popularity, while that of many around him declined. It encompassed the impeccable patriotism of a great soldier, a sense of duty transcending personal welfare, physical and otherwise, a massive belief in the greatness of the United States, an aversion to war but the will to wage it if need be, and a dedication to moderation.

The respect and love of many millions, in the United States and in the far corners of the earth, were held by this immensely human man, who could wield the awesome power of D-Day force and also exude warmth and friendliness through the famous smile that the world had hoped to continue seeing often for many more years.

---

[From the Springfield (Mass.) Daily News, Mar. 29, 1969]

GENERAL EISENHOWER

When they assess the life of Dwight David Eisenhower, historians will quite likely differentiate between Eisenhower the military man, Eisenhower the educator, and Eisenhower the President.

While these three distinct phases in his life must be considered separately by those who will assign him a place in history, there is no such compulsion for categorization on the part of people the world over who knew him best as Ike and made him one of the most popular figures in the 20th Century.

Perhaps as no other man in this century, with the exception of Winston Churchill, Dwight Eisenhower was the right man for the moment. During World War II, he gave Americans the military hero they so desperately needed. As commander of the Allied Expeditionary Forces in Europe, he was the tactician who shaped D-Day strategy and turned military togetherness into the formula for victory.

It can be said that Eisenhower—the general—was the most successful of the three Dwight Eisenhowers and that nothing he did afterwards—even as President—quite matched his World War II exploits.

His life—from the day he entered West Point in 1911—was oriented to military standards and thinking. However, it has become axiomatic in American life that military men do not translate well to other careers.

As president of Columbia University for several years after World War II, Gen. Eisenhower was not particularly at home as an educator.

As President of the United States for eight years, the military man never quite seemed comfortable in the new world of politics. The politics which is an integral part of the presidency was obviously foreign to his forthright nature and his military background.

Yet, the Eisenhower record during his eight years as President had no direct relation to his personal popularity. Almost certainly, had he been eligible and chosen to run for a third or fourth term, he would have been re-elected by large margins.

Whether he was president of a large university or President of the United States, he was still Gen. Eisenhower—the foremost military hero of our times.

In this sense, it is unfair to measure Dwight Eisenhower's place in history in anything but a military context. This was his special cup of tea. As Winston Churchill—despite his many other accomplishments—is primarily remembered as the World War II inspirational leader of Great Britain, so Dwight Eisenhower is inexorably cast as the great American general of this war.

He served his country well—with a full measure of devotion. He was a firm believer in—and a champion of—the ideals of democracy. He was—most of all—a champion for the people and the country he loved so much.

Whatever his eventual place in history, Ike will always be remembered with esteem and affection by countless millions.

## Hon. Daniel D. Rostenkowski

OF ILLINOIS

Mr. Speaker, I am deeply grieved as I join my distinguished colleagues who eulogize today the life and accomplishments of one of America's greatest soldiers and statesmen, Dwight David Eisenhower. Words alone cannot adequately delineate the omnibus contributions that this great man gave freely to his countrymen as well as to all the people who have inhabited this planet.

Few men in the annals of our civilizations have experienced so fully and deserved so entirely the public trust and confidence placed in Dwight David Eisenhower as General of the Armies, Supreme Allied Commander, and 34th President of the United States. He has held more positions of public responsibility than most all of the great men of history who have preceded him. But perhaps more significantly, former President Eisenhower was revered both at home and abroad not only for the offices that he held but for the man that he was.

Gentle of spirit, pillar of strength, and dedicated to liberty and justice for all, General Eisenhower was the epitome of the American dream. Born under the Texas stars, and raised in the open Kansas plains, his was a vision of a world without walls to contain the creeping ambitions of petty tyrants. He dreamed rather of a world where individuals could build their own future, free from the domination of others. It is to his great credit that the worst tyrant of the 20th century was smashed by the allied forces in 1945.

Of General Eisenhower, I believe, it may truly be said that although good men must die, death cannot kill their names.

## Hon. James B. Utt

OF CALIFORNIA

Mr. Speaker, without a doubt, the most popular President of several decades and probably of the history of our country, Gen. Dwight David Eisenhower, has passed away. But his popularity, great as it was with his infectious smile and his down to earth, "one of us" manner, is relatively unimportant when compared with his many and tremendous contributions to our Nation, and to the world.

Mr. Speaker, I had the pleasure of beginning my congressional service at the same time that "Ike" took over as our 34th President. I was honored to be a part of the Republican 83d Congress which helped to smooth the rocky path that faces new Chief Executives and which is especially obstacle-ridden for one who assumes the country's leadership without previous experience in the Congress.

With our help, his success came easier, but with or without it, "Ike" was bound to succeed since this was the pattern of his life. He never learned the definition of failure.

President Eisenhower had a deep and abiding faith in the Supreme Being and did not hesitate to admit his reliance upon Him. As every mortal man does, he made mistakes but these were not prompted by selfishness or greed. He did what he truly believed was in the best interests of the country he had served so many years. He led the Nation to victory in war and thereby brought to a close a bloody and shameful period of history. As Commander in Chief, he was called upon again to stop a conflict that had taken thousands of lives. His policies and his philosophy then allowed peace to continue through the rest of his two terms in office.

General "Ike" has now gone to his just reward. He sleeps in peace and no tears need be shed for him, but rather for his beloved wife Mamie and his family, who will personally miss him so intensely, and for the rest of the Nation who will now be deprived of his great wisdom, his sound advice and counsel.

Mr. Speaker, I extend my most sincere sympathy to his wife and family and know that the good Lord, whom Ike served so devotedly, will give them added strength of acceptance and joy that their loved one is now free of troubles and hardships and is resting in the House of the Lord.

## Hon. John S. Wold
OF WYOMING

Mr. Speaker, the Congress, the Nation, and the world have eulogized Gen. Dwight David Eisenhower. Words are never fully adequate, but they can be truly noble if men live by them. The general has passed on, but he has left us a legacy. Part of that legacy is the words he uttered and by which he lived. I believe they would be an inspiration to us and to our children also. Therefore, I have introduced a resolution to have the Librarian of Congress, in cooperation with the Committee on House Administration, publish the speeches of General Eisenhower.

Our grief and that of the world is unbounded. But it is lit by the hope and faith that the man, Dwight Eisenhower, inspired in the hearts and minds of men everywhere.

We pray for the comfort of those who were near to him at this time of bereavement.

He was, as has been said of our first President, George Washington, first in the hearts of his countrymen and in the hearts of the world—both in peace and war.

Who can forget this man who led the forces of freedom onto the shores of Nazi "fortress Europe" on June 6, 1944, with the knowledge that he alone bore the awesome responsibility for their success or failure? Who can forget this man who twice laid down the gauntlet of arms to take on the burdens of peace—first as the president of Columbia University and then of the United States? Who can forget the man who laid down a challenge in his farewell address as inspiring and far reaching as that laid down by President Washington in his farewell?

The man is gone—but not his spirit. We could do no better in these days of eternal crisis and challenge than to live by the ideals he stated in his second inaugural address:

May we pursue the right without selfrighteousness.

May we know unity without conformity.

May we grow in strength without pride in self.

May we, in our dealings with all peoples of the earth, ever speak truth and serve justice.

And so shall America—in the sight of all men of good will—prove true to the honorable purposes that bind and rule us as a people in all this time of trial through which we pass.

My district, the great State of Wyoming, is still very much a frontier place, similar to that where General Eisenhower was reared to hold great love for his God, country, and family. Therefore, I think it especially appropriate to have published in the Record the following editorial by Mr. James Flinchum, editor of the Wyoming State Tribune:

### Why They Liked Ike

In the hindsight of death, every man looms larger than life, miraculously purged of his sins and with his best qualities magnified. Only in rare instances do the eulogies match in the departed the individual in real life. In Dwight D. Eisenhower, there is such an exception.

The General was such a plain and simple man that his almost universal acceptance amounting to near reverence, seems an incongruity. His innate simplicity was manifested in many forms, many of them minor.

One of the highest ranking American military officials of all time, exceeded only by John J. Pershing, General Eisenhower studiously avoided trappings of rank. One small symbol of this was that he refused to wear gilt braid—"scrambled eggs"—on his visored military cap.

He constantly viewed himself as merely one of the millions of Americans who contributed to the winning of World War II; and when the Korean War began, he dismissed himself in one brief, typical statement when someone suggested that he consider himself for active duty in that conflcit: Korea needed young soldiers, said Eisenhower, not old generals.

Eisenhower, both as a soldier and as President, was so markedly unostentatious that it was like a silence in a great hall filled with people.

One of his great and enduring qualities was that he was so simple, so approachable and so possessed of the ability to not only put a stranger immediately at ease, but to establish a communion with that stranger at once.

This mystical quality that is not always obvious except on direct contact, somehow emanated from Eisenhower by indirect contact; so that he projected this image of simplicity and of simpatico from a great distance.

So in a sense he was everyman, and identified himself with all persons of all ages and backgrounds, races and creeds; and it is very possible that every person saw himself in the General, the person he thought he might be, or desperately desired to be.

UN Secretary-General U Thant said yesterday that Eisenhower was a good man, and he projected this image of goodness. Walter Cronkite, employing what now has become a cliche, said he was a man for all seasons. Someone else said to many women he provided a father symbol; to many old men the sort of son they would like to have had; to others the kind of leader they most admired.

It is best to remember that all of these things were true, simply because people believed them to be so; and that perhaps is the essence of truth.

Ultimately, the historians shall one day—possibly commencing a half century from now—get around to accurately assessing Eisenhower's place in history and the origin of his exceptional personal influence on others.

For our own part, we can point to the birth of the General, Oct. 14, 1890, and the place and circumstances—a humble home in what remained Frontier America.

Although Eisenhower's father was a railroad worker in Denison, Tex., when the future President and commander-in-chief of the Allied Forces in World War II was born, the time and place still were a part of the Frontier which did not end by agreement of most historians until a few years later.

Dwight David Eisenhower thus was a product of western, pioneer America, an essentially simple and unsophisticated place with a value system founded on what may be termed loosely the Puritan Ethic.

While basic virtues were not always observed by any means, and there was much lawless and wrongdoing in Frontier America, nevertheless the basic virtues represented chiefly by God, Home and Country were idealized.

People did not put on airs or assume exaggerated notions of their individual importance in the Denisons and Abilenes of the 1890's, and early 1900's, the millieu in which Eisenhower grew up.

If they were notable individuals it was because they were persons like Theodore Roosevelt, himself and easterner but who adopted the ways of the Frontier, an epitome of the direct actionist and the vigorous, simple and wholesome life. Or so it seemed.

Soldiering was an honorable and much-admired profession for that age was still influenced not only by a developing America that had been in vogue since Jefferson's time, and not only by the Spanish-American War just past, but also by the Civil War. Veterans of both these conflicts including such notables as Fighting Joe Wheeler, still lived in that era. Americans universally remained almost without exception, a proud people.

Essentially, then, General Eisenhower was a product of that age, a very different one from that in which we presently live in vast confusion, an era in which values were clear and definite and there was no obscuring of purpose either nationally, familially or individually.

Dwight David Eisenhower related that era to the present; he was a remarkable product of its virtues.

Despite what has happened in America in the past two decades and particularly in the past one, this nation was built on an ethical system best represented in such an individual as General Eisenhower.

For the older people he hearkened back to all that was good in an earlier America and what they liked to see in the present.

For the younger, he represented a solidity that the present fails of achieving.

In every respect, then, the General symbolized an ideal that seldom makes its appearance so notably in single individuals; he belonged to an America of heroic tradition, vested in such individuals as Washington, Lincoln, Lee and Pershing; startlingly similar to these persons in many respects, and yet different too in his own way.

Eisenhower was his own man, and yet he also was every man because he symbolized of the best in this country. That is what made him so unique—the very commonness of him, yet uncommon, too.

He was every American, or what every American really wants to be.

And so the man and the country that found such common identity, and a sharing of admiration and love, have come to the physical parting, as it must to all living persons.

It is a sad moment as on all such occasions whether the latter be one involving the great or the small; and as in these latter too, it may be said of General Eisenhower that the greater recognition must be that although death is sorrowful, the life that preceded it is so much more infinitely greater that the ultimate act is lessened thereby.

America and the world are fortunate to have had among its people such as Dwight David Eisenhower and we who lived during his life, have been particularly favored by his presence.

## Hon. Michael A. Feighan

### OF OHIO

Mr. Speaker, an era in the history of our country has ended with the passing of a great American, Gen. Dwight David Eisenhower. Born of sturdy pioneer parents, in humble circumstances, by his ability and determination he reached the pinnacle of success and popularity. He possessed an intuitive faculty of assessing the movements and motives of our enemies in combat, which was recognized by our allies. His was a life filled with accomplishments.

I had the privilege and honor of meeting General Eisenhower during the close of World War II and on many occasions thereafter.

Just to be in his company one could recognize his dynamic personality and his superlative aptitude for leadership. His brilliant direction of our Armed Forces in World War II won for him world renown. Not only our country but the entire world stood in proud salute to acclaim this able and remarkable man whose dramatic career will long live in the archives of our country.

General Eisenhower will be remembered and revered by all who have stood for the rights which our forefathers sought and those who have fought and are fighting for peace, freedom, and justice.

To his family and especially to his widow

who has shared his triumphs and who has stood bravely by him in sadness and sorrow, I extend my deep and profound sympathy.

## Hon. Ben Reifel

OF SOUTH DAKOTA

Mr. Speaker, during the past sad week I have shared the sorrow of all Americans at the loss of Dwight D. Eisenhower. General Eisenhower very literally gave his life to his country; first as a soldier who became one of our Nation's greatest military leaders, and then as a President who sought daily to bring peace to this troubled world.

General Eisenhower was a man to whom the words "Duty, Honor, Country" were more than just a slogan. He was a man of great stature, integrity, and patriotism. He will be justly remembered as one of our most beloved Presidents.

## Hon. Sidney R. Yates

OF ILLINOIS

Mr. Speaker, the world mourns the passing of a great American, Dwight David Eisenhower. To freedom-loving peoples everywhere, he was the symbol of the surge of a united world to eliminate the viciousness, the barbarism, the antihumanism. His reknown as an astute and victorious military commander was later succeeded by appreciation of his outstanding personal qualities as a man and leader for peace.

It is a measure of his strength that he was able to translate his wartime experience as a general into an earnest desire for peace matched by few national leaders in our generation. As one who has served at the United Nations, I recall particularly the speech he delivered while President before the United Nations in 1953. It made a profound impact. As President, it was Mr. Eisenhower's duty to preside over the assemblying of our nuclear arsenal, and he understood well the awesome implications of that activity. At the United Nations that day he made explicit the moral challenge confronting nations armed and capable of destroying the world. He was appalled at the prospect and urged a turning back before it was too late. His words were eloquent. He declared:

> But for me to say that the defense capabilities of the United States are such that they could inflict terrible losses upon an aggressor—for me to say that the retaliation capabilities of the United States are so great that such an aggressor's land would be laid waste—all this, while fact, is not the true expression of the purpose and the hope of the United States.
>
> To pause there would be to confirm the hopeless finality of a belief that two atomic collossi are doomed malevolently to eye each other indefinitely across a trembling world. To stop there would be to accept helplessly the probability of civilization destroyed—the annihilation of the irreplaceable heritage of mankind handed down to us generation from generation—and this condemnation of mankind to begin all over again the age-old struggle upward from savagery toward decency, and right and justice.
>
> Surely no sane member of the human race could discover victory in such desolation. Could anyone wish his name to be coupled by history with such human degradation and destruction.

Now, he said:

> There was no longer any alternative to peace.

One of the world's great military leaders, he knew the importance of peace, more important in the nuclear age than ever before.

I will remember Dwight D. Eisenhower as a man of peace.

## Hon. James A. Burke

OF MASSACHUSETTS

Mr. Speaker, I am deeply saddened at the passing of the late President Eisenhower. His death leaves a great void in the minds and hearts of the American people. He was a courageous man, one who I believe, truly reached heroic stature.

He will always stand in my mind as one of our greatest Americans. His record and accomplishments are all a matter of public knowledge and history. In a time of national disaster, Ike was there, leading his country with a moral force and courage unparalleled in our country's history. His decisiveness and brilliant leadership swept our Nation to victory during World War II, banishing the deplorable tide of nazism, and giving freedom-loving people, both at home and abroad, new hope for a better life.

It was fitting that a deeply grateful country would bestow its highest honor on this man. Following the mandate of his people, he restored his beloved country to a period of new calm and confidence.

The late President Eisenhower was all that was virtuous and fine in a human being. From a humble beginning, a glorious career ensued, one filled with faith in his fellow man, a great love of country, hard work and determination. This was the measure of the man. I cherish my memories of him. We shall not forget him soon.

## Hon. Harley O. Staggers
OF WEST VIRGINIA

Mr. Speaker:

> Soldiers, rest! Thy warfare o'er,
> Sleep the sleep that knows not breaking;
> Dream of battled fields no more,
> Days of danger, nights of waking.
> Soldiers, rest! Thy warfare o'er,
> Dream of fighting fields no more;
> Sleep the sleep that knows not breaking,
> Morn of toil, nor nights of waking.
>
> —SIR WALTER SCOTT.

Destiny reaches out her hand and with unerring accuracy places her finger on the man equipped by character and training to carry out her purposes. As the war clouds gathered over Europe in the late 1930's there was dire need for a man of uncommon virtues. In the armies of the United States there was an inconspicuous colonel. Who could have predicted that this colonel would be selected to lead the armed might of the free world against the violence of a military machine in the hands of a mad man? We must say that destiny—or shall we say, Divine Providence—interposed to save the world from slavery.

The record of General Eisenhower's achievements is placed clearly before the scrutinizing gaze of history. His judgment in military action, his skill in manipulating men and materials, his statesmanship in dealing with the complex problems arising from diverse personalities and independent governments, all have been analyzed in detail. Today they stand approved, without a dissenting voice. No such universal acclaim has ever been attached previously to any military figure in all history.

More than two centuries before the Christian era, Asia was the arena in which ambitious kings struggled for dominance. Out of the confusion of the times came an astonishing figure, little known to the Western World. His name was Asoka, and it was written of him that—

> He is the only military monarch on record who abandoned warfare after victory.

After uniting what is now India into a stable society, he put his genius to work in promoting the arts of peace. His accomplishments in economic advancement, in education, and in social welfare seem almost modern in scope and in application to the needs of the day.

Somehow the career of General Eisenhower seems curiously to rehearse that of this ancient and benign monarch. For with the general, after war came peace, and the reestablishment of stable societies in Europe, and the restoration of economic strength, and education, and political leadership.

Supported by the adulation of the millions, at home and abroad, he might indeed have been a monarch. The ego of a lesser man, fed on the approval of his countrymen, must surely have responded to the promptings of ambition. But he was not that lesser man. He chose not "pomp nor show, nor lofty place, not boast above the least." Clothed in the "majesty of humility, his scepter was his kindliness, his grandeur was his grace."

At this hour, a caravan of trains carries his mortal remains toward a little country town in the midwest. There, in a shrine as unpretentious as his life has been, the general will be laid to rest. But it is not the all-conquering general, but the wise and gentle and simple "father-figure" who will live in the hearts of his countrymen.

## Hon. Herman T. Schneebeli
OF PENNSYLVANIA

Mr. Speaker, the whole world mourns the passing of Dwight D. Eisenhower. We are fortunate to have had him as one of our country's foremost military and political leaders. We are all the richer to have been able to share him with his family.

Ike's boyhood ideals, supplemented by his strict family training and West Point's 4 years of emphasis on devotion to duty, all stood him in good stead for the rest of his life.

The puritan ethic was constantly an important factor in his life which resulted in his chief motivation: "to do good." His driving dedication pushed him forward into higher and higher responsibilities, so that he could implement the ideals which he held—to improve the welfare of his fellow man.

This ambition came into prominent focus at the height of World War II when the greatest military forces of the world were placed under his command, and he led them to ultimate victory.

It is no small wonder that this position of successful leadership led logically to a call from a grateful people, to pull this country together from the ravages of a war and to become President. He likewise served ably in the White House. Ike always remembered the strict precepts of his youthful upbringing. He was a God-fearing man, religious to the core, and motivated by only the highest ideals.

Despite his militaristic background, General Eisenhower was a patient, kindly, and humble man. His personality was warm and friendly. To know him, was to admire and love him. He was a special American and an exceptional world leader. Not only has he earned the respect and admiration of our citizenry, but citizens from all ends of the earth.

His fighting spirit was evident to the end. He fought valiantly despite countless odds, so that he could continue with his pursuit to "do good." We shall miss him.

Mrs. Schneebeli joins me in extending prayers and heartfelt sympathy to his grieving family.

## Hon. Harold T. Johnson

OF CALIFORNIA

Mr. Speaker, it is with a sense of deep personal loss that I rise today to pay tribute to a great man, a man whose dedicated service to his Nation in the military, as a civilian leader, and finally as President of the United States, offers to all of us in public life an outstanding example for each of us to follow to the full extent of our capabilities.

Dwight David Eisenhower was born on the Texas frontier and reared in the midst of a pioneer environment in the Middle West. He was a member of a family of limited financial means but of unlimited ideals and family spirit. This background and the strength of his family, provided the foundation on which he grew to become one of the greatest men the world has known this century.

Eisenhower, the general, earned a unique place in the history of this Nation because of his tremendous ability to mobilize not only the forces of our own country but the forces of our Allies for the greatest amphibious assault the world has ever known, crossing the English Channel on June 6, 1944, to commence the long march which he led to return freedom to Europe.

Eisenhower, the statesman, after World War II, served the free world as organizer and Supreme Commander of the North Atlantic Treaty Organization. Through his wisdom and guidance, General Eisenhower in this capacity contributed to the rebirth of free Europe. The healthy societies and economies these liberated nations enjoy today, especially as they are compared to their counterparts still behind the Iron Curtain, stand as a monument to the job which he undertook after achieving victory in World War II.

Eisenhower, the President, served all the people of this Nation, putting aside any thought of partisan differences. I can say personally that I felt it a privilege and a pleasure to work with this man who sat in the White House during the first 2 years that I was a Member of the House of Representatives. President Eisenhower, a soldier by education and profession, was truly a man of peace. His honesty, his open, warm personality, generated trust and faith in him as a leader not only on the part of the people of this Nation but on the part of the military and political leaders and individual citizens throughout the world. This confidence in his personal ability and integrity, I believe, were in large measure responsible for the fact that the Eisenhower years represent the longest period of peace this Nation has known for many decades.

Mrs. Johnson and I extend our deepest sympathy to Mrs. Eisenhower and the members of the family.

## Hon. William L. Hungate

OF MISSOURI

Mr. Speaker, I join in paying tribute to a great leader—a man whose life and devotion to our

Nation will continue to inspire people throughout the world for all times.

The people of the Ninth District and the State of Missouri share this period of mourning with all Americans and with all friends of freedom in every corner of the world.

As Commander of the Allied forces in Europe, General Eisenhower liberated millions from Nazi oppression and as the 34th President, he gave strength and courage to millions who recognized his smile and upraised arms as symbols of freedom.

Words are inadequate either to describe our loss or to retrace his contributions to mankind. History will have to record the full scope and significance of Eisenhower's deeds.

We can take comfort in knowing that the principles for which Ike stood have become more permanent as a result of his life and the future generations will not forget this great leader.

## Hon. Albert W. Johnson

OF PENNSYLVANIA

Mr. Speaker, I rise to pay tribute to one of the great men of American history, Dwight David Eisenhower.

How proud we citizens of Pennsylvania were when Dwight Eisenhower decided to spend his days of retirement in Pennsylvania. He chose the area of the historic Battle of Gettysburg. The American people literally plowed a furrow to his new door in our State. They not only visited his farm in large numbers, but also called on him at his office on the campus of Gettysburg College. How fitting that a great man like Dwight David Eisenhower would choose the area where Lincoln delivered his now immortal Gettysburg Address. Lincoln fought to free the body of man from slavery. Dwight Eisenhower, the hero of World War II, fought to preserve for free men that freedom won not only on the field at Gettysburg but also at Runnymede and at Belleau Wood.

I was one of those thousands who called on "Ike" at his office in Gettysburg. I was then a candidate for my first term in Congress. I had called for an appointment and was told to be there at 7:30 a.m. The General was always at his office in the early morning hours. He was most cordial and was especially nice to Mrs. Johnson. He said the only advice he could give me was to always campaign with my wife at my side. He said that Mamie was his constant companion and one of his greatest political assets.

In these last years of the life of our great President he was a tremendous force for good in this country. He had known happiness and love. He had suffered great sorrow, when he lost his 3½-year-old son through scarlet fever. He had known great anguish and uncertainty as he planned the great invasion on "D" Day. He had experienced the joy of having been elected President of the United States by the biggest majority in history up to that time. And he had the great satisfaction to know that he had a warm place in the hearts of his countrymen.

Dwight David Eisenhower has departed from this earth, but the principles for which he stood will be long remembered.

Dwight Eisenhower gave both strength and dignity to our Nation in both war and peace. He was a courageous man who deeply loved our country.

Eisenhower was the Commander of the Allied Forces in Europe during World War II, and later Supreme Commander of NATO. In both capacities he proved himself to be a great administrator and leader.

As our country longed for peace in the early 1950's Dwight Eisenhower again accepted a call to duty. He was elected the 34th President of the United States. During his two terms in office America experienced 8 years of peace, progress, and prosperity.

With a deep sense of loss we mourn his passing.

## Hon. John Kyl

OF IOWA

Mr. Speaker, in the history of this Nation there have been many individuals who have gained respect and admiration by virtue of their moving to high office. The admiration and respect sometimes goes with the important job. And there have been cases in which a good public servant has been overshadowed by the office. Dwight Eisenhower offers a different example.

In the typical mind's-eye picture, conjured by people here and abroad, Eisenhower the man stood before the uniform of Eisenhower the general. He was Eisenhower the general. He was not a general named Eisenhower. Similarly, they saw Dwight Eisenhower the President, standing before the White House. Conversely, Dwight Eisenhower considered himself to the end not a general, but a soldier; not President, but servant.

The President of the United States is always a symbol of America. And this is good, because he is the elected leader of our people. He was chosen to lead free men, by those who are served. But when the people can see in the President a man of integrity and honesty and strong moral convictions, they can identify with the man. They can take him for an example. They can draw confidence for themselves. They do not expect such a man to be infallible, yet they know that the decisions made, right or wrong, are made with the right processes, the right considerations.

Dwight Eisenhower showed us a lesson which we do well to recognize in these times. As General of the Army, as President of the United States, he demonstrated that there is but one moral code for all men at all times—for work and play, for government and those outside government, for those who serve and those who are served. No matter how spectacular are our accomplishments, or how great our affluence, we are reminded that it is the integrity of individual citizens which counts. There can be no truly worthwhile goals or movement to those goals without a deep spiritual strength. Any government which does not know this, which thinks there is a special code for itself, will perish in weakness. Dwight Eisenhower knew this truth. He lived this truth.

It is our belief that writers in some future age will echo Macaulay's prose in reference to Dwight Eisenhower:

> What a singular destiny has been that of this remarkable man! To be regarded in his own age as a classic, and in ours as a companion! To receive from his contemporaries that full homage which men of genius have in general received only from posterity; to be more intimately known to posterity than other men are known to their contemporaries!

## Hon. Joe L. Evins

OF TENNESSEE

Mr. Speaker, I want to join with other colleagues in paying tribute to Dwight David Eisenhower, a true patriot, a great hero, a natural leader of men.

As General of the Army and as President, he served with distinction and honor—but with humility and compassion. It is said that as he bade farewell to a contingent of young paratroopers boarding planes for a landing behind the Normandy beachhead in World War II, tears trickled down his cheeks as he turned away.

"I knew some of those boys would never return," he said later.

It was General Eisenhower, Supreme Commander of the Allied Forces in Europe during World War II, who welded together from allied nations a fighting force that spelled defeat for the aggressor.

His generalship of this multination force marked the first time that an American general had headed an army that included troops from many nations.

It was my good fortune as a soldier to serve in General Eisenhower's command in Europe—and later as a Congressman to serve in President Eisenhower's "command" in Washington. I served in the Congress while he was President.

I met General Eisenhower in southern France in World War II while I was a major in the U.S. Army. Again, in Washington I had occasion to meet him on several occasions during his Presidency.

Dwight D. Eisenhower—as general and as President—was always a warm, genial person. He was loved by the people, and he loved the people.

As general this great leader fought the fight for freedom in his generation and won. Later as he stood near the fields of white crosses marking the battlefields in France he said that nations of the world simply must discover a way to reconcile their differences without resorting to war and bloodshed.

He deplored the tragic waste of young men who gave their lives in the battles of World War II and in other wars.

As President he stood firm and yet he maintained the peace—he "waged" peace. His Presidency was noted for its tranquillity—the quieting of the frustrations and fears of our people. Among his domestic achievements as President was the initiation of the great interstate highway program which is continuing. This great limited access system of highways is comparable to the autobahn highway system in Europe.

Dwight David Eisenhower was a giant among

giants, a man among men. The fact that both major political parties sought him as their presidential nominee testifies and attests to his greatness as a natural leader.

We do not yet have the full historical perspective on the administration of President Dwight David Eisenhower—time will write this story.

However, we do know that his warm personality drew people to him. We do know that the American people felt comfortable and safe with Dwight Eisenhower in the White House. He will be greatly missed.

I want to extend to Mrs. Eisenhower, Col. John Eisenhower, and other members of the family this expression of our deepest and most heartfelt sympathy in their loss and bereavement.

## Hon. B. F. Sisk
OF CALIFORNIA

Mr. Speaker, there is nothing that can be said about Dwight David Eisenhower that can in any way add luster to his name. It has all been said. It has been said on the battlefields of World War II and in the councils of peace during his years as President of the United States.

And it has been said in a thousand different ways by millions of people around the world who have looked upon him as the dignified, much loved former leader of the free world living out the twilight of his life as the world's elder statesman and fighter for freedom.

It is in periods of national grief such as this that our Nation's better qualities become evident. We seem once again to be willing to acknowledge some of the eternal verities that in this age are all too often shoved aside for cynical vulgarities. And the measure of our love and affection for General Eisenhower can be measured, I believe, by the fact that no assassin's bullet was needed to elevate him or to trigger our response. He is of heroic proportions because of what he was an not because of the manner in which he died.

It was my pleasure to serve in the Congress for 6 years while Dwight Eisenhower was President of the United States. Though he was not of my party, he was my President, as he was President of all Americans. I am truly saddened at his passing and extend to Mrs. Eisenhower and all of their family my most sincere sympathy. We have all lost a great leader and true friend of peace.

## Hon. Julia Butler Hansen
OF WASHINGTON

Mr. Speaker, today with much sadness, I join the rest of my very distinguished colleagues in eulogizing our very beloved late President, Gen. Dwight David Eisenhower. Like many in this House of Representatives, I well recall the grim days of June 1944 when he led our allied forces through D-Day to victory. He became a symbol then of courage, tenacity, and a symbol of our freedom and our desire for the freedom of man in a world that had been too long held under the Fascist and Nazi heel. I know others here today remember those days while free nations of the world held their breath—and I may add these were not "simpler, easier times."

General Eisenhower later served with great distinction under President Truman as Director of SHAPE to keep the peace in Europe where it had been so painfully won. Those of us who recognize the inherent difficulties of working not only with people but with crowned heads, generals, and sovereign nations, give a special salute to General Eisenhower for his ability to deftly weave together from rather frayed threads a fabric that has become enduring. From some newspaper accounts, one might get the impression that courage, duty and honor today have become old-fashioned. I am glad that Dwight David Eisenhower never felt this way.

As a Member of the House of Representatives, I am proud to salute a courageous soldier, a calm politician, and a President of all Americans. To his wife and family, my deepest sympathy.

## Hon. Charles H. Wilson
OF CALIFORNIA

Mr. Speaker, Dwight David Eisenhower, general of the Army, President of the United States, is gone, and with him goes a small part of each of us. His career as one of this country's great leaders spanned both the tragedies of war and challenges of peace. The continuing pageant of history calls upon few men to bear the awesome responsibilities for the fortunes of both men and nations. General Eisenhower was among these few, not only as a defender of his country at war but, ultimately, of the free world at peace. His experience in battle—the violence, the destruction, above all the intimacy with the pain and suffering of death—led him not to the belligerency of a warlord but, rather, to a deep and lasting commitment to peace. For this, above all, he will be remembered.

An origin of simple but strongly principled beginnings propelled Dwight Eisenhower to the highest levels of military and civilian leadership. Often he described his boyhood home as a place of quiet tranquillity where the realities of an increasingly complex world seemed vague and distant. The values he held were not the compromising, coldly reasoned values of the intellectually cynical or the easily rationalized, unthinking values of the morally expedient. They were, instead, the basic human values which touch the heart of man's continuing effort to learn to live with his fellows in peace and security. It was his firm belief in and knowledge of what life could be and ought to be which sustained him through the infinitely complex and pressured trials that marked so much of his public career.

It can truly be said of General Eisenhower that he loved, above all, this country and his fellow man. In a world increasingly marked by cynicism and mistrust of established values, he maintained a remarkable example of principle, understanding, and warm humor. He cautioned his countrymen against indulging in self-satisfaction because of our successes during and since World War II. The demanding responsibilities of world leadership, he warned, and, especially, the maintenance of peace and freedom must summon the best that is in us.

He recognized also the serious implications of the intricate, new partnership between our vast military establishment and the modern industries which sustain it, saying that this situation was new to the American experience and warrants our attentive concern. His overriding desire for peace once led him to remark that, as a military man, he would like nothing better than to see the necessity for his own job eliminated. He viewed war not as the expedient tool of politics, but as the tragic social phenomenon of mankind.

So we bid farewell to this good and decent man who served us both as a great leader and a warm friend. May he find now the enduring peace and brotherhood which eluded his countrymen and himself for so many of his years; let us hope that the qualities he exemplified and the virtues he defended will guide our efforts to live together in peace and freedom throughout this troubled world which General Eisenhower has now departed.

## Hon. Don Fuqua
OF FLORIDA

Mr. Speaker, Dwight David Eisenhower is gone, but as long as men love freedom he will live.

He began as a soldier of war and completed his life as a crusader for peace. Perhaps only a man who has seen the terror and destruction which General Eisenhower saw could fully understand the ravages of war.

There is much to be said about the man that he requested to be interred in the simple metal coffin provided for a soldier. Perhaps this act of humility and devotion speaks much of the man.

He wore the five stars which only nine other men in the history of our Nation, which includes Pershing of World War I, have been entitled to wear. Who can know the agony he suffered as the final decision had to be made to invade Europe. He knew that thousands of lives rested in his hands.

One statement by a friend said that General Eisenhower was always the calmest when the tempest was at its height.

He served as the President of the United States. Twice the American people bestowed upon him the highest trust in the land. He served in a critical period of American history.

He followed the administrations of Roosevelt and Truman when this Nation was engaged in the greatest struggle for survival in the history of the world. At home, the Nation had undergone a peaceful revolution during the 20 years of these administrations.

Eisenhower brought a calm to the Nation. It was a period of reflection as we consolidated the programs of a hectic period. There was no looking back, only looking forward. I will have to leave to history to judge his Presidency. My feeling is that he was a man of the times—that he gave to the American people a sense of stability after such a hectic period in our history.

It has been 8 years since he has held any office, yet the heart of America went out to the general at his passing. There have been few men in the history of our Nation where the American people gave the affection they felt for Ike.

He was laid to rest in his "Eisenhower jacket" with his campaign hat at his side. He fought the good fight. His had been a rich and full life. While a Nation mourned his passing, there was also a sense of fulfillment and a deep note of gratitude.

As President Nixon intoned so eloquently, it was not so much the honors that came in such abundance that endeared him to the American people, it was his character.

Whatever historians may say in the future about the life and work of Dwight David Eisenhower, there is one thing for certain today. We liked Ike.

And his final words to Mrs. Eisenhower speak so much of the man.

"I have always loved my country."

His country will always love him.

## Hon. Ancher Nelsen

OF MINNESOTA

Mr. Speaker, the Nation this week mourns the death of a great American patriot, Dwight David Eisenhower. I would like to reminisce a bit about this warm and sunny personality, who made so many contributions to our country.

I came to know President Eisenhower rather well during the period I served as Administrator of the REA. He was always most gracious, very kind, and easy to talk to. He was pretty much the kind of a guy that people naturally like. He was surrounded by capable people and relied on them for the background and facts he needed to arrive at decisions. He seemed to decide questions easily.

My most delightful meeting with Ike occurred after I had decided to leave the REA and return to our farm near Hutchinson. It was necessary to visit the White House to submit a formal resignation, so I took along our daughter, Miriam, who was 10 or 11 at the time. The President could not have been nicer to our little girl. He was attentive to her conversation, jovial and fun to be with. He dug into one of his desk drawers, rummaged around for a little paperweight and presented it to her. He also gave her a silver dollar, minted in the year of his birth, and framed so that she could wear it as a locket.

I had brought along a camera, and asked the President if it would be all right to take a picture. He said, "Oh, yes, go right ahead." The photos we took that pleasant day are among the prized possessions in the Nelsen family scrapbook.

The incident tends to illustrate what were among the President's finest qualities—his genuine goodness and humility. These are among the qualities that define the very great among leaders in history.

I recall another incident that is somewhat revealing about Mr. Eisenhower. We had been having great difficulty settling an electric power controversy that had arisen between the Interior Department and some REA interests. Things had reached an impossible point. Finally, I suggested that the southern unit send up some new faces to Washington for discussions, feeling that the disposition of those arguing so stubbornly would never permit any kind of agreement. The new people came, and we went to the White House for some meetings with advisers. In short order, these lifetime Democrats from the Deep South—who held some pretty stout convictions about Republicans in general—were ushered right into the President's office. They seemed flabbergasted. When they found this Republican President to be reasonable and just, of course, the problem was quickly worked out amicably.

This story illustrates another of Eisenhower's great strengths. He was not a mean political partisan and he would not, for the sake of politics, do something cheap or wrong. His first and overwhelming concern was always for his country.

Few Americans in history can match Ike's many and varied accomplishments. He was a popular President, and his two terms were stable years of quiet peace and harmony. He was an outstanding wartime general. As Supreme Commander of the Allied Forces in Europe, he launched the biggest invasion in history and played a leading role in Hitler's defeat. He was an educator of note, serving for a time as president of a leading university. He was also a farmer and took a keen interest in his Gettysburg land and stock. He will be remembered for all such reasons. But he will be remembered, too, for his friendly ways, his infectious grin and his splendid spirit. These attributes of character will remain among Ike's greatest legacies to all of us.

I include at this point a further tribute to the late President, an editorial which appeared March 29 in the Mankato Free Press, Mankato, Minn.:

AMERICANS LIKED IKE

It can be said with considerable justice that Dwight Eisenhower was the most universally loved of all American presidents.

Lincoln and Franklin Roosevelt, perhaps, were revered in a more emotional way by their adherents—and, most certainly, were "greater" presidents—but they were also heartily despised by fairly substantial numbers. John Kennedy was achieving something of a love affair with Americans, particularly the young and the intellectuals, but the affair never really had to stand the test of election and time.

Ike was unique in generating the affection of all classes and parties. There was no shading. Americans just "liked Ike." And so did so many others, all over the world.

Eisenhower will not, in history's view, appear as a great man. He wasn't spectacular or political or responsible for great change.

He did his job.

He won World War II as Supreme Commander and he held the Alliance that fought that war together. He won election to the presidency on a plea for a "return to normalcy" and the ending of the Korean war and he accomplished both his objectives. He felt it was not a time for a political administration and he was, perhaps, the most unpolitical of our presidents.

It might be because of this, or because he embodied almost all the old, honorable American virtues, that the people followed him and respected him so very much. In an age of fetish for charisma in leadership, he was calm and really quite colorless.

Maybe this is why the people trusted him and believed in him.

They heeded his advice with consideration and it is, indeed, a mark of the man that his last official statement to his nation, his farewell warning about the dangers of a military-industrial complex, is becoming, nine years later, the catchword of an increasing national debate. The old soldier's syntax was involved but his thinking was clear and direct.

He is gone now, almost the last of the great figures of the 20 years that saw such a great upheaval of war and reconstruction. Only Charles de Gaulle and Chiang Kai-shek remain of those who fought and led in the war and only Harry Truman, who had so much to do with the peace and the rebuilding, are left.

However history records his immense career, most people will mourn his passing not as a great figure but as a friend in high places and this may, indeed, be the finest epitaph of all.

## Hon. Spark M. Matsunaga

OF HAWAII

Mr. Speaker, we mourn the passing of a great and beloved American, a victorious general and a President who strove for peace. We honor Dwight David Eisenhower for a lifetime of devotion to the ideals of "duty, honor, and country."

President Eisenhower, a son of America's heartland, touched the hearts of the people of the world with the American vision of tolerance, freedom, and compassion.

His memory will be honored as much for his character as for his deeds. The qualities which made him a great man were those that have made America a great Nation: Courage, integrity, vision, compassion, and loyalty.

He was a President above partisan politics; a general whose main concern was peace; a man at once kind, gentle, and stern in his pursuit of the right. He was calm, judicious, determined, hopeful, idealistic. Americans trusted and loved him, not because he was a great man, but because he was a good man. Thoroughly American, he elicited pride in America.

He enjoyed more widespread popular support than any public figure in modern American history.

His simple nobility never left him. His humor and humility were constant. First and foremost he was a down-to-earth American who treated everyone alike, whatever their station in life. This unique humility graced his enduring warmth and friendliness. It was as if everyone of us were a member of his closest family for whom he had a fatherly concern.

We will cherish his memory for as long as the qualities he possessed are valued by men of goodwill.

We citizens of Hawaii have even more reason to honor his memory, for it was President Dwight D. Eisenhower who signed into law that bill which made Hawaii the 50th State of this great Union.

To his grieving widow, our former First Lady, Mrs. Eisenhower and to members of his family, I extend deepest sympathy and heartfelt condolences for the people of Hawaii and for myself personally.

## Hon. Alexander Pirnie
OF NEW YORK

Mr. Speaker, the passing of Dwight David Eisenhower prompts people the world over to contemplate the outstanding career of a distinguished American, affectionately known as "Ike."

This great leader whose death we mourn today was in life the personification of all that is so dearly cherished by free people everywhere. As a soldier, he was a brilliant military strategist and inspirational leader during a period of great crisis. As a statesman, he was a cohesive influence at a time when certain forces were placing in jeopardy the democratic institutions we prize. As a general and then as our President, he earned our respect, confidence, and even love but it will be as a true patriot that he will be long remembered.

The personal struggle for survival against illness so valiantly waged by General Eisenhower was characteristic of his conduct through life. He was not one to back away from a challenge or to lose heart when the going got rough. It was this spirit that sustained him and permitted him to cling to life despite great physical attacks, attacks which would have long ago claimed men of less determination.

It was John Donne who said "any man's death diminishes me because I am involved in mankind." Today, I have that feeling. As one who proudly served in the Army under General Eisenhower in time of war and as one who was privileged to serve in the Congress during the final years of the Eisenhower Presidency, I prize the honor of having been personally so identified with this soldier, statesman, and patriot.

It is difficult to realize that Dwight David Eisenhower is no more. The loss is not ours alone, it is that of all mankind.

## Hon. Peter N. Kyros
OF MAINE

Mr. Speaker, I join my colleagues today in paying tribute to a great American, Dwight David Eisenhower.

A statesman among generals, Dwight Eisenhower's military leadership during World War II brought him the profound gratitude and respect not only of Americans, but of citizens throughout the world. This ability to lead men of diverse nationality and varying viewpoints came naturally to General Eisenhower, as a result of his character and dedication. No graduate of the U.S. Military Academy at West Point has ever better exemplified the creed with which Academy graduates are instilled: duty, honor, and country.

Dwight Eisenhower later sought and attained our Nation's highest leadership not as a war hero, although this he was, but as a man dedicated to true world peace. His ultimate quest was for that day, as envisioned by Tennyson, when "The war drum throbbed no longer, and the battle flags were furled." As our Nation yet continues to search for realistic relationships with allies and adversaries alike, it may be that history will regard as General Eisenhower's greatest accomplishment those steps which he took in furtherance of peace.

General Eisenhower inspired us, not only because of what he did, but because of his personal beliefs. He loved our country by loving its people. He sought to bring out in us those qualities which are most noble, and those ideals which he himself held dearest. In doing so, he summoned forth a unique affection among us.

Few Americans have served their country as long or as well as did Dwight David Eisenhower. We shall miss Ike.

## Hon. Jeffery Cohelan
OF CALIFORNIA

Mr. Speaker, as I ponder the life and passing of Dwight David Eisenhower, I am drawn to our great seal of the Presidency and the American eagle with its claws clenched on the sharpened arrows and a fragile olive branch.

It reminds me as I am sure it has served to remind the men who have held that office of the conflict of power and peace.

Dwight David Eisenhower dealt with power and peace as few other men ever have. He was first a military man whose career was culminated on the 6th day of June in 1944 when he led with daring and skill the most devastating army in the history of mankind. Our Nation had given the arrows of the eagle to Dwight Eisenhower. Use them, we said, so that we may have peace, and he did.

Can the fist that once clenched the arrows ever hold the delicate flower of peace without crushing it? I suspect not often.

Yet the United States found in Dwight Eisenhower a man who in war had learned to cherish peace and the 8 years of his Presidency and the remaining years of his life found him an untiring missionary for that cause.

The enormity of having held both the arrows and the olive branch of the American eagle in his lifetime left its mark on Dwight Eisenhower. So a devoted man of peace, he safeguarded his country with the most powerful military force in the world. A devoted soldier, still he warned his country of the great dangers he recognized in that force.

In fact, his warning against the power of the military-industrial complex is more timely at his passing that it was even at its uttering.

Dwight Eisenhower struck the balance of the American eagle and his passing must sorrow us all.

## Hon. Florence P. Dwyer

OF NEW JERSEY

Mr. Speaker, the significance of a man's life often emerges in clearer and more compelling perspective in the aftermath of his death, in the effect which that life and death are seen to have had in the lives of others.

The distinguished editor of the New York Times, Mr. James Reston, has captured one aspect of this truth about the life of our beloved former President, Dwight D. Eisenhower, in his column in this morning's New York Times.

Because it says so much and in so few words both about General Eisenhower and about our country, I want to bring it to the attention of our colleagues by including Mr. Reston's column as a part of my remarks in the Record.

The column follows:

[From the New York Times, April 2, 1969]

"Faith of Our Fathers, Living Still"?

(By James Reston)

It is hard to believe after the reverent public response to the Eisenhower funeral services that America is quite as indifferent to religion as the modern prophets and publicists say.

You can hardly pick up a paper these days without being told by somebody that God is dead. In fact, the Pentagon is now wondering whether it should banish Him from its instructions to the troops in Vietnam, which is scarcely surprising, considering the Pentagon's expansionist tendencies in all other fields.

Still the substitute gods of the modern age don't seem to be very satisfactory. The trend toward a secular society in America is clear, but when television demonstrates on a great occasion that it has the capacity to bring the whole nation into a common experience—almost to make us all part of a single congregation—then we find that at least the remnants of a common faith still exist.

FAITH AND DOUBT

The choir at the National Cathedral in Washington sang the old hymn. The opening line is: "Faith of our Fathers, living still," and despite all the modern denials of the point, it is probably still true. The first line of the chorus, however, is different: "Faith of our Fathers, Holy Faith, we will be true to thee till death"—and that is clearly not true for most Americans.

Nevertheless, for believers and unbelievers alike, some facts are plain. The political life and spirit of this country were based on religious convictions. America's view of the individual was grounded on the principle, clearly expressed by the Founding Fathers, that man was a symbol of his Creator, and therefore possessed certain inalienable rights which no temporal authority had the right to violate.

THE RELIGIOUS FOUNDATION

That this conviction helped shape our laws and sustained American men and women in their struggle to discipline themselves and conquer a continent even the most atheistic historian would defend. And this raises a question which cannot be avoided: If religion was so important in the building of the Republic, how could it be irrelevant to the maintenance of the Republic? And if it is irrelevant for the unbelievers, what will they put in its place?

"The liberties we talk about defending today," Walter Lippman wrote in 1938, "were established by men who took their conception of man from the great central religious tradition of Western civilization, and the liberties we inherit can almost certainly not survive the abandonment of that tradition. . . .

"The decay of decency in the modern age, the rebellion against law and good faith, the treatment of human beings as things, as mere instruments of power and ambition, is without a doubt the consequence of the decay of the belief in man as something more than an animal animated by highly conditioned reflexes and chemical reactions. For unless man is something more than that, he has no rights that anyone is bound to respect, and there are no limitations upon his conduct which he is bound to obey. This is the forgotten foundation of democracy. . . ."

THE COMMON FAITH

What the Eisenhower services suggested, maybe ever so vaguely to some and ever so strongly to others, is that the religious foundation of our common life—no matter how much we divide over creeds and sects and their relation to the state—is not "forgotten." It may be ignored or challenged or defied, but it is not lost. We may not believe, but we believe in believing, and the reaction to the old soldier's death dramatized the point.

It did something else. It demonstrated how national television can bring before the people the things that touch their noblest instincts, and in the process reminded us of how seldom we use their remarkable power for this purpose.

THE UNIFYING FORCES

Eisenhower and the church and television were unifying forces of tremendous power for good in America in the last few tragic days. They touched some old and worthy echo in the American spirit which politics, religion, and television usually repel.

These are very old questions but they are still with us. Plato saw man's problem as that of the charioteer driving a pair of winged horses: "One of them is noble and of noble breed and the other is ignoble and of ignoble breed" . . . and "the driving of them of necessity gives a great deal of trouble to the charioteer."

This is as true now as it was in Plato's time, but the old soldier gave us a glimpse of nobility, and through this remarkable instrument of television, the people responded to it with a solemnity and sincerity no cynic could deny.

## Hon. Lawrence J. Hogan

OF MARYLAND

Mr. Speaker, there is little I can add to the sincere outpourings of affection and esteem from my colleagues regarding Dwight David Eisenhower, but I would like to express my belief that he is uniquely suitable as an idol for our young people.

As President, he unified the Nation. Perhaps the solidarity of those Eisenhower years was due in large measure to the fact that he himself was the synthesis of America, the epitome of what our Nation can produce.

He possessed the qualities we all should nurture: courage, integrity, decency, humility, compassion, sincerity, selflessness, warmth, and patriotism. These qualities permeated his public and private life.

He was a farmer, an athlete, an artist, a soldier, a diplomat, an educator, a politician, a statesman, and a world leader. What an ideal here to emulate.

He loved peace, but he fought valiantly in war. His brilliant leadership as Commander of the Allied Forces in Europe during World War II contributed tremendously toward our success in that conflict. He ended the war in Korea, a war rivaling Vietnam in unpopularity.

He had a toughness of character, but it was tempered with a human gentleness. He was a strong competitor in sports, but he enjoyed the quiet solitiude before a canvas.

He was dedicated to civil rights, but he was equally committed to law and order. Under his leadership, the first civil rights legislation since the Civil War was enacted, and he used the full power of his office to quell the violence of those who opposed the exercise of civil rights.

President Nixon has said that two qualities about Dwight Eisenhower "stood out above all in both his public and his private life: one was his unwavering sense of duty; the other was that whatever he did, he did because he believed it was right."

When his country needed him in military service, he answered and served with distinction, rising to our highest military rank. When his country needed him in civilian service, he again answered the call and served in our highest civilian office, the Presidency.

Dwight D. Eisenhower was not a politician in the stereotype sense of that term. He was a citizen who involved himself in politics because he felt his country needed him in politics. He agreed to run for President on the Republican Party's ticket because he saw that party in such a weakened condition that he feared that the two-party system was in jeopardy. He involved himself in politics because he considered it essential to achieve a competitive balance between the two parties. He believed that, if the greatest form of government ever conceived in the history of the world is to be preserved, we must have two strong political parties to give the voters a meaningful choice at election time and to create a competition which will force both parties to be responsive to the needs and wishes of the people.

We mourn General Eisenhower's passing, but we pray that his spirit, his zest for life, his love of country will endure with us. We will honor his memory best by keeping these qualities alive and bequeath them to oncoming generations. These future generations should know the debt which we of this generation owe to him. They should know what a giant has lived among us.

There are no superlatives which any of us can utter which can add to the stature or deeds of Dwight David Eisenhower. We will miss him, but I hope and pray that we will continue to draw inspiration and guidance from the magnificent example of his life.

## Hon. Fred Schwengel
OF IOWA

Mr. Speaker, the death of President Dwight Eisenhower leaves all Americans with a deep sense of grief and sorrow. He was a great leader, both in war and in peace. We shall miss him very much. General Eisenhower's basic philosophy and outlook on life was dramatically revealed to me one day when I had the privilege of attending a luncheon at the White House. During the luncheon, the general mentioned the fact that he had just purchased a farm near Gettysburg, Pa. My immediate comment was that for good farmland he should have gone to Iowa. The general responded by saying that it was his belief that every person should acquire something during his lifetime and leave that something in just a little better condition than he found it. He went on to explain that he could do this more easily on a farm at Gettysburg than he could on the rich farmlands of Iowa. This was a wonderful tribute to Iowa, but even more important it pointed up a basic attribute which made this man one of our greatest leaders. And, indeed, he has not only left the farm at Gettysburg in better condition than he found it but also this Nation of ours and the world. In the 1940's he came to leadership in a world torn by war. He led us through wars to victory, and peace.

Again in the fifties he was successful in restoring peace, this time in Korea. His quiet and effective leadership provided the tranquillity which we so badly needed in the 1950's to complete the transition from war to peace. In the 1960's he continued his service to the Nation in the role of elder statesman. Here, too, it could be said that by his counsel to Presidents Kennedy, Johnson, and Nixon, he left our Nation in a better condition than that in which he found it. If all mankind were to subscribe to and follow this philosophy of General Eisenhower, what a far better world we would know and enjoy. About another great American, Edwin Markham once wrote, "Here is a man to hold against the world, to match the mountains and the sea"—this was a fitting tribute to Lincoln and it is also a fitting tribute for General Eisenhower.

Mr. Speaker, as might be expected several of the newspapers in eastern Iowa editorialized on the greatness of President Eisenhower. They expressed the high regard held for him by Iowans.

In addition, several of the newsmen recalled their own experiences with General Eisenhower. Somehow these recollections tell more about the the greatness of the man and unique place he will always have in the hearts of all Americans.

Some articles follow:

[From the Cedar Rapids (Iowa) Gazette, Mar. 31, 1969]

### They'll Always Like "Ike"

This nation isn't in as bad shape spiritually as it sometimes seems, when the long-anticipated death of a former President brings tears to the eyes of millions of Americans young and old. And we suspect that there were few wholly dry eyes throughout the country Friday when the word came from Washington that Ike's long and gallant fight against repeated strains on a weakened heart had ended.

It is significant that to most of those millions Dwight D. Eisenhower was simply Ike, not President Eisenhower or Mr. Eisenhower or even General Eisenhower, the designation he reportedly cherished most. By no means all of his contemporaries rated him as a great President or a great general or a great anything else—although historians may some day agree that he merited such distinction.

The key word for Ike was "good." He came across to people as a good man, in a wide variety of ways. Millions of individuals of all types, in all walks of life—even though they never came in close contact with him—had an instinctive rapport with him and felt that they understood him, and that if they could have been close to him he would have understood them and they would have been at ease together.

It is not exactly that they looked upon him as a hero in a bewildering age when people desperately need and yearn for heroes and find few. Rather it was that many Americans saw in him the personification of what they think a good American should be—not necessarily a faultless paragon but a kindly person, well intentioned, and trying hard to measure up to life's demands on the abilities God gave him. He made us all feel that we shared something with him.

Among all our public figures, no other projects that same sustaining image. And it is a time when we could use one.

---

[From the Burlington (Iowa) Hawkeye, Mar. 30, 1969]

### Memo From Mac

(By John McCormally)

Remembering President Eisenhower, Burlington Republican leader Jim Schramm recalled Ike's triumphal return to Washington after VE day,

"We all turned out to watch him drive down (it was actually up) Pennsylvania Avenue with his arms high over his head and grinning," Schramm, who was an Army lieutenant colonel stationed in Washington, recalled. "It was one of the most moving sights of my life."

I didn't know Jim Schramm then. Or Eisenhower either, for that matter. But I recalled with a start, when I read Schramm's recollection in Friday's Hawk-Eye, that, by golly, I was in that parade.

For all I know, I was one of the "heroes" he cheered as we paraded up the historic avenue in honor of Ike.

It was one of those crazy episodes which can only happen in war. I'd been preoccupied with the other end of that war and was only a casual reader of Ike's exploits in Europe.

But in the Spring of 1945, I'd worked my way back through a succession of hospital ships, planes, quonsets and wards from the Pacific, and across the continent, until finally I was a patient at Bethesda Naval Medical Center outside Washington.

When Ike returned for his hero's parade and appearance before Congress, someone decided it would add color to the festivities to include a platoon or two of patients from Bethesda and Walter Reed in the parade.

And, in the normal military way of things, I was notified that I had volunteered to be part of the sorry sample of the nation's sacrifice. (Presumably, we were chosen on the basis of looking beat up enough to stir patriotic emotions, but not bad enough to make anyone sick.)

It was an absolutely gorgeous morning: the brilliant sun bouncing off the well-scrubbed avenue and off the marble walls of the Federal Triangle; the flags whipping, the bands blaring, the troops clumping in splendid cadence.

We rode along, in our gray Navy bus, acknowledging the waves and cheers of the multitude with mock modesty, all the while cracking cynical jokes among ourselves about what the hell we, a bunch of Pacific Island dropouts, were doing in the celebration for the head dogface.

On the east steps of the Capitol, a platform had been erected, on which we were arrayed in our assortment of wheel chairs, crutches, slings and bandages.

When Ike arrived and got out of his car to go into the Capitol, he spied us. With a spectacular grin and a special grimace of recognition, he broke away from his escorts, mounted our platform and shook hands all around.

I remember that the high brass—political and military—stood fretfully waiting for him, while he chatted with several of the wounded, asking where they'd got it and how they were doing.

When he'd left, the mood of these wounded enlisted men had strangely changed.

"You know," someone said, and the others agreed, "he isn't a bad fellow. For a general."

And that, I suppose, is the kind of epitaph he'd like the best.

---

[From the Davenport-Bettendorf (Iowa) Times-Democrat, Mar. 30, 1969]

### Leader in War, Peace

Dwight David Eisenhower, dead at 78, led the nation with distinction in war and peace. And few if any Americans have won comparable love and respect in public life in our times.

The five-star general directed the World War II invasion of fortress Europe, then stood in a schoolhouse at Rheims to accept Germany's unconditional surrender.

He later became the nation's 33rd President, winning election on the Republican ticket in 1952 and again in 1956.

He finally succumbed after waging a long fight symbolic of the courageous life he lived in behalf of his country. His last, poignant struggles were reminiscent of his decision to seek the second term after he suffered first a heart attack and later a bout of ileitis.

Of his eight years in the White House, his "greatest disappointment" was what he considered a lack of progress in promoting better understanding in the world, particularly between the Communists and ourselves.

While this was his assessment, even critics would concede he expended enormous amount of time and good will in pursuits of peace.

Having viewed war firsthand, he regarded it with abhorrence, but thought it could be avoided only if this nation remained powerful both militarily and economically.

Of war he said, "It is an evil whose outbreak is the result of human errors, human ignorance, human greed."

Of peace, he said, "An enduring world peace must be founded on justice, opportunity and freedom for all men of good will. It must be maintained in a climate of international understanding and cooperation."

And of his country, he said "There is nothing wrong with America that faith, love of freedom, intelligence and the energy of her citizens cannot cure."

Mr. Eisenhower showed dislike for the rough and tumble of politics, but proved a formidable campaigner. Some disliked his unpolished syntax and his reluctance to step into party quarrels or to be stampeded on some public issues, among them civil rights. But even those who voted against him found it difficult, if not impossible, to dislike Eisenhower the man. He was an excellent imaginative cook. His love for golf helped to popularize the game. His trademark was an infectious smile that often lighted his blue-eyed, ruddy face.

He became a national institution; he was cast in the classic American mold. Born to relatively poor people in a small community, he graduated from the United States Military Academy at West Point and advanced through the ranks to become one of our greatest war heroes.

Persuasion was required to pull him into political life and the presidency, and there he did the best commonsense job of which he was capable, just as he contributed a sincere effort in whatever direction he turned.

His name will be etched in our history books as conqueror, liberator, educator, humanitarian, author, diplomat and President. He clearly strove with all his heart to promote better world understanding. It would be premature to try to assess all his achievements. But history will give him high stature as a man who dominated his era and gave greatly of his energies for both war and peace.

---

[From the Davenport (Iowa) Times-Democrat, Mar. 29, 1969]

### He Could Cuss, Then Could Purr

(Editor's Note.—Philip D. Adler, of the Times-Democrat, who interviewed former President Dwight D. Eisenhower in Paris in 1951, recalls that day and other meetings with the five-star general in the accompanying article prepared after Ike died Friday).

(By Philip D. Adler)

Eisenhower's life had many facets. In June 1951, at NATO headquarters in the Hotel Astoria, Paris, I had an hour with Ike.

With me for this interview was Don W. Anderson, publisher of the Wisconsin State Journal. I discovered Ike could pound the table and cuss like a cavalryman, and next moment he could purr like a statesman.

It wasn't an illuminating interview, mostly an extension of the briefing we had received the day before from Brig. Gen. Anthony J. D. Biddle Jr., former ambassador to Poland and Ike's troubleshooter at NATO.

General Eisenhower at this point of his career was a caged lion. He had set up a counterpart of SHAEF in Paris, with open-end authority to organize a European coalition to stop the onsweep of Communism. It was a thankless job, and Ike knew it.

In the light of Korea, which had erupted only one year before, Ike and his team of generals were trying with the remnants of the 1944 invasion machine to stem the Soviet tide.

Anderson and I were well aware of the political pressures that were on Ike at that time to go for the Republican nomination for President. We put the question to him squarely, and he simply smiled and said he wasn't interested.

He had said that before we had seen him, to others with special missions, and he said it many times afterward, until friends practically kidnapped him to go to Abilene and announce.

Going back nearly 18 years in memory, I recall Ike as a restless, chain-smoking dynamo of a man. He paced the office constantly while he talked. Every time we would reach for our pads to make notes he would give us the wave-off and talk about Poland or Berlin. I got the impression of a one man NATO, because it was Ike's drive and personality alone which held NATO together.

Before 1951 I had the privilege of hearing and seeing Eisenhower on other occasions, as Columbia University president, and as a five-star general in retirement. There was no perceptible change in Ike in those years. He was aways a fighter, and he was fighting back against odds which would have floored most men.

The Eisenhower we saw in the wartime newsreels, returning to London in triumph after D–Day and later as commander-in-chief in the Washington victory reception of 1945, was a strictly one-time phenomenon. He spoke easily then, with determination and conviction. Later as a political campaigner his speech in public was far from the rolling rhetoric of Franklin D. Roosevelt or the sparkling repartee of Harry Truman.

Out of uniform and in the tweeds of a Columbia University president before an Associated Press luncheon, Ike was ill at ease and straining for words. Somehow the direct, dynamic speech of a wartime commander never came through again.

But above all, Ike revealed himself to men who met him and spent time with him as a man endowed with special magnetism, a conscientious patriot doing his duty as he saw it. This is the Eisenhower I'd like remembered, and so would millions of other Americans who mourn him today.

---

[From the Davenport (Iowa) Times-Democrat, Mar. 26, 1969]

### Ike Added Warmth to Grid Event

(Editor's Note.—Dick Lamb of Bettendorf, news reporter for the Times-Democrat, tells of his meeting with former President Dwight Eisenhower at a Football Foundation Hall of Fame dinner.)

(By Dick Lamb)

It was unseasonably warm that late October evening in New York City 10 years ago. Most who were in the Grand Ballroom of Hotel Astor remembered that it was a Tuesday.

That same day, Oct. 28, a beloved Italian named Roncalli had been elevated to a supreme position in his church.

Henceforth he would be Pope John XXIII.

For 2,000 of us, the spiritual message of that day was a warm prelude to the excitement of the evening.

President Dwight Eisenhower was to supply the emotional thrill.

Waiting, as I walked to the dais, was the man who had led Allied forces to victory in World War II and was now President of the United States.

The occasion was the annual Awards Dinner of the National Football Foundation and Hall of Fame. My assignment as historian was to present the then President Dwight Eisenhower a program of the 1913 Army-Navy football game.

The presentation was in connection with Mr. Eisenhower receiving the first Gold Medal to be awarded by the foundation to persons prominently identified with the sport.

Mr. Eisenhower glanced over the program. His face broke into a smile as he recalled some of his teammates on that year's Army squad.

He turned to Gen. Omar Bradley, also at the speaker's table and a member of the same team. "You haven't gained a pound in nearly 50 years, have you?" he quipped.

Sitting nearby was Alexander Weyand, an All-American tackle that year.

"They wouldn't recognize you now, Babe," the President said. "You sure wouldn't make All-American to day."

I listened. The infectious warmth of the President was evident. He captivated everyone with his apparent genuine friendliness.

Mr. Eisenhower and I exchanged letters during the month following the dinner. He returned the football program to me for inclusion in the permanent files of the football Hall of Fame at New Brunswick, N.J.

Although Mr. Eisenhower's military and political accomplishments were monumental, it cannot be overlooked that an interest in sports through most of his 78 years also was very significant.

Golf provided most of his relaxation and physical exercise during the last 20 years, but a far more strenuous sport consumed his energies as a youth.

At the Hall of Fame dinner, the President told his audience, "Nowhere is competition, in its very highest form, better expressed than in the uniquely American game of football.

"To understand football," he said, "is to have an insight into an essential part of life."

He stressed that "Morale—the will to win, the fighting heart—are the honored hallmarks of the football coach and player, as they are of the enterprising executive, the successful troop leader, the established artist and the dedicated teacher and scientist."

Football was hardly a refined game of precision, speed or close coordination of men and maneuvers in 1911 when 21-year-old Dwight Eisenhower entered the United States Military Academy at West Point.

He had played tackle for Abilene High School in Kansas, and distinguished himself to such an extent his coach called him "the most outstanding tackle in the valley."

At West Point he went out for the freshman team and was shifted to the backfield. Game accounts at the time accorded him "star" status.

Against Colgate as a sophomore he was unstoppable in leading Army to a 15–7 victory.

Two weeks later, however, in a game against Tufts, Cadet Eisenhower broke his kneecap, his varsity career condemned to comparative obscurity by the permanently disabling injury.

Not content to be entirely severed from the game he dearly loved, Eisenhower turned to coaching the Cullum Hall freshman team.

Although never removing himself from concern over the fortunes of football at Army, Eisenhower fostered a genuine interest in the game in general after his return from Europe following World War II.

But his concern and interest in athletics and its byproducts extended beyond the boundaries of the gridiron.

"Fitness—in its deepest and broadest sense—is necessary," he said. "We know that it is far more than a healthy body, it is more than an alert and the disciplined mind."

THE WHITE HOUSE, *Washington,*
*Augusta, Ga., November 28, 1958.*

Mr. R. M. LAMB,
*Football Information Bureau,*
*Davenport, Iowa.*

DEAR MR. LAMB: Thank you very much for remembering our conversation of the night of the National Football Hall of Fame dinner. As you suspected, I was much interested in looking over the Army-Navy program for 1913. My secretary will return the program to you with this note.

With best wishes,
Sincerely,

DWIGHT D. EISENHOWER.

This is a reproduction of a letter sent by former President Eisenhower to Dick Lamb shortly after Lamb had presented the then President an official program of the 1913 Army-Navy football game. Eisenhower had been an Army football star. The presentation was made in 1958 at a Football Hall of Fame Awards Dinner in New York. Lamb was historian of the organization. The program now is in the Hall of Fame library archives.

"Fitness is the sum of all values which enable a man to act effectively in his nation's behalf. In this environment, fitness is man's maximum development to make all of us a stronger nation.

"Your fitness, in all its dimensions, is the proper concern of every American. To his task the inspirational coach is as dedicated as the most respected professor.

"And the whole field of sports contributes mightily toward that objective."

---

[From the Iowa City Press-Citizen, Mar. 29, 1969]

DWIGHT D. EISENHOWER

During his life as a public figure—and it continued for more than a quarter-century, an unusually long time—Dwight D. Eisenhower had more than his share of critics.

He wasn't much of a general, said the generals. He wasn't much of a politician, said the politicians. He wasn't much of an intellectual, said the intellectuals. And so it went.

But the American people thought he was a great American. They not only liked Ike, they loved him. And today we all miss the man who remained Ike from the time he first came to public attention in 1942 until his heroic battle for life ended.

He was a professional soldier who rose from relative obscurity at the beginning of the greatest war in history to supreme command of the greatest army in history; who later served his country for eight years in the highest position of responsibility any man can attain.

Yet he was always "Ike."

Looking back from the turbulent present, the years of the Eisenhower Administration seem calm and stable. They were not, but if they seemed so then as well as now, it was only because of the presence of this immensely popular president in the White House. There was something about this uncommonly common man that inspired confidence and unshakable faith that no matter how beset the nation was by crises and challenges, nothing dire would happen as long as Ike was there.

Beset the nation was:

Those were the years when the cold war was frigid; when a man named Khrushchev came to power in Russia to strut the world's stage for a time with his rhetoric of nuclear diplomacy and ballistic blackmail; when a man named Ho Chi Minh was mauling the French in Indochina; when a man named Joe McCarthy was finding Communists in every State Department closet and setting neighbor suspiciously against neighbor; when a man named Faubus in Little Rock, Ark., was fomenting the gravest federal crisis since the Civil War; when a U.S. vice president was being spat upon in South America; when the world hovered on the edge of Armageddon as war broke out in the Middle East; when freedom-loving men everywhere agonized as Hungary was ground under the heel; when the nation plunged briefly into its worst recession since the 1930s; when Americans indulged in the orgy of self-doubt because Russia had launched something into space called a Sputnik; when words like "agonizing reappraisal," "brinkmanship," "U-2" "summit" and "missile gap" became part of the vocabulary of reproach against the administration.

Yet, they seemed calm years, at least in part because Ike was there and because the people trusted him, the people stayed calm.

The years of Eisenhower are still too close for historians to present a balanced and dispassionate summary. Dwight Eisenhower, as general, president and elder statesman, in time will become a historic personage, drained of his humanity, accorded his proper place—no more and no less—among the heroes of the past as determined by the consensus of historians. That's what happens to all presidents.

But today his contemporaries mourn a man called Ike who, because he was a part of our lives, always will be more than a remote figure in history.

## Hon. Laurence J. Burton

OF UTAH

Mr. Speaker, General Eisenhower is dead. His passing, of course, was not unexpected, although the old soldier had fought with death and won so many times before that it was hard to believe he would not also win what proved to be his final battle. He died at age 78, his life full of both deeds and honors. And so his death was not tragic, not in the sense that his passing came before the essential part of his life's work was finished. General Eisenhower's was, indeed, a life fulfilled. As did Paul, he fought a good fight, finished the course, and kept the faith. Surely the supplication of Reverend Sayre, "remember Thy servant Dwight David, O Lord," will be heeded on high.

But the death of a man of the stature of Dwight David Eisenhower cannot occur without an accompanying sadness, whether he has completed his work or not. And truly we are sad, not only here in America, but throughout the world. He is gone, and we shall greatly miss him. His place cannot be taken by another. The famous Eisenhower grin, his strength of character, the easy charm, the essential goodness of the man are now but memories. But they are good memories and will, I am sure, cause the spirits of men everywhere to be uplifted for generations to come.

My generation remembers him as the peacemaker, a man trained for war who brought and maintained the peace. He led the most powerful military force in history to victory over a strong and evil aggressor enemy. It is doubtful that any man will ever again lead such a great army. General Eisenhower was already a hero, although the war was not yet over, when I became old enough to enlist in the Armed Forces in January 1945. I did not happen to serve under his command, but I have always been proud of the fact that I wore the uniform at the same time General Eisenhower did. All veterans of World War II, I am sure, share that same feeling of pride.

Having led our forces to victory in battle, General Eisenhower then fought to preserve the peace. After the war, he served as Army Chief of Staff, then later returned to Europe as Supreme Commander of the North Atlantic Treaty Organization. As President he again served in the role of peacemaker, bringing an end to the hostilities in Korea. And during his 8 years in the White House, Dwight Eisenhower, the man of war, took the necessary steps that preserved the peace.

My generation, of course, participated in the

Eisenhower years. We fought in battle with him, served under him during his terms as President, revered him as elder statesman. He was such a part of our lives and time--the hopeful, essentially happy, good period of years to which he contributed so much—that my generation cannot forget him.

My children and their friends of a younger generation have a less sure remembrance of him. Laurence Shupe, my youngest child, who was born in the last few months of the Eisenhower administration, is too young yet to understand fully why so much has been made of the Eisenhower passing. He will, of course, come to understand better as he grows older.

But to him and to those of his time I would say that what General Eisenhower did, important as it was, is not as important as what he was. And he was, in my judgment, one of the most genuine, honest, and deeply concerned men who ever served in public life. There was nothing hypocritical about Eisenhower, no phoniness, no posturing. He was as incapable of hiding behind an unreal facade as the Kansas countryside from which he came is incapable of hiding behind a mountain. Where some politicians are suspected of being devious, General Eisenhower was never suspect. Where some have been accused of being less than truthful, nobody ever seriously questioned "Ike's" honesty. When Dwight Eisenhower told you something, you could believe it. He was the diplomat, the conciliator, the leader who brought diverse personalities together and effected a working union. And, though mild in demeanor, he could be tough. It was Eisenhower who first moved in the direction of civil rights; it was Eisenhower who sent troops into Little Rock. When the situation became explosive in the Middle East, President Eisenhower didn't hesitate to send American troops there to restore order and prevent a Communist takeover. The deeds are many, and there is no need to recount them here. History will certainly note them.

I cannot say what place historians will assign General Eisenhower as a President, but I suspect that it will be high. There has been much speculation in this regard in recent days. I like what Newsweek Columnist Kenneth Crawford said the other day:

> He was the right President for a particular time.

Perhaps that is as fitting a judgment as any, at least until time allows for a better perspective.

Ike was the archetypical American hero, the poor boy who learned correct principles at home, practiced them in life and went on to accomplish deeds and win honors beyond the wildest of dreams. It is unlikely that my son will lead armies or be President. But though he may not emulate Dwight Eisenhower in deeds or vocation, I would hope that he would take him as an example, a model of the kind of man he wants to be. He could make no better choice.

## Hon. Page Belcher

OF OKLAHOMA

Mr. Speaker, mere words are always inadequate to express the deep feelings that flood over one in the loss of so great a man and so noble a leader as we have lost in the passing of Dwight David Eisenhower. And my words are more than inadequate to add anything to the stirring tribute delivered by President Nixon in his eulogy in the rotunda on Sunday.

The world has lost its most beloved and respected citizen. It is symbolic of the stature he attained that the world mourns the loss of this son of America's heartland and mourns him as deeply and sincerely as any in his native land.

Near the end of his eulogy, President Nixon expressed what to me is the most significant thing about the life of this late, great American hero. Each of us has been diminished by his passing, but as the President pointed out:

> Each of us here will have a special memory of Dwight Eisenhower.

That is true. And it is powerful.

It is true because no man who ever met him or saw him or heard him speak could forget him. Could anyone forget that smile, so full of kindliness and good humor? Could anyone forget his voice, so firm, resolute and assured, yet so rich in goodness and sincerity. There was strength in his manhood—boundless energy and enthusiasm—and such gentleness in his eyes and in his manner.

It is true and it is powerful. Powerful because it is a memory etched in the mind forever of a man who personified as no other of our era has all the noble qualities of America. Dwight Eisenhower was a man of great accomplishments who never lost his deep sense of humility. He was a man of great power whose first concern, whether as general or President, was always for the good of those he led. He was a target for thoughtless criticism who never learned to hate. He was schooled in the military, yet constantly devoted to the cause of peace and one of our most effective peacemakers. He was subjected to the greatest pressures, yet he never deserted the principles and ideals instilled in him as a youth by a devout mother, a firm but kindly father, and a community imbued with love of country. He is the kind of man every parent hopes his child will grow to be, and the challenge to emulate his example will be a powerful influence for good wherever it is taken up.

Yes, each of us will have a special memory of Dwight Eisenhower. My special memory is of playing golf with him at Burning Tree when he was President. He was a strong competitor, a great sport, a man it was tremendous fun to be with.

He was the most interesting man I have ever known; warm, friendly, and good-humored, with a deep compassion for all mankind; an American through and through. A great general, a great statesman, a great President. Yes. But more than that, he was a "great guy." That is my memory of Dwight Eisenhower. And in his passing I have lost a sincere friend. But my life has been specially blessed by having known him, and for as long as I live nothing can diminish that privilege, that honor, that great reward.

To his gallant and gracious widow, to his wonderful family, I extend my deepest sympathy and pray the blessing of God's peace upon them.

## Hon. Charlotte T. Reid

OF ILLINOIS

Mr. Speaker, during the 28 years the Honorable Frances P. Bolton served as a Member of the Congress from the 22d Congressional District of Ohio, she was privileged to work with the administration of five Presidents of the United States. One of our Presidents with whom she worked most closely for 8 years was Dwight D. Eisenhower. Her friendship and admiration for General Eisenhower dated back many years. In 1951 Mrs. Bolton was one of a small group of prominent persons who visited General Eisenhower when he was Supreme Allied Commander in Europe to urge him to become a Republican candidate for President.

Mrs. Bolton was appointed by President Eisenhower as the first woman Member of Congress to serve as a Representative of the United States of America to the Eighth General Assembly of the United Nations. Upon learning of President Eisenhower's death, Mrs. Bolton issued the following statement:

> To the many who have been privileged to work with him General Eisenhower's death is a grievous thing. Even in the last many months which he had to spend at Walter Reed Hospital, there was a courage emanating from him that gave each of us a steadiness and a strength that carried us over many stony places. For this we are deeply, deeply grateful—for we shall miss him more than words can possibly express.
>
> To him this country was indeed "one nation under God" and he served her selflessly and well. What light there was in his eyes! What strength and calm tenderness in his voice—what force when force was needed!
>
> One cannot grieve now that he has gone on to broader living, for has he not given us a rare legacy of patriotism? Surely it has been a wonderful experience to have known him—to have worked for and with him—to have watched his clear, open, honest ways. It will be many moons before another such as he comes into our midst.
>
> May Heaven grant his devoted wife and family a deep and abiding comfort and peace.

## Hon. Frank J. Brasco

OF NEW YORK

Mr. Speaker, citizens of the world mourn the loss of Dwight David Eisenhower, a dedicated leader who was beloved to friend and foe alike.

On the battlefront, in the White House, or in Gettysburg, Pa., this fine American inspired confidence and understanding in all with whom he associated. General Eisenhower was particularly devoted to the cause of better understanding among Americans, and among peoples of the world. I think it entirely fitting and proper that, in his memory, each of us strive a little harder toward achieving this marvelous attribute.

His passing leaves a great void on the American scene, and the memories of his brilliant service shall long remain.

## Hon. William T. Murphy
OF ILLINOIS

Mr. Speaker, I join my colleagues in paying final respects to a great American, former President, and general of the Army, Dwight David Eisenhower.

Not only was Dwight Eisenhower the embodiment of the ancient and honorable ideal of the soldier-statesman but he was a man blessed with an abundance of personal warmth and compassion. A devoted family man, a man of religion, and a stanch patriot, he was most of all a man possessed of deep feelings for this fellow beings.

I feel greatly honored to have had the privilege of serving in the Congress during the last years of the Presidency of Dwight David Eisenhower. He served his Nation and the cause of freedom well.

I join in expressing my deepest sympathy to Mrs. Eisenhower and the family.

## Hon. Richard L. Ottinger
OF NEW YORK

Mr. Speaker, I join with our colleagues, our fellow Americans, and men of good will throughout the world in mourning the death of a great patriot, soldier, and statesman, General of the Army Dwight D. Eisenhower.

General Eisenhower has now returned to the fertile plains of the Midwest of which he was so proud and which he loved. However, he will never be forgotten by the men and women of the world who loved him. He has left a rich legacy in which we can all take solace and encouragement. While his cheerfulness, energy, and great spirit will be deeply missed by us all, we will always remember his many contributions to his country and to the free world.

I am proud to join in paying tribute to General Eisenhower. His life, his moral courage, and his fine personal qualities serve as his best eulogy.

I wish to extend to Mrs. Eisenhower and her family my deep personal regrets and sorrow over their loss. We are all most grateful to them for having shared Ike with us.

## Hon. Leonard Farbstein
OF NEW YORK

Mr. Speaker, our Nation and the world have lost a man of unique qualities in the passing of Dwight David Eisenhower. For he was that rare military captain who genuinely renounced the very calling which put him among the historic great.

General Eisenhower first became known to the American people as Supreme Allied Commander in the European theater in World War II. What he did in those years made him a hero to all Americans and a liberator to many of the nations of the world.

He was a career soldier of a unique mold, for he embodied the best qualities of the American military even as those qualities went beyond the narrow confines of the military profession itself. In the words of the motto of the West Point Military Academy, he followed the principle of "Duty, Honor, Country." General Eisenhower carried this principle into the Presidency with him. Although a military man by background, he believed—and he made it very clear in his actions and statements as President—that the Armed Forces, just as the executive and legislative branches of the Government, are servants of the people and that their activities must stay within the confines of public policy, even if policy later turns out to be wrong. This is their duty to their country and it is what distinguishes a nation directed by its people from a people directed by their state.

As President of the United States, General Eisenhower translated this principle into action. He was the American President who negotiated an end to a war without insisting on capitulation. He made the first approaches toward a reduction of tension between the U.S. and the U.S.S.R. through his atoms-for-peace proposal. He created the first program for economic aid to Latin America. But most symbolic of his personal philosophy were the actions he did not take—the wholesome restraint he exercised on our use of power on major foreign policy decisions. In reacting to the French defeat in Indochina, he stood firm against involvement in the face of strong counsel by many of his top advisers to intervene militarily. And he refused to deploy an anti-ballistic-missile system which was so vehemently urged upon him by his former colleagues in the military.

General Eisenhower revealed his unique quality as a military hero able to step back from his background in his farewell address to the American public, warning that—

While a vital element in keeping the peace is our military establishment, we must recognize the immense influence that it has in every city, every State House, and in every office of the Federal government. We recognize the imperative need for development. Yet we must not fail to comprehend its grave implications. Our toil, resources and livelihood are all involved; so is the very structure of our society.

In the councils of government, we must guard against the acquisition of unwarranted influence, whether sought or unsought, by the military-industrial complex. The potential for the disastrous rise of misplaced power exists and will persist.

We must never let the weight of this combination endanger our liberties or democratic processes. We should take nothing for granted. Only an alert and knowledgeable citizenry can compel the proper meshing of the huge industrial and military machinery of defense with our peaceful methods and goals, so that security and liberty may prosper together.

General Eisenhower expressed so eloquently the principle that guided him as soldier, President, and private citizen in that farewell speech as well:

Crises there will continue to be. In meeting them, whether foreign or domestic, great or small, there is a recurring temptation to feel that some spectacular and costly action could become the miraculous solution to all current difficulties. A huge increase in newer elements of our defense; development of unrealistic programs, to cure every ill in agriculture; a dramatic expansion in basic and applied research—these and many other possibilities, each possibly promising in itself, may be suggested as the only way to the road we wish to travel.

But each proposal must be weighed in the light of a broader consideration: the need to maintain balance in and among national programs—balance between the private and the public economy, balance between cost and hoped-for advantage—balance between the clearly necessary and the comfortably desirable; balance between our essential requirements as a nation and the duties imposed by the nation upon the individual; balance between actions of the moment and the national welfare of the future. Good judgment seeks balance and progress; lack of it eventually finds imbalance and frustration.

With the Nation today so involved in the question of the antiballistic missile and the broader issue of how to channel our post-Vietnam economy, the greatest tribute we can pay Dwight David Eisenhower is not in our words a eulogy to his life, but by heeding the principle which governed his life and following the example he set as President by rejecting the antiballistic missile and the desire to channel our economy into bigger and better systems of mass destruction.

## Hon. Odin Langen

OF MINNESOTA

Mr. Speaker, the great honor of my life is to have personally known Dwight David Eisenhower.

Honesty, integrity, devotion to God and country, decency, courage—all describe our 34th President. He was the personification of all that is good and moral in America, and his countrymen responded manifold. He was a hero, a friend, a leader of the highest order.

Few men in our history have been so highly honored or so dearly loved by his people. Few in our history have so richly deserved it.

When America was provoked into war, he led the way to the swiftest victory possible, commanding the largest military machine the world has ever seen or may ever see again. But he remained a man of peace. General Eisenhower's words, spoken 14 years ago in Vermont, not only reflect his deep conviction and dedication to peace, but are particularly relevant to the world today. He said:

We merely want to live in peace with all the world, to trade with them, to commune with them, to learn from their culture as they may learn from ours, so that our sons may stay at home, the products of our toil may be used for our schools, and our roads and our churches, and not for the guns and planes and tanks and ships of war.

A military man himself, he warned upon leaving the Presidency against "the acquisition of unwarranted influence by the military-industrial complex."

We cannot and, as he would have quickly affirmed, should not turn to the past except to learn from it. But one cannot help harboring the wistful desire for a world less fraught with tensions and turmoil, as represented by the Eisenhower years of the Presidency.

Dwight David Eisenhower will live on as an inspiration to future generations of Americans.

The ideals for which he stood seem, in these days of national unrest, to reflect a simpler and more serene America. But these are the ideals that have always taken America through her most trying moments in history. They will be needed again and again in the future.

To the Eisenhower family, we express our heartfelt sympathy. To Dwight David Eisenhower, our eternal thanks and gratitude. Now committed to the ages, he can now take his rightful place in history as one of our greatest sons.

## Hon. John C. Kluczynski

OF ILLINOIS

Mr. Speaker, I am honored, as I am saddened, to share in these farewells to a friend, for it is as a wise and deeply respected friend to his countrymen that General Eisenhower will be remembered.

He was, in the long reach of mankind's years, a unique instrument of international cooperation and a national symbol of unity. But it is not of these achievements in themselves of which I would speak. The quality to which I wish to pay tribute was his active devotion to the moral principles upon which our country was founded, through which he became great, and to which it must return if it is to survive. To the extent that we compromise or abandon those principles on whatever pretext we court destruction, both personal and national, and to the extent that we sustain them, we will achieve the order, the peace, and the liberty we pride above all else.

General Eisenhower knew this and never ceased to live by it; through all the human contacts and experiences and events of his crowded days he was guided by that honesty of purpose.

It is the living example of a richly rewarding life, a life in which the satisfactions far outweighed the disappointments and the life guided by reverence by things we cannot see, for which we shall be eternally grateful.

## Hon. William S. Broomfield

OF MICHIGAN

Mr. Speaker, we allow few "great" men to walk among us. In all but rare instances, that is an adjective we reserve until the finality of death permits us to safely sum up a man's life and decide whether it will be bestowed.

Dwight D. Eisenhower was one of those rare great men permitted to wear that mantle in his lifetime. He did so with grace, humanity, and restraint.

He was a simple man in the best sense of that word who seemed to live a life filled with contradiction.

He was a great soldier, but a President who was a peacemaker. He made momentous decisions, but sometimes appeared to make none. He was a statesman who unified the Nation, but who confessed humbly his ineptitude in politics.

But the contradictions of his life were not to be found in the man. They arose naturally from the great variety of responsibilities he assumed. They were enhanced because the man did not vary with the role.

Whatever his undertaking, he applied the same principles, of duty, dedication, honesty, and humanity.

As a general he led history's most massive assemblage of men and weaponry to free the continent of Europe from tyranny.

As a President he maintained peace on a warlike globe for 8 years and presided over a world which history may credit with renouncing great wars.

He was a soldier who never permitted himself to cease cherishing human values.

He once said:

> The only thing I can bring to the White House is the values that a man thinks are important.

No man could bring more.

He left us with a restatement of those simple values in words spoken to his wife on his deathbed.

He said:

> I've always loved my wife. I've always loved my children. I've always loved my grandchildren and I've always loved my country.

In a confusing and complicated world people have not always understood the depth of those simple values and all they imply. But they have always recognized intuitively how well Mr. Eisenhower understood them.

People have always responded with affection and trust.

Even after he retired to Gettysburg every American President sought out his advice and counsel whenever a great issue required national unity and bipartisan support. For they knew that with Mr. Eisenhower's approval came the confidence and trust of millions of Americans.

Mr. Eisenhower claimed often that he did not understand politics. Yet, as commander of the Allied forces in Europe during World War II he welded brilliant military men from diverse backgrounds and with diverse ambitions to achieve the most ambitious military undertaking in history.

As President, this man who claimed not to understand politics unified for 8 years a nation weary from war and social change.

It was those same qualities of humanity and tolerance and an outstanding ability to work with others to enlist their trust and cooperation that enabled him to do so.

During those 8 years of peace and stability he worked with quiet strength to maintain the United Nations and the North Atlantic Treaty Organization. He gave permanence to a sweeping foreign aid program and offered Americans a new, mature approach to relations with the Communist nations, an attitude whose wisdom and realism we have not yet fully grasped.

He preserved and maintained these institutions for the future often in spite of formidable and determined opposition without bombast or personal recrimination.

He did so with a quiet strength and resolve that often belied the deep inner conflicts which must have enveloped him.

It was his simplicity of motive and purpose that always came through that won him such great rapport with the American people.

And, in turn it was the trust and affection of the American people which provided him with the strength to prevail.

More than any President in modern times, he exemplified the qualities that we like to claim as truly American.

He once said:

> I came from the heart of America.

He was referring to the broad expanse of Kansas countryside in which he grew up.

I believe historians will conclude the truth of that statement rests only partially in geography.

## Hon. Carl D. Perkins

OF KENTUCKY

Mr. Speaker, the people of the Seventh Congressional District of Kentucky, which is generally known as the heart of Appalachia, are truly anguished by the departure from the national scene of a great military hero and a great leader in line with the tradition of great leaders of our country.

Dwight David Eisenhower will not be known in eastern Kentucky because of any bricks or mortar erected in his memory, in any bridges or roads constructed during his era of leadership, in any tangible public works or economic development, but Dwight David Eisenhower will be remembered in the hearts of every eastern Kentuckian for what to me is worth far more. Our departed general and great President will be remembered by us for the strength of spirit with which he gave Kentuckians and all Americans, for a renewed faith in our democratic principles, in our Christian heritage and in the noble task which confronts America.

Few Americans have given so unselfishly of their total lives in public service and dedication and I am pleased to rise today with my colleagues—pleased and greatly honored to have this opportunity to speak what I believe to be in the hearts of every one of my constituents.

## Hon. George A. Goodling

OF PENNSYLVANIA

Mr. Speaker, many fine tributes have been paid to a very fine man, the late Dwight D. Eisenhower.

On March 30, 1969, Rev. Edgar Henshaw Steedle of the United Church of Christ of Glen Rock, Pa., offered a splendid tribute to General Eisenhower at his church's day service. Because this is a particularly meaningful expression on a truly great man, I submit it to the CONGRESSIONAL RECORD and commend it to the attention of my colleagues. The tribute follows:

TRIBUTE

Dwight David Eisenhower, 34th President of the United States.

What does one say about a man who has served his fellow men so well for so many years?

If you list his accomplishments you must be extremely selective or you will run the risk of rambling on into the night.

If you speak of his personal attributes, and love this man as I have, you may be accused of trying to turn a man into a saint.

If you compare him with other great men of the century you will find that his unique contributions place him beyond the bounds of legitimate comparison.

I can say this, for me, Dwight David Eisenhower lived a life dedicated to the people of the nation into which he was born. He governed his life by principles founded upon eternal values, not upon selfish desires or human expediency.

He set the standard for a good life in his day and exemplified, for generations to come, those things which make a person truly human.

We thank God for the life of Dwight David Eisenhower. He answered God's call to service among his fellow men. He has now answered God's call to eternal life.

## Hon. John J. Rooney
OF NEW YORK

Mr. Speaker, on June 14, 1911, a group of plebes gathered at West Point and one of them many years later said of that occasion:

> With the American flag floating majestically above us, we were sworn in as cadets of the U.S. Military Academy. It was an impressive ceremony. As I looked up at our national colors and swore my allegiance, I realized humbly that I now belonged to the flag. It is a moment I have never forgotten.

So spoke Dwight David Eisenhower, General of the Army and 34th President of these United States. We shall not forget him either.

"Duty, honor, country" is the code of the Cadet Corps at West Point and it was Dwight Eisenhower's code all his life. But this was a man who could also say on his deathbed "I have always loved my wife. I have always loved my children. I have always loved my grandchildren. And I have always loved my country." He was a man who could receive every honor that a military career could offer, lead the largest and most victorious army in the history of the world and at the same time call war a "damnable thing" and express the hope that his military colleagues would eventually find themselves unemployed. He was a man who, as 34th President of the United States, could lead the wealthiest, most technically advanced country in the world and also warn her citizens of a threat to "the very structure of our society" by a military-industrial complex and a "scientific-technological elite." He termed these two threats, very real today, "a hostile ideology—global in scope, atheistic in character, ruthless in purpose, and insidious in method."

President Eisenhower was a very human and trusting person and so at times made mistakes and was betrayed by some of those in whom he put trust. But the basic decency, honesty, and warmth of the man could never be doubted. He was without doubt one of the most popular Presidents this country ever had. Nor was his popularity limited to this country. "We like Ike" was a worldwide chant in an area when "Ami, Go Home" was much more popular.

President Eisenhower was proud to be an American and in 1953 I think he summed it up perfectly when he said:

> The things that make us proud to be Americans are of the soul and spirit. They are not the jewels we wear, or the furs we buy, the house we live in, the standard of living, even, that we have. All these things are wonderful to the esthetic and physical senses. But never let us forget that the deep things that are America are the soul and the spirit. The Statue of Liberty is not tired, and not because it is made of bronze. It is because no matter what happens, here the individual is dignified because he is created in the image of his God.

Dwight David Eisenhower, gone from us now, made us all proud to be Americans.

Mr. Speaker, I should like to add a personal footnote to the foregoing. When I first became a Member of the House of Representatives on June 6, 1944, I was assigned to the House Committee on Military Affairs. As a member of that committee and in the months of November and December 1944, I had the privilege of joining 16 other members in a visit to our military installations and activities in England; France; Liege, Belgium; Maastricht, Holland and the entire western front. Subsequently, we visited such activities in Italy and the icy cold Italian front, which was then up in the Apennines, south of Bologna. It was while we were in France in 1944 that I first met General Eisenhower. Following that time, it was my pleasure and privilege to meet him on innumerable occasions. He became, as you know, president of Columbia University in New York City and subsequently the Supreme Allied Commander, Europe, where I visited him a few times.

31-935 O—70——7

He was my host in the White House on many occasions during his 8 years as President of the United States. So you see, I have lost a valued friend.

## Hon. William B. Widnall

OF NEW JERSEY

Mr. Speaker, since March 28, 1969, the Nation, through the television and radio networks, has been able to share in and be a part of the dignified and solemn ceremonies following the death of our beloved Dwight David Eisenhower.

The general was truly a man of the people, and through the fine efforts of the broadcast media, the people were able to share throughout the days of mourning the warmth of his personality.

Dignity and taste best describe the manner in which this last tribute was carried out. Dignity and taste also describe the way in which these days of mourning were reported to the Nation. Television did what it does best—capture a mood with fine camera work and a minimum of commentary. The restraint which the newsmen on the scene exercised was laudable, and realistic, since the participants and the observers were not listening to a flow of words describing the scene. The radio commentary I heard was also excellent—low-keyed, restrained and yet complete.

During those parts of the observances I attended, particularly the eulogy in the Rotunda, and the state funeral at the Cathedral, the media were not obtrusive, and I am told the coverage was excellent.

I want to commend both television and radio executives and newsmen and technicians for their thoughtful presentation of the events of these sad days. That their excellence allowed the Nation which loved Dwight Eisenhower to participate in his funeral is to their credit. The Nation is grateful.

## Hon. Robert N. Giaimo

OF CONNECTICUT

Mr. Speaker, I join with the people of this Nation and the people of the world in mourning the passing of Dwight David Eisenhower. Men of peace and goodwill have lost a true champion of their cause.

First as a soldier, then as Supreme Commander of Allied Forces during World War II, and finally as the 34th President of the United States, General Eisenhower served his country in war and in peace and he served it well.

Though General Eisenhower rose to fame as the commander of the largest fighting force ever assembled, he will be remembered by the people of the world as a soldier of peace. He knew, more than any man, the havoc war wreaks on both mankind and nations. Because of this awareness of the tragedy of war, he strove diligently during his Presidency to erase this ugly menace from the world.

"Ike" represented America at its best. He was a man of great moral courage, and he possessed an overwhelming sense of duty. But more importantly he believed in the basic goodness of his country and of mankind.

At this time, when many are questioning the fundamental values of our country, we have only to look to this great man for inspiration and strength. We shall always be grateful for his many outstanding and wonderful contributions toward making this a better world in which to live.

## Hon. Louis C. Wyman

OF NEW HAMPSHIRE

Mr. Speaker, the comments of the distinguished, patriotic, and dedicated American philanthropist H. L. Hunt concerning the beautiful eulogy to former President Eisenhower by President Nixon in the Capitol Rotunda on March 31, 1969, are particularly timely. I believe they are deserving of consideration by all readers of the Record.

The comments by H. L. Hunt follow:

President Nixon's unparalleled eulogy of the late President Eisenhower was truly magnificent. While his words were clearly spoken for no other reason than to express what he and a grieving nation felt for a good man and a good leader, the impact of his oratory, the depth of his feeling and the warmth with which he expressed what he and the nation felt, will doubtless have the effect of raising his popularity rating of 60% in March to at least 70%.

In addition to enhancing the President's popularity noticeably in the polls, his words, spoken with such feeling, are also quite likely to have the effect of setting back the cause of crime and rioting which have been at least sympathetically tolerated, if not actually encouraged, by members of the Administrations of Mr. Nixon's predecessors and a vast number now in government.

In his masterful eulogy, Mr. Nixon literally grasped the mind of America and turned it, for 16 minutes, upon itself. Through a departed soldier of the Republic, he did something that is almost never done: the President reminded us of what is good about Republic USA. Sad though the nation was at the loss of a beloved man, who declared that "I am from the heart of America," refreshed it assuredly was at the convincing words of a man at the helm, that "America is Okay!"

## Hon. Carleton J. King

OF NEW YORK

Mr. Speaker, there is little one can add to the many magnificent tributes which have already been paid to our distinguished former President, Dwight D. Eisenhower. His leadership at a time of great danger to the free world is a matter of history and his place in it is secure.

One of the most memorable events of my career in Congress took place several years ago when I and several of my colleagues were invited to General Eisenhower's farm in Gettysburg for an afternoon visit. We conferred with the former President, viewed his beautiful farm and were taken on a guided tour of the Gettysburg battlefield. I could not help but think that here was a five-star general, former President of the United States, willingly taking the time from his heavy schedule to welcome a few freshmen Congressman to his farm, personally guiding us through the historic battlefield and giving us the benefit of his wisdom and knowledge.

I do wish to pay my respects to this great statesman. We have suffered a great loss in his passing but freedom will continue to live in the world because Dwight David Eisenhower lived and defended it.

Mr. Speaker, General Eisenhower's passing was the subject of an editorial eulogy published March 29, 1969, by the Saratogian newspaper of Saratoga Springs, N.Y. I would like to share this exceptional expression with my colleagues:

IKE WAS THERE

If the essential greatness of Dwight David Eisenhower could be summed up in one-word epitaph, it would be simply: "Ike."

Here was the professional soldier who rose from relative obscurity at the beginning of the greatest war in history to supreme command of the greatest assemblage of armies in history; who later served his country for eight years in the highest position of responsibility any man can attain.

Yet he was always "Ike."

Looking back from the turbulent present, the years of the Eisenhower administration seem calm and stable. They were not, but if they seemed so then as well as now, it was only because of the presence of this immensely popular President in the White House. There was something about this uncommonly common man that inspired confidence and unshakable faith that, no matter how beset the nation was by crisis and challenges, nothing dire would happen as long as Ike was there.

Beset the nation was:

Those were the years when the cold war was really frigid; when a man named Khrushchev came to power in Russia to strut the world's stage for a time with his rhetoric of nuclear diplomacy and ballistic blackmail; when a man named Ho Chi Minh was mauling the French in Indochina; when a man named Joe McCarthy was finding Communists in every State Department closet and setting neighbor suspiciously against neighbor; when a man named Faubus in Little Rock, Ark., was fomenting the gravest federal crisis since the Civil War; when a U.S. vice president was being spat upon in South America; when the world hovered on the edge of Armageddon as war broke out in the Middle East; when freedom-loving men everywhere agonized as Hungary was ground under the heel; when the nation plunged briefly into its worst recession since the 1930s; when Americans indulged in an orgy of self-doubt because Russia had launched something into space called a Sputnik; when words like "agonizing reappraisal," "brinkmanship," "U–2," "summit" and "missile gap" became part of the vocabulary of reproach against the administration.

Yet they seemed like calm years, because Ike was there.

Now the general has lost his last battle, after besting the scythe-bearer in encounter after encounter. He went down fighting, he surrendered reluctantly. More than that can be asked of no soldier.

The Eisenhower years are still too close for historians to be able to give us a balanced and dispassionate summary. The full figure of Dwight D. Eisenhower as President and elder statesman remains to be limned by a future generation.

Of one thing we can be certain, however:

If, in their study of this man, his life and his accomplishments, Americans of the future can come at all close to knowing him as his contemporaries did, they will call him "Ike."

## Hon. J. Irving Whalley

OF PENNSYLVANIA

Mr. Speaker, a time of sorrow has again blanketed our Nation. The loss of Dwight David Eisenhower touches the hearts of many individuals not only in America but throughout the free world and inspires the emotions of people everywhere who cherish freedom.

I had the pleasure and privilege of meeting President Eisenhower on many occasions. Dwight Eisenhower exemplified compassion, dedication, and integrity. His charismatic personality and distinguished character promoted respect and admiration in practically everyone he met.

Dwight Eisenhower fought for freedom for all people and made tremendous gains. His biggest battle, however, was lost to time.

Words cannot truly express our heartfelt condolences to Mrs. Eisenhower and family. I am thankful for being able to bear witness to the era of Dwight David Eisenhower for he was an inspiration to all of us.

## Hon. F. Bradford Morse

OF MASSACHUSETTS

Mr. Speaker, our country and indeed the world has lost one of its greatest leaders. We mourn him in death as we loved him in life, for Dwight David Eisenhower, General of the Army, 34th President of the United States, had a very special place in the hearts of men and women everywhere. He had lived a full life, accomplishing more than most men would dare to dream, and when the end came he was peaceful, and he was ready. I watched some of the thousands of people who filed quietly by his casket as it lay in the Rotunda of the Capitol. They came out of a deep and profound respect for one of the best loved and most humane men of our time. That is a great tribute.

But there is a greater tribute still that we can, and should, pay to a man who dedicated his life to the causes of his country and its people. That tribute is to look to the lessons of his life and to see that what he stood for, what he tried to accomplish, and what wisdom he passed to us, is not lost, but woven into the fabric of our national future.

Dwight Eisenhower was a professional soldier and he was a man of peace. Perhaps one of his great accomplishments was in showing us that the two are not incompatible. Only a man of his inner strength, patience, cheerfulness, and good humor combined with rare modesty, could have molded together the diverse elements needed to mount the great Allied offensive that landed at Normandy and culminated in the surrender of the German armies 11 months later. For that accomplishment he will forever hold a place of affection and respect in the hearts of all free men.

In 1948, General Eisenhower refused to run for the Presidency, indicating his strong belief that the subordination of the military power to the civil power, wisely structured, was best served if professional soldiers did not seek high political office. As Tom Wicker has pointed out:

> Only a general of Dwight Eisenhower's human quality, of whom there are precious few, should ever be exempt from (that) reasoning.

He was exempt, and he was elected President in 1952, in the midst of a "conflict" in Korea that frustrated the American people much as the Vietnam conflict does today. And President Eisenhower brought us peace, a peace which he sustained throughout his years in office.

In his administration the North Atlantic Treaty Organization was forged; an International Finance Corporation was created; the International Atomic Energy Agency was approved; and a U.S. Development Loan Fund was established. All these, and more, were solid contributions to building peace through international cooperation.

We sometimes tend to forget—because those were peaceful and tranquil years—that President Eisenhower presided over major contributions to domestic progress, contributions that formed the basis for much that has come since. The Department of Health, Education, and Welfare was created; the research and assistance program on air pollution was enacted; the National Defense Education Act and the Interstate Highway Act were passed; and the basic Civil Rights Act, the first legislation in this area in some 80 years, was brought into being.

Before leaving office General Eisenhower delivered an eloquent farewell address, and in it he gave us some advice we would do well to heed carefully now. He understood before many of us that "the potential for the disastrous rise of misplaced power exists and will persist." And he tried to tell us that, "in the councils of government, we must guard against the acquisition of unwarranted influence, whether sought or unsought, by the military-industrial complex. We must never let the weight of this combination endanger our liberties or democratic processes."

We are engaged today in a great national debate which involves, at its heart, the determination of important priorities for ourselves and for generations to come. What should be our guides to a wise decision? Dwight Eisenhower made a start on what have become some of our most pressing national problems. We have done more and there is still more to be done. If we can bring a part of the wisdom and a fraction of the generosity of heart and of mind to the task that remains as he did to his, we shall have served his memory well.

## Hon. William F. Ryan

OF NEW YORK

Mr. Speaker, I join with millions of Americans who mourn the passing of Dwight David Eisenhower.

The affection which General Eisenhower earned from his countrymen is perhaps unique in this era. In a period of our history when many Americans have come to view the purposes and motivations of politicians with cynicism and even hostility, the nationwide respect for General Eisenhower is a reminder that honesty and openness are still essential to the formulation of public policy. For when public trust is lacking, essential programs will fail to engender the support necessary for their success.

The many accomplishments of General Eisenhower's career are well known. As Supreme Commander of the Allied Expeditionary Forces in World War II, Chief of Staff of the Army, and the first Supreme Commander of NATO, General Eisenhower achieved the highest honors which can be bestowed on a military man. In addition, he served with distinction as president of Columbia University from 1948 to 1950. And, of course, he was twice elected President of the United States.

As the victorious military Commander of Allied Forces in Europe during World War II, and the first head of the NATO forces, General Eisenhower's place in our military history is assured. It was his plan which resulted in the successful invasion of Normandy in June of 1944, and it was under his direction that that invasion was carried through to the successful defeat of Nazi Germany. With the fate of the entire Allied Expeditionary Force on his shoulders, General Eisenhower made the right decisions at the right time. His leadership earned him the gratitude of all of Western Europe, as well as his own fellow countrymen.

As the head of NATO, General Eisenhower molded separate and competing military powers into a successful defense force and laid the basis for the military security of Western Europe. The unity which he helped to forge has made possible the two decades of peace which Western Europe has known and the increasing cooperation between European powers that has characterized postwar European development.

As President, General Eisenhower's record is mixed. While he failed to attack many of the longstanding problems—including poverty and discrimination—which have had so great a significance for the future of America, he did not—as some of his supporters thought he might—dismantle the social programs and institutions which he inherited from his Democratic predecessors. His decision to send Federal troops to Little Rock in 1957 in support of the Supreme Court's order that schools must be integrated also laid the basis for future Federal action in support of desegregation.

In his farewell radio and television address on January 17, 1961, General Eisenhower issued a warning to America that in recent years has taken on greater and greater significance. Although he was himself a military man, he warned in that address of the escalating power of the military and the potential implications of the encroachment of the military-industrial complex on our democratic processes.

He said:

> In the councils of government, we must guard against the acquisition of unwarranted influence, whether sought or unsought, by the military-industrial complex. The potential for the disastrous rise of misplaced power exists and will persist.

The rise in the military budget which has occurred since General Eisenhower issued that warning, and the initiation and perpetuation of the war in Vietnam, testify to the validity of his fears of an ever growing military influence on the conduct of public policy. As the General himself said:

> Only an alert and knowledgeable citizenry can compel the proper meshing of the huge industrial and military machinery of defense with our peaceful methods and goals, so that security and liberty may prosper together.

The growth of the military-industrial complex since 1961 has failed to bring increased security, and today poses very real dangers to the future of our democratic processes. As a country dedicated to liberty and the democratic formulation of public policy, we can ill-afford to ignore the threat of increasing military and industrial dominance which General Eisenhower pointed out.

Americans have traditionally reserved their greatest respect and admiration for those who serve their country with honesty and dedication. General Eisenhower brought both qualities to his long and distinguished career as a public servant. His dedication and his contributions will endure as standards by which to judge the careers of those who come after him.

## Hon. J. J. Pickle
OF TEXAS

Mr. Speaker, this country and the world all mourn the loss of one of our great sons.

Dwight David Eisenhower stands as one of the most outstanding figures in the American heritage. Born in the heartland of our country, he reflected the kind of spirit and enthusiasm which gives this Nation the dynamic force it has in the world today.

But at the same time, he had a deep understanding of human emotion and a sense of compassion for those ideals which truly urge man to his highest goals.

It was this combination of driving force tempered by compassion which made "Ike" the great man he was.

He was the most capable military commander in the world, and the hand of fate directed that he appear on the scene at perhaps the most critical time in world history. He was an efficient and able President who guided his country through a period of complex transition. And his success was the embodiment of the dream of the real America.

Dwight David Eisenhower, General of the Armies, President of the United States, was one of the few men in American history who only had friends, and no enemies.

## Hon. Donald Rumsfeld
OF ILLINOIS

Mr. Speaker, when the general who commanded history's greatest army turned to civilian life in 1948, he stated that he would not be changing the fundamental purpose of his life—"the protection and perpetuation of basic human freedom."

Dwight Eisenhower had protected the freedom of men by forging unity among the Allies and maintaining that unity until Hitler's "Fortress Europe" had been broken. After the war, he turned to perpetuating the hard-won freedom.

Although most of his life had been devoted to war and preparation for war, he was a man of peace. He believed as an article of faith that peace was the only climate in which human freedom could endure.

As President of the United States, he brought us out of war and then gave our Nation a period of growth and progress with uncommon tranquillity.

His success in maintaining the peace derived from a quality often underrated in leaders—good will. He trusted people and in turn they trusted him. He appealed to the best in people and they responded with their best. He reasoned with others and they refrained from shouting when disagreeing with his policies.

Hugh Sidey of Life magazine, a man who has covered many presidents, commented on this quality last August after the general's last TV appearance:

> There are even those who dare suggest that his soothing spirit, the innate goodness of the man himself, did more to lift up the hearts of Americans and hold them together in a reasonable state of public happiness than many social reforms that have been propounded since.

His unending good will made him a unifier of men and allowed him to become an instrument of peace. The name Eisenhower translates to "hewer of iron." I prefer to remember him as a "hewer of peace."

## Hon. Don Fuqua

OF FLORIDA

Mr. Speaker, the outpouring of affection for General Eisenhower across the length and breadth of America has been an inspiration to all of us.

The simple wave of a hand as the funeral train passed through the heartland of America was refreshing in this period of history which has been so fraught with controversy.

A memorial service for General Eisenhower was held at Florida State University in Tallahassee, Fla., March 31, and I think much of what was said by Acting President Stanley Marshall; Student Government Supreme Court Justice James Tait, speaking for the students; and Dr. Robert Spivey, chairman of the department of religion, who spoke for the faculty; represents the real heart of America.

The material referred to follows:

REMARKS BY ACTING PRESIDENT STANLEY MARSHALL, FLORIDA STATE UNIVERSITY, AT THE MEMORIAL SERVICE FOR DWIGHT DAVID EISENHOWER, MARCH 31, 1969

We assemble here briefly today to honor the memory of a good man—of a loved and respected American citizen who gave a lifetime of service to his country. We pay tribute to a soldier—a military man who commanded troops from throughout the free world—an administrator who served as president of one of this country's most distinguished universities—a politician who held this nation's highest office when he served as the 34th President of the United States—and, a statesman who enjoyed the respect and affection of peoples on every continent.

Dwight David Eisenhower was an average man who rose to challenges faced by few men in our lifetime. From a modest background in the rural heartland of America, this Texas-born, Kansas-raised boy became a leader not only of his compatriots, but of men everywhere who were dedicated to freedom. He was thought of by millions as a decent, honorable man who did his best to find decent and honorable solutions to the problems faced by mankind.

A military man who was skilled in forging together other military men from a number of nations to fight an awful war, Eisenhower also served as a soldier in the battle for peace. A military man in an establishment that sometimes wished it could throw off the yoke of civilian control, Eisenhower insisted that civil government and civil control were and should be superior to the military. A military man who had spent virtually his entire adult life in uniform, President Eisenhower warned the American people of dangers involved in a powerful military-industrial combination.

Although he was President of the United States, most people seemed always to think of Dwight Eisenhower as General rather than President. Perhaps this is true because as President he may have been less a partisan politician than many of his predecessors. President Eisenhower wanted to heal the ravages of war and strife, external as well as internal. He wanted the American people to recognize their obligations to the freedom of nations throughout the world, and to the freedom of the individual at home. This battle-tried soldier yearned for peace for all mankind and during most of his administration our nation fought only a cold war of words rather than a hot war of bombs.

Only history can truly and objectively assess the contributions of David Eisenhower but to the men and women of my generation Ike holds a unique and a very warm place in our hearts. He represented to us and for us, those age old tenets of the worth of American society and democracy. He believed in God, in country, in family, and in duty; in essence, he believed in the simple virtues that have, despite many imperfections, brought greatness to our country and our system of government. He was, as all of us are, an imperfect man in an imperfect world who gave the best of himself and urged us to give the best of ourselves. As one historian has written, President Eisenhower sought national unity and not personal power as he attempted to reconcile the differences among Americans and among nations. To what greater task can any man dedicate himself than peace and brotherhood? What greater tribute can we pay to Dwight Eisenhower than to carry forward and to implement his goals of national unity and reconciliation of our differences with other nations of the world?

Soldier, administrator, President, statesman—man of unbounding courage and good will—man of unquestioned loyalty to his beliefs—man of untiring dedication to the tasks set before him—the name of Dwight David Eisenhower will be remembered as more than a great general and a great statesman. He will be recorded in history as a man of courage and integrity and virtue who believed in the goodness of man and took account of that belief in everything he did.

---

REMARKS BY JAMES TAIT, CHIEF JUSTICE OF THE SUPREME COURT, STUDENT GOVERNMENT, SPEAKING FOR THE STUDENTS OF FLORIDA STATE UNIVERSITY, AT THE MEMORIAL SERVICE FOR DWIGHT DAVID EISENHOWER, MARCH 31, 1969

In this time of strife, both domestic and international, this nation will sorely miss the wise counsel of our most outstanding "soldier for peace." General Eisenhower had that rare ability to create in all men a will, a drive for peace. He was able to turn the energies of freedom-loving, peace-loving men toward the betterment of man, rather than against one another. When necessary he would vigorously defend the democratic ideals of this nation. However, he showed a deep respect for the basic dignity of man, individually and collectively, in assisting them to determine for themselves the best approach to peace and freedom. His record speaks for itself—General of the Armies, Supreme Allied Commander, welding together men of many nations to overthrow the tyranny of one man, of one nation over the lives of many and posing a threat to others; President of the United States, bringing an end to a deadly war and also assisting in the overthrow of a man threatening the individual freedom of many Americans, presiding over a peaceful era.

Although we will sorely miss him, he has left us a legacy. I hope that all men will accept this legacy and commit themselves to the ideals for which he stood—to allow his rare ability to continue in spirit. He was such a man.

---

Memorial Service for Dwight David Eisenhower—Remarks by Dr. Robert A. Spivey, Chairman of the Department of Religion, Speaking for the Faculty, Florida State University, March 31, 1969

Supreme Commander of the Allied Military Forces during World War II, President of a distinguished institution of higher education, and President of these United States. Yet in all these offices, Dwight David Eisenhower towers as a person.

In his column from yesterday's New York Times, James Reston captures the spirit of this man:

"The nation mourns the death of President Eisenhower almost as if it were grieving for the loss of its own youth. For Ike was a symbol of a simpler age, and he lived long enough to become part of all the old American legends of the frontier.

"The '60s have enhanced his reputation. They have been years of solemn, clever, and calculating men, and in contrast the old soldier seems open, straight, natural, joyful, and trustworthy.

"It was not so much what President Eisenhower did in the White House but what he didn't do that seems in retrospect so much more important than it did at the time.

"He did not misuse power. He did not allow his former colleagues on the Joint Chiefs of Staff to drag him into unnecessary military adventures, and while his native caution and conservatism limited his achievements on the homefront, they also limited his risks and blunders overseas. . . .

"Few men at the top of American politics in recent years have managed to make their way through the tangles and conflicts of Washington with so little personal rancor as Eisenhower. There was nothing mean or petty about him, and he never allowed political differences to loiter down into personal animosity.

"The historians so far have not rated him among the great presidents, but his contemporaries are certainly agreed that he was a remarkably warm, fair, and attractive human being. It was the personal Eisenhower rather than the political Eisenhower that triumphed, maybe because he was the living model for so many popular American myths.

"To the present young generation, he may be a magnificent square, but in his own time he proved once more that the squares usually inherit the earth. . . .

"Ike will have his place in the story of this tremendous time. He proved that simple goodness can still be a power in the world and that luck helps. He didn't "fade away" like the rest of the old soldiers but fought for life years after his obituary got dusty on the stone.

"This may be why this cynical age has taken his death with such genuine regret and sorrow."

In a sense his death represents the reaffirmation of simplicity, goodness, trustworthiness, and normalcy. During recent years we have become accustomed to unexpected, catastrophic, tragic ends for our national heroes—Martin Luther King, Robert and John Fitzgerald Kennedy. The unexpected and seemingly unexplainable violence that has characterized our recent past causes many Americans to believe in hidden, sinister forces at work to destroy our nation and its heroes. But in President Eisenhower's death, there is a certain triumph of normalcy, a simple, dignified ending to a man's days that were spent in service and loyalty.

It is altogether fitting that his funeral and our memorial be on this day, at the beginning of holy week in which religious folk throughout this country celebrate the triumph of life through Jewish Passover and Christian Good Friday and Easter. It is altogether fitting that he be buried in the spring of the year when dogwood and azaleas declare the goodness and beauty of life. In all these manifestations of triumph, Eisenhower shared. Toward religion he was unreflective, yet broadly committed. He exemplified affirmative trust, not so much to the institutional church, but to his offices and in his presence among other human beings. Few could resist his person or resent his popularity—"we do like Ike."

Eisenhower's stature with the intellectual community was never particularly great. Probably the least distinguished part of his career was his tenure as president of Columbia University. Certainly he never considered himself an intellectual. Yet the university community does indeed respect and honor him as a leader and as a person. His finest hour, in the view of many educators, was his sharp criticism of the "military-industrial complex" as he left the office of the Presidency of the United States. He was able to remain critical of that very "complex" which helped catapult him into national prominence.

His real stature was that he towered above by not elevating himself. He expended himself in service to country and others; he did not seek to expand himself. He was not an intellectual, but he did quietly serve truth.

A review of a recent movie ("The Prime of Miss Jean Brodie") about a teacher and her students points to the relevance of the example of President Eisenhower: "Those charged with the education of the young are responsible not only for the distribution of information, but for the stimulation of character. And often it takes a character to make a character. There is a desperate need for innovators who are able to stimulate unrealized potential and nourish the humanity of a student. But how risky the enterprise becomes when those who are unwhole attempt to make others whole; when the frustrated try to mold the young in their own defective image." President Eisenhower served the truth in his own quiet way, without making the mistake of imagining himself a savior. He liked to play the game of golf.

President Nixon shared the last words of President Eisenhower. "I have always loved my wife. I have always loved my children. I have always loved my grandchildren. I have always loved my country." That was Dwight David Eisenhower. That also represents his triumph, and ours if we will, of normal, simple, trusting goodness.

## Hon. John W. McCormack
OF MASSACHUSETTS

Mr. Speaker, on March 31, 1969, at St. Matthew's Cathedral in Washington, D.C., a mass for peace was celebrated as a tribute to the late President Dwight David Eisenhower.

At the mass, His Eminence Patrick Cardinal O'Boyle, archbishop of Washington, delivered a homily as a tribute to our late, beloved President, the text of which homily I herewith include in my remarks:

### Cardinal's Homily at Mass for Peace

My dearly beloved friends in Christ, we have met together many times in this beautiful old cathedral. We have met in joy and in stark tragedy. We have prayed for peace and unity among our people, and have asked the guidance of Almighty God for those whom we have delegated the awesome responsibility of governing this great nation.

Today, although our hearts are saddened by the passing of a beloved figure from our midst, we meet with a certain sense of fulfillment. For although General Eisenhower would be the last to claim personal credit for the progress achieved in the years over which he presided, his footsteps on the beachhead of human progress are sharp and deep.

General Eisenhower served his country well in many fields—as soldier, author, educator, chief executive and world statesman. Yet although he commanded the greatest military force in history, it was his accomplishments in pursuit of world peace that gave him the greatest satisfaction. He quickly perceived that the world would never find lasting peace and tranquillity as long as the nuclear bomb hung like a Sword of Damocles over the head of mankind. This led to development of the "Atoms for Peace" program which President Eisenhower presented in person to the United Nations.

General Eisenhower's outgoing temperament made it easy for him to perceive both the impossibility of isolation in an expanding world and the benefits of free intercourse between nations.

By every measurement of inclination and training General Eisenhower fitted perfectly into this mold. He was the right man in the right place at the right time, and the country showed its confidence by giving him two resounding victories at the polls.

The former President's critics have argued that he sought to stay "above politics," and that no man can do that in a democracy and govern effectively. Perhaps. But the record will show that an American general successfully put together a complex striking force manned by professionals from half a dozen countries, and led them to victory.

Dwight Eisenhower was able to accomplish this military miracle because he had learned the secret of getting people to work together. He was marked for greatness even then. And try as he might to escape his destiny, the Normandy beachhead led inexorably to the White House.

In these informal recollections of a great and popular figure, I have left to the last one facet of his character that would clearly set him apart in any age. Perhaps President Nixon said it best in a tribute to his former chief shortly after his death.

"For a quarter of a century," the President said, "he spoke with a moral authority seldom equaled in American public life. This was not only because he held the nation's highest honors . . . but because of the kind of man he was."

It was true. People sensed in Dwight Eisenhower a rock of integrity that inspired not only confidence but affection. Through his humility, his dignity and his unselfish willingness to spend himself on any task that might benefit the land he loved, General Eisenhower richly earned the love and respect of his countrymen. May God rest his brave and noble soul.

In the April 3, 1969, issue of the Catholic Standard, the official newspaper of the archdiocese of Washington, appeared an editorial entitled "Dwight David Eisenhower," which I also include in my remarks:

### Dwight David Eisenhower

The death of General of the Army Dwight D. Eisenhower marks the passing of an era in the history of this country. He served as the key military leader of our armed forces and later as a two-term President of the United States when our nation reached its highest point of world political and moral leadership.

Although he was not the prime architect of the grand strategy that led to final victory in World War II or of the policies that pledged our nation to serve the world community, it was his unique talent that molded the essential ingredients into the harmonious effort necessary for success. It was a period when this nation, although a victorious world power, neither demanded nor acquired a single foot of alien territory from either friend or foe. On the contrary, this nation both instituted and supported the national aspirations of any number of emerging new nations in direct contrast to the actions of the Soviet Union and other Communist-controlled countries.

It is a matter of historical record that Gen. Eisenhower played a profound, even though at times a somewhat intangible, role in determining the future courses of this country. His ability to persuade the brilliant and sometimes domineering men with whom he was called upon to associate to put aside their diffuse interests for common causes resulted in the achievement of many successes which otherwise would have been unattainable. He was a truly remarkable man and a dedicated patriot.

There is little that we can add to the accolades he has received from the nation and the world. We can only urge all men of good will to work toward the accomplishment of the same spirit of harmony that he so richly prized and was so effective in achieving. This could be our greatest tribute to him, and the one he would cherish above all else.

We join with our fellow Americans and men of good will throughout the world in asking God's mercy for a great American—Dwight David Eisenhower.

## Hon. John T. Myers

OF INDIANA

Mr. Speaker, the world has lost a friend with the death of former President Dwight David Eisenhower. He dedicated his entire life to his Nation and mankind around the world.

General Eisenhower's devotion to man's fight against tryanny, his constant quest for peace, his sense of justice and equality place him alongside the great leaders this Nation has known.

The memory of this old soldier's devotion to God and country will never fade away so long as this Nation cherishes the ideals he championed in a lifetime of service to his fellow man.

In the brief period since his passing, tributes to his life have come from around the world. To me, President Nixon struck the most significant theme when he eulogized that General Eisenhower's life reminds us "there is a moral force in this world more powerful than the might of arms or the wealth of nations."

The citizens of the Seventh Congressional District of Indiana, who gave General Eisenhower overwhelming support in his two presidential campaigns, joined the world in paying tribute to this great man as demonstrated in this sampling of editorial comment from district newspapers:

[From the Bloomfield Evening World]

May God grant that generations will continue to produce such men who place great value on religious faith, family and country.

---

[From the Bloomington Courier-Tribune]

Among General Eisenhower's most important qualities was his ability to bring men of diverse views together and to infuse them with his own spirit of generosity and service in a common cause.

---

[From the Bloomington Herald-Telephone]

The kind of man you'd want your son to be.

[From the Brazil Times]

Not since George Washington has America seen a leader such as Dwight David Eisenhower. Had he lived forever the world could never repay her debt to him.

---

[From the Crawfordsville Journal & Review]

There was something about this most uncommon common man that inspired confidence and faith that, no matter how beset the nation was by crises and challenges, nothing dire would happen so long as Ike was there.

---

[From the Greencastle Daily Banner]

General Eisenhower was so many things that most Presidents are not—a military hero and a national symbol—that it became customary to minimize his accomplishments as a political leader.

---

[From the Plainsfield Messenger]

A soft-spoken man, Eisenhower's image of being the nonpolitician but possessing that man you could trust look, will be greatly missed in government.

---

[From the Putnam County Daily Graphic]

This man has a world that will remember and never forget one of the men who did not ask or hesitate but gave of himself, all of himself, for the betterment of his world.

---

[From the Rockville Republican]

He was a humble man. He was a good man. And was there ever a man more human?

---

[From the Terre Haute Saturday Spectator]

The name of Eisenhower is deeply carved in the marble tablets of history, as a leader, a man of integrity, outstanding character and compassion.

---

[From the Terre Haute Star]

His openly friendly and sincere character, although at times a matter of consternation to his political associates, endeared him to both great and small.

---

[From the Terre Haute Tribune]

In his military role he did as much as any man to save the world from totalitarianism. His abiding concern as president was to build a more stable world order.

## Hon. Edward G. Biester, Jr.

OF PENNSYLVANIA

Mr. Speaker, President Nixon and the American people have lost in the death of former President Eisenhower, a powerful voice and good counsel at a time when we can ill afford that loss.

Few men in American history have given so much to the American people. I join with all Americans in mourning his passing.

I would like to take this opportunity to insert two editorials in the CONGRESSIONAL RECORD regarding Dwight D. Eisenhower from the Philadelphia Evening Bulletin.

The articles follow:

[From the Philadelphia (Pa.) Bulletin, Mar. 31, 1969]

A LEGACY OF DECENCY

As long as free men cherish their freedom, Dwight Eisenhower will stand with them, as he stood during war and peace; strong, confident and courageous—President Nixon proclaiming today as a national day of mourning.

Most men who make their mark upon the world and who die in greatness leave behind as their legacy some specific deed or thing, or some words expressing inspiring or profound thoughts.

Dwight D. Eisenhower has given more. He has left behind, for all who will accept it, a legacy of decency.

As 34th President of the United States, as most respected citizen in retirement, as General of the Army, Mr. Eisenhower held to a strong and basic faith in his country and its people.

There was, he was certain, a strength, a resolve and a basic goodness in the land and in its people. To him the qualities of honesty, tolerance, self-reliance and patriotism were not to be described as old fashioned. They were part of each day.

When Mr. Eisenhower saw these qualities held up to ridicule he became concerned. He saw the young people of today as perhaps the finest the nation has ever produced. But he expressed fear that so many of them have been taught nothing of responsibility and self-discipline or the real meaning of life.

"You accepted hard work and a concern for others as a way of life," Mr. Eisenhower once said in describing his formative years. "We would have sneered at anyone who said we were underprivileged or anything like that."

Mr. Eisenhower was indeed, as President Nixon said yesterday, a product of America's soil and America's ideals. Mr. Eisenhower was, as he said in his London Guild Hall speech in 1945, from the "heart of America."

There is a tendency today to brush aside the qualities that were so much a part of Mr. Eisenhower as something of value only in a past, unsophisticated and simplistic era. But in truth they are as relevant and more needed today than ever before in the nation's history.

And, despite the cynicism and the skepticism that is part of America today, the vast majority of the nation holds to the same beliefs that Mr. Eisenhower held—a faith in themselves and in their country and a respect for their fellow man.

The difficulty today, as it has been in other periods of this country's history, is that it is difficult to hear the voice of this majority above the shrill shouts of those who seek confrontation rather than conference and conciliation.

President Nixon, in the eulogy delivered yesterday in the Rotunda of the United States Capitol said that these days of national mourning should also be days of gratitude for the inspiration and the strength which Mr. Eisenhower has given his countrymen.

These days can be something more. They can be days of rededication to the basic beliefs and the truths that were Mr. Eisenhower's. They can be the time of acceptance of Mr. Eisenhower's legacy of decency.

Nothing, in a nation so divided and torn by dissent, could be a finer tribute to a man who believed that his nation's future rested upon its moral strength.

---

[From the Philadelphia (Pa.) Bulletin, Mar. 30, 1969]

DWIGHT D. EISENHOWER

There is nothing wrong with America that the faith, love of freedom, intelligence and energy of her citizens cannot cure.—Dwight D. Eisenhower.

The Eisenhower presidential years now seem a time of serenity and untroubled acceptance of the virtues which make us a great people.

The era has a placid, sunlit quality to it.

This tranquillity and amiable consensus derived from circumstances and General Eisenhower's demeanor, his faith in God and belief in America, and in the American people.

The circumstances, of course, was the relatively brief period of calm intervening between the end of one war, the Korean War, and the gathering storm of another, the Vietnam War.

Probably no President could have made such a respite more purposeful.

His contribution was a renewal of the spirit, a general sharing of his instinctive sense of decency, a time of weighing values and the inevitable reassertion of the virtues which went into the making of the nation.

As recently as last summer, he told the GOP National Convention by television from his hospital room that the vast portion of the people are law-abiding and proud of their country and ready to sacrifice on her behalf—that all but a tiny percentage of Americans are patriotic, optimistic and loyal.

Dwight David Eisenhower was sure about important things like that, things which perhaps he made sound more simple than they are, but which are nonetheless the basis of Americans' faith in their country and in one another.

Ike, as the American family called him with fond familiarity, trusted his countrymen and his countrymen trusted him. That relationship—the affection, confidence, and respect—may not come through in the history books. Youngsters, even today, may not feel it. But it explains a great deal about the America of the nineteen-fifties, about Mr. Eisenhower's years in the Presidency, and about the inexhaustible reservoir of goodwill on which he drew among the generation of World War II.

It was this great confidence, this respect that helped to elect him President: Americans had ample cause to remember and be grateful for the services of the commander in Europe who carried such massive responsibilities in the battle against Nazi evil that threatened this nation and mankind.

But it was more than gratitude or the remembrance of past glory that put the general in the White House. In 1952 the Korean War was the sort of agonizing issue that the Vietnam War is today. Americans trusted Mr. Eisenhower to find a solution to it. They were willing to accept what he would do as necessary, in the nation's interests, honorable.

And something else: the American political atmosphere was also befouled then by those who spread fear, hate and distrust to gain their ends. Mr. Eisenhower did much to clear the air in the fifties simply because he was the kind of man he was—towering above the demagogs in public esteem, restrained, patient, moderate in speech and trusted.

There was added to Mr. Eisenhower's world reputation as a military man a universal recognition of his qualities as man genuinely desirous of peace. He was at once able to inspire caution in potential aggressors to extend the olive branch. His countrymen trusted him to be firm without being bellicose and peace-seeking without appeasing.

Let historians deal with the specifics of his political leadership and of his Presidency. To his nation, and to the world, he gave a strength of leadership, a new sense of resolve. And although he sat long with the great, his was an open and unassuming greatness that raised him to a place above the others.

He served his country in war in one of the highest of commands. He served his country and the free world in time of relative peace and in the most powerful office in the world. The "Eisenhower Years" may blur with the passage of time, but the quick and friendly grin of the man will never be forgotten. His was a great and rare gift, the gift of measuring problems and seeking solutions in terms of people.

The American nation mourns a great soldier, a high-minded President, a good and trusted man.

## Hon. Charles W. Sandman
OF NEW JERSEY

Mr. Speaker, the death of President Dwight Eisenhower leaves all Americans with a deep sense of grief and sorrow.

Yet there is also a feeling of quiet pride in the very full and very rich life which he lived.

It was my honor to serve under General Eisenhower as a navigator in the Army Air Force in Europe during World War II.

I was privileged to visit with our former President in 1967, when he greeted Republican freshmen at his home in Gettysburg.

I was struck by his modesty, by the clarity of his mind, by his intellectual articulation of basic truth, by the force of his expressions, and by his constant consideration for those of us around him.

Soldier and statesman, his life was one of distinguished and disciplined devotion to service.

Ike's life and achievements and the high principles for which he stood will continue to serve over the years as an inspiration to us all.

I join my colleagues in extending my heartfelt sympathy to Mrs. Eisenhower and family at their great loss.

## Hon. J. Herbert Burke
OF FLORIDA

Mr. Speaker, a tyrant is one who demands respect. A statesman is one who commands respect, but a great man earns respect.

One such man, who earned the respect of all who knew him, was Gen. Dwight D. Eisenhower.

He was truly one of our country's greatest Americans and the respect that he earned was worldwide, from both his friends and foes alike. He lived his life among the great people of his time and yet, prior to the time of his death when he selected his burial site, he requested that he be laid to rest in the town where he spent his boyhood, Abilene, Kans.

He loved his country, his family, and people from all walks of life, and he never forgot his beginnings as humble as they were.

Much has been written and spoken about the admiration and respect the American people had for General Eisenhower, and this is true because year after year even following his retirement from active public service he was selected in poll after poll as one of the most admired Americans and one of the most respected men throughout the world.

As for me, I feel indeed fortunate to have had the opportunity of not only seeing General Eisenhower, but meeting and talking to him on a number of occasions. I first met the general when I was a second lieutenant with the 90th Infantry Division in England, just prior to the D-day invasion where I served as a courier instructed to deliver certain information to him regarding division deployment in connection with "Overlord," the overall plan for the invasion of Normandy.

I remember him well, although I only saw him two times in May and June of 1944, because many of us who would shortly land in France were deeply concerned about our futures. Despite the great problems and worry that were on his shoulders, he remained cheerful, but most of all humble, courteous, and unusually friendly to me even though I was only a second lieutenant and he was a general charged with winning the largest war in history.

I had seen him several times after that, but my next personal meeting with him was at the White House in 1955 when I was requested to be the Republican nominee for Congress from the old Sixth Congressional District following the death of Dwight Rogers.

Here again, my meeting with President Eisenhower was unusual because he was the President and I the candidate for Congress, and despite the fact that he had the problems of the world confronting him, he spent more than an hour in conversation with me at the White House. I might add that it was one of the most pleasant hours spent in my lifetime.

The fact that he had become President had not changed him and to me he was the same, quick-smiling "Ike" that he had always been.

The final time I personally saw General Eisenhower was about a year ago and then I had been elected to the U.S. Congress and he was retired with his lovely wife, Mamie, in Gettysburg. A group of us had lunch with him and I was still impressed by his quick wit and charm, but what stood out in my mind was that Ike was still the kind, humble person he had always been.

General Eisenhower had a great influence on many people and in his quite but firm manner, he instilled confidence in the American people. He gave us the feeling of pride in being part of this great Nation.

His record as a military leader cannot be questioned and his ability to unify our allies into one smoothly run unit during the invasion of Europe will go down as one of the most superb military maneuvers in history. But even while he was noted as commander of the greatest expeditionary force ever to be assembled, General Eisenhower was respected as a peacemaker.

He was never one to believe in retribution, thus following World War II Europe was nurtured and rebuilt and once again joined in the brotherhood of free nations.

As a military man, he lent his efforts to ending the bloody conflict in Korea and from that time forward, no American boys were killed in battle while he served America as President.

He accepted his share of criticism while President, but I feel much of it was undeserved. A look at his record shows great accomplishment—for instance, the largest roadbuilding program in the history of any nation was inaugurated; he ended inflation; provided medical care for the aged; added two new States to the Union; created the Department of Health, Education, and Welfare; advocated and built the St. Lawrence Seaway; sought to balance the budget; initiated the American space program; conceived and advocated the need for strong ballistic missiles as a preventive to war; extended social security benefits to an additional 10 million Americans; and worked to contain the spread of communism and to generate good will among our allies.

Some say the Eisenhower years in the White House were boring, but it seems that it is nice to be bored to the extent that during those years there was no civil strife and no militant threats by certain groups to destroy life and property; and disrupt our colleges. There was peace with prosperity and the threat of communism was merely talk for we militarily strong.

Dwight D. Eisenhower is to me a great and compassionate man, and truly a great American and now we as fellow Americans can best show our respect for him by rededicating ourselves to accepting our responsibilities as Americans as he did.

To do this we must stop being afraid to fight for what is right for our country. We should be proud to get a lump in our throats when we hear the "Star-Spangled Banner" and look to our flag. We should recognize that appeasement is a step backward into the road of national destruction.

We should accept national pride in relationship to the true greatness of our Nation dedicated to the principles of the golden rule instead of the rule of gold. We should recognize that those who strive to divide us are the enemies of our Nation.

General Eisenhower was a brave American and a good soldier. He made mistakes because he was human, but no one can honestly doubt his dedication to his fellow Americans. It is men like General Eisenhower that gave our country the proud heritage and courage to become the strongest people and the greatest Nation on earth.

To dedicate ourselves to our country as General Eisenhower did will insure our greatness in history.

## Hon. Lester L. Wolff

OF NEW YORK

Mr. Speaker, our late beloved President Dwight David Eisenhower has left an indelible mark on our Nation. It is the mark of a proud American who provided outstanding leadership in war and in peace. President Eisenhower's mark is that of a soldier-statesman who saw his duty and then filled it in the highest standards of the United States and the free world.

There have been appropriate eulogies for President Eisenhower since his recent passing. Among those that I feel best captured the spirit, drive, and success of this great man were editorials on March 29 in Newsday and the Long Island Press.

In memory of President Eisenhower I include those editorials in the RECORD:

[From Newsday, Mar. 29, 1969]

DWIGHT D. EISENHOWER

Commander of the mightiest armada the world has ever known, he hated war. Twice elected to the White House by landslide votes, he detested partisan politics. A national and world hero, he never lost touch with the values he learned as a Kansas farm boy.

Dwight D. Eisenhower was an American original, his life a mirror of traditional virtues: honesty, hard work, religious faith, respect for authority, love of country, honor and devotion to duty. An Horatio Alger in uniform, he fulfilled the American promise that a boy from the humblest origins can grow up to be President of the United States.

Faith in America and in its democratic institutions was the central theme to which Ike was devoted. "I am proud to say," he once declared, "that I am a fanatical devotee of the American system of democracy. I believe that the two fundamentals of the American democracy are, first, a deep and abiding religious faith, and second, a system of freedoms and rights for the individual that we generally refer to loosely and roughly as 'free enterprise.' "

Although he had devoted his life to the military, Ike wished to be known as a "soldier of peace." "You help man the fortress for which freedom still finds need," he told the West Point Class of 1947. "But this service does not imply subscription to the rule of might. War is mankind's most tragic and stupid folly; to seek or advise its deliberate provocation is a black crime against all men. Though you follow the trade of the warrior, you do so in the spirit of Washington—not Ghengis Khan."

Dwight D. Eisenhower never lost faith in America, though his concern for the future of his country increased with each passing day. As he watched turmoil and disorder sweep the nation, be pleaded with his countrymen to heed the rule of law and to fight for the concept of an orderly society—lest society be destroyed.

In time, history will write its verdict on the eight Eisenhower years in the White House. Whether Ike was a weak President who failed to inspire the nation to attack the urgent domestic tasks at hand . . . or whether he was a strong President who, by holding together the western alliance, saved the world from a new holocaust . . . will be debated endlessly.

But whatever the findings of history, Americans of his generation have already made their own judgment about Dwight D. Eisenhower.

They said it loud and clear: We Like Ike.

---

[From the Long Island (N.Y.) Press, Mar. 29, 1969]

DWIGHT EISENHOWER, 1890–1969

In mourning Dwight David Eisenhower, the sorrow is eased by the fact that his 78 years of life mirrored a glowing picture of all that is best in American life.

His initial impact upon his countrymen was as a military leader, but his first achievement as President was as a man of peace, fulfilling his campaign promise to go to Korea to end the slaughter.

Born in Denison, Tex., he grew up in near-poverty in Abilene, his mother a pacifist who wept when her boy was appointed to West Point. Perhaps that is why he was a warrior who hated what he called "this damnable thing of war," and as a President he wielded power sparingly.

He was also a politician who told a news conference: "I think in the general derogatory sense you can say . . . that I do not like politics."

As a soldier he commanded the greatest military machine in the history of mankind and led it to victory over the most infamous enemy in memory.

A measure of this man was his popularity with the troops. Traditionally generals are fair game for the men in the ranks, but not General Ike. One of the reasons may have been his "enlisted man response" to the ingrained "chicken" of Army life.

For example, at the end of the war soldiers on leave flocked to Berchtesgaden, Hitler's Bavarian retreat. Only one elevator was available to take visitors to the top of the mountain fortress. The alternative was a long, winding climb up a path. The elevator bore a sign: "For Field Grade Officers Only." When Gen. Eisenhower saw it, he yanked the sign off and scaled it down the hillside. After that, field officers stood in line with privates to ride the elevator.

As President, he gave America no ringing slogans and made no glowing promises, but he was elected by majorities matched previously only by Franklin D. Roosevelt.

The same warmth that existed between Gen. Eisenhower and his troops carried over to civilian life. "I like Ike" was more fact than slogan, and his appeal was so magnetic that the Democrats sought him as a candidate before he identified himself as a Republican.

As he rode in an open car through Long Island—as in other parts of the nation—tens of thousands turned out to see the tanned, fit hero, and to smile back at his famous grin.

Under the Eisenhower Administration the Korean War was brought to an end, the hydrogen bomb was developed and America entered the space age.

It was President Eisenhower who appointed Earl Warren Chief Justice of the Supreme Court, and later sent federal troops to enforce the court's order to integrate the schools in Little Rock, Ark. He sent Marines into Lebanon at that country's request, but he avoided massive involvement in French Indo-China when Dien Bien Phu fell.

The cocktail party psychologists talked glibly of the "father image" when he was in the White House. And there may have been some truth in the trite phrases because he came at a time when America yearned for the comfort of a fatherly leader.

Although he was of the military, his outlook was never narrowly militaristic. The generals and admirals enjoyed no special influence over policy or budget decisions while he was President.

His military leadership made him aware of the parallel interests of the makers of arms, and military careerists. When he left the Presidency, he warned the nation to beware of an alliance between these parallel forces, and to guard against the danger of inertia in the defense establishment.

History may not rank him as our most brilliant general or our most extraordinary President, but history occasionally does not measure the quality of integrity or nobility in a man.

He was as popular when he left office as when he entered it, and there is little doubt he could have won a third term had he not been barred by the Constitution from running again.

The affection the nation felt for Ike did not diminish in the years afterward. He was always the elder statesman of the nation more than of his party.

His typically American optimism was deeply rooted in his firm faith in the strength of America. In his last public address—via television to the 1968 Republican convention in Miami—he said: "Let us first remind ourselves of the greatness of this nation and of its people. Let's not waste time this year searching out someone to blame, even though some seem more disposed to concede rather than to stand firmly for America."

A gentle man and a patriot has left us.

## Hon. Edward Hutchinson
### OF MICHIGAN

Mr. Speaker, the death of General Eisenhower, though not unexpected, was a shock to a great many people, among them the millions of veterans of the Second World War who served under his command. One in my congressional district, sharing his grief with me, wrote that he sort of identified Ike as another dad. In every veterans post throughout the land there are numbers of men, now in middle age, who in their youth fought in North Africa and in Europe, always proud of their service to our country and of the general who led them to victory. And after the war was over these millions of American veterans enthusiastically voted him twice President of the United States, finding him first in peace as he had been first in war.

Indicative of the genuine sense of personal loss felt by so many veterans is the following tribute from James Drumm, a member of Hice-Shutes Post No. 170, the American Legion, at Three Rivers, Mich. The tribute was published as a letter to the editor of the Three Rivers Commercial on March 29, 1969, the day following Ike's passing, as follows:

TRIBUTE

To the EDITOR:

Yesterday at work a friend who is also a veteran said to me, "Do you know that Ike is dead?" Twice more I heard practically the same words expressed and I thought, "What a ridiculous idea, Ike losing a battle."

My thoughts drifted back to the dark days at the start of World War II when each succeeding day brought only defeat and despair.

The leaders of the Allied Nations finally decided that we needed a Supreme Allied Commander to unite all of the troops of all of the nations. They picked the right man, Dwight D. Eisenhower. Very soon things started looking a little brighter. The tide of battle turned our way. It was a long, hard road back, paved with broken bodies and shattered equipment, ending eventually in final victory. To me Ike's leadership was decisive.

His quiet confidence, grim determination and superior judgment was an inspiration to all of the Allied Nations and the more you think of it, the more ridiculous it sounds. Ike lost a battle.

Not to me he didn't, rather he gained a final promotion. Now he is as high as he can go.

JIM DRUMM,
*Hice-Shutes Post No. 170, American Legion, Three Rivers, Mich.*

## Hon. James A. Burke
OF MASSACHUSETTS

Mr. Speaker, I would like to bring to the attention of my distinguished colleagues in the House of Representatives the following editorial which appeared in the Quincy Sun, Quincy, Mass., on Thursday, April 3, 1969, entitled "A Bell and a Prayer":

A Bell and a Prayer: Would That God Might Give Us Others To Take His Place

The bell tolled sadly and solemn words were spoken this week at Quincy's historic United First Parish Church in a farewell tribute to Dwight David Eisenhower.

The Rev. Stephen W. Brown, pastor of First United Presbyterian Church, Quincy, pinpointed the feelings of a mourning nation with these words:

"Dwight David Eisenhower is a symbol of that which is good, and right, and strong in our nation.

"Would that God might give us others to take his place."

His eulogy to the 34th President and General of the Army was given during an Ecumenical Memorial Service at the "Church of the Presidents" Monday noon.

And at 4 p.m. the big, 2,000-pound bell in the belfry tolled for five minutes as funeral services were being held in Washington, D.C.

The church's bell has thus been sounded in tribute at the death of every President since George Washington.

"Dwight Eisenhower," said the Rev. Brown "was a warrior whose chief aim was peace.

"Our time is a time of extremes when some are willing to have peace at any price, even the price of chains, and others are willing to have war at any price, even the price of annihilation.

"His words are to be remembered. He said, 'I hate war as only a soldier who has lived it can, only as one who has seen its brutality, its futility, its stupidity.'

"He also said, 'Today . . . we still must be wise and courageous enough to live fully, confident in the knowledge that we have taken every reasonable step to deter aggression, and that we shall always be ready to defend liberty . . .'

"His words need to be heard in our time."

The Rev. Brown's eulogy was listened to attentively by approximately 150 persons attending the service at the church that contains the remains of Quincy-born Presidents John and John Quincy Adams and their wives.

Other Quincy clergymen participating in the service were:

Rev. Bradford E. Gale, minister United First Parish Church; Rev. Demetrics Michaelides, St. Catherine's (Greek Orthodox) Church; Rabbi David J. Jacobs, Temple Beth El; Rt. Rev. Richard J. Hawko, pastor Sacred Heart Church; Rev. Dean E. Benedict, Quincy Centre Methodist Church.

Dwight David Eisenhower: His Passing Is More Than the Passing of a Man

(Text of the eulogy to former President Dwight D. Eisenhower given by the Rev. Stephen W. Brown, at the Ecumenical Memorial Service Monday in Quincy's historic First Parish Church)

We are gathered here this afternoon to remember one, Dwight David Eisenhower . . . Supreme Commander of the Allied Forces in Europe during World War II and the 34th President of the United States.

His death on Friday last leaves our land a sadder place. And yet, because Dwight Eisenhower was full of years, because he was covered with honors and praise, because his efforts, perhaps more than any other man of our time, bore much fruit and because death is the inevitable precondition of life . . . the passing of Dwight Eisenhower does not have the overtones of tragedy that would be quite evident in the death of one not so successful, not so full of years and not so highly esteemed.

It is for that reason that the passing of Dwight Eisenhower should inspire in us not only sadness and hurt, but even more, a feeling of somber thoughtfulness, for his passing is more than the passing of a man . . . it is the death of an era in which giants walked the land, the passing of a period in history when men seemed taller and heroes were easier to come by, the passing of a quality of life that we have somehow lost.

Dwight Eisenhower was a warrior whose chief aim was peace. Our time is a time of extremes when some are willing to have peace at any price, even the price of chains, and others are willing to have war at any price, even the price of annihilation.

His words are to be remembered. He said, "I hate war as only a soldier who have lived it can, only as one who has seen its brutality, its futility, its stupidity . . ." He also said, "Today . . . we still must be wise and courageous enough to live fully, confident in the knowledge that we have taken every reasonable step to deter aggression, and that we shall always be ready to defend liberty." His words need to be heard in our time.

Dwight Eisenhower was a politician whose aim was statesmanship. He was a man who invested in the word "politics" its rightful qualities of honesty, integrity and service. In a time when there are those who would place self-interest above national interest, who would sell their souls for a vote, who would rather have position than honor, his life would guide us.

Called to serve his country as President, he found the business of politics distasteful and at the same time to give that business the depth and quality that a nation governed by political forces must have if it is to survive. He prayed in his first inaugural address, "Give us, we pray, the power to discern clearly right from wrong and allow all our words and actions to be governed thereby . . . May cooperation be permitted and be the mutual aim of those who under the concepts of our Constitution, hold to differing political faiths, so that all may work for the good of our beloved country and Thy glory."

Dwight Eisenhower was a citizen whose aim was to

serve his country best by the life that he lived. There was in him a quiet simplicity that seems alien in an age of sophistication and cynicism. He loved his God; he loved his family; he loved his country . . . sentiments, if expressed by a lesser man, would bring on the snide, knowing smiles of a generation that has outgrown that kind of naivete.

However, those were the sentiments with which he worked as he forged together a group of nations and articulated those nations' goals. Those were the sentiments with which he worked as he led his own country in a time of crisis. Had Dwight Eisenhower been only an unknown private citizen who operated the general store in Abilene, Kansas, I doubt that the qualities that he personified as a Supreme Commander, a university president and President of the United States . . . I doubt that those qualities would have been different.

Let us once again listen to his words: "As friends of free people everywhere in the world, we can by our own example . . . our conduct in every crisis, real or counterfeit; our resistance to propaganda and passion; our readiness to seek adjustment and compromise of difference . . . we can by our own example ceaselessly expand understanding among the nations."

We must never forget that international friendship is achieved through rumors ignored, propaganda challenged and exposed; through patient loyalty to those who have proved themselves worthy of it; through help freely given where help is needed and merited. In this sense there is no great, no humble among us. In rights and in opportunity, in loyalty and in responsibility to ideals, we are and must remain equal. Peace is more the product of our day-to-day living than of a spectacular program, intermittently executed.

The best foreign policy is to live our daily lives in honesty, decency, and integrity; at home, making our own land a more fitting habitation for free men; and abroad, joining with those of like mind and heart, to make of the world a place where all men can dwell in peace. Neither palsied by fear nor duped by dreams but strong in the rightness of purpose, we can then pace our case and cause before the bar of world opinion . . . history's final arbiter between nations, Dwight David Eisenhower is a symbol of that which is good, and right, and strong in our nation. Would that God might give us others to take his place. Amen.

## Hon. Richard L. Roudebush
OF INDIANA

Mr. Speaker, many fine eulogies to President Eisenhower have appeared, but one of the best I have read appeared in the Indianapolis News, the largest afternoon daily newspaper in Indiana.

Mr. Fremont Power is the author of the eulogy which emphasizes the human qualities that President Eisenhower possessed to such a great degree.

Fremont Power has long been recognized as a writer and columnist of exceptional talent, and his column about President Eisenhower is typical of his ability to get to the heart of a situation and interpret the importance of an event.

The article from the April 7, 1969, edition of the Indianapolis News follows:

### Ike Tributes Renew Flood of Loyalties

(By Fremont Power)

Dwight D. Eisenhower is dead and properly eulogized and, with simple dignity, interred in Abilene, Kan., whence he sprang.

The Eisenhower era in American history is thus closed.

But some thoughts of last week remain and they don't go away.

The man, even in death, seemed still to be speaking to America, for whom he gave so much. And the essence of the message was that the old verities remain and that more millions of Americans adhere to them than may ever be counted.

It is easy, particularly in this business that deals with the unusual rather than the ordinary, to acquire, unconsciously, an impression that this whole country is caught up in quarreling, bitterness, legal pornography, defiance of authority and a predilection for anarchy.

#### NOT SO SELF-SUFFICIENT AFTER ALL

It just isn't so. The way the nation responded to the old soldier's passing made this very plain once again.

Godless as we may seem to be, how many millions of breaths must have been caught as the old hymns came pouring forth from the organ of the Washington National Cathedral, played, incidentally, by Indianapolis-born John R. Fenstermaker Jr. These simple expressions of faith stir old memories, old loyalties, old ideas of rightness.

Not all feel as self-sufficient as they might pretend.

As pictures of these solemn ceremonies came flooding over the news wires and the television screens, there was one recurring, refreshing feature: The young faces, looking on in seeming awe.

#### NO OCCASION FOR NEW OUTBURST

When Eisenhower died, a grisly thought crossed the mind: What if the rebellious misanthropes took even this said opportunity to insult and shock those who feel there are still some things worth saving in this country?

Considering some of the other outbursts, it didn't seem beyond possibility. But it didn't happen. Instead, there were these young faces, looking on as respects were paid one whom they could only have known as an old man long passed from the stage of public affairs.

Even they seemed to reflect some of the love that America held out to this man.

As the funeral train went west, there was this picture of a girl at Washington, Ind., holding up a penny flattened by the wheels that carried Eisenhower home. More memories came springing up, of small towns in another day where, if there was nothing else to do, there was always the putting of things on the railroad tracks to be flattened: Nails, pennies, a washer.

SOLDIERING NOT WHOLLY DAMNED

Now this girl has a proper souvenir which surely she will want to show her children some day and tell them how it was when the train went through bearing a man they could know only from their schoolbooks.

Perhaps if she conveys to those children that he meant something to her, he will mean something to them.

Eisenhower showed us in death that we are still capable of gratefulness to one who gave so much, that soldiering is not universally damned, that there are principles worthy of cruel sacrifices, that simple religious faith has not been completely computerized from the American psyche.

These old verities are still cherished by the masses of Americans.

As in any other death, we must return now to today's battles and not dwell overlong on yesterday's sorrow. But it has been good to have this pause, to see that decadence has not become a way of life for so many.

## Hon. Charles W. Whalen, Jr.

OF OHIO

Mr. Speaker, I would like to take this occasion to pay tribute to the memory of our 34th President.

Dwight David Eisenhower was a great public servant who had the respect and admiration of the American people perhaps more consistently than any other American Chief Executive.

He first captured these feelings as the planner and leader of the invasion of Europe and held them for the rest of his life.

His personal popularity was immense after D-day and, once established, never really declined. It remained strong enough for him to run for President successfully some 8 years later.

Ike was an honest and uncomplicated man. And these qualities enabled him to achieve his many successes both in war and in peace.

His direction of the European invasion is cited as the best example of his uncanny ability to influence people to follow his leadership. That war effort involved men of many nationalities, including some with major reputations.

They were placed under the command of a junior American general who was not even well known in his own Army.

Despite this, the enormously dangerous and complicated operation of retaking Europe from the Nazis came off and exceedingly well.

As President, Ike did not accomplish everything he advocated. No President ever does.

But his 8 years in office were a reflection of the man himself. His tenure was characterized by a general tranquillity, a period of consolidation.

The 1950's, it turns out, really represented a period of transition. We were still recovering from the aftereffects of World War II when we were plunged into the Korean war. Thus, the stability we desired right after the Second World War was delayed until the Korean conflict could be resolved.

Ike presided over that transition. Toward the end of his term of office, the first signs of the turbulence that was to mark the sixties appeared.

Although a general and a war hero, Ike was a man devoted to peace. It was he who issued the warning about the military-industrial complex just before leaving office, words that have equal validity today.

It also was Ike who cut back military expenditures to the bone after ending the Korean war.

As many were moved to comment during the 5 days of mourning for this great man, his death may mark the passing of another era in our history.

Ike was the storybook hero come true. The product of small-town America, he became part and parcel of the international America. And he did it all on his own, the very model of the traditional American virtues of hard work and self-reliance.

So now he is gone after a hard year-long fight against a weakening heart. He confounded the medical profession by surviving as long as he did. Of course, he had excellent medical care. But it would have meant little without Ike's tremendous will to live.

He was a great American who spent virtually his entire adult life in the service of the Nation.

It is a monument—

The Cincinnati Enquirer editorialized—

that when death came to him, it found his stature undiminished in the eyes of his countrymen.

## Hon. Ed Foreman
OF NEW MEXICO

Mr. Speaker, Sarah McClendon, Washington News correspondent for the El Paso Times and other leading newspapers, has written a column about a great American, the late Gen. Dwight David Eisenhower. I especially appreciated this review by Sarah McClendon of the Eisenhower years.

Mr. Speaker, under unanimous consent I include this article from the April 5, 1969, edition of the El Paso Times in the Record:

A West Texan in Washington

(By Sarah McClendon)

Washington.—If any man ever could, Dwight D. Eisenhower probably could have become dictator of the U.S. The people were at times that close to adoration of the man. But he did not seize or use power in that manner. He was never a dictator at heart.

He wanted to be doing the right thing for his country and his government at all times, so much so, that when a mistake was made, he just could not understand it. And when there was any implied criticism, he just blew his top. It was not that he thought no one should criticize him. It was just that he was trying so hard to do his best, he could not see why others did not acknowledge at all times that his motives were high.

President Eisenhower actually did not forget the grass roots. It was probably this reason why he gave to the American people a great gift, a new institution in this country—the presidential press conference as it is today. Now the questions and answers of the President of the U.S., on the record is probably the most watched show on earth. Even the poorest minority groups and the most backward nations are now watching it. The nation had never had a presidential press conference like this before. President Truman for the first time let reporters sit down in a special room and thus make it possible for them to write. But once reporters were slow with their questions, Truman cut off a press conference in six minutes. Ike gave reporters a full 30 minutes of writing on their laps and let the conference be televised.

Early in the game, he was advised by some high-level officials not to accept questions from a certain busy-body woman reporter who might ask sharp questions. She was from the smaller papers and thus was not important anyway. A member of the President's staff spoke up and said, "She will always ask questions from the grass roots and it is important that a President know what the grass roots are thinking." Ike thought that was good advice apparently. James Haggerty, his press secretary, said "Therefore, we will always take your questions." The President did so.

Other people, however, adored Mr. Eisenhower so much that they had no brief for any persons who might imply criticism of his administration. Feeling was so high on his side that most newspapers in the country were strong for him and many people wanted to ostracize any one who criticized him. One woman wanted to drop any member of a club who raised any question of his actions publicly.

The President wanted so hard to give the best type of reorganization to the military machine that he was particularly sensitive to any doubts about his action in that regard. He felt hurt to the core when someone asked if he were building a one-man military rule. Being perfectionist, he was put out when someone suggested a slip in getting copies of his speeches and messages to the members of Congress.

But one thing about him, when this was called to his attention, he immediately saw to it that the situation was corrected. Even today, members of Congress get copies of messages to read by the time they are presented to Congress.

President Eisenhower did not seize the opportunity which reporters gave him to use White House leadership to avert trouble between races in the civil rights field. He was strong about desegregation of schools at Little Rock. But when reporters made suggestions that he later try to avoid schism in the country by appealing to the citizens through ideological or educational methods, he stood apart.

Ike was a man who was ever trying not only to do his best, but to do better. He studied. He made numerous contributions. He was able to smooth over issues of division between sections, like on tidelands, natural gas rate structure, civil rights to some extent. He was once asked if he favored large dams downstream or small dams upstream where rain fell. At the time this was a big issue before the country, internally, but a new one for the less background White House press corps. A year later, Ike recommended to the press a book he said he had been reading, called "Big Dam Foolishness." He had learned.

He understood that reporters were trying to get news for their papers when they asked him questions. On two occasions, he demonstrated this. Once this writer asked him a question about public works, an urgent matter at the moment to many communities, and implied that perhaps too much time was being taken up with his golf to give to public works considerations. Feeling deeply later in the day that this implied he should not be playing golf for his health, she sent him a letter of apology, pointing out she was glad he played golf for relaxation and had slipped, in her zeal for getting out information to readers, on the issue. He replied immediately with a beautiful personal letter (which this writer keeps in her lock box at the bank for grandchildren to cherish) thanking her for the apology and acknowledging he knew of her interest in development of waterways resources.

The thing I like best about Ike was the time he responded so quickly and willingly to a question about why could not the nation match up hungry people in Appalachia who had had nothing but carbohydrates and fats in their diet, from surplus commodities for months with a surplus of green vegetables, in this instance, cabbages which could not be marketed, in South Texas. The growers were going to plow them under. The people in Kentucky needed green in their diet. The President rose to the occasion at once and said he would do everything he could. He did, too, and although several government agencies wrestled with bureaucracy to overcome barriers and the railroads were stopped in their efforts by their own red tape, Ike's responsive leadership enabled national volunteer organizations to accomplish the mission.

This simple man was truly a leader because he never forgot simple people.

## Hon. Albert W. Watson
OF SOUTH CAROLINA

Mr. Speaker, in a very stirring tribute to the late Dwight D. Eisenhower, Mr. Thurman Sensing, of the Southern States Industrial Council, has written an article which should be read by all Americans. For that reason, I commend it to the attention of the Congress and the Nation as follows:

### A Man Who Believed in America

For millions of Americans the passing of Dwight D. Eisenhower, 34th President of the United States and commander of the allied armies in Europe, provided a solemn occasion for recalling the vital qualities of leadership in this Republic.

Gen. Eisenhower was a product of the American experience and embodied patriotic virtues which are essential to this country if it is to endure. At a time when there is disorder in the land and not inconsiderable disloyalty to its values, as evidenced among the militants of the New Left, it is timely to bear in mind what is basic to greatness and to the survival of the American system.

Nowadays, militants angrily denounce "The System," and call for its overthrow or radical alteration. The militants have their camp followers in politics who try to sell the idea that the United States is riddled with imperfections and in need of radical reconstruction. Some officeholders, sad to say, believe that it is smart to adopt the New Left's slogans about this being a land of hunger and hardship.

Dwight Eisenhower was a product of the American System, and his success in life demonstrates how effective and worthwhile that system is. He was born into a family of modest means. His father was a worker in a creamery in Abilene. Today, "liberals" no doubt would describe his family as "deprived" or "disadvantaged." But the Eisenhower family didn't see itself that way. Members of the family worked hard; they had faith in America. Not only the future President but his brothers did well in careers, achieving substantial success. The story of the Eisenhower family is the story of countless other American families of modest means who believed in the virtues of work, thrift, and loyalty to God and country.

The man who later in life was to command the largest force of free men ever committed to battle was a man brought up to believe in self-reliance. He didn't have the comforts and pleasures of other young men from more affluent circumstances, but he didn't complain. He relied on his own abilities and energies. He didn't expect an OEO or any other agency to provide him with instant prosperity.

For the young Eisenhower, service to country was a wonderful opportunity, not something to be avoided by taking refuge in graduate school. Throughout his life, he adhered to West Point's injunction to follow the path of duty, honor and courage. These concepts are a million light years away from what the New Left intelligentsia teaches today. Instead of stressing duty, the "liberal" intellectuals urge young men to avoid national service. Honor is scorned by the Left intelligentsia as an outmoded concept. Instead, they urge the young to seek peace at any price, to believe that it's better to be "Red than dead." Finally, courage in defense of one's country is dismissed by radicals as a shopworn concept. They speak of the virtue of anarchy.

In the eight years that Dwight D. Eisenhower was President, he displayed none of the arrogance of power characteristic of some of his predecessors and successors. Though his administration disappointed some conservatives who hoped for a thorough housecleaning of entrenched radical elements in the federal government, President Eisenhower was not afraid to show his belief in free enterprise. He brought businessmen into the Cabinet. As a result, America's affluence gained greatly in the 1950's. Home ownership grew enormously during the Eisenhower years. American society was strengthened and stabilized.

Like other outstanding men, Gen. Eisenhower made mistakes in his appointments and his policies, but he acknowledged mistakes. He was extremely reluctant to give moral approval to court-ordered experiments with public education. It has been written that he felt he erred greatly in using troops at Little Rock in 1956.

In the main, however, Gen. Eisenhower was in the central current of American thinking. He understood the strength of the American "system," and upheld it as a model of opportunity and enlightenment. He had no use for the strident doctrines of social revolution. He rejected the demagoguery and truth-twisting that is involved in describing America as a land of hunger and poverty. His confidence in the United States and its essential goodness and greatness should be remembered for years to come.

## Hon. Robert McClory
OF ILLINOIS

Mr. Speaker, tributes to the late Gen. Dwight D. Eisenhower will continue to be paid for a long time—as the impact of his passing penetrates our consciousness. Each day brings to our attention a new and expressive acknowledgment of the integrity of this great leader. Only today I noted a guest editorial in the Lake Forester-Lake Bluff Review, a weekly publication circulated widely in the 12th Illinois Congressional District. This editorial is from the pen of the Honorable James H. Douglas, a resident of Lake Forest, who served as Secretary of the Air Force and Deputy Secretary of Defense under President Eisenhower. I offer it to my colleagues for their respectful consideration:

A TRIBUTE TO PRESIDENT EISENHOWER

(By James H. Douglas, Secretary of the Air Force and Deputy Secretary of Defense under President Eisenhower)

It is an honor to join with you in expressing our respect and affection for President Eisenhower, our gratitude for his leadership, and our sense of loss in his death. He was a warm and friendly man, whose life was simple in its complete dedication to the service of his country. He had a quality of straightforward integrity which gave confidence to all those who served under him and knew him. GIs knew he was interested in them as individuals, and commanders and staff officers had unflagging trust in his judgment. Difficult problems of disagreement at high levels of authority were sometimes solved—as I have seen—by his asking a single question and quietly stating his decision.

Sometimes in a press conference President Eisenhower would produce a perplexing non sentence, which seemed to please his critics, but his sincerity and persistence in expressing his purpose left no doubt as to his position.

As a nation we were fortunate when General George Marshall selected the Chief of the War Plans Division of the War Department, Major General Eisenhower, to command United States forces in the European theatre. The war had gone badly for England, France and Russia, and few soldiers ever faced and mastered more complicated problems of command. I remember a tribute to Marshall of the Royal Air Force Lord Tedder, Deputy Supreme Commander, who wrote "There was little cheerful about the last stages of the war except the wonderful spirit which existed throughout the allied team, and for which we should be eternally grateful to General Eisenhower."

When he became President in 1953 his first concern was to bring the Korean War to a close. This goal was achieved six months after his inauguration.

His command of great military forces, his understanding of war, and what nuclear war could be, led him to declare that there is no alternative to peace.

I think he would like to have us remember that when he made his "Atoms for Peace" proposal to the United Nations General Assembly, he was seeking the cooperation of the Soviet Union in peaceful uses of atomic energy, and to begin to turn nuclear science from destructive to peaceful purposes.

In his account of the White House years he says that underlying his atoms for peace effort was "the clear conviction that the world was courting disaster in the armaments race, and that something must be done to put on a brake."

Then at Geneva in 1955 President Eisenhower proposed the plan which was called "Open Skies"—for international arms control—under which nations would deliver to each other maps and descriptions of all military installations and permit inspection by air reconnaissance by crews including representatives of the country inspected.

And he would want us also to keep in mind problems inherent in what he called "the conjunction of an immense military establishment and a large arms industry"—something new in American experience. He expressed concern "that our scholars not be dominated by federal employment, project allocations and the power of money," and also that "public policy should not become the captive of a scientific-technological elite."

General Eisenhower was always concerned with protecting and building the dignity of the individual, regardless of race or creed, in the armed services and in all of American life. He left us a great example. He greatly loved his country, and there is undying mutual respect and trust between him and his countrymen. We shall miss him.

## Hon. Richard L. Roudebush

OF INDIANA

Mr. Speaker, many excellent newspaper stories have been written about Gen. Dwight D. Eisenhower and more will be written.

I would like to share one of these stories with my colleagues. This was written by the fine Washington correspondent for the Indianapolis Star, Ben Cole.

Cole recommends that a town be named for Eisenhower but he warns that this town will have to live up to its name.

The article follows:

TOWN OF EISENHOWER WOULD HAVE CHALLENGE

(By Ben Cole)

WASHINGTON.—It would be a nice thing if somewhere in America there could be a town called Eisenhower.

It would be a far better tribute to the late soldier-President than any other.

Eisenhower, USA, shouldn't be a big, crowded city but a homey town with church spires sticking up through the hardwood trees and a good basketball team the whole town roots for.

Of course, most of the towns in America already have names—and they're proud of them and want to keep them.

When the country was expanding westward and new towns were springing up like mushrooms, finding names for them all was a challenge if not a chore.

Many took their names from some strong men who founded them—hence places like Logansport, Sullivan, Crawfordsville, etc. Some got made-up names like Indianapolis or Minneapolis. A few looked to a classical age—Athens, Ithaca, Syracuse, Cairo, Rome, Carthage.

Others took their names from geographical features—South Bend, Crown Point, Riverside. And the music of foreign language remained to describe the features of many—Terre Haute, Buena Vista, Monticello, Champagne.

Many new towns took the names of Presidents out of pride in the new country and the infant government—Washington, every state has one), Adams, Jeffersonville, Madison, Monroe, Van Buren, Jackson, Harrisonburg, Tyler, Polk, Filmore, Lincoln. . . ."

In recent years there have not been many new towns—only a few real estate developments that get named after motivational psychology—Pine Manor, Heather Hills, Cloistered Woods, Colonial Shores, etc.

But if somewhere in America there is a neat and pretty town with an ordinary name that would like to make of itself, a living memorial to a beloved soldier and statesman—then it ought to change its name and become Eisenhower. And then live up to it.

## Hon. John Brademas
### OF INDIANA

Mr. Speaker, I wish to include in the Record at this point the text of an article which I wrote for the local newspapers of the Third Congressional District of Indiana:

### Congressional Corner: John Brademas Reports From Washington

Few Americans have been so genuinely respected and loved not only by their fellow countrymen, but by people all over the world as Dwight D. Eisenhower.

Destiny chose Dwight Eisenhower to play a leading role in the drama of Twentieth Century history both as Supreme Commander of Allied Forces in World War II and as President of the United States for eight years. He was always equal to the challenge.

Dwight Eisenhower was a warm and generous human being. To millions of Americans he was also a symbol of the basic strengths and virtues of the American character.

President Eisenhower once said, "I come from the heart of America."

He did, and America took him to its heart.

As we mourn General Eisenhower's passing, let our tribute to his memory be a heightened resolve to continue the quest for peace which dominated his extraordinary career.

As one of the greatest military leaders in history, General Eisenhower was all too familiar with the horrors of war. His experiences made him a passionate advocate of peace. Yet at his final news conference, when asked to indicate what he regarded as the greatest disappointment of his eight years in office, he answered in this way: "The big disappointment I felt is one not of mere incident, it was the fact that we could not in these eight years get to the place where we could say it now looks as if permanent peace with justice is really in sight."

The Eisenhower years were years of cold war, of armed peace. And no one was better situated than the President who was also a general to measure the effects upon the institutions of American democracy of a development which was totally new to American life—the growth of an enormous standing military establishment in a time of peace.

In his famous Farewell Address to the American people on January 17, 1961, President Eisenhower spoke at some length about what he termed the "conjunction of an immense military establishment and a large arms industry."

He solemnly warned that "we must not fail to comprehend its grave implications." Here is President Eisenhower's parting advice to the American people:

"In the councils of government, we must guard against the acquisition of unwarranted influence, whether sought or unsought, by the military-industrial complex. The potential for the disastrous rise of misplaced power exists and will persist.

"We must never let the weight of this combination endanger our liberties or democratic processes. We should take nothing for granted. Only an alert and knowledgeable citizenry can compel the proper meshing of the huge industrial and military machinery of defense with our peaceful methods and goals, so that security and liberty may prosper together."

President Eisenhower's statement seems today, eight years later, to have been truly prophetic, or we are only beginning to realize the truth of his words. For example, the American people are now being asked to shoulder the burden of an expensive antiballistic missile system which an extraordinary number of scientists and other experts have criticized as useless or even dangerous; which they warn would increase our security only minimally, if at all; and which nearly everyone agrees will divert funds from vital programs in our own country.

Moreover, this controversy arises at a time when we are learning that the Army has spent $1 billion on the development of a tank for which there is no ammunition; that the costs of developing a new Air Force transport have exceeded original estimates by $2 billion; and that contracts awarded by the Department of Defense are effectively exempted from the normal auditing processes of the government.

Could such developments as these be examples of the "disastrous rise of misplaced power" of which President Eisenhower warned us?

Surely all of us want a military defense powerful enough to assure the security of the United States against potential enemies—and so did President Eisenhower.

But surely we must also all take to heart President Eisenhower's admonition to be concerned lest what he described as "the military industrial complex" acquire such "unwarranted influence" as to "endanger our liberties or democratic processes."

President Eisenhower's plea for "an alert and knowledgeable citizenry" that will "take nothing for granted" may come to be regarded in decades ahead as the most significant legacy of wisdom this great man has left us.

## Hon. Martin B. McKneally

OF NEW YORK

Mr. Speaker, when I learned of the Army's decision to have chaplains refrain from making any reference to God during its moral guidance lectures, I voiced my shocked disbelief. I asked what kind of moral guidance can there be without a Supreme Being.

I simply cannot fathom the motive, purpose, or objective of the American Civil Liberties Union in pressuring the U.S. Army into such a decision. Certainly it stretches the doctrine of separation of church and state beyond rational limits.

If, in conducting these moral guidance lectures, it is the desire of the Army to make good soldiers out of these young men, I commend to the gentlemen who are reconsidering this policy, and to my colleagues, the philosophy of one of the greatest soldiers ever to wear the uniform of the U.S. Army, Gen. Dwight D. Eisenhower.

General Eisenhower prepared the article which follows before his death and it appeared in the Washington, D.C., Sunday Star on April 6, 1969:

### A Soldier Recalls "Why I Believe"

(By Dwight D. Eisenhower)

Of the many instances when faith and Christian prayer have sustained me in life, the first came when I was a teenager and marked a turning point in my life. I had fallen, skinned my left knee and, when a painful infection later became so bad I couldn't do my farm chores, my parents discovered my swollen and discolored leg. Old Dr. Conklin, the family physician, took one look at the poisoned limb and immediately advised amputation to save any part of the leg or even my life.

When the horror of this prospect swept over me, I raised my 14-year-old frame from the bed to shout, "Not me! I won't allow it! I'd rather die!" Later I made my older brother Edgar promise not to let the doctor cut off my leg no matter what happened and he literally stood guard duty outside my bedroom. At the same time my parents, probably recalling my River Brethren grandfather and his belief in miracles, began a prayer vigil at my bedside. First, father and mother prayed, taking turns in leading one another; during the second night, Edgar—and finally my other four brothers—would kneel from time to time and join the prayers.

The next morning Dr. Conklin's experienced eye noted that the swelling was going down and the discoloration fading. Later in the day I was able to sleep soundly. In two weeks I was out of bed and able to walk. To me, this demonstration of the power of prayer did more than save my leg; it strengthened my faith for life.

Often during World War II, I turned to God when I had no one else to turn to. Two such crises involved our paratroopers. One night during the invasion of Sicily an armada of American aircraft was reported off course and there was an imminent danger that thousands of our sky troops would be dropped into the sea. I remember praying, "Save them and deliver them, O God. For they are in Thy Almighty Hand." Incredibly enough, the lead plane later regained its bearings and the drop was successful.

Similarly, on the eve of the massive D-Day assault on Europe, the soul-wracking problem arose as to whether to send two American airborne divisions against the Nazi-fortified Cherbourg Peninsula. British Air Chief Leigh-Mallory himself advised against what he termed "this futile slaughter," and yet to cancel the airborne attack would endanger the whole critical invasion of Utah Beach. I could only go to my tent to think and pray, to review every step of our elaborate planning and to ask God's guidance in making the right decision. I finally decided that the aerial attack would go as planned and, with what seemed to be the Almighty's Blessing, the paratroopers accomplished their dangerous mission with comparatively light casualties.

When in peacetime it became my high honor to serve the nation twice as President, I tried to ensure that the government and every person in it was dedicated to honesty and moral principles. To a large extent, I believe, we succeeded. Personally I tried to set the new administration's tone before delivering my inaugural address when I asked all present to bow their heads and I offered a prayer I had written that morning: "Give us, we pray, O God, the power to discern clearly right from wrong and allow all our actions to be governed thereby and by the laws of the land. Especially we pray that our concern shall be for all the people regardless of station, race or calling." During the ensuing eight years I never opened a cabinet meeting or made a major policy decision without a minute of silent prayer.

A lifetime of soldiering and public service only confirms my conviction that I am as intensely religious as any man I know. Nobody goes through six years of war and two terms of the presidency without faith. And, although I have seldom displayed or discussed my religious philosophy with anyone, a deep Bible-centered Christian faith has colored by life since childhood. Devout Evangelical parents, who loved the Bible as dearly as life itself, made sure of that. Indeed, before I was 18, I had read through the entire Bible and discussed it, chapter by chapter, with my mother.

Recalling the long years and the cascade of crisis through which we have passed, I realize that a strong spiritual experience has literally been the staff of life to me. Back in Abilene, Kans., my mother, who was never happier than when reading the Bible, and my father, who balanced his career as a mechanical engineer with the study of scriptures in the original Greek, stressed one truth over and over again: Religion, placed in man by God, is most natural to him. How often, both in war and peace, was I to rediscover this changeless truth.

With equal fervor I believe that faith in God and the Judaic-Christian ethic inspired the founding fathers of the United States. These remarkable men—Washington, Jefferson, Madison, Hamilton, Franklin, Paine, John Adams, John Hancock, and Patrick Henry, to name a few of them—were men of deep religious conviction and in the new world they were trying to establish an entirely new form of government. They succeeded because during the fateful decade of deliberation and decision, the 1770's, they put their final trust in Almighty God and his moral law. We are a religious nation today because in the Declaration of Independence they stated their full reliance on "the laws of nature and nature's God" and because they published before the world "these self-evident truths: that all men are created equal; that they are endowed by their creator with certain inalienable rights; that among these are life, liberty and the pursuit of happiness. . . ."

In contrast with this concept of the sacredness of life, modern atheistic dictatorships treat men as nothing more than animals or educated mules. How many materialistic psychologists and smart-alec professors sneer that men invented God in a childish search for security; yet, I have noticed that these same men in the fox-holes or at the moment of death turn to some higher power for comfort and courage. Thus, it is that I believe there is nothing wrong with America today that the faith, love of freedom, intelligence and energy of her citizens cannot cure.

Thus, in hope and eternal vigilance, I recall again for America my favorite biblical lines: "Except the Lord build the house, they labor in vain that build it; except the Lord keep the city, the watchman waketh but in vain."

## Hon. Joe L. Evins
### OF TENNESSEE

Mr. Speaker, a great void has been left in the American scene with the passing of Dwight David Eisenhower, President, General of the Army, and citizen.

General Eisenhower's presence and his counsel were reassuring to the Nation even after his years of public service. He was regarded by millions as an anchor to the bedrock traditions and principles of our great Nation.

In memory of his passing, I herewith place in the RECORD my recent newsletter, Capitol Comments, because of the interest of my colleagues and the American people in this great American.

The newsletter follows:

DWIGHT DAVID EISENHOWER, PRESIDENT AND GENERAL: A TRUE PATRIOT, A GREAT HERO, A NATURAL LEADER

(Capitol Comments by JOE L. EVINS, Member of Congress, Fourth District, Tennessee, Apr. 7, 1969)

Volumes of eloquent eulogies have been given in our country and throughout the world in tribute to the memory of the late Dwight David Eisenhower, President, and General of the Army.

My personal eulogy must include my vivid recollection of meeting General Eisenhower in southern France during World War II. He, at that time, was Supreme Commander of the Allied Forces in Europe, and I was a major serving under his command. General Eisenhower was warm, friendly, with a magnetic personality and the famous, engaging smile that became his trademark. He projected sincerity and interest as we met.

Later when he was "in command" as President and I was serving in Congress we met on a number of occasions, including several special, memorable occasions at the White House. He was always the same warm, genial person—a natural leader of men.

President Eisenhower's life was filled with a record of magnificent achievements. He was the first American General to head an army that included troops from many nations, and he was masterful in pulling together these troops into a powerful instrument for freedom. As a military leader, he led our Nation to victory into a time of peace, ending the Korean conflict and establishing a period of tranquillity. His Administration was a period of calm, quieting the fears and frustrations of our people.

One of his outstanding domestic achievements was the inaugural of the great interstate highway program which is continuing under construction. This great system of limited access highways is comparable to the autobahn highway system in Europe and has expedited safer travel throughout much of our Nation.

President Eisenhower enjoyed the confidence of the people. He was loved by the people—and he loved the people. He had a special sense of the greatness of America and its traditions, and he believed fervently in the vital importance of preserving, promoting and perpetuating our cherished American way of life. The fact that both political parties sought him as the Presidential nominee attests and testifies to his greatness as a natural leader.

We do not yet have the full historical perspective on the Administration of President Eisenhower—time will tell this story. However, we know that the American people felt comfortable and safe with President Eisenhower in the White House. Dwight David Eisenhower will be missed—a friend of the people has gone.

## Hon. Henry C. Schadeberg
### OF WISCONSIN

Mr. Speaker, I wish to call to the attention of the House a review of a new book, "The Real Eisenhower," by Frank L. Kluckhohn. The review appeared in the Philadelphia Bulletin of April 10.

Incidentally, Mr. Speaker, I was astounded recently to read in a nationally syndicated column that the same Frank Kluckhohn was maligned without cause and by innuendo was accused of being a neo-Nazi. The charge, of course, is utterly ridiculous and without foundation. I have known Frank Kluckhohn since the days we found ourselves under attack on the cruiser *Louisville* during World War II, I as chaplain and he as war correspondent for the New York Times. As I recall those day, I remember that Frank received a high commendation from the ship's captain, Captain Hicks, as he left the *Louisville*.

The attack against Frank seemed to be directed against a new association he has formed along with such distinguished writers and reporters as Walter Trohan and Edgar Ansell Mowrer. The new group calls for the formation of a press ethics committee which I am certain we would all agree is an excellent idea.

Having received permission, the book review follows:

PERCEPTIVE STUDY OF EISENHOWER

(By Saul Kohler)

WASHINGTON, April 9.—Two weeks before General Eisenhower's death, Frank L. Kluckhohn and Donald Ackerman put the finishing touches on a biography of the former President, and the product was stored in a warehouse to await the inevitable.

As a consequence, even as the funeral was taking place, booksellers across the country were stocking their shelves with "The Real Eisenhower," a readable and highly informative little work which sums up the general-statesman-politician-educator in one sentence: "Ike was a very human guy."

Too often, when a national hero dies (or even while he still lives), his biographers attempt to give the impression he could walk on water. On the other hand, there often is an attempt to be hypercritical in an effort to push the sale of books by injecting controversy where it doesn't exist and magnifying it where it does.

This is not the case here. As Kluckhohn, a long-time Washington correspondent for the New York Times and an even longer-time observer and participant in national politics, points out, one pays for leadership with the loss of friends.

So it was with Dwight David Eisenhower, who sometimes has been called a mediocre officer, an ineffective politician and a do-nothing President who avoided making decisions.

The biography notes that as general and as President Eisenhower did what he thought was right, even though on several occasions he tried to protect the men he liked.

Kluckhohn himself was suspended for 10 days as a war correspondent by the supreme commander after writing something which Ike didn't like, yet the author displays an admiration for the man who came from the heart of America eventually to control its entire nervous system—and that of the free world.

When he left office, General Eisenhower was the most admired, and yet the most criticized, man in the nation. Despite the criticism, and despite the physical ailments which began to manifest themselves even while he was the tenant at the White House, he probably could have won a third term if he had wanted it and were it not for the constitutional limitation on the Presidency.

The biography points out that General Eisenhower made mistakes and President Eisenhower made mistakes. But it notes, too, that he was good for the country, and that he did what he thought right.

As a military commander, General Eisenhower could send an officer home or to another station if he so desired. As a politician he had to use other methods. To his credit, and to the credit of Mr. Nixon, the differences were resolved and teamwork prevailed.

Indeed, the general's indorsement of Mr. Nixon last year probably was what iced the cake for the President. This despite the national defeat in 1960 and the California loss two years later in a race for governor which almost everyone had urged Mr. Nixon to forego.

To General Eisenhower, the 1968 election was a final "win" and it embodied his sentiments that an individual cannot and must not reject what he considers to be a genuine desire by his party for him to bear the standard.

The biography quotes Churchill as having said of his political enemy Neville Chamberlain that the sincerity of a man is a shield to his memory, and with such a shield, he marches in the ranks of honor.

Because he was sincere—though a human guy capable of making mistakes as well as being the darling of a nation and a world—the biography concludes that Dwight Eisenhower was entitled to join these ranks—"as man, soldier and President . . . he always marched and always shall."

# Hon. John H. Dent

OF PENNSYLVANIA

Mr. Speaker, it has been almost 1 month since the death of Gen. Dwight David Eisenhower. We are reminded of this sad event each time we have occasion to see the Stars and Stripes flying at half mast in his memory.

The month-long official period of mourning for this great American will extend but a few more days, but he will certainly be remembered long afterward. His contributions as leader in time of war and leader in time of peace will be forever recalled by his grateful country.

Dwight Eisenhower exemplified what is best in America: courage, devotion, strength of character, humility, respect for mankind, and love of homeland. He was ever ready to serve his country in any capacity: warrior, educator, Chief Executive.

We would all do well to rededicate ourselves, public officials and private citizens alike to those ideals for which the general stood, especially during these chaotic times. This would be the most fitting memorial we could devise to honor our former President.

When our flag is again raised to full staff, may it fly over a more wholesome, united America.

## Hon. James C. Cleveland

OF NEW HAMPSHIRE

Mr. Speaker, Edward DeCourcy, editor of the Newport Argus-Champion in my district, wrote a superb editorial at the time of President Eisenhower's death. Of all the tributes which I saw and heard I have found none finer or more moving than this. I congratulate my friend E. DeCourcy. One of the measures of Dwight Eisenhower's noble character is surely in its power to evoke as beautiful a tribute as this. I offer this at this point in the RECORD:

THE SPECTATOR

(By Edward DeCourcy)

*"No man is an Iland, intire of it selfe; every man is a peece of the Continent, a part of the maine; if a Clod bee washed away by the Sea, Europe is the lesse, as well as if a Promontorie were, as well as if a Mannor of thy friends or of thine owne were; any mans death diminishes me, because I am involved in Mankinde; And, therefore never send to know for whom the bell tolls; it tolls for thee."* JOHN DONNE (1573-1631)

It was not only General Eisenhower who died last Friday. A little bit of a lot of us—many right here in Newport—died too.

When that coffin was lowered into the rich Kansas earth yesterday, midnight passed. It was the final end of a day whose night had fallen almost a decade ago.

It was the end of an era that had been a major part of our lives, those of us who can still hear the General's stern, calm midwestern voice on June 6, 1944, as he reported that a landing had been made that morning on the coast of France and said, "I call upon all who love freedom to stand with us now. Together we shall achieve victory."

Nostalgia burnishes the pleasant and banishes the unpleasant. We'd rather think about the joys of V-E Day than the horror of Pearl Harbor. We'd rather remember the photograph of Ike recuperating in Denver with "Much Better Thanks" embroidered on his pajama pocket, than the shock when John Daley interrupted the "Weston Family" broadcast at dusk on April 12, 1945, to announce, "President Roosevelt is dead."

We'd rather remember the turn of full gas tanks, the scramble to buy new cars, the birth of the ballpoint pen, the ruptured duck, than the Bulge, Anzio, Guadalcanal, Omaha Beach or ration points. We'd rather remember that little red schoolhouse in Reims where Jodl and Friedeburg stood in defeat before a five-star General Eisenhower, than those days of November, 1942, when troops in North Africa under Lt. Gen. Eisenhower were temporarily being thrown back by Nazis.

Today's woes may have been budding during the Eisenhower presidency, but we remember Eisenhower's efforts to prevent them—the White House Conference on Education urging massive new efforts to make education adequate in quantity and quality for the enormous need ahead—thawing of the Cold War—the NATO conference in Pairs—admission of Alaska and Hawaii to the statehood—the offer for an end to atomic testing—creation of the National Aviation and Space Agency—heroic efforts to unify the armed forces—trips to many foreign lands to build peace—that ominous and prophetic warning of the military-industrial complex.

What died in each of us was our part in an era that we now realize is gone forever.

If we did not know it before, we knew it this week when we talked to young people to whom that era that we regard as hardly passed, is an obscure page in ancient history; young people who knew that the name Eisenhower was famous, but weren't quite sure why. Millions of today's voters were tender teenagers when Dwight Eisenhower turned the White House over to young John Kennedy, and most of today's voters think Edward Kennedy is a Senator from Massachusetts forgetting that it was a man named Edward Kennedy, chief of the Paris bureau of the Associated Press, who stirred the Eisenhower wrath when he barked into a telephone on May 7, 1945, "Germany has surrendered unconditionally," hours before Supreme Headquarters was to give the official release.

Something did die in a lot of us who are over 30 last Friday, our part in an era that has passed.

But something more important has been given new life. In death General Eisenhower has made the world recognize anew the virtues that made him widely loved and respected, virtues that hordes have been trying to discredit. Frank Reynolds of ABC put it crisply the night President Eisenhower died when he asked his listeners to "try to think of somebody else in public life you trust."

## Hon. Thomas J. Meskill

OF CONNECTICUT

Mr. Speaker, Dwight David Eisenhower, the 34th President of the United States, was a truly great American in every sense of the word. He was an individual who exemplified everything that we strive for. General Eisenhower's passing is mourned by all Americans.

The Hartford Courant carried a fine tribute to this great American which I would like to bring to the attention of my distinguished colleagues. It tells about another side of one of our outstanding leaders:

GRIST FROM THE SPORTS MILL

(By Mike Caruso)

A great man was laid to rest last week in Kansas under the floor of a chapel where a cornfield once stood. He led his nation through war and peace. He requested that he be buried in a simple steel $80 G.I. casket. Simplicity was his style and mark of greatness.

During World War II he was known as "the boss" to many of us in uniform. No wonder that we experienced pride, admiration and melancholia when we watched the young servicemen of this era execute their duties during the four-day ceremony with such precision and dedication.

As is the case more times than not, the military and athletics seem to go hand in hand. The latter was another facet of Dwight D. Eisenhower. One reason that he wanted to go to West Point was the hope that he could continue an athletic career. "It would be difficult to overemphasize the importance I attach to participation in sports," General Ike once stressed.

The farmer's son from Abilene felt while he was in grade school that his first idea of glory was to become a member of the high school baseball team. His boyhood dream was to toe the mound and whiff three batsmen on just nine pitches with the bases jammed in the bottom of the ninth.

Ike performed nobly as a tackle and end on the Abilene High School football team in addition to playing baseball. When he reached the Hudson Highlands in 1911, Ike became a 150 pound plebe halfback who sometimes played on the varsity squad. He was also a center fielder with the baseball club. He was alert afield but had problems at the plate. Ike was told he would have to overcome his method of chopping at pitches and learn to hit away. He was also a boxer of repute.

In 1912, the determined cadet from the long gray line improved his speed by running distances and strengthened his muscles through devotion to a gymnastics program. His weight increased to 174 pounds and he showed well in a practice football game against a rugged squad of soldiers.

While Ike was trotting off the field in ill-fitted gear, Coach Ernest Graves stopped him. The Army mentor instructed the team manager to outfit Ike properly—which was a way of indicating Ike would make the varsity. Ike later recalled the incident saying it was not only a thrill but a highlight of his football career on the plain overlooking the Hudson.

Ike's spirit made up for lack of size. He set his sights high. Army downed three of its first four opponents but succumbed to a 27–6 defeat against the legendary Jim Thorpe and his Carlisle Indians.

Disaster struck. Two weeks before the annual battle with Navy, Army met and defeated Tufts 15–6. But Ike suffered a twisted leg that brought an end to his athletic career. The injury was taken lightly at the time but during a riding drill a few days later the cartilages and tendons were torn.

Ike mused that there must have been a multitude of Jumbos on the field that day he was incapacitated, because in later years at least three dozen men who claimed they were Tufts players apologized to him for inflicting the injury.

Navy beat Army that year while Ike was encased in a cast from hip to foot. The finish of his football career had a demoralizing effect on Ike. Baseball and boxing were dropped also because of his lack of lateral movement. During vacation he umpired baseball games in a semi-pro league in Kansas. Many years after, Ike referred to the knee injury as one which "kept me from small town baseball and big league football."

In 1913, the U.S. Military Academy had a new football coach—former three-time all-American quarterback Charles Daly. The academy tried diligently to get Ike back in harness but the knee never responded. Daly did induce Ike to coach the Cullum Hall squad, better known as the Jayvees.

Later that autumn, Army won 22–9 over the rival Midshipmen from Annapolis. Ike reveled in the fact that he collected $65 from fellow Cadets to put up against a naval officer's wager the Middies would win. The Navy man never showed up after he let Ike hold the money.

Ike's Cullum Hall squad was the breeding ground for an undefeated Army team that won the national title in 1914 with a 9–0 record. Ike was acclaimed by "Howitzer," the West Point yearbook, gaining more plaudits than the varsity, which beat Navy and accomplished an unblemished record.

In 1915 while stationed at Fort Sam Houston in Texas, Ike coached Peacock Military Academy's football team. He originally turned the position down but reconsidered when the post general persuaded him to take on the extra duty so that his coaching would encourage youngsters in military training and give them a favorable impression of the Army.

The following year, Ike took the head coaching job at St. Louis College, which hadn't won a game in five years. Ike replaced a staff of priests and achieved a winning season. The happy Fathers invited Ike and his young wife, Mamie, to a victory dinner. The gesture started a friendship that lasted to Ike's death. Ike returned to the Roman Catholic institution in San Antonio, now known as St. Mary's in 1962 for a reunion with the faculty.

Ike coached football while stationed at Camp Meade in Maryland for four years in the early 20s. He quit when the club ended a dismal season by losing to a Marine eleven. In the late 20s, he rejected a military-coaching assignment for a battalion command at Fort Benning, Georgia. As one might have guessed, another friendly persuasion brought Ike back to coaching as an aide at the Georgia base. Service football talent was limited in those days.

During World War II, Ike was on a continual lookout for natural leaders. In his popular informal biography, "At Ease," Ike recounted his respect for athletics—especially football.

"Athletes take a certain amount of kidding, especially from those who think it is always brawn versus brains. But I noted with real satisfaction how well ex-footballers seemed to have leadership qualifications and it wasn't sentiment that made it seem so—not with names that turned out to be Bradley, Keyes, Patton, Simpson, Van Fleet, Harmon, Hobbs, Jouett, Patch and Prichard. Among many others, they measured up. I think this was more than coincidence. I believe that football, perhaps more than any other sport, tends to instill in men the feeling that victory comes through hard—almost slavish—work, team play, self-confidence and an enthusiasm that amounts to dedication."

There was another general's expression that has perhaps meant more to any cadet at West Point in the academy's 167 year history. And he was manager of the Army football team that sank Navy in 1902. So penned Douglas MacArthur, "Upon the fields of friendly strife, are sown the seeds that, upon other fields, on other days, will bear the fruits of victory."

## Hon. Durward G. Hall

OF MISSOURI

Mr. Speaker, the "American War Dads" were formed in Kansas City, Mo., during World War II. Their program consists very simply of how they can best help the men and women in service. The qualification for membership is that the member have a son or daughter in the service.

Mr. Elwyn S. Woods, the Americanism and patriotism chairman of the Missouri State Association of American War Dads, has written this tribute to Dwight D. Eisenhower. Under unanimous consent I insert this article at this point in the RECORD.

DWIGHT DAVID EISENHOWER

(By Elwyn S. Woods)

Unworthy as our effort may be, we must pay our tribute to one who lived so generously for others.

His first altar at his mother's knee, and her great faith when his childish tantrums obsessed him must have tempered his life and laid the foundation for the altar of devotion to his country upon which he placed his life and his fortune, in later years.

The titles of Soldier, Statesman, General and President do not truly indicate his greatness. They but epitomize the inner qualities and talents which made their attainment inevitable. So many aspire to greatness but fall short of the goal; he never was ambitious for honors but acquired them all.

Abilene, Kansas, can rightfully claim the distinction of his boyhood days, but his death, as was said of Mr. Lincoln, "makes him belong to the whole world."

We know not how historians will record him—nor do we care. One thing we know for sure—this great American Patriot was loved by all. He will be long remembered when others are thought of no more. Let us think of him often that we may be reinspired by the rare characteristics he possessed so abundantly.

How better could we close than by quoting from the old-fashioned motto that hung in his bedroom at Abilene, "Thy Will Be Done."

## Hon. Silvio O. Conte

OF MASSACHUSETTS

Mr. Speaker, the death of our beloved former President Dwight D. Eisenhower occasioned many moving tributes to his greatness and humanity.

None, I feel, excel the following lines by Gordon Hawkins, formerly of Westfield, Mass., for their eloquent simplicity and sincerity. I would like to insert his poem, eulogizing President Eisenhower, into the Congressional Record:

DWIGHT DAVID EISENHOWER: 1890–1969

(By Gordon Hawkins)

Delayed by his tenacious grip on life
He now rejoins his comrades of the past—
Those valiant ones who sought to quell world-strife
In hope that freedom for mankind might last!
In their long bivouac in foreign lands
And in America, he joins the hosts
Of World War dead, in comradeship joins hands
With those immortals that our nation boasts;
Our hallowed dead and those of our allies—
The titan Churchill, others fine and great,
All those whose fame and honor never dies
Who curbed the Nazi menace and its hate!
His epitaph—"He had his country's love, deserving it all other things above."

## Hon. Howard W. Robison

OF NEW YORK

Mr. Speaker, William A. Grace—of Freeville, N.Y., in my congressional district—has been a participant here, these recent months, in a study group of State University of New York students and others examining "The American National Governmental Process," during which time he has had considerable contact with my office.

I have come to know and appreciate Mr. Grace who also is a contributing reporter to the Inter-County Press, of Dryden, N.Y., writing a column of "Washington Comment" based on his observations while here in the Capital City. One of his recent columns was a tribute to Dwight D. Eisenhower which, under leave granted, I now include as a part of my remarks:

WASHINGTON COMMENT

(By William A. Grace)

"The death of President Eisenhower takes from our midst a great American, a great statesman and military leader who served our country in peace and war with sound judgment and outstanding courage."—Speaker of the House John McCormack.

In Washington tonight, the heart of Dwight David Eisenhower is still. He passed gently from us at 12:25 this afternoon. President, General of the Army, Chairman of the Joint Chiefs of Staff, Supreme Commander of N.A.T.O., author, and former president of Columbia University; all prove an inadequate measure of the man. For Dwight Eisenhower was the embodiment of an American dream.

Only history can judge the ultimate significance of the "Eisenhower Years." It will have much to assess; implementation of containment, the peaceful uses of atomic energy, establishment of coexistence, the first enforcements pertaining to civil rights, the ending of the Korean conflict, and the espousal of the Eisenhower Doctrine, but perhaps most the fact that he moderated the fury of our domestic politics. Only time can validate whatever judgment we hold.

Official Washington, as well as the world, has paid profuse tribute to this great American. Richard Nixon spoke of his "unique place in American history." Lyndon Johnson declared him "A giant of our age." Truman praised his military acumen, and Hubert Humphrey his international foresight. Ted Kennedy cited his "quiet dignity" and Earl Warren stated that he felt an illustrious chapter in world history had closed. Everett Dirksen, the Republican Senate Minority Leader, had the most definitive comment: "The World Liked Ike."

Yet the significance of Dwight David Eisenhower lies not in the world of Washington's movers and shakers. It lies in the genuine and sincere affection with which he was held by his fellow citizens. Of all the beautiful tributes paid to this former President the greatest was given by an anonymous negro woman who, when asked, stopped before the local television cameras and said: "I think he was a nice man. I'm sorry he died, and I hope he goes to heaven." Dwight Eisenhower's spirit lives in the hearts of those who knew him. There was no facade. His intense humanity has not been lost upon us.

## Hon. James G. Fulton
OF PENNSYLVANIA

Mr. Speaker, the Senate of the State of Pennsylvania has recently adopted a resolution honoring the late Dwight David Eisenhower. A letter from the senate secretary, Mark Gruell, Jr., and the resolution follow:

SENATE OF PENNSYLVANIA,
*May 13, 1969.*

Hon. JAMES G. FULTON,
*House Office Building,*
*Washington, D.C.*

GOOD MORNING CONGRESSMAN FULTON: At its session on May 6, 1969, the Senate of Pennsylvania unanimously adopted the enclosed Resolution.

In accordance with the directions contained therein, I am forwarding a certified copy to you.

Sincerely,

MARK GRUELL, Jr.

RESOLUTION

Dwight David Eisenhower, thirty-fourth President, was the embodiment of patriotism both as a military man and as a statesman. His ethical code of behavior and fear of God was expressed in his every action.

The Commonwealth of Pennsylvania was honored for many years by the presence of the Eisenhower family while living near Gettysburg; therefore be it

*Resolved,* That this Senate of the Commonwealth of Pennsylvania memorialize the Congress of the United States to adopt the proposed commemorative stamp honoring Dwight D. Eisenhower, depicting the Civil War monument and United States flag in Center Square, Easton, Pennsylvania; and be it further

*Resolved,* That a copy of this resolution be transmitted to the presiding officer of each House of Congress of the United States, and to each Senator and Representative from Pennsylvania serving in the Congress of the United States.

I certify that the foregoing is a true and correct copy of Senate Resolution Serial No. 28 introduced by Senator Jeanette F. Reibman and adopted by the Senate of Pennsylvania the sixth day of May, one thousand nine hundred and sixty-nine.

MARK GRUEL, Jr.,
*Secretary, Senate of Pennsylvania.*

## Hon. Philip J. Philbin
OF MASSACHUSETTS

Mr. Speaker, under unanimous consent to revise and extend my remarks in the RECORD, I include therein an excellent tribute to our great, beloved, and late friend, President Eisenhower, written by my dear friend, Dr. Charles H. Bradford, outstanding doctor, medical and civic leader of Boston.

This lovely, inspiring poem is composed with rare sensitivity and charm, and it impressively portrays the rugged character, great ability, extraordinary spirit of dedication and marvelous achievement for the Nation, and the American people of our illustrious world and national leader and friend, Ike, as we knew him here on the Hill.

Certainly, no one is more qualified by reason of background, patriotism, learning and talent to pay this tribute, than this great son of Massachusetts, Dr. Bradford, because he and his family spring from the early sources and very foundations of American freedom, democracy, and the spiritual values and beliefs upon which they rest.

He and his brother, Robert, another distinguished friend and outstanding former Governor of the Commonwealth, and family, trace their lineage to a long line of ancestors, including the first Governor, whose wise leadership and magnificent contributions helped so greatly toward the origin, development and glory, which peculiarly belong to the Bay State.

Many tributes have been and will be paid to our fallen leader, President Eisenhower, but most assuredly, none could be more sincere, more feelingly expressed, or more appropriate than this stirring poem by Dr. Bradford, which reaches such a high pitch of eloquence and emotional truth.

This timely, well-written verse will continue to inspire generations of future Americans and give them full understanding of the rare components of character, ability, training, and unselfish dedication, which made it possible for President Eisenhower to take his place as one of the truly great leaders of the Nation and the world.

We may all prayerfully join Dr. Bradford in his beautiful poem, and reflect upon his closing lines:

> But our affection follows on his name,
> And never fading laurels crown his fame.

I am sure that our beloved general would have liked this great poem and these words, and his gracious wife and family, and all of us who knew and loved him for the great American he was, will always cherish them. The poem follows:

TRIBUTE TO GENERAL EISENHOWER

At our great General, let us look again
As once we knew him in his wartime days
When battles waited on his word, and when
The thunder of great guns echoed his praise.
Soldiers from every land and every race
Served under him in Freedom's vast crusade,
When the world's armies struggled to displace
The Empire of Evil, Hitler made.
From every race, indeed, and every land,
These soldiers gathered to sustain the Right;
While over their array, he held command,
And marshalled them in their heroic fight.
To Africa and Italy, they went
By Eisenhower's conquering orders, sent.
At Fortress Europe, next he aimed a blow
To free the peoples who were there enchained
Under a reign of slavery and woe
That Nazi terror-tactics had ordained.
Wickedness, unparalleled before,
Such as no other nation ever knew,
Kept millions, who were victims of the war,
In death camps, where the stench of horror grew.
Murder and frightfulness and torture ruled,
Like beasts of prey that through the jungle ranged;
And in a cult of vicious hate were schooled
The leaders, from all decency estranged.
'Twas this that Eisenhower sought to free
From the blackout of crime and misery.
With armies centered in the British Isles,
He carefully prepared plans to attack
The foe's defences, where for miles on miles,
Huge gun emplacements lay, to hurl him back.
His word unleashed the storm of blood and war
That like a tempest struck the coast of France.
There, under sweeping shellfire, his troops bore
Their banners in a conquering advance.
With fearful fighting, then, they battled on
And step by step, they breached the German wall,
And victory after victory they won
Until the rule of Hell was forced to fall.
Tragic, the cost in wounds, and blood, and death;
But free men, now, once more, might draw free breath.
As Peace returned, it showed the greatest need
Was for strong men to bear the nation's cares;
Then Eisenhower once more took the lead
In civil life and government affairs.
For eight long years, as President he served,
Meeting each strenuous crisis as it rose.
He never from the path of duty swerved,
Nor failed in tasks his office might impose.
Around the world, his influence was felt,
Establishing a sound, straightforward course;
While in his policies, he ever dwelt
On principles of reason, not of force.
By a wise use of his authority,
He led the nation with firm dignity.

His character, above all else, we prize
For throughout life, he made his life worthwhile:
Gazing on all mankind with friendly eyes,
And greeting every new task with a smile.
Wholesome and hearty was his attitude,
With skill in making men cooperate;
His judgment keen, intelligent, and shrewd,
And in his manner, friendly, yet sedate.
Despite his great fame, he was humble still,
And to life's simple duties, remained true;
Genial at heart, and with sincere goodwill,
His soul was filled with honor, through and through.
As he departs, we offer this great man
Our tribute, as a true American.

L' Envoie

Gone are the mighty armies that he led;
Faded, the grandeur of his lofty place;
And down the highways of the Past have fled
The great events he was called on to face.
But our affection follows on his name,
And never fading laurels crown his fame.

## Hon. Glenard P. Lipscomb
OF CALIFORNIA

Mr. Speaker, during these times of riots, disrespect of law and order, and advocacy of extremisms, the voice of moderation is critically needed. Dwight D. Eisenhower bequeathed to us that creed of moderation.

The general's legacy is reviewed in a May 19 editorial of the Progress-Bulletin, Pomona, Calif., which I am inserting in the Record under leave to extend my remarks:

[From the Progress-Bulletin, May 19, 1969]

EISENHOWER LEFT VALUABLE LEGACY

Dwight D. Eisenhower accomplished many things in a long and brilliant career of public service. It may be, however, that he will be remembered longest for the legacy of moderation that he has left the nation. Moderation was the basis of the General's Middle-of-the-Road political philosophy. But, moderation was obviously more than a political philosophy to Eisenhower. It was a creed. And, in these critical, turbulent times, the creed of moderation bequeathed to us the former president is a foundation upon which all Americans can stand and face the future with confidence.

In one of his last messages to his fellow citizens—an article appearing in The Reader's Digest, under the title "We Must Avoid the Perils of Extremism"—General Eisenhower applied his philosophy and his creed to the contemporary scene, and he did so with a heartening sense of optimism. In one passage he said, ". . . I for one refuse to become pessimistic about America's future. Granted that storm signals are up, I believe nevertheless that we as a people have the good sense to place patriotism and human understanding above the arrogance of personal prejudice—and that we can and will solve peacefully the problems that beset us. I believe that we will do so through our traditional reliance upon the philosophy of moderation—or Government by Common Sense."

As a student of American history, Eisenhower noted that most of our great presidents—Washington, Lincoln and Theodore Roosevelt among them—were men of the Middle Way. He characterized the extremists of both left and right as people who spill off the ". . . one-way highway of progress" into the gutters. He believed that extremism comes easily ". . . to men who have doped themselves with delusions of their own unblemished virtue and the rascality of others . . . The Middle-of-the-Road American—Negro or white—has put up with a lot from the extremists." Eisenhower never felt that a Middle-of-the-Road American is simply a fence-sitter and pointed out that it often takes more courage to occupy the center than any other position ". . . for you are then subject to attack on both flanks."

Eisenhower was not above compromise and considered it a highly useful tool within the limits of basic principles. He was keenly aware of the dangers of today's extremism. On the one hand, he pointed out that there are those who want to socialize everything. On the other, there are the far-out conservatives who want to do away with the graduated income tax, stop social security, abolish all regulatory agencies, smash the labor unions and confine the functions of the federal government to running the military establishment and the post office and conducting our foreign affairs. While accepting a measure of governmental responsibility in social welfare, he warned, ". . . I have said to those who espouse the completely paternal government that they are advocating the road to national bankruptcy and human ruin . . . you cannot place millions of citizens on a permanent dole and leave them there to rot in mind and spirit . . . This today is at the root of our tragic difficulties in the slums."

Eisenhower left a word of advice to youth: "It will soon be your country to run . . . When you have a just and reasonable cause, protest all you wish, but remember that there can and should be order and decency in democratic protest. Stand up and be counted when troublemakers try to rob you of your right to an education. If it becomes necessary for the forces of law and order to move in and quell such disturbances, give them your support." At the conclusion of his brief article, the General and former President of the United States said, "In this article I have tried to set forth some of the guideposts of the Middle Way. I would hope with all my heart that during the next few years our country will unite under the President in giving this Common-Sense approach a chance."

The Eisenhower legacy of moderation will be considered by many the foundation on which to build an even greater nation in the future.

## Hon. Seymour Halpern
OF NEW YORK

Mr. Speaker, June 6 marks the anniversary of D-Day, that historic moment in history when the eyes of the world were focused upon the invasion forces of the Allied army and the activities of its Commander in Chief, Dwight David Eisenhower. It is fitting that at this anniversary of that landing we again pay tribute to the man who left his mark on history not only as a military leader but as a political leader as well.

But it is perhaps the mark of a man that we remember him more for his human qualities than for the imprint that he leaves on mankind. Dwight David Eisenhower certainly engraved his name in the history of the 20th century—commander of the greatest invasion force ever assembled in the history of man, university president, author, the President of the United States—yet he is best remembered in the hearts of Americans as a man loved by the people.

He was of the very essence of America. Born to a poor hard-working family in Texas, his warm, outgoing personality engendered the friendship, admiration, and trust of those who came to know him. Upon graduation from West Point, he began in 1915 one of the most successful military careers in the history of the United States. To have led the legions of democracy against the armed might of tyranny would have been reward enough for most men but for General Eisenhower a life of public service could not be so easily ended no matter how richly deserved. After a short term as president of Columbia University, he again returned to the service of the United States in the capacity of commander of the newly formed North Atlantic Treaty Organization. As he had done during the Second World War, he succeeded in welding into a single fighting force the many diverse armies that are part of the common European defense.

Recognizing his talents, the American people called upon him to give yet more of himself to public service. Rising to the call, he spent 8 years providing the American people with that determined, studied leadership ever mixed with a depth and breadth of human understanding that he had so amply displayed in the past. As President of the United States, he placed principle above expediency both at Little Rock and Suez. He sought to maintain democracy wherever it was threatened, whether Lebanon or Berlin. He strove constantly for peaceful coexistence with the Soviet Union while maintaining security for the free world. As new nations emerged from old empires, he remembered that America, too, had fought for its independence against empire and consequently he devoted considerable effort on behalf of these nations struggling with the manifold problems that attend newly won freedom.

At home he provided Americans with great leadership amidst crisis. After the Soviet technological successes of 1957, he pressed for and succeeded in obtaining significant Government assistance to education. So that all of our citizens would be equal under the law, he sought and obtained far-reaching civil rights legislation.

It is possible that other men of similar devotion to duty and general excellence might have accomplished some or even possibly all that President Eisenhower did. But in such a case, one would only be recounting deeds rather than telling of a man and above all things, Dwight David Eisenhower was a man that America knew it could look to for leadership, honor, respect, and, from the very depths of his heart, love of everything America has ever stood for.

## Hon. William H. Bates
OF MASSACHUSETTS

Mr. Speaker, I wish to add my voice to those who pay tribute to a great American.

General Eisenhower was one of our Nation's most patriotic and dedicated leaders of all time. His great contributions, both as a soldier and as a statesman, toward peace in the world will continue to inspire others to work for that cherished objective.

Ike was a tremendously human and understanding individual, whose sincerity and warmth of spirit will live on in the memory of everyone who was privileged to know him. I am especially grateful for the personal kindness and counsel he extended to me, both while he was in the military service and in the White House.

While the world shares the sadness of his passing, I know that former President Eisenhower's beloved family finds comfort in the knowledge that he was so widely admired, respected, and loved.

## Hon. M. G. (Gene) Snyder
OF KENTUCKY

Mr. Speaker, Dwight David Eisenhower can be regarded as perhaps America's last true hero. In an age when heroes are fashioned from blind and emotive desperation—and, at a time when our citizens are beckoned forth to the recurrent apotheosis of mediocrity—the image of this man can be clearly discerned through it all—surrounded by the serenity of confidence and swathed in the memories of all those Americans who believed in him and in what he stood for.

Dwight Eisenhower in his calm and unassuming manner received the respect of America and became what we are likely to see little of in the future—a true leader. In seeking out the finest qualities of leadership, I think we must agree that the tendency to heroism should be included on the list, together with executive ability and, in the rare case, accompanied by a genuine proclivity for modesty.

These have been the qualities of all the outstanding heroes of our national history—from George Washington through Abraham Lincoln to Dwight D. Eisenhower—all of whom could reach decisions with dispatch, carry them out firmly and without trepidation. And all of them would know, ultimately, that they acted not so much as the direct agents of divine intelligence but merely as humble human beings acting with whatever talents they were fortunate enough to have at their command.

Such are the qualities of our great men, and such are the qualities we witness all too seldom in this age of turbulence, weakness, confusion, and periodic chaos. The traditional and honored institutions of our great land are under furious onslaught by the marshaled forces of philistine error. Dwight Eisenhower, the man, is gone, but Dwight Eisenhower, the constant symbol, remains to serve as an example to recall, to praise, and to salute with pride. His record in battle inspired our country in time of war, and brought us from the brink of horror and destruction to the point of glorious victory. He brought us victory as a general. He brought us peace and prosperity as President of the United States.

General Eisenhower captured the spirit of the citizen-soldier, and, therein, lay the secret of his great popularity which buoyed our Army and drove us to victory. And how did he accomplish this? By bold, straightforward policies, unmixed by political pettifogging. He was uncomplicated and direct—and his soldiers loved him for it.

President Eisenhower captured the spirit of the citizens of this country—the voters—and therein lay the secret of his great popularity at home, which buoyed our country and brought us peace and prosperity. This he accomplished in the same fashion as he accomplished his military success—by bold, straightforward policies—uncomplicated and direct. The American people loved him for it—and they always will.

Ike was a winner. He knew that war had only one purpose; to win. And when the war was over and General Eisenhower returned, to what could have been the greatest hero's welcome in the history of our planet, he requested and obtained a modest welcome. If he had wished, he could have paraded in every city of America—every city in the Allied world, in fact—and he would have been assured of a jubilant and cheering turnout. But that was not his style. He knew that victory was his only purpose and that applause is not the stuff of victory.

As long as America remains great, she will be in the vanguard of the struggle for freedom. We will always be well advised to emphasize the spirit which Dwight Eisenhower engendered; the spirit of victory; the spirit of democratic triumph—a spirit which electrified the Republic in those dark days, and which, if permitted to flourish, will electrify the Nation once again.

Ike will endure not simply as a great man, but as a symbol—a symbol which unified America. He stood and stands above the petty machinations of small men as the wise and understanding leader, the eminent counselor.

In trying times, it is, indeed, a credit to the memory of this great man that his final tribute was not a vast and cacophonous caterwauling from the brutish mob, but a thunderous silence of dignified respect for the man and for what he represented.

Dwight David Eisenhower is dead. But he has quietly and indelibly emblazoned his memory on the past, present and, hopefully, the future of our Nation.

## Hon. Thomas J. Meskill

OF CONNECTICUT

Mr. Speaker, the death of Gen. Dwight David Eisenhower on March 28, 1969, brought sadness to the entire Nation. The general was undoubtedly a great soldier, a true humanitarian, and a distinguished President.

General Eisenhower will long be remembered in history for his outstanding leadership of the Allied Forces in Europe in World War II. He demonstrated that he was a man of great courage and wisdom. Every serviceman who had the privilege of serving under his command will testify to his leadership and genius.

But it was Dwight David Eisenhower's humanitarian concern which brought him back to the United States to serve as the president of one of this Nation's most distinguished universities. His service to Columbia University and to the role of education in our society tells us much about the depth of this man's personality.

As President of the United States for two terms, General Eisenhower made some of the most outstanding contributions to the world community. He was a true statesman who was fully dedicated to bringing peace and stability to the conduct of affairs between Nations. President Eisenhower was a peacemaker first, last, and always. He set the tone for his administration by concluding the Korean war and followed through by maintaining peace in a troubled world.

All Americans owe a debt of gratitude to this man who, throughout his life, served as an example of everything that we strive for in America.

## Hon. Margaret M. Heckler

OF MASSACHUSETTS

Mr. Speaker, the passing away of President Dwight David Eisenhower has been mourned by millions all over the world. Old and young alike, people of every race, have experienced a deep sense of personal loss. Eisenhower knew no boundaries in his love for mankind; he sought not just the peace of a nation but the peace of the world. For a few moments in time the world rests in peace as all men join together to grieve the death of this great man. Perhaps this is the highest tribute that can be paid to Eisenhower. Although his career was military in character, his life was devoted in actuality to his hope for peace among men.

I welcome the opportunity to express, as others have, my own love and deep admiration of Dwight David Eisenhower. I speak for many Americans whose unspoken thoughts are easily read in their sad faces as they recall their memory of this wonderful man.

Our beloved Ike played an important role in my own life—he was a significant influence on my personal direction. While I was a student in college, I followed every step of his distinguished career. I quickly grew to love that warm smile and reassuring tone of voice which drew people to him wherever he went. His art of leadership was unique. Every national or international problem was attacked by him as if it were his own personal problem. His patience was boundless, and his high degree of perseverance to solve the Nation's problems was exemplary. Eisenhower made me proud of America. He inspired me with his contagious zeal to serve America.

The accomplishments of Eisenhower are countless. The diversity of these contributions seem truly remarkable. The world can ill afford to lose such a brilliant soldier and statesman as he was. The Republican Party is proud to have had this giant of a man lead us for so many years. Eisenhower may have been "no politician" as he so often claimed, but he commanded the respect and affection of the people in a way that far surpassed the skills of politicians of any era.

Eisenhower's true greatness lies in the unspoken compliments that dwell in the hearts of the people he served and to whom he devoted his life. Eisenhower has not really died; he has not even faded away. For as long as the spirit of liberty lives in the minds of men, so long will the memory of Dwight David Eisenhower remain with the American people—Forever.

## Hon. William V. Roth, Jr.

OF DELAWARE

Mr. Speaker, after I was elected to Congress, a group of my colleagues and I traveled to Gettysburg to speak with Dwight David Eisenhower. I had met the former President previously, but in that summer of 1967 I was so impressed with his clarity of mind and perception of world politics, I felt the United States would be remiss if we did not put Ike's knowledge to use. After consultation with the general's aides, and after being assured that he looked favorably on the idea, I drafted the following resolution:

H. CON. RES. 476

CONCURRENT RESOLUTION

Whereas General of the Army Dwight David Eisenhower has served the United States of America with distinction for more than fifty years as soldier, President, and statesman; and

Whereas as President of the United States he has gained great knowledge and understanding of this Nation's relations with other nations; and

Whereas he has rendered this Nation and the free world invaluable service as Supreme Commander of the Allied Expeditionary Force in Europe during World War II, and, later as Supreme Commander Allied Powers Europe, and, because of this service he knows well the aspirations, potential, and problems of the North Atlantic Treaty Organization; and

Whereas during his eight years as President of the United States this Nation cemented its ties of friendship and understanding with free world nations through a policy of mutual defense binding these nations together against the common threat to their security; and

Whereas developments in recent years have seen a disturbing deterioration in the close ties among members of the Western alliance: Now, therefore, be it

*Resolved by the House of Representatives (the Senate concurring)*, That it is the sense of the Congress that General of the Army Dwight David Eisenhower should be requested to undertake a factfinding mission to investigate and report to the Congress and the President on the state of the relations of the United States with other nations of the world, with particular attention to the North Atlantic Treaty Organization, and the politicomilitary effort in defense of the Republic of Vietnam.

Unfortunately, the general took ill 2 days before 80 other Members of the House of Representatives were planning to introduce the resolution with me; out of respect for this great leader, we delayed our plan. After that first weekend in August 1967, Mr. Eisenhower never regained the good health and robust constitution with which he was blessed for most of his life; the resolution was never formally set forward. I wanted to record it here, Mr. Speaker, because I think it articulates most clearly how I felt about Dwight David Eisenhower. I mourn his passing, as do millions of people around the world; I particularly regret that in times such as these Dwight David Eisenhower is not here to offer us wisdom, counsel, and a firm, guiding hand.

## Hon. William S. Mailliard

OF CALIFORNIA

Mr. Speaker, I would like to join my colleagues in paying tribute to Dwight David Eisenhower, soldier and statesman, general, and President, who dedicated his life to serving our country. His death brought great sadness to all Americans, especially to those who served in Congress during the 8 years of his Presidency.

His warm smile, his dedication, his honesty, and courage endeared him to the world and kindled in Americans patriotism and statesmanship, in the finest sense of the words.

Ike lived a full and rewarding life, inspiring faith in the democratic process in his fellow Americans. His heroic and courageous struggle to continue living under adverse and often painful conditions was itself a memorial to his great personal integrity and unyielding spirit. Distinguished men require no tributes; their actions, decisions, and character cannot possibly be heightened by any additional adornments. Simply because of their existence the world is changed, and continues to improve.

All men of the world will continue to express their affection and admiration for Dwight David Eisenhower, a true citizen of the world. His unselfish and dedicated leadership in times of war and peace will never be forgotten. Ike will be remembered as an outstanding example of leadership in a world which could certainly use many such examples.

# INDEX

31–935 O—70——8

## Memorial Services and Tributes in the Senate of the United States

# Memorial Tributes in the House of Representatives of the United States

## State Funeral and Memorial Services Held in Washington, D.C., and Abilene, Kans.



U.S. GOVERNMENT PRINTING OFFICE: 1970 O—31-935